a man
of much
importance

a man of much importance

THE ART AND LIFE
OF
TERRENCE McNALLY

CHRISTOPHER BYRNE

APPLAUSE
THEATRE & CINEMA BOOKS

Essex, Connecticut

APPLAUSE
THEATRE & CINEMA BOOKS

An imprint of Globe Pequot, the trade division of
The Rowman & Littlefield Publishing Group, Inc.
4501 Forbes Blvd., Ste. 200
Lanham, MD 20706
www.rowman.com

Distributed by NATIONAL BOOK NETWORK

British Library Cataloguing in Publication Information available

Library of Congress Cataloging-in-Publication Data

Names: Byrne, Christopher, author.
Title: A man of much importance : the art and life of Terrence McNally / Christopher Byrne.
Description: Essex, Connecticut : Applause, [2023]
Identifiers: LCCN 2022058266 (print) | LCCN 2022058267 (ebook) | ISBN 9781493053773 (cloth) | ISBN 9781493053797 (epub)
Subjects: LCSH: McNally, Terrence. | McNally, Terrence—Criticism and interpretation. | Dramatists, American—20th century—Biography. | Gay dramatists—United States—Biography. | American drama—20th century—History and criticism.
Classification: LCC PS3563.A323 Z58 2023 (print) | LCC PS3563.A323 (ebook) | DDC 812/.54 [B]—dc23/eng/20230124
LC record available at https://lccn.loc.gov/2022058266
LC ebook record available at https://lccn.loc.gov/2022058267

♾️™ The paper used in this publication meets the minimum requirements of American National Standard for Information Sciences—Permanence of Paper for Printed Library Materials, ANSI/NISO Z39.48-1992.

Piece out our imperfections with your thoughts.

—Shakespeare, *Henry V*

For Michael G. Jackson

CONTENTS

AT RISE

"AT RISE" IS, perhaps, an arcane term. Coined in the eighteenth century when proscenium curtains entered common usage in the theater, it is a stage direction used by a playwright to describe the first images an audience sees. Literally, when the curtain rises. The term has fallen out of common usage for many years as very often there is no proscenium curtain in contemporary theaters. "Lights up" is the much more usual direction.

Yet there is something resonant—and wonderfully old-fashioned—about "at rise." It hints at discovery and surprise, at something being slowly revealed, at the start of an adventure.

It's fitting that it's the term that playwright Terrence McNally used most often at the beginning of his scripts. The term fits Terrence. A little formal, respectful of tradition and yet always capturing the sense of excitement an audience feels in the moments before a show begins. Will we be transported? Challenged? Amused? Upset? There is no moment in the theater—or anywhere really—like that, where a group of strangers is united in anticipation, where magic is, one hopes, about to happen. "Astonish me," the audience is saying in so many words or that delicious moment of silence, much as Sergei Diaghilev of the *Ballets Rousse*, said to artist Jean Cocteau (Terrence would write about Diaghilev and his impact on twentieth-century art in a later play, *Fire and Air*.). What they are about to see has never happened before . . . and will never happen again. For better or worse, this performance exists only in this moment.

"At rise" is so much more than a stage direction, at least where Terrence is concerned; it speaks to his deep, abiding love of the theater. He even puts his wonder at the phrase in words in a speech by the character Alfie Byrne, in *A Man of No Importance*, who wonders at just this moment when magic may—or may not—begin.

Over his long career, Terrence's art lived in that moment of possibility. He was a gimlet-eyed observer of the human condition, a passionate activist, and a believer in the transformative power of theater. Above all, though, Terrence was honest, unvaryingly so. As Mr. Darcy writes to Elizabeth Bennet in *Pride and Prejudice*, "disguise of every sort is my abhorrence." In a period when it was dangerous to be openly gay, Terrence was out. If people were uncomfortable, so be it—if there was a greater truth to be told. Where his contemporaries went to great lengths to conceal their sexuality, Terrence didn't. In part, he had no choice. Nor did he ever really understand the need to hide, and based on his own observations as a young man, he knew how soul-draining the closet could be. (He would explore this in *The Wibbly, Wobbly, Wiggly Dance That Cleopatterer Did,* in which a supposedly straight man can only explore his homosexual feelings with a hustler.) From his very first major production, he was written about as gay, but that was because he had the courage to put a gay character on the stage. Terrence was committed to holding the mirror up to nature, to paraphrase Shakespeare. And it was nature as he saw it and experienced it.

It was Terrence's honesty—and fearlessness about being honest—that made him stand out early on. He faced the consequences of his honesty in, at times, critical outrage over his willingness to go after the shibboleths of the commercial theater and the culture around him.

He was not alone. There were many playwrights in the Off-Off Broadway movement of the late 1950s and early 1960s who took on the theater establishment and rebelled against what they saw as the falsity and commercialism of Broadway. Their plays giddily and dangerously pierced the mythos of postwar America. Much of their work came out of the absurdist theater, but their influences can also be traced back to Shakespeare, pantomimes, or indeed any theatrical work that took on the art form itself—that was self-reflective, or as we say today, "meta." These were plays that challenged all kinds of cultural norms and the established theatrical forms, engaging audiences directly and creating a thrilling immediacy that was largely absent uptown. This was the theater that Terrence encountered when he arrived in New York in 1956—the "at rise" moment for his career, if you will, as he matriculated at Columbia.

During this excitedly transformative time, playwrights such as Terrence, Robert Patrick, Charles D'Innocenzio, Ruth Kraus, Charles Ludlam, Adrienne Kennedy, Jean-Claude van Itallie, and many more got their starts at downtown theaters like LaMama, the Judson Poet's Theatre, Theater De Lys, Caffe Cino, and in countless lofts, churches, and black boxes between 14th and Houston streets. These playwrights, producers, and tiny theater companies thrived—after a fashion, since funds were scarce—as they redefined plays and playwriting. Their work ultimately attracted audiences, and spoke feelingly to the nascent anti-establishment sentiments that would flower in the latter part of the 1960s—and would drive unprecedented creativity in theater, music, and art that challenged the prevailing culture.

These writers used their art to mount an assault on what they saw as the stultifying conventions that limited expression, suppressed the individual, thrived on conformity, and were inherently dishonest in a dynamic world. While the older generation had sought comfort and peace after the upheavals of the Great Depression, World War II, and the Korean War, these artists raised angry and reactive voices, and a growing audience headed downtown looking for theater that was more authentic, more real, and more reflective of the emerging *zeitgeist*. As television was becoming the dominant form of entertainment, it felt increasingly urgent to assert theater as an art form and to combat the bland, strictly heterosexual diet of idealized pablum being fed to the masses. Small wonder that for a time these writers were seen as a threat.

If there was precedent for the shared sensibility of these playwrights, it would be the work of writers like Ionesco, Genet, Shelagh Delaney, and Samuel Beckett, whose plays were staged in uptown productions that attracted the *cognoscenti* and could land reliable "snob hits," as William Goldman refers to them in his book *The Season*. By this, Goldman meant plays that find an audience not because of what they are about—indeed many were obscure or challenging or, to some, downright boring—but because having seen them confers on the audience member a kind of intellectual credit, a sense that they were somehow superior to the masses who were delighted by lighthearted comedies like *Any Wednesday*.

Aside from the handful of snob hits, however, the newly fledged American writers couldn't get produced in the so-called legitimate theater of the time. Their use of absurdism, camp, breaking (sometimes shattering) the fourth wall, profanity, and taboo subjects was a threat to much of the mainstream. They didn't have the name recognition that could guarantee box office sales for potential producers. So, they mounted the shows themselves and found an audience that was the direct antithesis of Broadway, where shows like *My Fair Lady* reigned. In fact, it was as much a badge of honor for them to loathe that now-classic musical as it was for the well-to-do to pretend to understand Ionesco. (In *Merrily We Roll Along*, Sondheim lampoons this exact point when he has the character Charlie say, "I saw *My Fair Lady*. I sort of enjoyed it.")

Time, as it inevitably does, passed. Playwrights and small theaters continued to experiment, push limits, and mount productions. And the culture changed. Downtown became hip, and the avant-garde began to coexist with the tried-and-true. That's no surprise since the theater always wants one thing: novelty. When a group of Off-Off Broadway playwrights approached Lynne Meadow, early on in her tenure at Manhattan Theatre Club, asking to be produced, downtown moved uptown, and New York theater was changed forever.

Even if people didn't understand it or were offended by it (as many mainstream critics were), attention had to be paid. The theater always reflects the culture at large, so as the world changed, the Vietnam conflict escalated, and the focus shifted to youth, theater adapted—and playwrights, as they always do, continued to respond to the world and reflect it. If the audiences were slow to follow, they eventually caught on, and what had once been the radical fringe spoke to theatergoers in a new way.

Many of the plays of this era are lost or languish in obscurity in collections of plays. Terrence was in the rarified group that successfully made the leap from the fringes of Off-Off Broadway to Off Broadway and ultimately Broadway. John Guare, A. R. Gurney, Edward Albee, David Rabe, and Sam Shepard all became "mainstream" as the world changed to embrace their visions of what theater was—or should be—in the second half of the twentieth century.

Even with all the groundbreaking new work of that era, Terrence stands out among all of his contemporaries for several reasons. First and foremost, fearless honesty resonates through all his plays. He never shied away from the dark, the taboo, or the things "nice people" didn't talk about. He openly and enthusiastically embraced sex—particularly gay sex, often graphically at a time when the closet was the norm and at least the pretense of Puritanical values was dominant. Sex in mainstream plays could be used for comedy . . . and not much more. Real passion, real bodies, and real sexual feelings were not tolerated. Second, Terrence was passionate about the theater. Though he adapted his plays for the screen and had a few forays into television, mostly in the form of one failed series and pilots that never really went anywhere, the theater was his home. He understood its history, its conventions, and he understood the experience of an audience as well. Third, he never stopped growing. He was working on projects to the end of his life, and he branched out into musicals and opera, always bringing a playwright's sensibilities to those forms. In fact, he always maintained that libretti should always be written by playwrights. Who else could craft a dramatic story for the stage? Finally, he was an artist. It was always about the work; it was always about the exploration and expression. Not everything worked. In show *business*, he was not a guaranteed moneymaker and given his fearlessness, he encountered controversy. He never courted it, but given how he was, how could he not find it?

Nonetheless, through success and failure, Terrence kept showing up and telling the truth, and the theater was transformed because of his work. He never set out to be a pioneer, hero, or a game-changer; he set out to be a working playwright. Yet he managed to be all three, and along the way had a profound impact on the art form he loved and to which he dedicated his life.

II.

I first encountered Terrence's work when I rescued him from the trash.

Let me explain.

I was a theater geek in high school. At the Tower Hill School in Wilmington, Delaware, I was a faculty kid. My dad was the head of the middle school, and my mom taught English and Latin as a substitute and directed the middle school plays, writing many of them, including the annual Christmas musical. We lived on the school grounds and had the run of the campus. I had a grand master key, which I had swiped from my father and had copied at Hoy's 5&10, though it was clearly marked "Do not duplicate." I'm not sure why I wanted it; we never did anything truly untoward, but it conveyed a kind of power and we thought ourselves daring. I think my brothers had their own copies, but it was a secret. If mom or dad would send me across the yard into the school after hours to fetch papers or grading books or some such, I would always borrow my dad's key.

In fact, at this far remove, I can only remember one time when I used my illicit key, and that's the one that introduced me to Terrence.

Our drama teacher, Mr. Shearer, routinely ordered scripts from Dramatist's Play Service. He read them to consider what the school would do. Mr. Shearer fashioned himself as someone "in the know" about theater, and around 1970, that meant scripts from the Off-Off Broadway theaters had found their way into the mix. For all his desire to seem avant-garde, the school was WASPy and highly conventional, bordering on Edwardian. As a result, we did plays like *Pygmalion, The Heiress,* and (God help us) *Dark of the Moon.* Probably the most daring play we ever attempted was *The Skin of Our Teeth,* and Thespis only knows what a hash we must have made of it. It certainly raised a lot of eyebrows among the parents and other faculty.

At the end of my ninth-grade year, school was out for the summer, but having nothing really to do, I was banging around the abandoned halls, enjoying the quiet. I saw Mr. Shearer in his classroom, and I stopped in to wish him a good summer and perhaps talk about my stellar performance as the Broadcast Official in Act Two of *Teeth.* Mr. Shearer was flipping through scripts, tossing them into the wastebasket. I asked why he was throwing them out, and he said they were plays we would never do, and he was making room for the new candidates that would arrive in August.

I'm not sure why I didn't ask if I could take the scripts he was throwing away. Mr. Shearer knew I was a theater geek, and I'd been reading Shakespeare, Kaufman and Hart, and basically making my way through all the scripts in the school library, as I imagined my future life on the Broadway stage. I suppose it didn't seem right to ask for things my teacher didn't think had merit, but I was curious.

I expect you can see what's coming. Later that afternoon, the school now almost completely deserted, I used my key to open Mr. Shearer's room, gathered up the multi-colored, cardboard-bound scripts, and headed home. It was a treasure trove.

I can still remember where I was when I first read *And Things That Go Bump in the Night,* Terrence's controversial first Broadway play. (More on that in a bit.) I was sitting in a folding lawn chair on the stone patio outside the large faculty house where we lived. I was surrounded by rhododendrons and in the shade of an elm tree, almost hidden from view. My interest was piqued as I pulled the script out of the dozen or so I had stacked up. I looked at the muted red cover of the "acting edition," with the title in all caps and saw that Mr. Shearer had written on it: "Inappropriate. No rewrite possible." Clearly, this was where I needed to start.

Can I say I understood it fully? No. But I was captivated immediately by the rhythms, the brazenness of the characters. The anger and the fear of "something out there," a nameless threat that seemed to loom over the family in a basement shelter. The twisted domestic comedy appealed to my teenage sense of irony that was, if I do say so, pretty well-developed for someone my age. And there was a gay character in it who believed in love, or the possibility of love. Of course he's destroyed, but his loneliness and despair and determination that love existed against all odds sounded like me. Not literally, of course, but theatrically, in a sense that was larger than life and that seemed in all the abstraction of the play to capture the chaos and fear that I lived in. I was also completely aware that I was gay, but as with many young gay people at the time, there was no place for that, no validation, just a dark secret that haunted the edges of virtually every aspect of my life. It was not an answer, but I didn't feel so alone, no matter how dark the story was.

What I also remember is that I *heard* the characters as I read. While I would never see the play on stage—being "inappropriate" and all and having come and gone at least five years before—it appeared nearly fully formed in front of me on the page. I was changed by it. Many years later, I was able to tell Terrence that story, or an abbreviated version of it. He was very gracious, and I think was most impressed that I was able to remember lines from the play, that they had stayed with me for decades. He was intrigued by people who could retain lines and speeches, and in the latter part of his life, he tried to memorize some of Shakespeare's famous speeches, and was not overly successful at it.

I tell this story for a very specific reason: it's not unique. Virtually every person I spoke to as I developed this book has a similar story. The play might have been *The Lisbon Traviata*, *Frankie and Johnny in the Claire de Lune*, or *Love! Valour! Compassion!*, and it was discovered in the stacks of a library, offered by a drama teacher, or stumbled on in some other way. The actor Michael Urie talked about staging a one-act version of *Lips Together, Teeth Apart* in his high school, adding that he could figure out what it was about but not what it *meant*. And yet, he was drawn to the material—much more than that of other gay playwrights who by the nineties were mainstream.

The common experience was that in reading one of Terrence's scripts for the first time, something shifted, a door opened, a light went on . . . whatever metaphor you want. It was the power of his characters, the situations, the pure theatricality, the language that had transformative power. The question, obviously rhetorical, that was asked over and over was, "How did he know that?" It was the underlying humanity and, as mentioned earlier, fearless honesty of his work that touched people and made them want to know more. In many cases, it made people want to become actors or writers or find themselves in the theater. Many of them did . . . and got quite good at it.

III.

"Is this going to be the *definitive* biography of Terrence McNally?"

That's a question that was often asked as this process began, and it's ridiculous. For all the facts and chronologies one can assemble, a biography, like a play, is an abstraction. It is filtered through what information is available, what fallible memories can dredge up, and the perspective of the writer. It is accurate to a point with details that can be corroborated, but it is largely an impression of the subject.

With theater people, it's doubly or triply challenging. Events have been turned into legends; facts are, shall we say, massaged in order to make a good story. In a business that is largely presentational, with some very rare exceptions, stories have been honed over the years with constant retelling for ultimate audience value, even if it's an interviewer—an audience of one. It's not from any malicious intent, but it is theater in its own right. We all present curated lives—even more so now in the age of social media—and wherever memory and subjectivity are in play, "truth" is at best inexact.

That's not to say that biographical stories aren't interesting, but rather than a recounting of dates and places, it's far more useful—and interesting—in Terrence's case to look at the process of becoming an artist, his lifelong expression of that art, the challenges he faced, and the ways he challenged them. Most importantly, though, it's vastly more interesting to consider how he was changed by the world and in turn changed it and the theater. It's also important to see how the uniquely collaborative nature of the theater, unlike any other art, shaped the final product, for want of a better word. That is something more likely to be a catalyst for deeper understanding of the process of an artist in a dynamic world than knowing who dined with whom at Sardi's and when, particularly when those bold-name diners are people we will never meet in life. After all, to be frank, we all look to find ourselves in whatever we read or see.

The actress Ruth Jaroslaw, who appeared in the original cast of Terrence's *The Ritz* on Broadway, once said to me, "Honey, here's how I read a script." (Grumbling and miming turning pages.) "Bullshit. Bullshit. Bullshit." (Stopping as her face lights up.) "My part!" Whenever we encounter art in any form, that's the reality; we look to see ourselves. That's also the intention of the artist—to touch people on an elemental level through the work.

The story of Terrence's life is in his work. It is in the challenge to get it written and get it seen. Terrence steadfastly believed that the work was more important than the story of his life; what he felt was important to say about himself is in the scripts and libretti. He resisted writing an autobiography, saying that he wasn't sure how to structure it. He could create an arc for a character he invented, and he could adapt books and movies, even interpret life events into opera, but he was baffled by writing his own life. The closest he came is in an anthology, *Selected Works: Terrence McNally, A Life in Plays*, with each of the plays introduced by a page or so of backstory on its development. Beyond that, his literal life story wasn't one he wanted to write. You can find information in a Google search, but the heart and humanity remain steadfastly resistant to algorithms and those were what drove Terrence as a playwright.

Case in point: Terrence told me that *Master Class* is his most autobiographical play. While it was revelatory to me when he first said it, turns out it was one of the things he said in countless interviews. And why not? It played well. It's certainly not autobiographical in the way that *Long Day's Journey into Night* is drawn from Eugene O'Neill's life. Yet look below the surface of *Master Class*, and it is about an artist's process, the challenges of success and fame, and ultimately the confrontation with aging and inevitable obscurity. These are issues that Terrence explored in his art and his life, which were inseparable for him. He wrote about what intrigued him, what inspired him, and what he was passionate about. He found truth not in events but in the hearts of his characters, which is why they live so vibrantly on stage and reach audiences so powerfully.

Theater is essentially false. It purports to show us life, but for it to do so an audience must be complicit in believing what they're seeing is real, even if they know those actors aren't those characters and through that door upstage is not the bedroom the characters are talking about, but a dusty building. Theater is an abstract construct, a story delivery system, if you will. We flock to it, though, because humans love their stories. They define us. They have more power than empirical fact (as you can see in any religion or political movement) to motivate passions and behavior.

Shakespeare's Henry V made up St. Crispin's Day to inspire his beleaguered army and to show them that they were the center of the day. It worked, far more than recounting how they were outnumbered, doused with rain, doubled over with dysentery, and without any apparent chance of prevailing—which is closer to the factual reality of the day. Shakespeare created that both to lionize Henry and to inspire his audiences about the great heart, courage, and inherent superiority of the English.

Terrence was a consummate storyteller, and if his plots were subtle, his talent was in knowing how to create compelling characters and situations. Like many playwrights, he wasn't interested in talking about the work as literature. It's a lesson I learned directly from Edward Albee who, when asked about the literary meaning or structure of a play, after a somewhat grumbling and annoyed response came out with, "I leave that for other people to determine." Lesson learned. As Ernest Hemingway wrote about *The Old Man and the Sea* in a letter in 1952, "There isn't any symbolism . . . The sea is the sea. The old man is an old man. The boy is a boy and the fish is a fish. The sharks are all sharks no better no worse. All the symbolism that people say is shit." Plays are even less illuminated by criticism, as they live in front of an audience. The experience is—or at least always was with Terrence—visceral and immediate.

Piecing together Terrence's journey as an artist has, in fact, left me a confirmed skeptic about literary analysis as a discipline, particularly as it relates to theater. Plays are not meant to be read or analyzed; they are meant to be seen. And seen in a particular moment in time. As Terrence said, "that moment in the theater at that performance will never come again in the same way." In the case of Terrence's work, there are only a few of his many plays that have been successfully revived, and we're talking critically if not commercially: *Frankie and Johnny in the Clair de Lune* and *Master Class* foremost among them. These are the plays that are more timeless, though the number of potential audience members who even know who Maria Callas is dwindles with each passing year. Terrence wasn't writing for the ages, however. He was writing things that had to be said *now*. The fear that throbs under every character in *Lips Together, Teeth Apart* seems blunted today as HIV becomes, often, a chronic condition, rather than life-or-death in the here-and-now. He was a radical political writer of his moment, who when asked why he wrote about certain subjects—HIV and AIDS in particular—he responded, "How could I not?"

A play affects people or it doesn't as it is being seen, and no analysis of underlying themes or theoretical approaches to the work as a whole will change that. What matters to an audience—and playwrights and producers—is how a show is experienced in a particular moment. Terrence knew this and was tireless about editing and adapting plays—even at times creating anxiety among his companies and threats of run-ins with Actors' Equity as edits came once performances had begun and actors were terrified about how changes would ever be accommodated. That was his process, however, and Terrence's passion was always to be clearer, truer, and more authentic—and, of course, more theatrical. (He never pretended that what he wrote was *real*.) When he had the chance, he would rewrite for a production, or even for publication, meaning that what's on the page in perpetuity may not have been what was on the stage in the first production. So, following Albee, and encouraged by Hemingway, we'll leave the analysis to others.

Finally, as we talked about this book and what it might be, Terrence said on several occasions he wanted himself presented "warts and all." Nice try. In all the conversations with people about Terrence and his work, it was nearly impossible to find a wart. Perhaps he reacted strongly to people and situations that he felt challenged his work. He was an ardent collaborator but also believed in his vision. His Irish temper sometimes let him feel wounded—and he could hold a grudge. Yet he was always happy when those issues resolved—also characteristically Irish. So, no disfiguring warts: a few minor abrasions, perhaps, but nothing serious—and little that was lasting. Even when wounds lingered, there is no one who was touched by Terrence and his work who was not changed for the better, as they all happily admit.

Terrence approached everything he did with passion and dedication. He cared deeply about people and from all I can tell was generous with his time and his heart. He delighted in others' successes and took his own in stride . . . as well as his failures.

This is the story of a man who made connections, who loved his work and who was a true artist. He was fallible and flawed, but how could he have created what he did if he was not . . . and owned that? It is an imperfect chronology. As with any life, there are gaps, events forgotten, entire shows that are not to be spoken about, at least by some. People whose thoughts we'd love to know are gone. Others aren't talking, or their stories are so curated as to inspire skepticism about their literal truth, however publication-ready the tale might be. People who inspired Terrence are gone, and the whirligig of time has changed the world and with it the theater.

And so, I'll ask, as Shakespeare does at the beginning of *Henry V*, for you to "piece out our imperfections with our thoughts." Terrence certainly understood and requested that, and it's important to recall, particularly as we stand "at rise."

1

The Last Man of
the Theater

I.

IN THE FINAL DECADES of the twentieth century, the theater changed. The millennium approached—and passed. It became more challenging to get plays mounted, largely due to economics and the skyrocketing costs of every aspect of production. The ever-increasing price of tickets made going to Broadway if not elitist at least not a regular event for most people. (In 1981, tickets for the two parts of *Nicholas Nickleby* shattered box office standards with a top price of $100, which was shocking and made headlines internationally.) In the 2020s Broadway prices can top $500 for hot shows—and resale tickets for hits such as *Hamilton* could, at the peak of its "hotness," command multiples of that—and that's now the case for any "hot ticket."

It wasn't just money, however. Audiences were changing, too. DVRs were introduced in 1999, and home-based entertainment became more prevalent. By 1992, more than 60 percent of American homes had cable TV. For many, going to the theater became an event. The "Disney-fication" of Broadway starting in 1994 with the arrival of *Beauty and the Beast* made theater an "attraction," with New York as the larger theme park. Going to a Broadway show, or any show for that matter, was no longer a habit. The actor and playwright Martin Moran, who has taught playwriting at Yale, notes that his students were encouraged not only to write for the stage, but to create screenplays and teleplays too. The reality is that if they ever hope to make a living as dramatic writers, they're going to have to go where the money is—and it's not in the theater. It can take years, decades even, for a piece to get on its feet—and even then, it may never make a dime.

Economics and changing entertainment platforms aside, the artistic influences on young artists has changed. Whereas theater in the twentieth century was to an extent self-reverential, in essence responding to itself and innovating within and in response to the conventions of the stage, by the end of the century and in the 2000s, it was popular culture, video, social media, and TV that were shaping young writers. That's not altogether surprising. What audiences wanted from a theater experience—and in particular a Broadway experience—had evolved to reflect the changing culture.

Now, this is to some extent an exaggeration. There is still some experimental work being done Off- and Off-Off Broadway, but in many cases the tropes (and technologies) that inspire them are not exclusively of the theater, which makes sense when an audience has not been raised with these conventions as part of their experiences.

And it's very hard to make money in the theater. On Broadway, it is the rare play that recoups. Even the starry revivals of Terrence's play *Frankie and Johnny in the Clair de Lune* failed to recoup their investment in either the 2002 Broadway outing with Stanley Tucci and Edie Falco or in the 2019 production with Audra McDonald and Michael Shannon, though both productions received stellar reviews. Nor did his last Broadway play, *Mothers and Sons*, make money on Broadway, but Terrence never did it for the money. Asked later in life why he chose to be a playwright, he said, simply, "I wanted to be heard."

II.

Coming of age in the mid-twentieth century, Terrence's experience, his sensibilities and appreciation of the form were almost completely shaped by live theater. He worked in it throughout his career. It was his greatest joy and source of success, though it's a difficult and often heartbreaking business, to be sure, an observation he would share with anyone inclined to pursue that life . . . even as he encouraged them to do so.

From an early age, Terrence was exposed to theater, and the form spoke to him. He grew up during the so-called Golden Age of musicals, conventionally thought to be the 1940s and 1950s. They were mainstream entertainment, a source of many popular music and cultural events. After making a splash on Broadway, leading stars like Mary Martin toured in their productions, which was the only way to cement their national stardom before television was widely adapted. Even when TV became the norm, much of early TV was inspired by theater. (It wouldn't be until 1951 when Lucille Ball and Desi Arnaz introduced the three-camera shoots of sitcoms that much of TV stopped looking like filmed theater.)

Terrence's introduction to Broadway was largely due to his paternal grandfather, who lived near Port Chester, New York, and who took Terrence to shows.

For years, Terrence said the first Broadway show he was taken to was *Annie Get Your Gun* with Ethel Merman. In many interviews over his career, Terrence recalled being around five years old when he saw it. However, as Terrence admitted later, that wasn't true, and he finally wanted to "set the record straight" about the first show he saw. His first trip to Broadway was the revival of a 1906 Victor Herbert operetta, *The Red Mill*. However, the show made little impression on him, and all he could remember was a windmill spinning on the stage, whereas he retained—and could describe—images from *Annie Get Your Gun* even late in life. As to why he created the story, Terrence was always the storyteller with an eye for dramatic detail. Terrence thought that it "made a better story" for someone with a prominent theater career to have his first encounter with Broadway be with no less an icon than Ethel Merman. After all, who would remember the revival of an obscure show few people had ever heard of, despite its respectable run of 531 performances from 1945–1947? It's also not possible that Terrence was five when he saw it, as *Annie Get Your Gun* didn't open until May of 1946, at which point Terrence would have been at least eight. (His Wikipedia biography was later updated to reflect that.) *Annie Get Your Gun* was a memory for a lifetime, and he recalled Merman shooting out candles on a motorcycle. Of course, he said Annie was supposed to be the kids' older sister, but Merman looked like their mother. ("And when she did *Gypsy*, she looked like their grandmother.") Terrence loved Merman all his life, however. He said that she was one of the first women he was attracted to in the theater, largely because she could never be mistaken for anyone else, much like Gertrude Lawrence. In 1976, when Merman announced she was retiring from Broadway, Terrence wrote a column for *New York Guide*, one of the many papers that came and went during that period and for which Terrence wrote a regular column, saying that she owed her fans one more Broadway show. Merman replied thanking him but noted the rigors of doing eight shows a week (most before musicals were amplified with microphones) and that she was happy in her retirement.

The second Broadway show Terrence always said he had seen, though it was the third actually, was a matinee of *The King and I* with Yul Brynner and Gertrude Lawrence when he was on a trip back to New York. Small wonder it intrigued him, "*The King and I* is about a little boy lost in this exotic kingdom with his wonderful archetypal mother who's there for him all the time," as Terrence described her. This was decidedly not the case with his own mother, who was distant and a heavy drinker, more interested in her own good times than being a mother. Gertrude Lawrence represented the classic preteen fantasy of a protecting, caring mom—shared with countless young, gay boys.

Although Terrence often was quoted as saying he was ten when he saw *The King and I*, given the show's dates, he would have had to have been at least thirteen, which would make more sense as he experienced the emotional toll of his disengaged mother. He also recalled that as it happened, he saw the next to the last performance of Lawrence. She died of cancer on September 6, 1952, just over two weeks after he had seen it. Terrence remembered that show throughout his life and the grief he felt at Lawrence's death and felt the loss deeply on a personal level. He grieved for the loss of Lawrence who had dazzled him—and for the realization that he had never had a caring, maternal figure in his own life.

On the day he saw *The King and I* at the matinee, Terrence saw *Pal Joey*, a successful revival after the original had bombed, at night with Vivienne Siegel and Harold Lang. What he remembered of that performance was a young Elaine Stritch as Melba singing "Zip," a novelty number about the intellectual thoughts running through Gypsy Rose Lee's head as she strips.

Needless to say (almost), on one day he got two very different portrayals of women, but more importantly it cemented the experience of theater as something very special; "Zip" amused him, even if he didn't get all the references to Schopenhauer and Dali, it touched him on a deeply emotional level. He also remembered seeing *Paint Your Wagon* on that trip as well, but that show had little impact on him. That's not surprising. Despite some hits from the score, such as "I Call the Wind Maria," the sprawling tale of love during the Gold Rush would never hold the emotional complexity of shows that touched Terrence's developing sense of self. (Ironically, he would write the book for the ill-fated musical *Here's Where I Belong*, which partly failed due to its plot-heavy structure.)

As for the chronology, in the greater scheme of things, exact dates don't really matter. Terrence liked to say that he was terrible with dates, which always gave him a plausible excuse for any errors, and for several years as a young man, he regularly shaved a year off his age, thinking, as many artists do, that as a younger man, he was more likely to be seen as an *enfant terrible*. The point is that theater and the experience of going to the theater was part of his life from his earliest years, and that the images of those early shows stayed with him throughout his life. As he was approaching eighty, he said that he could recall Lawrence in *The King and I* with more clarity than something he had seen last week.

Theater would have an even bigger impact on the dramatic arc of Terrence's life—and not from a seat in the Orchestra. His father Hubert and mother Dorothy had had a bar and grill in St. Petersburg before the war, the Pelican Club. The club was destroyed by a hurricane, and not knowing exactly what to do, Hubert enlisted, which as Terrence recalled was before he would have been drafted. (The first peacetime draft was established in 1940, and by enlisting, Hubert would have more options in his service and less risk of going to the front lines.) Dorothy and Terrence moved to Port Chester and lived with her parents. Hubert's father, who was a prominent New York lawyer, and according to Terrence, a bit of a playboy, lived nearby and was the huge theater fan—and regular audience member.

When Hubert returned from the war, he came back to Port Chester. Terrence only recalled that his father was working for General Foods, and he wasn't very happy. However, after seeing *Death of a Salesman* on Broadway, he was inspired to change his life, uprooted the family and moved to Dallas, later to Corpus Christi where he bought a Schlitz beer distributorship, around 1951, just as Terrence was entering high school. Hubert wanted to be his own man, more like Bernard, the young character in *Salesman* who is on a path to success while Willy Loman, the title character, finds himself increasingly irrelevant in a world that moves past him. Many years later, Terrence wrote in a note to playwright Arthur Miller that throughout his childhood, he remembered seeing the playbill from *Salesman* on the coffee table in the living room, an almost permanent reminder of the power of theater to change lives.

His parents also returned to New York annually to see shows, so Terrence got to know the big shows of the time from the programs they brought home and the cast albums he would listen to. He had vowed on his trip to New York to see *The King and I* that he would live in the city one day. Like many who are lucky enough to get to New York and Broadway at a young age, the luster and lure of the town marked him forever as a future resident.

Musicals and theater may have had another appeal as well. Terrence recalled the excitement that his parents expressed and the happiness theater brought them. Given that the relationship between his parents was otherwise strained and that tension and anger hung over the house like a cloud, he couldn't help but notice the power of theater to lift that cloud and create, if only for a short time, a level of escape from a limiting life, if not actual happiness.

III.

Why or how theater—or any art form—has an impact on people is unknowable. Terrence certainly had no idea. "I wasn't aware of it then," he said looking back later in life, "but now I can see it in myself. I knew from an early age that I would be a writer. I just liked writing." When he was in school during the war in Port Chester, Terrence started writing "little stories." In those early days, he hadn't seen a play yet, but he recalled "words never frightened me." Throughout the rest of his education, he said that words came very easily to him. "It was easier to do that than try to be good in science or math, which I didn't take to very naturally."

Once he began going to the theater, the scale intrigued him as well as the potential for storytelling. He felt the same way about opera (well, most operas. In his notes, he writes that he is "done seeing operas I don't like a second time.") and the power for something larger than life, abstract and inherently false—as the theater is—could nonetheless be so emotionally powerful.

His theatrical sensibilities were developed at an early age, not merely by his trips to the theater but also by his exposure to opera. His first exposure to the artform he could remember came in fifth grade at Christ the King Catholic School in Dallas. One day the nun who was his teacher brought in a phonograph and 78-rpm records and said, "Children, I'm going to introduce you to something called opera." She played "Vogliatme Bene" from *Madama Butterfly* sung by Licia Albanese and James Melton, and he said, "the moment I heard it, I just loved it." (That recording can still be heard on YouTube.)

Over the years, the story acquired a little more detail. In *Terrence McNally: A Memoir in Plays*, the teacher Sister Mary Margaret took on a more terrifying demeanor. From a purely narrative standpoint, one has to admit that the image of a draconian and punitive 1950s nun in full habit, who was quick to rap errant kids' knuckles, becoming the instrument by which Terrence was introduced to an art form that would change his life *is* a pretty darn good story. Nor, as noted about stories of this nature, does the absolute truth matter. What matters is that at a young age, Terrence was first exposed to opera, and the experience of a moment had a lifetime of impact. Terrence was always a storyteller, and what mattered in his plays was never the actual veracity of a story but the emotional impact and theatrical effect of it. So, we'll stick with that, too.

Continuing the story, Terrence describes himself as the only one in the class who paid any attention to the music. If it were a movie, from his description, you would see little Terry, as he was called then, in a glow of light, transfixed by the music while all around him eleven-year-olds were acting out.

As he describes that moment:

> I was drawn into this world of melody and feeling without a moment's hesitation. I wanted to live there forever and in that moment, I think I knew I would. There was no barrier between reality and art. I lived fully in one; I lived more fully in the other. I wanted both. . . . I knew if I couldn't express my own feelings in my life and work, I would explode. Art wasn't an escape from reality, it was a *heightened* reality all its own, perhaps a more truthy one. Art was an escape *to* the truth, not a turning away from it.

No doubt it was a profound experience, but his writing about it more than sixty years later is an adult's interpretation of a child's experience. Nonetheless, he did recall that his first impression was that it was a beautiful voice, like nothing he had ever heard, and he knew right away that he liked her. When he later discovered Maria Callas, he said her voice was beautiful and unique, something he treasured in an actor or singer throughout his life. He loved singers who sounded like themselves, not some generic product, and near the end of his life he was pleased that there seemed to be a rising trend toward unique, even idiosyncratic, voices, after a period when to his mind, American acting and singing became "generic." One of the defining characteristics of a "McNally actor" is that they could never be mistaken for somebody else.

From that one hearing of *Butterfly*, as he tells it, Terrence became fascinated with opera and began following it in the same way his contemporaries followed sports teams. Where other kids had pictures of sports heroes on their walls as kids, Terrence had opera stars. He began to follow and recognize opera stars and was very likely the only teenager in Southern Texas who knew Kirsten Flagstad from Maria Callas. The other important element of this is that the language and dramatic conventions of opera in terms of scale, scope, and emotional power became a language he understood; well, more felt than comprehended. They would influence how he would score speeches intent on the rhythm, the arc of a speech. The artistry of the language was always as important as what was being said, and he would wrestle with words to find that precision, something he did when he came to writing opera libretti, thinking about the physical demands of producing a single word. By his own admission, he wrote operatically . . . and had no interest in writing any other way, even if he could have.

As he often did, and as noted earlier, Terrence put his biographical reflections in the mouths of his characters. Many of Terrence's thoughts about opera are expressed that way in *The Lisbon Traviata*. He knew his obsession with opera was not something his parents, for example, understood.

> **Stephen:** My father always wondered why I wanted another *Aida*. "Because it's different from the other ones, Dad. You go to the Army-Navy game every year. Same game, different players. Same opera, different singers." He didn't see my logic. I thought it was brilliant for a toddler.

Later, he explains opera in the simplest of terms:

> **Stephen:** Love and death. That's all they're ever singing about. There's an occasional Anvil Chorus, but it's basically boy meets girl, boy gets girl, boy and girl croak. That's all you need to know, from

Aida to *Zaide*. . . . Opera is about us, our life and death passions—
we all love, we're all going to die.

Like Terrence, these characters understood themselves, their lives,
and their passions in the context of art. Despite its abstract nature, it
was real, the lens through which he saw and tried to come to grips with,
offstage reality. Terrence understood art and experienced on the highest
level how art affected the art and soul, or as Stephen suggests, "some
even more intimate place." He wrote for audiences that "got him," and
he loved working with actors who likewise "got him." Many of his plays
would also deal with the theater at all levels. Whether it is *It's Only a Play*
that deals directly with Broadway or Chloe in *Lips Together, Teeth Apart*
who revels in her own community theater triumphs, theater in its many
guises was the *lingua franca* of his work. Throughout his life, Terrence
would always go to the theater, wherever he was. Whether it was in the
capitals of Europe, or at a community theater production of *The Sound
of Music* in Ojai, California, theater is what fed his soul and helped him
make sense of life.

IV.

Terrence had another early influence that shaped his writing: the television show *Kukla, Fran and Ollie*. Terrence didn't have a TV in his house
when he was first in Texas, he recalled. At the time much of TV in
Texas was controlled by Lady Bird Johnson, and Terrence recalled Corpus Christi was the biggest city in America without television. However,
when he visited cousins in Dallas for the weekend, he always wanted to
watch TV. He was immediately, he said, captivated by the puppets and
the human star, Fran Allison. He also became a big fan of creator and
puppeteer Burt Tillstrom. The show was almost entirely ad-libbed and
featured rapid-fire wordplay and a lot of puns. By 2022 children's TV
standards, the show would be far too sophisticated for how executives
perceive children's grasp of topics, but Terrence loved the quick-witted
Allison and her interaction with the puppets, the dragon Kukla and

The television show Kukla, Fran and Ollie *had a profound impact on Terrence's early appreciation of theater.*
HISTORIC COLLECTION / ALAMY STOCK PHOTO

"Kuklapolitan Players," especially the retired opera star Madame Ogle-puss, not surprisingly. (Her voice may have been shot, but that trope was necessary since she was voiced by Tillstrom.) To Terrence's mind these characters were "realer than real," and he loved the concept of puppets as well, saying, "I was especially intrigued by them, and I realized that I preferred making them talk, rather than being the person out in front." Years later, Terrence would regularly speak aloud in different voices as he worked out the dialogue, something his husband Tom loved hearing because it indicated that Terrence was indeed in the thick of writing— and enjoying it. This may seem to contradict the earlier statement that Terrence was influenced more by theater than pop culture, since no show was more pop than *Kukla, Fran and Ollie*. Look closer, though, and you'll see that it used many more theater conventions than what are generally thought of as TV conventions; it was intrinsically simple. The show was shot by a single, stationary camera, and when Fran wasn't talking to the puppets, she was talking directly to the camera—often singing to solo piano accompaniment. These weren't so-called kiddie songs, either. Arranged by Jack Fascinato, who had worked with Tennessee Ernie Ford among others, the songs sounded like they could have come from the Broadway stage. Indeed, many of the episodes that weren't ad-libbed were complete musical productions and even parodied Gilbert and Sullivan. Kids couldn't get enough—and neither could many adults. When he began writing for Off-Off Broadway in the early 1960s, Terrence discovered that other writers, including Edward Albee, had also been influenced by the TV show. During their relationship, Terrence once said to Albee, "You were really influenced by Burt Tillstrom." And he said, "You're the first person who's ever noticed that." What Terrence added was that the characters from the show inspired many of the characters in Albee's plays, largely because they were such archetypes. The presentation also informed a style of comedy and quick-witted banter that almost seems like it's improvised, which is much more evident in Terrence's work than that of many others at the time.

Terrence began to understand and study classic theater in high school where he was introduced to Shakespeare and Chekhov, who remained his favorite playwrights throughout his life, and from whom he learned structure and language, and, to a large extent, how to observe people and the human condition. Along with opera, they created the backbones of his theatrical sensibility: Shakespeare for scale and grandeur and Chekov for the mordant comedy of living and observation of the tiniest details of life and how they resonated. He continued his study at Columbia, and in one paper wrote about the scale of tragedy in Shakespeare, particularly in *King Lear* and *Hamlet*, how it's juxtaposed with the quotidian concerns of the characters, and how the scale of the drama facilitates—and is essential to—understanding.

Terrence embraced the abstraction of the theatrical form, the "heightened reality," he wrote about. He also referred to his style as "poetic reality." If his characters were realistic, they were not naturalistic, and that's what makes so many of them memorable. Mendy in *The Lisbon Traviata* is, fittingly, an operatic character, larger than life, but even in his excesses, there is an emotional truth about a man who has devoted his life to his passion for opera and obscure recordings at the expense of more serious, deeper, personal relationships. This play is particularly operatic, not just in its subject matter but also in the relationship between Mendy's best friend Stephen and Stephen's boyfriend Mike, simple challenges of fidelity and love in a gay relationship ultimately take an operatic turn. He never intended it to be taken as reality.

This may have been one reason that Terrence's plays didn't transfer well to the movie screen. The abstraction of theater, the character-focus rather than an emphasis on plot, don't translate well between media. The two notable movies made from his plays, *Frankie and Johnny* and *Love! Valour! Compassion!*, also became bloated—and blunted—on the screen. Additional characters and all of the settings detracted from the inherent simplicity of the pieces—and their power. While *L!V!C!* won the Tony award for Best Play and John Glover for featured actor (as the twins John and James Jeckyll), the transfer to the screen received mixed reviews and garnered only $2 million in U.S. box office on an estimated $2.9 million budget. Reviewers criticized its conventional three-act structure and that it was too much like a stage play. *Frankie and Johnny* fared better in the reviews, though Terrence and director Gary Marshall turned it more into a romcom (following Marshall's hit with *Pretty Woman*) than the story of two people struggling to find intimacy. According to the production notes of the time, the cast featured ninety-four people. The sharpness of Terrence's lines endures, and there are some comic bits introduced, such as Nathan Lane as a gay neighbor, but it is more facile and predictable than the two-hander on stage—aiming at the romcom audience happy to see two great big stars playing ordinary people. What made *Frankie and Johnny* work on stage was the sense that in the middle of the night, two people lost in the big city found themselves alone together in an intense negotiation of intimacy. On stage, the play is delicate yet unrelenting. That feeling that the characters were trapped in their own stories was diluted in the broader world of the film. The simple fact is: Terrence didn't write romcoms. He wrote life-or-death situations for his characters. When the thing that is "out there," in this case intimacy beyond sex—is relieved by opening up the story, the urgency is diminished, and the characters become ordinary. Terrence never wrote anyone who was ordinary. Still, *Frankie and Johnny* was more successful as a movie than *L!V!C!*, largely due to Michelle Pfeiffer and Al Pacino in the title roles, grossing $67 million worldwide on a reported budget of $29 million.

The movie *The Ritz*, a farce set in 1976 in a Manhattan gay bathhouse, didn't make the transition easily from stage to screen, either. What was a classic door-slamming farce on stage got bogged down and, according to reviewers at the time, missed the poignancy of the play and that the comedy was overdone. Again, what worked on stage couldn't be re-created as effectively on film. Surprisingly for 1976, the review in the *New Yorker* suggested that one of the reasons that the movie fell flat was because director Richard Lester, mostly known previously for the direction of The Beatles' two movies and *The Three Musketeers*, was not himself gay and so couldn't effectively convey gay characters on the screen. However, it's more likely that trying to force a farce onto a larger—pardon the pun—stage, as with the other transfers, watered it down.

Terrence never considered himself a screenwriter. Reflecting on both *L!V!C!* and *Frankie and Johnny* later in life, he didn't think they were "particularly outstanding examples of my work." He also wrote two original screenplays, both of which are lost. One is completely forgotten, and the other is remembered because it was written for Barbra Streisand. He said,

> It was a commission from a producer who thought the world
> needed a big, big, expensive movie made about the life of Puccini,
> and I was the only person who could write it. I think I wrote a really
> good screenplay, but it was suddenly budgeted at $100 million.

It was going to have openings at La Scala and the Met, "and you can't green screen that."

He spent time with Streisand in the Bel Air house, which he described as "pretty nice," and he thought it was going well, until one day Streisand's manager came to Terrence and said, "She's decided to pass, and she's going to make something called *The Mirror Has Two Faces.*" Terrence recalled later that they also told him at that time that Barbra's audience didn't want to see her in a comedy. (Though she had been in *What's Up Doc* in 1972.)

And Terrence thought, "Well, that's the end of that." He did note that he had gotten an advance. ("When I write a play, nobody pays me in advance"), and he didn't recall what he had been paid, but he knew at the time Streisand pulled the plug he had already spent it.

He didn't fare much better in television. The disastrous, one-season 1984 CBS TV series *Mama Malone* (rhymes with "baloney") was pure Terrence. The premise was a cooking show that came live from a Brooklyn apartment, and every recipe began with chopping onions. Because it was in an apartment, life intervened, and no recipe was ever completed. The comedy was antic and the characters extreme (somewhat like *The Ritz*), and it got strong initial reviews in the industry. It was praised for its concept, and as a send up of cooking and lifestyle shows. Norman Lear was the producer, who was about as hot as anyone could be in television at the time, so everyone in show business was predicting big things for the show. At the time, Terrence said there wasn't much respect for TV writing in the theater community. Hits like *All in the Family* that were sophisticated and daring were the anomaly, and while there was a lot of money to be made, people who wrote for TV were spoken of with contempt by "real" writers, as Terrence recalled. Working with Lear, however, Terrence thought he basically had it made. He imagined giving up the theater, living in Malibu and not having to worry about the arduous and emotionally draining process of getting a play up. Because he was getting a lot of Hollywood buzz—and because he hadn't understood the process of television writing—he had insisted from the outset that he be the only writer on the show.

CBS had initially slated *Mama Malone* for 1982 and production was completed on thirteen episodes, but release was held till 1984, a move Tom Shales, while reviewing it for the *Washington Post*, inferred was because it was not good. In his review, he wrote, "*Mama Malone* is one long bray of coarse sitcom noise, cold and clammy as a politician's handshake, though perhaps less deeply felt." Ouch. The show was also criticized for the ethnic stereotyping of Italian Americans and in perhaps one of the earliest criticisms of cultural appropriation, English star Lila Kaye was criticized for her performance as an Italian. Even though CBS had programmed it as a lead-in to the Monday Night Movies, it was consistently a ratings disaster. It was up against Monday Night Football on ABC, and as Terrence learned later, there's no way that CBS was ever going to put a show that anyone thought was going to be a hit up against that ratings giant. He realized that the network had used the show to fill a slot with something already bought and paid for, and no one was going to watch it. At the time, *Variety* ran a list of the top fifty shows on television. *Mama Malone* opened at number forty-nine, and thirteen weeks later, it was in the same slot. CBS aired the thirteen episodes that had been produced, took whatever financial hit associated with it, and cancelled the show.

The failure of *Mama Malone* was difficult for Terrence. He wasn't bothered by the critics and the low ratings as much as surprised. As he said, at the time he was working on *Mama Malone*, he was in limbo as a playwright, and the initial Hollywood industry response led him to believe that, as noted, he would become a wealthy TV writer. He had bought that house in California, which he kept for about five years. Contributing to his reaction to the failure was that at the time he was two years sober and was trying to figure out what that meant to him as a playwright. (More on that in a bit.)

Terrence told another story about working with Lear. Given his admiration for Lear, it was a big deal for Terrence that Lear was producing *Mama Malone*, and they hit it off. Together, they developed another show that they pitched to CBS. Tentatively titled *The Education of Young Henry Blair, Esq. or The Way of the World*, it was a sitcom set in England in 1700 and was about which of two brothers—one legitimate, one illegitimate—was more worthy of the family fortune. *Mama Malone* was still in the honeymoon phase pre-premiere, Terrence, still presumed to be a hot up-and-comer, was the writer, and he and Lear got a meeting with top CBS executives to pitch the show.

It didn't go well. Terrence recalled that at the time Lear had a fax machine in his car (Hollywood!), and by the time they got out to the car in the CBS parking lot, a rejection had been faxed to them. Terrence didn't know for sure, but he speculated that within the TV industry there was a lot of resentment for Lear's success, and that it gave the programming executives particular pleasure to turn something down from the man who had single-handedly changed the sitcom forever. That might have been the case, but one wonders how a semi-comedy set in the Age of Enlightenment would fare in a TV lineup that featured *Dallas*, *Dynasty*, *Miami Vice*, and *Who's the Boss*? Period clothes and sets alone would have required enormous budgets. It also reads like a classic McNally play. It had lots of wit and complex characters, but that was just the opposite of what TV was buying. Whether *All in the Family* or *Dynasty*, subtlety and nuance were not what sold to the mass audience. Whatever the reason, this rejection would be the only time that Terrence felt that resentment of success colored a response from executives or producers. Though he and Lear remained friendly, they only tried to pitch one more show, which also never was picked up.

When Terrence's work succeeded on screen, it was, ironically, on television. Two of his short plays, *Next* and *Botticelli*, were produced for channel 13 in New York, in 1967 and 1968, respectively. He won an Emmy for *André's Mother* starring Richard Thomas and Sada Thompson. *André's Mother* in 1990, produced for PBS's *American Playhouse*, was an adaptation and expansion of an eight-minute one-act he had written for a 1998 omnibus evening at Manhattan Theatre Club called *Urban Blight*. The TV script won an Emmy Award. His other most successful teleplay, *The Last Mile* starring Bernadette Peters, was set in a dressing room at the Metropolitan Opera where a singer was about to make her Met debut in *Tosca*. Part monologue, part interaction with an array of backstage characters and a memory of her brother who had died of AIDS, the piece was presented in 1992 as part of the *Great*

Performances 20th Anniversary Special. Although written and produced for television, both are theater pieces. They are smaller, more intimate, and deeply personal, and they conveyed characters at a turning point, always with love and death in the background, exactly what Terrence did best.

He also wrote a teleplay with Wendy Wasserstein, which aired on ABC on May 31, 1988, as one part of a three-play omnibus called *Sam Found Out: A Triple Play* starring Liza Minnelli. (John Kander and Lanford Wilson wrote the other two pieces.) In the McNally/Wasserstein piece, Minnelli plays Maxine Evans, a tap dance teacher, who fumbles into a fairytale and is swept off her feet by the crown prince of a small country, played by Louis Gosset Jr. The fairytale storyline is pure Wasserstein, but the jokes are pure McNally, including inside theater gags. Still, it's a static piece that might have worked on stage but feels labored on TV and received lukewarm reviews, though Terrence and Wasserstein fared best of the three. Over the next years, Terrence kept trying his hand at TV, and his archives have many pilots that he wrote, some of which got nearly to the point of production. At the same time, he hated the fact that as a TV writer he was a slave to the ratings and that one's value could change every week with each new ratings report. He hated not having complete artistic control over his work. While in the theater he, of course, had to collaborate, he often had the final word. Not so in the world of TV where the "suits" and the ratings drive the writing. Terrence's experiences with Hollywood weren't happy, but they did turn his focus back to the theater . . . where failure is forgiven, at least to some extent. Or at least you can keep trying.

And so, the now-sober Terrence found out who he was and discovered that the theater was where he belonged. He jumped fully into the world of musicals, wrote opera libretti, articles, and much more. In fact, he wrote nonstop. As an artist, perhaps the soulless harshness of Hollywood and the challenge of getting sober did him a favor. Some of his greatest work was yet to come, and the theater would be the home for the rest of his life.

V.

Like many writers, despite his love of words and the fact that writing was easier than math or science, writing didn't always come easily to Terrence. Also like many writers, he often would write in bursts, and when he was in the thick of it, he was the happiest he could be. As he said of the writing profession, "If you can feed yourself and keep a roof over your head, it's the best possible life."

He loved the story he often told of having writer's block, and his partner at the time, Dominic Cuskern, apparently said to him, "Honey, how difficult can it be? One character says something and the other character says something and so on. And pretty soon you have a play." Like so many stories, this one had several versions, depending on who's telling it and their fallible memories, but Terrence said that this conversation—or something very like it—got him writing again after the long dry spell from his TV experiences.

Writing, however, didn't always come easily. One of his assistants, Sam Myers, said that when they were supposed to be having a working session, Terrence would suddenly have a need to organize the CDs—and have a story about each one. His husband Tom said that when Terrence had set out to write, he would suddenly have a need to clean out the refrigerator or undertake some other task. Another assistant, Logan Reed, said that one day he arrived to find Terrence with a bunch of broken awards which absolutely had to be super-glued back together before he could start writing. Logan dutifully complied, and then the awards were put away in a box not to be seen again. Or the bookshelf needed reorganizing, or any number of things.

Certainly, any writer can relate to that process, as they can to what the novelist Frank Norris wrote in a letter to a friend, "Don't like to write, but like having written." It's all part of the creation, and Terrence's friend and onetime producer Edgar Bronfman maintained that interruptions were not distractions or avoidances but an important part of the process of writing, giving time for ideas to develop in the subconscious before they materialized on the page. In other words, on some level Terrence was always writing, especially when he was working on a specific project.

In short, he loved being a writer, and more particularly he loved being a playwright. Like Dickens, his characters lived for him, and even when they went through a long gestation, he knew who they were and what they were after. It was the power of making them talk that he had discovered watching *Kukla, Fran and Ollie* and allowing them to reveal themselves to him that fascinated him. While he would write his plays alone in his office—often with opera blaring—he loved the interaction and the collaboration with all the people involved in a production when that was happening. It was the balance of these two experiences that propelled his writing and fed his creativity.

He loved hearing his words in the mouths of actors as well and said that the best actors showed him things about the characters he might not have known were there. That was another reason the theater suited him so well; plays are constantly evolving and changing during rehearsals (and sometimes even afterward), and even when it could get trying, Terrence loved the collaborations and the problem-solving once a show began to be on its feet, as they say. He was famous for rewriting plays, up to the last possible minute. When he was working on *Fire and Air* in 2018, for Classic Stage Company (CSC), the director John Doyle sent him away from rehearsals because the constant changes he wanted were making it hard for the actors to get the show up in the limited rehearsal time they had. Even when a show had closed, that wasn't the end of the edits. Published versions of his scripts often have been either tweaked or substantially rewritten from what they had been on the stage. *Fire and Air* was substantially revised prior to being presented as *Immortal Longings* in Houston in 2019, where it was billed as an entirely new play.

He also worked closely with actors to help make the words fit. In the rehearsal room, he was always listening. If an actor said they needed something for a character, almost every time he would come back with something brilliant. That interaction was important to him in shaping a play. As many of the people who worked with him pointed out, he wasn't like some of his contemporaries who insisted that the script be presented exactly as written. Nonetheless, he also could be exacting when a script was finally set.

The actor Benjamin Eakeley, who was in one of the industry readings for the musical *Anastasia*, remembered Terrence giving the cast a speech about the integrity of the language and how he didn't want to hear any added "ums" or "pauses." After all, the soprano doesn't add notes to Verdi.

He was also exacting about creating jokes that landed. That often happened in the rehearsal room. Reed, who by this time was an assistant director on the Broadway production of *It's Only a Play*, remembered that Terrence would work and work with the actors on getting just the right words and actions to make a gag land. Reed remembered working with Nathan Lane, who as we'll see was one of McNally's beloved muses, and working the joke down to the granular level of where Lane should move his foot to make the joke work. Reed said he was watching two exceptional showmen doing what they did best.

Terrence was always trying to dig deeper, be clearer, and more honest as his characters and his plays lived for him.

Although much of his early work was one-act plays, Terrence loved the three-act format. Of his major works, however, only *And Things that Go Bump in the Night*, *Lips Together, Teeth Apart*, and *Love! Valour! Compassion!* were presented in three acts. Many of the works were presented in two, and later works like *And Away We Go* and *Mothers and Sons* had no intermissions, in part in response to changing tastes in the theater, where audiences no longer want to spend three hours watching a straight play. As he always did, Terrence adapted to the conventions of the time. In the early 2000s, it was common to hear critics—and audiences—say, "My favorite words in the language are ninety minutes, no intermission." Although he acknowledged the convention, he never liked it. Having cut his artistic teeth on Chekhov, he wanted to delve deeply into small, intricate moments, and he wanted the audience to go along.

Nor was Terrence overly concerned with plot, an approach that can often work in the theater but not so well in films or television. It's not that things don't happen in Terrence's plays; they do. However, the plays are about people in situations, and it's the people and how they respond to those situations and interact that give the plays their life. The situations are, as we've discussed, often operatic in scope, but the stories could be relatively small. The lack of traditional storylines didn't always sit well with critics or audiences. Nathan Lane recalls during the run of *The Lisbon Traviata* that at one point a man in the audience stood up and hollered, "Where's the plot?" before storming out. Lane wanted to respond, "Wait till act two." (This is another one of those theater stories that has been told in various ways by different people over the years.)

As a writer and in working with actors, Terrence was famous for his attention to punctuation. Bronfman tells a story, which he repeated at Terrence's memorial service, of taking down revisions over the phone from Terrence during *It's Only a Play*, and when he read them back, Terrence said he hadn't heard the semi-colon. That's the point: he hadn't *heard* it. For Terrence punctuation was critical. He believed that just as music was scored with notes and rests, language was scored with words and punctuation. The best actors, he said, were those who knew how to act the difference between a comma and a semi-colon or a period. Actors like Richard Thomas, who had a major hit with Terrence's short play *Prelude and Liebestod*, a stream of consciousness monologue from a conductor as he is leading the orchestra, believed scoring was a gift to an actor.

As a writer, to Terrence, the key to the acting was all there on the page. If actors simply performed the words as written and punctuated, there would be no need for a director. This may seem to contradict his desire to work with actors on what was comfortable to them, but he often wrote with the voice of a particular actor in his ears. The comment about directors, one suspects, was—at least partly—waggish, as Terrence had great relationships with many of the directors he worked with, though not all. However, he heard the language as music, and though he claimed he was not a musician, when read with an attention to the punctuation, his text can sound like music—staccato, legato, obligato, and, yes, cadenza. There is a musical sensibility in the arc of his phrases that rivals any of the great operas, classical or modern.

As a subject, Terrence loved the theater. Plays like *And Away We Go*, *Golden Age*, *Fire and Air*, *Master Class*, *Dedication or the Stuff of Dreams*, and *It's Only a Play* deal directly with theater as a topic, as his opera *Great Scott* deals with opera as a subject. In other works, his characters are steeped in theater: Mendy in *The Lisbon Traviata*, Buzz in *L!V!C!*, and Chloe in *Lips Together, Teeth Apart* all derive a portion of their identity from their relationship to the theater. He also believed that any working playwright was part of an unbroken line from Aeschylus forward.

In one of his most theater-centric plays, *And Away We Go*, which is a time-traveling piece imagining theater as it's being created throughout history, a character says: "Somewhere out there is a young person who will write the great American play and I think it will be because someone kept the light on for Ibsen and Chekhov."

Having found his home in the theater, he never wanted to leave, and he didn't think anyone else who had followed the difficult trail to get there should either. When actors he loved would go off to take more remunerative roles in film and TV, he would tell them to come back because the theater needed them. Actors such as Richard Thomas, Nathan Lane, and Christine Baranski he always felt belonged in the theater primarily.

Once he came back, Terrence never doubted that he would be able to make a living as a writer. There were lean years to be sure, but he always felt lucky to be able to do what he did.

He encouraged people to see as much as they possibly could. He would tell people to buy the most expensive seat they could afford and sit as close as possible. "What you're going to see will never happen again in the same way," he said, acknowledging the uniqueness of live theater.

He also knew what the theater was about. While he was ultimately seen as a mainstream playwright with a Broadway career, his commitment was first and foremost always to the art. He knew the techniques of the stage, and he worked tirelessly to shape plays up to—and even at times beyond—opening. (He never did quite get that when a show was in technical rehearsals he couldn't easily change the script because that would change light cues, staging, and more.) For Terrence, it was always about the words . . . and how they communicated to an audience. He would say, "Theater isn't life or death, but it should be approached that way."

In his blood from his youngest days, his love of theater was the part of himself he was most eager to share, and he was the last artist perhaps of all time who was completely shaped by theater and his art ultimately found its fullest expression in live performance on stage. It might have been a rocky road at times, but the theater was in him and it couldn't be avoided. He believed passionately in the power of theater to change hearts and minds, and he was perhaps the form's biggest cheerleader. No playwright since has had such a varied career, triumphed in so many forms, was so consistently original and daring and unwilling to rest on his laurels, or searched so diligently for truth in the abstraction that is the world behind the proscenium. He was knocked down and got up again and again, and arguably he had no choice; it was what he was born to do. In doing so, he changed the theater, and then the world changed to accommodate his vision. As an artist, he was unquestionably the last man of the theater.

And here's how he got there . . .

2

And Away We Go
Home and School

I.

IF TERRENCE WAS the last man whose art was shaped almost entirely by the theater, or quasi-theatrical experiences, he is one of the first playwrights of the Internet age, which presents a challenge to any would-be biographer. The online repository of everything about everyone from kindergarten photos to catalogs of work of public figures hadn't been invented. So, in trying to reconstruct Terrence's early life, there are no teenage journals, nor is there a trove of letters to friends, stored away. The few that exist are about where he was going, plays he'd seen, and were for the most part informational, not to mention sites like Wikipedia, which can be edited. Portraying the artist as a young man must, for the most part, be pieced together from bits and fragments, fading decades-old memories, and, as mentioned earlier, stories that have migrated from tale to legend to accepted fact, not to mention that many people want to control how things are remembered . . . as if a book is that old "permanent record" so many were threatened with in school.

With regard to Terrence, it's not surprising that records should be so scanty. What has been retained in his archives are papers, clippings, early scripts, and notes all to do with what is so coldly referred to as "work product." Throughout his life, Terrence was not a man given to deep introspection, though he did go to therapy for a brief time in his middle years. He lived very much in the present and for what would happen next. That is perhaps why faced with lacerating criticism, deep personal tragedy, and his own worries about his work, he kept moving forward. As an artist, he was always looking for the next thing to spark his creativity.

What we know is that Michael Terrence McNally was born November 3, 1938, in St. Petersburg, Florida. (He never used Michael again and was known as "Terry" until he was in college.) He didn't recall much about life there, nor did he recall much about life in Port Chester. He did recall that his mother worked at Abercrombie and Fitch on Fifth Avenue in Manhattan and commuted in every workday. He remembered that he went to Catholic school and that was the time he realized that he wanted to be a writer. As he said later, he didn't think his life in Port Chester was important enough to remember.

He did recall the birth of his brother Peter in 1944, largely because it came as a total surprise to him. His mother got pregnant when his father was on leave, and Hubert, who was stationed in the Pacific, wouldn't meet his second son until around eighteen months later when he came home. Terrence said he was completely unaware that his mother was pregnant. That came as a surprise to her because she later said she was clearly showing. At the same time, he added that in 1944 people didn't talk about pregnancy the way they do in the contemporary world; it was just a fact. He said he came home from school one day, and his maternal grandmother was in the house. "I said, 'What are you doing here?' She said, 'Your mother's in the hospital. She just had a baby.' I was shocked, and they're all equally shocked that I could not have been aware of it."

After the life-changing performance of *Death of a Salesman*, the family moved to Dallas. When his father quit General Foods, he'd been working in beverages, and he became a wholesale distributor. However, all that was available to him in Dallas were the franchises for unpopular brands, so he wound up distributing a long-discontinued brand called Birley's, an uncarbonated fruit drink. Terrence remembered it as being awful, and that when his father showed up with it at a class picnic, the kids would complain that "the McNally's are going to make us drink that awful stuff." The kids, of course, wanted Coke, but Hubert never would have enough money or power to secure a Coke franchise in Dallas.

Other than the embarrassment of offering a second-tier refreshment and again the story of being introduced to opera in fifth grade, Terrence didn't recall much of his life there. He wasn't very happy, and like his early years in Port Chester, he never considered it very interesting. What he did recall was that he saw *Pal Joey* outdoors at Broadway Dallas in 1949 (later Dallas Summer Musicals) starring Vivienne Siegel in a production that transferred to Broadway the following year, was far more successful than the original Broadway outing, and was the production Terrence saw for a second time on the day he had seen *The King and I*.

He recalled seeing other theater in Dallas as well, but not with the same kind of specificity. What he did say was that he was always happy whenever he got to see a play. Dallas had—and has—a robust theater community so when they moved to Texas, theater was still a part of his life. It's also where he became more and more interested in opera after his classroom experience and began listening to opera on the radio. His parents indulged him even if they didn't appreciate his fandom. Terrence told the story of how, in a rare moment of consideration, they listened to a football game in the car one Sunday so he could listen to opera on the better radio in the living room.

What's significant about the time in Dallas for his future as a playwright is that the theater he did see helped shape what he liked and would later write. He said, "I guess the actors I've always been most attracted to are those who plant their feet and perform for the audience. They're not mumbly hesitant." Moreover, he appreciated actors who performed appearing to know that they were in a play and had an obligation to deliver that play to the audience. Small wonder that many of the actors who would later be deemed "McNally actors" were highly skilled at balancing human truths and theatricality.

II.

The family moved to Corpus Christi when Terrence was entering ninth grade, which would have been in 1952, and though he only lived there for four years, it's the place that had the deepest impact on his then

Terrence in Florida, age three (approx.).
COURTESY TERRENCE MCNALLY ESTATE

present and future life. He always maintained that he was *from* Corpus Christi, and that was more reflected in who he became as an artist and the influences on him rather than as a function of chronology.

According to his brother Peter, Corpus Christi in the early 1950s was a sleepy town. With a population of just over 108,000, it was a small town with a large naval base, fishing, and a branch of Texas A&M that had been established in 1947.

Hubert had purchased a beer distributorship, Ace Distributors, and he represented out-of-state beers. However, it wasn't an easy sell. Most people drank Lonestar, which was produced in Texas, and cost about sixty cents a bottle. The Schlitz or Budweiser Hubert was selling was seventy-five cents, and most people went for the cheaper option. Since payroll was every Friday, Terrence remembered that Thursday nights were very stressful because Hubert had to reckon what he owed, and it would get tense between his parents as his mother was now the book-keeper for the distributorship. He also remembered his father borrowing money because he was $1,800 short and trying to work out how to pay the drivers of the trucks and others. In a bit of dramatic irony, Hubert ended up having more in common with the darker side of Willy Loman as he struggled to make a living with a product that was challenging to sell. Terrence became keenly aware that their family was among the less well-off in Corpus Christi, certainly among his peers.

The McNally's lived in a medium-sized home, and Terrence and his brother Peter shared a room. As Peter recalled, the walls were deco-rated with pictures of opera stars, and he, Peter, had a small area where he could display pictures of his sports stars. Terrence also had a record player on which he was incessantly playing opera and musical comedy records, and Peter loved to stamp the floor and make the needle bounce, which enraged Terrence, behavior highly recognizable to legions of older and younger brothers as the younger tests his own ability to get a rise out of the older.

Terrence's record collection was easily his most prized possession. He said that by the time he had graduated from high school, he had thirty or forty complete operas. His parents didn't stand in the way of his passion, but at the same time, they didn't pay for the records either. "They weren't going to just give me five dollars to buy another *La Bohème*."

As he recalled,

> My main job for years was working in a place called the Robin Hood cafeteria. I wore a hat with a big plume and green tights.

Terrence and friend Pat, 1956.
COURTESY TERRENCE MCNALLY ESTATE

My job was to carry trays for older people, and I stood by the cash register.

With that money, I would buy an album. I remember that LP records were $5.72 each, and the guy who ran the music shop was a Mr. Green. He would not let me have the record until he had $11.44. I could give him $5, but until I brought in the remaining $6.44, I could not have the *Tosca*. [This was the 1953 recording featuring Maria Callas and is considered one of the most important opera recordings of the time.]

And so I learned a lot about opera that way, since I didn't see it. I would read the reviews of this remarkable new voice, and I would get the records or mail order from Sam Goody in New York. [Sam Goody in the 1950s was primarily a mail-order company.]

The pleasures, and presumably the escape, of the opera aside, Terrence's home wasn't a happy one. Though he later downplayed it, it was clearly an alcoholic home, with all the consequences and issues that

brings. He remembered people being at the house and drinking virtually every day. At times there was so much drinking and partying that
their mother might forget to get supper for him and his brother.

Terrence and his father had a strained relationship. It could have
been that since Terrence was already aware that he was gay, it made his
father uncomfortable and angry. Neither Peter nor Terrence used the
word "alcoholism" in describing their family, but there was no question, drinking played a huge role in the family dynamics—and with
both parents. Though he was sober thirty-eight years at the time of his
death, Terrence himself didn't use the words "alcoholic" or "alcoholism"
in talking about his parents, nor did Peter. As Peter said, "it's just the
way things were at the time," though he was upset by it.

It was particularly difficult for Peter as the younger brother watching
Terrence whom he idolized. He recalled that after his father had been
drinking, he could get belligerent and would hit Terrence, or chase him
across several backyards yelling at him, and it would happen with some
frequency.

Terrence described one incident:

> We lived in Corpus Christi without air conditioning, and everyone
> had a patio because the houses would really get hot. Ten months
> of the year, we ate on our patio, which was a concrete slab right
> adjacent to the kitchen just to get a little bit of Gulf breeze and air.
> People did not have fences, and all the neighbors would be out on
> their patios eating dinner. And my father would chase me across the
> yards because of something I'd done to provoke him. I really don't
> remember. But once I do remember, I don't know what possessed
> me, but I went and put on one of my mother's skirts. I was never
> interested in drag, but I knew it would annoy him, and I loved to
> twirl in it and see it as it would flare out. So, I did that, and he got
> really angry. At the time, I also had a rubber-tipped dart gun. He
> was watching Lucille Ball, and I guess we had just learned about
> John Wilkes Booth, and I shot him in the head and said "*sic semper
> tyrannis*," and that got him out of his chair, and he chased me for

several blocks, and I'm in my mother's skirt. My mother liked the Mexican clothes with the big, really full skirts. Eventually, he would catch me, and he would hit me pretty hard.

Peter tells a portion of the story in the 2018 documentary about Terrence's *Every Act of Life*, and even all those years later it made Terrence uncomfortable because it was revealing family secrets. It wasn't that he was angry; he was surprised that his brother was able to talk about it. Looking back, Terrence didn't think how he was treated was remarkable. He figured that if you gave your father lip, you would get hit, whether it was with a belt, or if sitting at the table, Hubert would just backhand Terrence if he was within reach.

Terrence said that at the time he didn't have strong feelings about the way his father treated him. He wasn't the only kid living in a home where there was a lot of drinking, but it wasn't talked about, though it was obvious. There was, however, one time when Terrence's friends saw firsthand how difficult his home life was.

Terrence lived a couple of miles from the school. At that time in Corpus Christi, kids as young as fourteen could get a driving license, which was the result of farmers saying kids needed to be able to drive farm equipment. Terrence had a bike, but he didn't want to ride it to school; he thought that was "uncool."

> All my friends had cars, and one morning, some guys came by to pick me up, and for some reason they came into the house where we're still having breakfast. And my father punched me for something that I'd said or done, and he'd bloodied my nose. And I was glad because people could see how horrible he could be.

Peter thought there might be an additional source for the friction between Terrence and Hubert: envy. With no TV in Corpus Christi (the first station KVDO wouldn't go on the air till June of 1954), Terrence was always on top of the news. As Peter recalled, Terrence always seemed to know what was going on in the world, with events like the

Korean War, and he would engage his father's drinking buddies in adult conversations about that, and his father would have felt left out of the conversation and upstaged by his son.

Peter also was aware that he was the favorite son, at least his father's favorite. He was involved in sports, which Hubert could relate to, rather than Terrence's immersion in opera, musical theater, and journalism.

Amid the chaos, Terrence said he was basically left alone, and looking back he said his biggest problem in his home was sharing a room with his brother. He couldn't do anything without being watched, and he recalled that when he finally got old enough to masturbate, he always wondered if Peter was asleep. Denial is also a characteristic of alcoholic homes.

As far as his relationship with his mother, Terrence simply felt disconnected and ignored. He thought that his parents were married too young and that they were essentially party people, and having kids put a damper on it. His parents mostly had as friends childless couples, and Terrence remembered coming home from high school and seeing four or five cars outside the house, and Terrence would know that they had already started drinking. Terrence and Peter would often have to fend for themselves, as his parents sometimes wouldn't even think about dinner till around 9:00 p.m.

Yet even with what was revealed in the documentary, and the stories Terrence told later in life, for the most part when the brothers were adults and their parents had long passed on, neither wanted to be overly critical of their parents. Terrence said that he never really resolved the issues with his mother during her lifetime. She loved the glamour of coming to New York and being in the theater. Peter said that when theater people visited from New York, they loved Corpus Christi. Still, his mother never wanted to know anything about Terrence's romantic life and discouraged him from talking about it. Criticisms were implied, and certainly there were some questions about whether his mother was inappropriate with him when he was young. There is no definitive answer, but a poem he wrote in high school appears to be an early attempt to deal with what was an incredibly complex and unhappy relationship. It also indicates what Terrence only once obliquely alluded to in that his mother was at least once what we euphemistically call "inappropriate" with him.

SECRETS FROM MY MOTHER

In my bed you wait
I see you in the mirror
You lurk to see what happens
Your hand rests on my shoulder.
You touch my things. you want to know
My secrets. Would you find out
My only hiding place?
Gently, I say no more.

It's inevitable that these experiences would shape Terrence's work where rage, resentment, and power struggles would provide a foundation for his characters—more overtly in the early works and more subtly as he matured. Like his characters, and as often happens in an alcoholic household, everyone was a prisoner to their secrets.

The family was nominally Roman Catholic, but Terrence didn't recall being terribly active in a church. What he remembered was that his mother always wanted to watch Midnight Mass from the Vatican on TV on Christmas Eve. It was the way she felt that Christmas had finally arrived.

Terrence would fortunately find release from his difficult home life, or at least to the extent possible, in the halls of W. B. Ray High School. The school had opened in 1950, and it was pretty much the model of a postwar, mid-century high school. It was also the time when the teenager and adolescent had become a force in American culture. At Ray, almost like a cliché of Texas, football was everything. The focus on the program was enormous, and, as he said:

The pressure on these young 15, 16, 17-year-old young men was enormous. I know there was betting on the games, and the grownups had a lot to say about how the team members were treated like royalty. They didn't really have to do anything [academically]. The rest of us did.

Terrence was, by his own description, never athletic, and he grew very late. His high school friend Peggy Dobbins (née Powell) remembered that she had first seen Terrence in freshman Latin class, and he was so small that his feet didn't touch the floor when he was sitting at his desk. Terrence recalled that he didn't really begin to grow till sophomore year of high school, though it never seemed to bother him.

Terrence was also keenly aware of where he stood in the social hierarchy of the town. Peggy's father was a major doctor in town, and Peggy herself was a debutante with a white Thunderbird, whom Terrence described as a "Grace Kelly blonde." Terrence said her family didn't approve of him, and he would never be invited into their house, nor wanted to meet his parents, and he was aware that they felt the McNallys were beneath them, and Peggy's family wasn't the only one who looked down on them, something Terrence knew hurt his mother, though he was helpless to do anything about it. It was a big deal to be one of the "first families of Corpus Christi," and the McNallys were definitely not one of them. Oil money made for rich families, and he remembered fancy cars, wonderful clothes, and hundreds of thousands of dollars spent on debutante balls, and Terrence even remembered one where Nat King Cole performed, the trappings of wealth. Though he and Peggy would remain lifelong friends, for most of his life Terrence carried with him a sense that as a result of his life in Corpus Christi he didn't really belong in many situations. He always felt for the outsider—and the person marginalized for no fault of his own.

In high school, he was the editor of the school paper *El Tejano*, and with Peggy a co-editor of the literary magazine, *Viva*. That took a great deal of Terrence's free time, and his brother remembered that the big table in their dining room would often be covered with proofs of the paper as Terrence worked on it all night.

By the time Terrence got into high school he already knew that he wanted to be a writer, and though he thought he would be a journalist, he had also already written a play—one that he often talked about in later years.

The script is undated, but it was written when Terrence was in high school. The first few pages are handwritten with the rest closely typed on legal paper. It begins backstage on the opening night of *Girl Crazy*, and two of the main characters are George Gershwin and his wife, Ira. Terrence had no reference material but the album liner notes (*sans*, obviously pictures of the composer and lyricist) and his own imagination and experience of theater by that time. He was probably also heavily influenced by backstage movie musicals. Though the writing is clearly juvenile, there are glimmers of themes that would intrigue Terrence for the rest of his career: the challenges of putting on a show, the lives of actors, and real stars in unexpected situations. There are appearances by Al Jolson, who suggests that Gershwin may have a future, and Ginger Rogers as a nervous ingénue going on for the first time. "After tonight, you'll be the toast of Broadway," one of the characters says to her. Terrence knew even then that irony can be comedic. At one point, someone runs down the aisle of the theater saying that George Gershwin was dead at thirty-seven—his earliest incident of breaking the proscenium.

The untitled play is also character-driven, rather than plot-driven, and even has hints of the wordplay and repartee that would become a hallmark of Terrence's writing. He plays fast and loose with time and place as scenes reveal George's challenge as being taken seriously as a composer. ("Nobody wants his type of music," a producer tells him, instead asking why he can't write a popular hit like "Glowworm." This prefigures what Stephen Sondheim would write in *Merrily We Roll Along* when a producer criticizes the work: "There's not a tune you can hum.")

Reading the play is entertaining, perhaps because it is the earliest complete work of Terrence's. The fluidity of time and place, with scenes moving from backstage to a producer's office back to the Shubert Theatre, is a tool he would employ later, yet even here there's a clarity of what's going on. It bordered on absurdism with characters appearing and disappearing for no real reason, and Terrence thought much later that it probably would have been something Charles Ludlam of the Ridiculous Theater might have produced when he was at the height of his career. Much of his insight and style and sense of humor are all already there, if you look. There are even some elements of camp. Dialogue was always one of Terrence's strong points, and it shows even in this early piece. In a high school writing assignment where the students had to write dialogue, his teacher at the time wrote on the paper, "This sounds like real people talking." Even as an adolescent, he was listening, reflecting, and revealing a level of sophistication that was an anomaly in Corpus Christi, Texas, in the early 1950s.

He wrote other plays as well, and inspired by *Kukla, Fran and Ollie*, he built a puppet stage and performed in the garage, but those plays are lost both to memory and the archives, outside a few scraps. The point is: in high school Terrence was already writing plays.

It was at Ray that Terrence first discovered Shakespeare and Chekhov, and some of his high school papers on those playwrights have a level of sophistication that is unusual for a high school student.

Aside from his trips to New York, Terrence's experience of live theater in Corpus Christi was largely a local community theater. He would go occasionally if a friend was in something. He remembers that one of their teachers was in a production of *Picnic*, playing Rosemary, the Rosalind Russell part in the film, and they were more interested in seeing her in a tight sweater than in the Pulitzer Prize–winning play. "We went to shows for the wrong reasons," he said, laughing. "It was not for the literature."

The person, however, who would have the most influence on Terrence as a young writer and set him on the course of his life was his English teacher, Maurine McElroy, "Mrs. Mac." Even as they remained in contact until her death at ninety-one in 2005, Terrence always referred to her as Mrs. McElroy, or "Mrs. Mac."

Mrs. Mac had come to Ray High School when her husband, who was in the oil business, had been transferred to Corpus Christi. She had a master's degree from Hardin Simmons University, where she had specialized in Shakespeare and Renaissance playwrights, and she arrived with the reputation that she was very tough, so, as Terrence said, if you weren't interested in English, you avoided her class. There were several other teachers with whom it was much easier to pass.

Mrs. Mac arrived in time for Terrence's junior year. As Terrence said, "It was just my good luck that I was at Ray High School the two years she taught junior and senior English." She was an exacting teacher, however, and she set the bar high for her students. In her notes on Terrence's papers, she questions his arguments and consistently encourages him to be better organized in presenting his ideas. At the same time, she was very supportive and encouraged Terrence and the other students to reach further. Peggy Dobbins remembered that at one time she, Terry, and another boy named Bill Traylor wrote a collaborative paper on *Macbeth*. "It was a big paper, and we were proud that we had collaborated. So, we turned it in, and she gave us each a score of thirty-three-and-a-third." Terrence and Peggy thought that was unfair, since both were accustomed to getting high marks on their work. It was the last time Terrence collaborated on a school project, becoming a solo writer from that point forward. Terrence and Peggy weathered that storm and stayed close, even doing their homework together, "I was very honored," she added. "He thought of us as George and Emily in *Our Town*." And yet, close as they were, just as Terrence had never been invited into her home, she never visited Terrence at his home. Peggy, too, was the child of an alcoholic, despite being one of the "first families." There were some secrets they didn't, or couldn't, share.

Peggy Dobbins remembers that Mrs. Mac held "salons" at her house. A bunch of kids would come over and sit on the floor in the back room of Mrs. Mac's house, which was on the bay in a wealthy part of town, and they would talk about books and literature. Peggy remembers it as a terrific group of people, though she said, "But of course every one of us who went to Mrs. Mac's was a couple of standard deviations to the left or the right of the norm." Not surprising, given that these were the intellectual kids in a school and a community that revolved largely around sports.

Terrence remembered those meetings and Mrs. Mac's influence with a little more detail:

> We were maybe six of the brighter kids in our class. Kids who loved the English language and loved reading Shakespeare and Keats and Shelley, and she loved poetry. I felt understood by her in a way that my parents did not. They had very little interest in me or my impressions of *Hamlet* or *King Lear*. Mrs. Mac made us write a three-paragraph essay every day, five days a week. And it had a specific organization: state your theme, develop it, conclusion. We just got in the habit of it, so writing became about organizing your thoughts and not something you were scared of.
>
> Mrs. Mac was just an extraordinary teacher, which I think is my great fortune that she was in Corpus Christi when I was in high school. Looking back, Mrs. McElroy probably knew I was gay, but I never discussed that.

More importantly, Terrence felt that Mrs. Mac was the first person to see and appreciate him as a writer, who in contemporary parlance "validated" him. Both he and Peggy said that she was the first person who let them feel they could do something more. As Terrence said, "The big movie of my adolescence in Corpus Christi was *East of Eden*, and the other one, *Rebel without a Cause*. Peggy was the "girl" version of that, just rebellious, and insistent that there had to be more than "you go to college to join a sorority and marry a rich guy and become a leader of Houston or Dallas society." Mrs. Mac's belief in them and their talents helped them to see possibilities for their lives away from the stultifying South Texas town.

Terrence said,

> The desire to move away from Corpus Christi was always present. It was a holding place, but no one really—or not many people—wanted to stay there.
>
> It's just really hard to imagine my life without Mrs. McElroy. Looking back, I'm sure she knew my secret: that I was gay. She

was certainly sympathetic. I've often wondered about her as an adult. She had two kids of her own who were, I'd say, in maybe the fifth and sixth grade, but they would come home from school, and there'd be ten of us sitting in Mrs. Mac's back living room, taking all her time, and I wondered how they felt about us.

They were probably fed up with us as was her husband, who we never saw. But it was obvious that we made her life, too. She loved being our teacher. I think even then I knew she was overqualified to be teaching high school English in Corpus Christi.

She only taught there for two years and went off to the University of Texas in Austin, and within a year or two was made head of the freshman English department. By the time she retired, she was a very respected scholar and had seminars on Elizabethan and Jacobean drama. She was a very beloved person.

In an often-cited letter from Mrs. Mac to Terrence in his senior year, she wrote:

> Your integrity is your armor. I am glad you are planning to write professionally; I had assumed that you might but had never heard you say so until recently. Writing is a highly competitive occupation; it can be heartbreaking. But you have already learned that if you must write you simply must: nothing else can substitute for writing. And so my hope and my prayers go with you in this life you have chosen.

All the kids who went to the salons went on to bigger things in their lives. Some became scientists, Dobbins became an artist and an activist for women's rights, writer and performer, and, of course Terrence became, well, Terrence, and he said that Mrs. Mac was as responsible as anyone for the career that he had. His gratitude was lifelong, and he would write many tributes and acknowledgments of Mrs. McElroy in later years, including Easter egg–style mentions in *Frankie and Johnny* acknowledging how she helped instill a love of Shakespeare, one of the

most heartfelt is in another one of his plays. In *The Last Mile*, Bernadette
Peters as the soprano about to make her Met debut as Tosca, is sitting at
her dressing table, where a photo of Mrs. Mac is displayed, and amid all
her worry and jitters looks into the mirror, and says:

> I'm from a small town in Oklahoma where Nat King Cole was
> a major lieder singer, and art was Barbra Streisand singing "Ave
> Maria" on the Christmas album.
>
> You gave me music, Mrs. McElroy. And the ears and the heart
> and mind to hear it with. How do you thank someone for a gift like
> that? You can't.
>
> Next to our parents, the most important people in the world are
> our teachers.
>
> Good ones are rare, and you were a good one Mrs. McElroy—a
> very good one.

This group of kids spent time together away from Mrs. Mac's as
well. And there was a good deal of sex. Peggy said that at the time she
didn't know that Terrence was gay, and they did kiss once when they
were sitting by the bay after their prom. Peggy remembered that she
didn't respond to Terrence's kiss as she did to kissing another boy, Bill.
Terrence was otherwise occupied. During high school, he had sex with
several boys, all of whom he said were friends, but they didn't think of
themselves as gay, or "queer" at the time. Though Terrence knew that
he was gay, the sex with the other boys was casual, recreational, and all
of them that Terrence knew about many years later had gone on to live
heterosexual lives.

It wasn't easy to be gay in Corpus Christi in the early 1950s. As Peter
McNally says, anyone who was known to be queer was likely to get
beaten up. There were known places where gay people would meet—a
public restroom near the piers, or a dance pavilion down by the water.
Navy men or locals cruising had to be circumspect, and beating up
queers was a pastime for some of the high school boys. Peter even tells
the story of a sailor who was beaten up and thrown in the water. He

drowned, and it was swept under the rug, the prevailing attitude was that he had been drunk and careless, though the murder was more or less an open secret. Peter also recalled a popular teacher who was essentially run out of town because it was rumored that he was gay. Given that survival, quite literally, depended on hiding one's nature, it's not surprising that Terrence knew almost from the start that he wanted to get out of Corpus Christi. "After graduation, I'm taking the first plane out of here," he recalled saying often.

III.

When it came time for Terrence to go to college, Mrs. Mac played a central role in Terrence going to Columbia. She assumed that her students were going to college, not a given at the time, and that there was more to life than the University of Texas or SMU. Terrence had, of course, heard of Yale and Harvard and was aware of the Ivy League, but it had never occurred to him to go there. He applied to Yale, Harvard, and Columbia, all looking for scholarships, but not for any understanding of the schools, he said, but because they were the most famous. Mrs. Mac promoted college outside Texas for all her star students. Peggy Dobbins, for example, went to Wellesley because her mother had gone there even despite the fact that one of her female classmates told her that Wellesley would "turn her lesbian."

Terrence wasn't accepted at Harvard, but both Terrence and his best friend at the time, Pete Walsh, were accepted to Yale and Columbia with full scholarships, but which one they would accept came down to chance.

Terrence and Pete talked about which school they should go to. Neither of them had a preference, especially since neither of them knew that much about the schools as institutions. They did think it was stupid to be the first people who had ever traveled more than 1,800 miles from Corpus Christi, then go to Columbia together or even be roommates. So, they flipped a coin, and Pete headed to New Haven and Terrence to New York.

Maria Callas and Rudolf Bing at the Metropolitan Opera . . . before their falling out.
PHOTOFEST

Terrence's parents were far from thrilled at the results of the coin toss. His mother had only a high school education, and his father was a college dropout, so Terrence going to the Ivy League, he thought, was intimidating, much as Terrence's grasp of world events had intimidated his father a few years earlier. If he was going to the Ivy League, however, they were not happy that Terrence had selected Columbia over Yale.

Yale, to his parents, meant wealth and connections, and Columbia was a hotbed of radicalism and communism. This was especially disturbing to Hubert who was very much anti-union and had decided to move to Texas in part because the state at the time was anti-union. Terrence, however, was thinking practically. At the time, he was intent on becoming a journalist, and he reasoned that after four years of undergraduate study, he could simply walk across the campus and go to the journalism school.

By the time Terrence was getting ready to go to college, all of his family had moved to Corpus Christi. Terrence's paternal grandfather was living with the family in an apartment at the back of their lot. His mother's family, what was left of it, had moved down as well. As he prepared to move up there, Terrence knew no one in New York, but there was extended family, his Aunt Marie, who he says was really more like a cousin. He arrived at their house in Westchester, and they drove him to Columbia. However, Terrence remembered that they were frugal bordering on cheap, and they knew a way into Manhattan that would allow them to avoid tolls. His first introduction to Columbia and his new home was a somewhat harrowing drive through run-down neighborhoods that looked at best sketchy. When they got to Amsterdam Avenue, they said, "Here you are." Terrence was pretty upset and said that in the Columbia catalog they had managed to get a few strategic pictures of fountains and trees, and it looked nothing like a campus. He had an idea of what college was going to be with kids hanging out, playing guitars, singing along with The Kingston Trio. It wasn't like that. It was a bit of a culture shock. He had anticipated that it was just going to be an extension of high school, but it turned out to be a bit rougher than that.

He went in anyway and found his room. His roommate, an engineering major, was already there and writing to his girlfriend back home. Terrence remembered he had a big, glossy photograph of her. Terrence stashed his stuff, made peace with the fact that small as he was, he was going to be in the upper bunk, and asked his roommate if he wanted to go to Times Square.

Terrence, of course, knew it and the theater district from his earlier trips. When his roommate said no, Terrence was surprised, but he headed down anyway, and within an hour of arriving in New York, he was on the subway going down to Times Square. His destination was the Mark Hellinger Theatre on 51st Street where he promptly walked up to the box office to buy a ticket for *My Fair Lady*, which had opened a few months before. Of course, the man in the box office looked at this eager seventeen-year-old like he was crazy and told him to come back in a year. However, they also told him that if he really wanted to see it, standing room tickets went on sale when the box office opened at 10:00 a.m., but he'd better be ready because by 10:01, the thirty places at $1 were gone. Worse yet, the line formed overnight, so in order to get one of those elusive spots, one would have to sit on the sidewalk all night to hold a place. Disappointed but still eager to see a Broadway show on his first night in New York, Terrence walked over to 46th Street and saw Gwen Verdon in *Damn Yankees*, which had been running over a year at that time, so walk-up tickets were available.

After the show, he headed back to the Mark Hellinger and took his place to wait. He remembers that it was a mild September night, so he'd be comfortable on the night watch. However, he said, people came out of the show as it was letting out, looked at the line of people sitting on the sidewalk, and told them they were crazy. "It's great," he remembered being told, "but no show is that great." Undeterred, Terrence waited, and his second night in New York, he saw *My Fair Lady*.

It lived up to all his expectations. By the time he had gotten to New York, he had practically worn out the cast album that had been released the previous April (and would top the *Billboard* charts for forty-eight weeks), and what he remembered in later life was how beautiful the production was and that it had three turntables. He would see the show eleven times, and the size and scale of it impressed him. He also recalled seeing celebrities and even President Eisenhower on his many trips to the show. Especially after having seen *Damn Yankees*, he felt that *My Fair Lady* was remarkably innovative and, more importantly, he began to appreciate the power of writing for the specific talents of a certain actor, in this case Rex Harrison as Henry Higgins—and the ineffable power of stars to simply walk on a stage and hold an audience.

Now that he was in New York, Terrence embraced the theater, saying that he attended something easily five nights a week—theater, opera, ballet. It was a time when it was easy to walk up to the box office and get a seat for a dollar or two for standing room. Although his professors at Columbia included Eric Bentley, the British playwright, translator, and critic, and Lionel Trilling, one of the leading literary critics of the twentieth century, Terrence always maintained that his larger theatrical education came from actually going to the theater, something he encouraged everyone who wanted to work in the theater to do throughout his life.

He graduated in 1960 in Phi Beta Kappa, but admitted he wasn't a particularly dedicated student. "That's where being a writer, I think, was lucky," he said. "Because Columbia is the kind of school where the questions in your finals were such that a good writer could, frankly, bullshit in a way that my roommate, the engineering major, could not."

One of the friends he met in college was Michael Kahn. Kahn went on to have an illustrious career as a director, teacher, and artistic director of the Folger Theater in Washington, D.C. He also directed many operas and Broadway shows. Kahn said that it was during their time at Columbia that "Terry" became "Terrence." He thought at the time that Terrence wanted to be a journalist, but they became theater friends, sharing a passion for Maria Callas.

Kahn had attended the High School of the Performing Arts in New York, and to Terrence, he was already a sophisticated New Yorker, something Terrence aspired to become. Kahn says that it was he who took Terrence to see Callas at the Met for the first time, but when he tried to explain who Callas was, Terrence cut him off and told him that he already knew about her. Michael and Terrence stood in line, trading places, for almost two days to get standing room tickets and finally saw her perform *La Traviata* on February 6, 1958, in a production staged by Tyrone Guthrie. They never forgot the performance, and sixty years later could easily recall details and how they were completely blown away by

it. Guthrie had also directed the first opera Terrence saw at the Met—
Carmen with Risa Stevens in December of his freshman year.

Kahn recalled that he and Terrence would buy every record and
listen closely, and the two of them would then discuss the differences
minutely. Their shared attention to detail, arguing about minutiae, and
the budding connoisseurship would provide the basis for the passion for
opera shared by the characters in *The Lisbon Traviata*.

Terrence always lived for the big, dramatic moments in opera, but
not every opera had the impact of a Callas performance, though he went
regularly, and if he'd seen an opera already, he very often did his reading
for school while the opera was going on. As he described it, standing
room was in the Family Circle at the "old Met," when they let the audience in, he would race up the stairs, and since he was young and fast, he
could usually get a place closest to the center of the stage. There was a
railing standees could lean on, but on the three steps up to that railing,
it was lit so people didn't trip, as he said:

> You could sit on the top step with your back to the stage and put
> your book down. You could do your homework or your Columbia
> work during the part of the opera you didn't care about—a lot of
> whole sections that were more like a play. "I've seen this scene; I
> don't need to see it again." I want to see Hedda Gabler shoot herself,
> not the scene with the nurse and the aunts at the beginning.
>
> So, I did a lot of my work at Columbia on the subway or
> hunched over in the Family Circle. And I could get away with it
> because I was a good writer.

It wasn't just opera that engaged him. New York was alive with creativity and artistic exploration. Terrence saw the premiere of Balanchine's
Agon with music by Igor Stravinsky. It was widely hailed as a triumph of
modernism, and the opening night response was wild. Balanchine also
challenged convention by using a Black male dancer in the *pas de deux*
with a white, female dancer, which complemented the black-and-white
theme of the piece but was highly controversial at the time.

The sophisticated Kahn also introduced Terrence to jazz. Terrence's father had listened to Edith Piaf, Nat King Cole, and the ubiquitous Broadway albums, but it was Kahn who introduced Terrence to Mabel Mercer and others. For Terrence, it was exciting to be continually opened up to new things, new ways of hearing, and be surrounded by so much going on in the city—and seeing something groundbreaking and challenging nearly every night.

Michael and Terrence's passion for opera and Maria Meneghini Callas, as she was billed in the programs when married to Giovani Meneghini (Terrence would have her proudly proclaim her full name in *Master Class*: Maria Cecilia Sophia Anna Kalogeropoulos), also led them to an act of righteous vandalism.

Callas was famously temperamental, and her offstage exploits often made headlines, as did her diva-like behavior. In January 1958, she walked off the stage at a gala production of *Norma* in Rome, and just over a month later she was fired from the Met by director Rudolf Bing for refusing to sing Verdi's Lady Macbeth, albeit in a new production, so soon after singing *La Traviata* because of the demands of both roles. Despite the fact that she had signed a contract saying she would alternate roles, she refused. When negotiations finally broke down—and the role would go to Leonie Rysanke—the Callas/Bing *contretemps*, to put it mildly, made worldwide news.

Kahn said that by that time—later in 1958—he'd already been thrown out of Columbia for not taking any exam, and he was working for an interior decorator, and saw the headline. Outraged at the displacement of the diva, he and Terrence that night took cans of red paint and plastered "Viva Callas" all over the Met building. They were never found out, it seems, and it would have been a stunt worthy of Bing, who hired a claque to shout "Brava Callas" on Rysanke's entrance to outrage her fans and generate sympathy. The production was a success, protests notwithstanding.

Kahn did return to Columbia, though by that time he was not in Terrence's class, and their next joint project would be Columbia's 66th Annual Varsity show in 1960. Terrence had seen a note in the campus paper that there was no one to write it. So, he did. He was intrigued by the challenge, he said. Fellow student Ed Kleban contributed the music, and Kahn directed. Titled *A Little Bit Different*, according to the review in the Columbia paper:

> The music was snappy, the lyrics were funny, the situation and characters were ridiculous, the girls pulchritudinous, the scenery was imaginative, the production went smoothly enough, the choreography was sprightly, and the actors and actresses played their roles well and actually even managed to sing more than acceptably. And though the script often plays footsie with bad taste—race, sex, and sadism are bandied about rather freely, albeit extremely mirthfully—Terrence McNally's well-conceived and finely frothy book never quite goes too far.

The story, which was intentionally ridiculous, was likely largely inspired by the silly Jerome Kern/P.G. Wodehouse musicals of the early years of the twentieth century, which served as the template for the typical, joke-laden college musicals. The plot, such that it was, concerned a film crew stranded in Africa. Hilarity—and the threat of cannibals—ensues. (Likely inspired by the Kern/Wodehouse show, *Sitting Pretty*, and cannibals, particularly the image of missionaries boiling in a pot were popular in cartoons, though contemporary sensibilities deem such humor racist.)

One story that Terrence remembered about the show had to do with how it was promoted. Apparently, a poster had been printed up that omitted Kahn's name as director, and, as the story goes, Kahn ran around campus with a Magic Marker, adding his name to the credits.

Terrence also remembered that the Varsity Show was one of the only times his parents were proud of his time at Columbia. When he stepped up to write it, he was aware that "a lot of really cool people" had written the show, and he did very much want to be cool. His parents apparently agreed, and they had told him that there was a time when the Columbia show was done for two weeks on Broadway and that the famous writing team Richard Rodgers and Lorenz Hart had met doing the Varsity

Show, and that some of their first hits had come from that show. Terrence was finally in a company his parents admired.

During his time at Columbia, Terrence wrote one other play, a one-act called *The Rollercoaster*. It won the Boar's Head prize, a $50 award presented by the *Columbia Review* for the best fiction, poem, or play written by an undergraduate. The play is set in a dilapidated amusement park where a young man, Rudolph, who has been afraid to ride the roller coaster comes back to face his fears. Gerty, an abrasive woman who minds the coaster, at first refuses to let Rudolph ride it, though he's prepared by riding many other coasters and swears he's ready, actually pleading with her to let him ride. Gerty finally allows Rudolph to ride, and tragedy ensues as Rudolph falls to a grisly death.

The play is significant in Terrence's development as a playwright for several reasons. First, the threat of something large and dangerous looms over the action. In this case, it's the roller coaster, but it prefigures the unknown threat "out there" in *And Things that Go Bump in the Night*. Second, it's one of the first instances of an aggressive, powerful, and angry woman controlling a situation, a trope he would use with Ruby in *Bump* and in other serious guises in plays like *Cuba, Si!* and to comedic effect in Chloe in *Lips*, and even comedically with Googie Gomez in *The Ritz*. Finally, this is one of the first instances of Terrence writing a long monologue for a character that tells a story and in doing so reveals a great deal about the emotional state of that character. And then there's the darkness. Mordant, absurd, and unexpected darkness would characterize much of his work, not just in the plays about AIDS, where agonizing death is always just offstage, but even in pieces like *A Perfect Ganesh* where a violent murder comes as a surprise. For Terrence, unexpected and terrifying violence in many guises, at times arriving unexpectedly, would become a standard feature of his work—very much like a child's experience growing up in an alcoholic home.

The success of the Varsity Show and his prize-winning play notwithstanding, Terrence still intended to pursue a career in journalism, at least outwardly. He had spent his summers during college back home working as a reporter for the *Corpus Christi Times-Caller*. He needed the job of course to have spending money at school, and it paid a fairly generous $100 a week. Of his stint as a "cub reporter," he liked to tell the story of the time he interviewed Lyndon Baines Johnson when he was in the Senate. During the interview, Johnson took a call from his wife Lady Bird, and while he spoke to her was flipping through a copy of *Playboy*. This was too good for Terrence, and he included that detail in the piece, which prompted Johnson to call the editor and complain—resulting in a reprimand for Terrence. Even then, the nuances of a story that are unexpectedly revealing had more appeal to Terrence than simply writing a puff piece. He thought the detail was both funny and a great perspective. Neither Johnson nor the paper's editor agreed.

Whether it was this experience or Terrence's off-campus education in theater, ballet, opera, and art while at Columbia, he knew that his life was going to take a more creative turn. As he said, "I totally love the education I got at Columbia, but I totally also love the experience of going from Corpus Christi, the town with really no culture, to being in a town with a lot of culture." He was glad he stayed at Columbia. Early on in his freshman year, he had gone to visit his friend Pete in New Haven and had fallen in love with the Yale campus. To Terrence, at the time, Yale was everything Columbia was not.

He had begun his career at Columbia with a resentment. His freshman advisor told him that he had only been accepted because of "geographical distribution." At the time, Terrence said, Columbia was primarily a college for New Yorkers who didn't live on campus. Having just made it there, he hated being told that he hadn't earned his place in the class on his own merits. That stung. After seeing Yale, then, he inquired about transferring there at the end of his freshman year, but as he considered it, he realized that had he moved to New Haven, he would not have been able to see Maria Callas as *Norma* at the Met. And that, more than anything else, decided that he would complete his four years at Columbia.

Yet, Terrence's big secret as his time wound down at Columbia was not that he was gay. That was never much of a secret to him, or anyone else. He managed to have plenty of sex during his time at Columbia, some of it anonymous with random men he'd meet at bars in Greenwich Village, on the street, or even with other students, but none of it had any real import outside of just being sex. He said he never really felt oppressed or inhibited about being gay, and there was something fun and exciting about the secrecy surrounding it.

No, his secret was that he didn't want to be a journalist: he wanted to be a playwright. "That's pretentious of you to say, 'I want to be a playwright,'" he remembered, which is one of the reasons he didn't talk about it. Furthermore, he wasn't quite sure how to go about it, but his course was set . . . at least in his heart.

He graduated and matriculated into New York during what was arguably one of the city's most exciting and creative periods.

3

The Bumpy Beginning

I.

DIPLOMA IN HAND, Terrence left Columbia to be a writer. He also had in hand a prize he had won at Columbia of about $1,800, enough for him to go write. In the fall of 1960, he headed to Puerto Vallarta, Mexico, which at the time was, he said, nowhere, and a place reached only by two flights a week, which landed in a cornfield. It was about as remote a place, though, as he could find and afford with a beach and a chance to experience being a writer on his own.

He had intended to write a novel, but he said that he soon realized that he wasn't suited for expository writing, at least not as a novelist. While he was at Columbia, in addition to his prize-winning play, he had won third prize in a *Columbia Review* short story competition for a tale called *Mona Lisa and the Matador*, an ironic tale about a Mexican whorehouse where a famous matador is expected, and the madam wants him for herself. It has an O'Henry-like twist, and the prose is a bit labored, but it was published in the *Columbia Review* in 1959. Still, McNally realized that prose wasn't for him, and "I was never going to write 'the Great American Novel.'" In hindsight, this shouldn't be that surprising. Reading *The Rollercoaster* and *Mona Lisa and the Matador* side by side, it's clear that his gift was putting words into the mouths of characters. Where the short story bogs down, the play is crisp, appropriately harrowing and manages to convey a sense a menace and that "heightened reality" Terrence wanted in his plays.

During his time in Mexico, Terrence also wrote another play, and he sent it to the Actors Studio in New York for consideration. That play, called *The Elevator*, appears to be lost; it is not with other writings in Terrence's archives. The play was not accepted for production, but Molly Kazan, wife of Actors Studio founder Elia Kazan, wrote and suggested that when he returned, if he wanted to, he should come and observe actors and acting classes, and get a better sense of the theater. With only sixty or so mediocre pages of his novel written, which he himself had called "thoroughly bad," Terrence thought, "why not?" And when he returned to New York, he took on the role of stage manager . . . and observer.

The Actors Studio was one of many small groups producing plays in the early 1960s. The Off-Off Broadway movement was developing fairly rapidly, with companies like La Mama Etc. (founded 1961), Caffe Cino (founded 1958), which presented gay theater at a time when portrayal of gay people on stage could get an establishment raided, and Judson Poets' Theater (founded 1961) were the training ground for many playwrights of the time. Terrence found himself in the middle of all of this, and he remembered especially the creative energy surrounding the theaters and plays of this time. "It seemed like you could finish a play on Friday and have a reading on Sunday," he said, though he acknowledged that this was probably not literally true.

The Actors Studio was also noted as the mecca for "method acting," a style that originated with Konstantin Stanislavsky in Russia, then came to America and was further developed at the Group Theatre in the 1940s under the direction of Strasberg and cofounders Harold Clurman and Stella Adler. The Actors Studio was intended as a laboratory where professionals could work, explore, and grow without the pressures of commercial production, or professional criticism. Terrence certainly observed a great deal of this type of acting in rehearsal and performance, but it was a style that never really resonated with him. He said, "I never really cared for Marlon Brando's or James Dean's style of acting. It was far too mumbly." Of all the criticism that has been hurled at Terrence's characters over the years, no one has ever accused them of mumbling.

While he was at the Actors Studio, one day Molly Kazan came to him and said that John Steinbeck was looking for a tutor for his two teenage boys, Tom (15) and John (13), as they were about to embark on a ten-month long world trip. In later years, Terrence loved to tell the story, which he did in the documentary on him, *Every Act of Life*, that he said to Molly, "You mean like the writer?" She said, "It *is* the writer."

Terrence wasn't sure why he got the job when there were clearly more qualified tutors available. However, he always considered it a stroke of luck and perhaps had to do with Steinbeck feeling more simpatico with Terrence who aspired to being a writer than a professional tutor. After all, Terrence would become part of their family for a year.

He embarked on the trip with the Steinbecks in the fall of 1961, and he writes feelingly of the time that he spent with the Steinbecks and the theater that he saw on that trip in his *Memoir in Plays*. One of the greatest revelations for him on the trip was how important language was—and how important it was for a play to convey a kind of truth, however poetically that was expressed.

Steinbeck also told Terrence, "Don't write for the theater. It will break your heart." Although Steinbeck had great success with *Of Mice and Men* in 1937, the two subsequent plays he wrote, *The Moon Is Down* in 1942 and *Burning Bright* in 1950, were total failures.

Terrence always felt that the critics were overly harsh on Steinbeck; he certainly wasn't a critics' darling, though he would win the Nobel Prize for literature in 1962. *Of Mice and Men* had succeeded on stage, Terrence thought, in part because George S. Kaufman, who directed the original production on Broadway, had said that the novella was virtually a play as it was structured and written. Through Steinbeck, Terrence observed firsthand the harshness of the critical world and the ways in which it could hinder or impede an artist. Especially with the publication of *Travels with Charley* in 1960, Terrence remained perturbed, if not outraged, for the rest of his life that critics didn't want Steinbeck to be other than he had been in the past. He also observed, however, that painful as it was, Steinbeck didn't let that hinder him—a lesson that would be more valuable for Terrence than he knew at the time.

On the trip, he also began work on the play that would become *And Things That Go Bump in the Night*, and he began discussing with Steinbeck writing the book for a musical based on Steinbeck's novel *East of Eden*. Considered by Steinbeck to be his magnum opus, and based on the success of the novel and the 1955 film directed by Eliza Kazan and starring James Dean, Burl Ives, and Julie Harris, it was anticipated that a musical based on the material would be a huge hit, particularly with household name Mitch Miller (of *Sing Along with Mitch* fame) producing. It would be Terrence's first book of a Broadway musical.

The trip ended, and Terrence returned to New York in the summer of 1962, thrilled to be living in the West Village. It was, he said, an apartment that would have made his mother cry, "a slum" as he described it, but he was exactly where he wanted to be—and wanted to belong.

II.

Back in the Village, Terrence devoted himself to writing, though he took various so-called survival jobs to pay the rent. He was writing, but like many young artists and writers, it was difficult to work all day and then come home and write. He was hired to do rewrites for the Franco Zefferelli production of *The Lady of the Camellias*. The production was a bomb, but Terrence pocketed $1,500 for his work. He was also writing film criticism for a journal, *The Seventh Art*, but he was only making $10 per published column. As he later said, it was one of the lean years.

During this period, however, he wrote his next play, *This Side of the Door*. It is the most literally autobiographical play Terrence ever wrote. It expresses the fear, vulnerability, and uncertainty of a young boy, Edmund, growing up in an alcoholic home, how he tries to exact revenge on his drunk father, almost always locked away on the other side of the door. The father, a failed insurance salesman, rages at his son, who he calls "a fairy" for having dressed up as Carmen Miranda for Halloween. He seeks solace from his mother Hebe, who ultimately abandons Edmund, at least emotionally, in favor of her drunk husband. It is a verbally and physically violent play, and like *The Rollercoaster* has a surprising and deadly twist at the end, but in this case, it's a ruse and a desperate move by Edmund to be seen by his parents and claim some vestige of power.

The play won first prize in the New York City Writers Conference (later the Stanley Award presented by Wagner College on Staten Island), which came with an award of $500. Judges in March 1962 were Edward Albee, Willard Mass, David Susskind, Kim Stanley, and Geraldine Page. Along with the award, the play was produced in January 1963 by the Playwright's Unit at the Cherry Lane, with Estelle Parsons in the role of Hebe, the mother.

There was some question at the time about the award because Terrence was in a relationship with Edward Albee, though that would not have been widely known outside of the close circle in New York. The official history of the award on Wagner's website also suggests that the play had been previously produced, which was against the rules. They, however, misquote the date, as the program from the play at the Cherry Lane lists January 1963 as the date of production. It was part of their *Theater 1963* series, not 1962, as they state. It was legit.

Over the years, Terrence distanced himself from that play. He was dismissive of it and in conversation downplayed it, perhaps a bit embarrassed by some of the interactions between Edmund and Hebe that border on bathos and Edmund's clear and desperate neediness. He would never again write with such naked emotion about something so close to his personal story. He also said that after the production at the Cherry Lane, he had put the script away and had completely lost track of it, but a typed version exists in his archives. What's particularly fascinating about that script is that Terrence has marked beats with slashes throughout to orchestrate how the lines would be said and the rhythms of the speech. It's the closest he could get to how he heard the lines in his head. One of Terrence's additional realizations from writing this was also that he didn't want to write autobiographically. He felt that it was limiting, and that "Once you've exhausted your family, where else is there to go?" He also had a sense that he had cut a bit too close to the bone, that he had revealed more about himself personally than he wanted to and he felt that he exposed too much . . . that the puppets had maybe gone a bit too far.

The Wagner College website also suggests that *This Side of the Door* was an early draft of *And Things That Go Bump in the Night*. This assertion strains credulity when the scripts are read side by side. First, the stories, such as they are, are completely different. There are no parallels between Hebe in *Door* and Ruby in *Bump* other than that they are women who are coping with fear and threats. What the plays do have in common is that much of the action in both is in response to a threat. In *Door* that threat is the drunk father, Henderson, while in *Bump* it is undefined. In both, that threat is unseen and provides an undertone of menace, but it is the same element that was in Terrence's earlier play *The Rollercoaster*. What's clear is that Terrence was developing themes and dramatic structures—and his own tropes—that would inform all his later work. One can take his entire *oeuvre*, in fact, and always, always find that thing lingering just offstage or in the background that raises the stakes of what's happening onstage.

Before going on to talk about *Bump* in particular, it's important to talk a little bit more about the Playwright's Unit and Terrence's relationship with Albee. Both would have a major influence on his life and career.

The Playwright's Unit was founded in 1963 by Albee, Clinton Wilder, and Richard Barr to support the work of young playwrights. Barr had set out with another producer H. B. Lutz to create the program *Theater 1960*, which produced Beckett's *Krapp's Last Tape* and Albee's *The Zoo Story*. The following year Barr was joined by Wilder to produce *Theater 1961*, which included Albee's *The Death of Bessie Smith* and *The American Dream*. They also produced the first production of *Who's Afraid of Virginia Woolf?* in 1961, and that went on to win the 1963 Tony Award when it moved to Broadway. If there was a *Theater 1962* season, there is no record in either Terrence's archives or those of Wilder and Barr. Albee joined them, and they formalized the organization, which Terrence believed was largely funded by Albee's proceeds from *Who's Afraid of Virginia Woolf?*, which, he said, "were considerable."

Terrence holds a photo of himself with other playwrights in Greenwich Village in 1968.
COURTESY JEFF KAUFMAN / EVERY ACT OF LIFE / FLOATING WORLD

The organization also produced other early works by Albee, as well as playwrights Sam Shepard, Le Roi Jones (Amiri Baraka), Jean-Claude Van Italie, A. R. Gurney, John Guare, and Terrence, among others. The Playwright's Unit was pivotal in establishing Off-Off Broadway as viable theater, though Terrence noted what they got was a showcase. Everyone was paid very little, if at all. Nonetheless, the role of this organization in transforming theater is undeniable. It remained active until 1968.

He tells the story in *Every Act of Life* that it had been after a party following a performance of Marc Blitztein's 1937 political opera *The Cradle Will Rock* presented by the New York City Opera at City Center in February of 1960. They shared a cab after the party. Albee invited Terrence up for a drink, then as always a coded invitation to have sex, and they began a four-year relationship. Terrence said, "I asked him if his wife would mind if I came up; I was that naïve."

Their time together would have been broken up by Terrence's writing journey to Mexico, and his trip with the Steinbeck's. It was neither a good nor an easy relationship for Terrence. Throughout the rest of his life, he said very little publicly about the relationship. He did say that they drank a lot and they fought a lot and that Albee wasn't particularly supportive of Terrence's writing, nor did they really talk about writing. Terrence did say that it was interesting to be around during all the excitement about *Virginia Woolf*, but publicly he was very much in the background, and he was never fully comfortable with that. Even during the relationship, Albee, who was ten years older and had a lifetime of hiding that he was gay, would say that he was single publicly and in interviews. As he had with his parents back in Corpus Christi, Terrence felt invisible. The breakup was acrimonious and damaging to Terrence, at least that was what he implied. He hated having to hide and said that he truly loved Edward and didn't really understand the need to be secretive. It would take ten years for the scars to heal before the two men could develop a cordial, professional relationship. Over the years, Terrence delivered many tributes to Albee, and wrote the introduction to a collection of his plays, but there were always some sly digs, suggesting that Albee wasn't that good with people or that even though he hadn't had a hit play in years (this was long before Albee won the 2002 Tony Award for *The Goat, or Who Is Sylvia?*), he was still a force in the American theater. More tellingly, despite several requests from theater critic Mel Gussow, Terrence declined to be interviewed for Gussow's 1999 biography of Albee. Biographies, as noted at the outset, are imperfect things, and until he finally married Tom Kirdahy, Terrence largely preferred not to discuss details of his private life publicly. He wanted to matter—and not let his personal story detract from the work.

Still, without that fateful cab ride, there might not have been a *Bump*.

III.

In the summer of 1963, Terrence started working seriously on the play that would become *And Things That Go Bump in the Night*. As he would for the rest of his career, Terrence was always eager to hear his words in the mouths of actors, and while the script was in development, he had a reading at the Playwright's Unit.

Bump is set in a cellar in a dystopian, futuristic world. The family includes the mother Ruby, a former opera diva, the disconnected father

Fa, Grandfa in a wheelchair, son Sigfrid, and daughter Lakme. They play dark games with one another, mostly having to do with destroying each other's spirits as they cower in the basement, afraid of the thing "out there," and unable to go out after dark. Into this mix, Sigfrid brings Clarence, a guest for the night with whom Sigfrid has sex and who becomes the object of the family's dark games, including hiding his clothes and forcing him to make a speech about "The Way I Live." It's a long monologue—typical of Terrence's style for revealing character. As he would throughout all his plays, Terrence puts his philosophy in the mouths of his characters:

> **Clarence:** I love life. I suppose that's a corny statement . . . I know how fashionable it is to be morose these days . . . but I do. I really do love it. There are just too many good things in the world not to want to be alive. Just think of all the beautiful things men have made. Music, art, literature . . . Shakespeare alone is a reason to be alive. How could anyone not want to be alive after there's been a Shakespeare on this earth?
>
> . . .
>
> Everybody loves somebody . . . or they will . . . sometime in their life. Anything that makes you want to live so bad you'd . . . you'd die for it . . . Shakespeare, Florence . . . someone in the park. That's what I believe in. That's all. That's the way I live.

It's a hope-filled speech, but the family destroys Clarence for it. Lakme forces Clarence to watch a slideshow of his tryst with Sigfrid and cruelly humiliates him. At the end of the second act, Clarence runs away, and we hear him being killed on the electric fence, or that's what the audience—and the family—infer. The play continues in Act Three to its even darker conclusion. At the end of the play, the family, more or less, waiting for the inevitable arrival of the unknown thing, which appears to be getting closer and closer. They are still. They hear,

Bump. (pause) Bump. (pause) Bump. (pause)
Silence.

Clarence's final speech, however, reflected Terrence's life. His relationship with Albee was deteriorating as he was writing—and would be over by the time the play was produced—and it reflects the promise of hope in a dark and incomprehensible world. Terrence would be in a relationship with actor Robert Drivas by the time *Bump* was fully in development.

The reading apparently went very well, and as a result, directors Alan Schneider and Harold Clurman recommended that Terrence apply for a Rockefeller Grant that had been established to support new playwrights. The Rockefeller Foundation had given the University of Minnesota a grant of $75,395 for the development of new playwrights. It's important to note, given the controversy that was to follow, that what the foundation was funding was research, not a commercial, out-of-town tryout production. The goal of the research, which was administered by the school's theater department under the Office for Advanced Drama Research, was to provide a laboratory for a playwright to develop work and, as described by the department, "opening the vistas of 'American theatre.'" From a research perspective, the idea was to remove the pressures of commercial theater from the mix and allow an unadulterated audience experience—and to see how that affected the creative process. One of the premises of the research was that if a show opened and was reviewed by professional critics, that would affect how a future audience approached the play, or if they went at all. Was it possible, they wondered, to have a pure and unadulterated sense of how an audience would respond to work based just on their own perspectives, personalities, and preconceived notions? So, the idea was to mount a production and bring in an audience essentially *tabula rosa* and see how they responded without outside influence. Indeed, one element of the research proposed that an audience was actually detrimental to artistic development. The goal was, if not noble, at least pointed. As American commercial theater was in flux, this was both an attempt to gauge what audiences liked and perhaps were looking for and to try to define "success" in the theater in non-financial terms. It's an interesting premise but an inherently flawed one because it can't be achieved without an audience, and audiences, in research terms, are a self-selecting sample. In a larger world as long as criticism existed—and this was during a time when newspapers had vibrant drama desks and multiple theater writers—it would be impossible to transfer anything they might learn to the real world.

Theater is an art form that stands firmly at the intersection of art and commerce. Theater, as Terrence always knew, demands an audience. A play on the page is no more theater than is a cry of players talking to an empty house. And that means financial concerns. The better goal of the research would have been not to advance the art *per se* but to determine what people in 1964 were willing to pay for. The realities of theater have never been more succinctly stated than by Irving Berlin: "The opening when your heart beats like a drum. / The closing when the customers won't come."

With the promise of a fully mounted production at no less than the prestigious Guthrie Theater in Minneapolis, which was available because they were dark during January and February, Terrence was given a grant of $1,500, and in January, Terrence, with his cast, headed to the Midwest. Along with *Bump*, the University of Minnesota selected playwright Arthur Kopit whose two short plays were *The Day the Whores Came Out to Play Tennis* and *Mahil Daiim*.

Both Terrence and Kopit claimed that they had been unaware that the productions would not be open to the public, and they accused the University of Minnesota of censorship. Kopit left, returned to New York, and went on a public tear accusing the university of "censorship of a most insidious kind." The Guthrie had offered Kopit a public performance in an eighty-eight-seat theater separate from the research project, as opposed to the 1,400-seat main stage, but Kopit declined. He was later able to produce the plays under a different Rockefeller grant at the Actors Studio.

Terrence stayed and created a minor firestorm in the press. In 1964, theater got a lot more space in newspapers, and a *contretemps* with New York theater folks pitting the young artist against the big university was red meat. Over several weeks many column inches in both the Minneapolis *Star* and the *Tribune* were devoted to the situation.

Terrence claimed that in allowing only an audience selected by the university for the four "viewings" of the pieces—carefully avoiding the word "performances"—they were being censored. The university shot back that it couldn't be censorship because they hadn't reviewed the scripts and thus could not be censoring them. Though we only have statements from the university to go on, the focus appears to be on the research project, and there is no mention of public performances being planned or guaranteed. Even director Lawrence Kornfeld said there was no censorship of the material, even adding that no one from the university had objected to the homosexual content.

Still, Terrence persisted on his own. On January 10, 1964, he released a lengthy statement that told his side of the story, with an abundance of purple prose. As he tells it, the university had decided to withdraw support of any public "viewing" on January 4. (Throughout his statement, he places "viewing" in quotes to diminish the concept, as opposed to a performance.) He and the cast and director arrived in Minneapolis on January 6 and were informed of this decision the next day. His upset at the closed nature of the "viewings" was palpable:

> The man on the street was specifically not welcome at the theater, and indeed would be turned away at the door should he try to enter the theatre. The University felt it could not give its support to my play, unless the audience was first selected by the Board of Directors of the Office for Advanced Drama Research.

He continued claiming that he and the play were "on probation" and objected to the university wanting to select the audience and adding that they were not acting in good faith. However, what he was missing was that the Rockefeller grant was for research, and the university was structuring the research in accordance with that grant. Terrence admitted as much:

> A legal right, they have; a moral right, no. I do not ask that they endorse my play. I only ask that they endorse my right to present

my work to the public and the public's right to see and judge my
work. Their stand is an insult to myself, my director, my cast and
the people of Minnesota. Naturally, we resent this . . .

We are willing to perform for 3 people as long as those 3 people
are in the theater because they *want* to be there. Not because they
were selected.

And we protest. Our protest is to stay and continue rehearsing.
. . . We do not play to present the play to *anyone* unless the University reverses its decision as to the nature of our audience. . . . Under
no circumstances will we play for an audience hand-picked by the
University. Either everyone is invited to these plays or no one sees
them.

He continues, stating conditions under which they will continue to
work, portraying him and the play as the victims: "And we are not especially flattered to be cast as the 'heroes.' We simply want to work and
perform for the public. We cannot subscribe to a dictatorship. . . . It is
up to the University and the people of Minnesota to come up with a
happy ending."

It was ultimately resolved that there could be an audience, and Terrence allowed that audience to be invited by the university. Evidently,
the compromise was reached so as not to invalidate the parameters of
the research and at the same time put butts in seats. In a letter to both
Terrence and Kopit, the university took responsibility for any misun-
derstanding that had occurred as they assumed "ultimate importance
on the possibility of sizeable audiences." Moreover, the letter stated that
their assumption all along, which they admitted was erroneous, was that
just as universities want to relate to the current state of the theater, they
"might be helpful for distinguished artists from the theater to live for a
brief time in relationship to the University."

At the opening, which was not an opening since everyone received
a statement saying that the play was a work-in-progress and that this
was not an official production, 237 people attended in the 1,400-seat
house. The other three performances were attended by "relevant viewing

groups" (talk about the language of research!), which included local critics and academic, amateur, and theater professionals.

Terrence's initial assumption that there would be open, public performances was not unfounded. The director of the program, Dr. Arthur
H. Ballet of the university, had been quoted in the Minneapolis press
in December of 1963, saying that the decision to have a live audience
would be determined by whether or not the playwrights thought that
their work would be helped by it. (Not to put too fine a point on it:
duh!)

A component of Terrence's reaction to the situation may also have
been more deep-seated in his personality. Since he started writing plays
as he said "to be heard," and throughout his life said that it was important to him to do things that matter, the idea of putting on a play that
no one would see was forcing him to hide his work at a time when he
was willing to be vulnerable about it. After all the work—and all the
courage—it took to get the play to a place where it could be seen by an
audience, it was unthinkable to be in a position where he might not be
heard and, worse, that his work didn't matter.

So, the production went on, and it was generally well-received. The
critics who reported on it steered away from going full-on in their analysis but were generally positive about the play and had high praise for
the cast. It was received by the press as a timely horror story and noted
for the sophistication of its language and willingness to grapple with the
darkness and the threat of what's "out there."

Throughout his career, Terrence, perhaps as a result of this experience,
would hate audience research. He felt that art shouldn't be subjected to
mass opinion which inhibited playwrights. How could anyone's voice be
heard if it's in response to other's opinions on a single viewing? A valid
point. Rather, Terrence felt that each individual takes away whatever
they take away from the playwright's work; it was, to some extent, a
sacred relationship. Nonetheless, the audience research that the University of Minnesota did on *Bump* was revealing to an extent. The audience
members who attended the "viewings" had been given a questionnaire,
and their responses were very positive. Given that the sample came from

people knowledgeable about theater, educated, and somewhat sophisticated, it couldn't be inferred to reveal anything about a general audience, but at least to this cohort, they got the play and knew what Terrence was going for. One comment, in particular said, "It's like a combination of *Who's Afraid of Virginia Woolf?* and *The Visit*," demonstrated that this wasn't the generic "man on the street" Terrence wanted to have access to the work. (It's also a bit prescient in that, decades later, Terrence would spend nearly fifteen years on the musical adaptation of *The Visit*.)

Though it had never been intended to be such—and really was designed *not* to be—the production at the Guthrie turned into a *de facto* out-of-town tryout. Michael Kahn, Terrence's college friend, now an increasingly important Off- and Off-Off Broadway director, flew to Minneapolis to see it and said he loved it. "It was just the period of awful mothers, right? You know families." Kahn and others were excited about its potential, and it's undeniable that the amount of publicity the play received raised its visibility, and several producers came out to see it.

Kermit Bloomgarden was the first producer to secure the rights to *Bump* with plans for a production in the fall of 1964. Noted director John Dexter was attached, Irene Worth was slated to play the mother, Ruby. As often happens, however, the financing fell apart.

The option was picked up by Ted Mann. Mann had founded Circle in the Square in 1951 with director Jose Quintero and the company was known for having reignited interest in the works of Eugene O'Neill after staging a production of *The Iceman Cometh*, which starred Jason Robards Jr. Their revival of *Summer and Smoke* in 1952 had launched the career of Geraldine Page. By 1964, Quintero and Mann had parted ways, and Paul Libin had joined the company as managing director after a series of meetings with Mann. Libin had been producing Off-Broadway, but the two men decided to join forces—and would work together for the next fifty years. In addition to revivals of O'Neill and Tennessee Williams, the theater was known for nurturing young talent, and its two hundred–seat theater at 159 Bleecker Street in Greenwich Village had steadily grown in prestige as a place where name talent could do serious work. After the critical and audience success of their revival of *Summer and Smoke*, Mann was very interested in *Bump*, but he didn't want it for downtown; he wanted to take it directly to Broadway. Libin was initially skeptical but jumped in when Mann said he believed this was Broadway material. It would be breakthrough and mainstream, particularly after the success of *Virginia Woolf*. The belief was that modern audiences were ready for something a bit more provocative—a *lot* more provocative as it turned out.

Libin doesn't recall the exact production budget for *Bump*, but noted that at the time, they were producing shows downtown for about $17,500 for their two hundred–seat theater and that to mount a show on Broadway would take $150,000 to $200,000. They booked the 1,100-seat Royale Theater on 45th Street (now the Bernard B. Jacobs Theatre)

Even though the producers and directors who had flown out to Minneapolis had loved the play, the first thing they did was fire the director and all the actors except Robert Drivas (who, as noted previously, was now Terrence's lover). Even then, Terrence was aware that to make such wholesale changes to the piece and how it was presented was to make the play significantly, if not entirely, different. It wouldn't be the only time that the decision to play on Broadway would change a play—and not necessarily for the better.

Michael Cacoyannis was signed on to direct. He had had a major hit for Circle in the Square with his production of *The Trojan Women* and a year later had been nominated for an Academy Award as the director of *Zorba the Greek*. He was, as they say, hot, and his history with the classics seemed to make him right for the scope of *Bump*.

Eileen Heckart signed on to play the mother Ruby. Heckart had made a splash on Broadway in the original 1953 production of William Inge's *Picnic* and had appeared in movies *Bus Stop*, *The Bad Seed* (for which she was nominated for an Academy Award), and *My Six Loves*, among others. As Terrence recalled, Heckart was a big name and was eager to return to Broadway—and to do something modern and edgy. (She was not alone in this. One of the characteristics of the Off-Off Broadway movement had been to redefine new forms of theater as art, and stars of all magnitudes were eager to push boundaries and be involved in something new and groundbreaking.) Moreover, it was the first time Heckart was going to have her name above the title, and she reportedly had visions of a Best Actor Tony Award to match her Supporting Actress Tony for *Picnic*. The rest of the cast included Robert Drivas as Sigfrid, Susan Anspach as Lakme, Marco St. John as Clarence, Clifton James as Fa, and Ferdi Hoffman as Grandfa.

Rehearsals were rocky from the beginning. As Terrence recalled:

> Michael Cacoyannis is making his Broadway debut with an unknown American playwright. It was a big deal, but in actuality he and I were not a good combo. Eileen Heckart and Bobby Drivas were all method actors, very much committed to the Stanislavsky, Lee Strasberg school of acting, and Michael believed in giving line readings very strongly, and he was giving them in the first five minutes, and he had a very thick accent . . . and the cast was not amused.
>
> One of the first lines of the piece is "Good morning." And Eileen said it about three times, and he said, "No, no, no." So, the battle lines were drawn, and we hadn't even had our first lunch break, and you could feel the animosity between the star and director, and I knew we were probably doomed.

Terrence was also apprehensive because it was the first time the play was being given a commercial production. It had had the imprimatur of academia in Minnesota, and the other production at the Playwright's Unit had been done for free.

He was also concerned that perhaps the play wasn't cast correctly and had a healthy dose of insecurity about himself in that he had never worked on Broadway before. Secretly, he felt that Ted Mann and Paul Libin were insane to put the show on Broadway, but there was a huge appetite for new American plays and playwrights, and with a name like Eileen Heckart on the marquee, all signs pointed to at least a healthy run. Knowing that the play was going to be different than it had been in Minneapolis, Terrence tried doing rewrites, but they weren't well-received by the cast. He was afraid that the script wouldn't work, but he kept all those fears—the fear of something threatening "out there"—to himself.

All of that happened privately behind closed doors, however, and Libin remembered that after the play was announced, ticket sales were strong. Heckart's name carried some weight, and Libin said, "It was just, I think the title had some kind of inherent intrigue. And we thought we had a hit." Terrence did as well: "Not in the sense that it's going to be a 'smash hit,' but I thought it would be acknowledged as ambitious, written by a 'talented young man with a future.'"

The critics had another thought altogether. The play opened to what Libin called "the worst set of reviews imaginable, and suddenly ticket sales disappeared." In talking about *Bump*, Terrence often cited reviews that called for his death or suggested it would have been better if he had been strangled in his cradle than write this play. Howard Taubman in *The New York Times* was not as violent, but he was dismissive of the characters as "zombies" and derisive, writing at length about the character of Fa and whether actor James was earning his money "the easy way or the hard way" since he mostly had to sit and listen to what's going on around him. Taubman archly comes down on the hard way. He also makes a joke out of Ruby's last live line, as the threats are closing in—expressed through a series of ever-louder bumps—"We will continue!" It is an assertion of going on despite the threats and their vulnerability. Taubman, however, asks, "Wanna bet?"

It's a bet Taubman would have won, and it might have closed that night as shows often did back then, if Libin hadn't stepped in and, somewhat, saved the day:

> It was a disaster, and we were in a quandary, so I tried to get a meeting with Lawrence Shubert who was then running the Shubert organization. He was very hard to tie down because he liked to spend his afternoons drinking and other "responsible" things.
>
> So finally, I decided to go to the lawyers who were Bernie Jacobs and Jerry Schoenfeld at the time, and I said to them, "Look, we've

got enough money to keep this thing going for a couple of weeks," and then what I wanted to do was charge a dollar for weekday tickets and two dollars for the weekend.

"Oh, we can't do that," he said. "It would be embarrassing for us. We're charging $15 and $18 a ticket. How could we have a Broadway show selling tickets for a dollar or two dollars?"

I said, "It's got nothing to do with what you're doing now. Obviously, we're just trying to get an audience to come in and see the play. We just thought we had a good chance of this play catching on."

But they just kept saying no, no, no, you can't do it. And I just said, I'm going to keep talking to these guys until they throw me out of their office. Finally, they said to me, "Look, get the hell outta here and go do whatever you want." I went out and changed the ticket prices.

There was a powerful response, and people started coming to see the play. Frank Rich [later chief theater critic of *The New York Times*] admitted to me that he took a date at a cost of two dollars. He never did tell me what he thought of the play.

Of course, all of a sudden, we thought we were going to make it, and I realized that if we could change the prices to $2 and $3 we could keep running. Well, that was the acid test. I suppose people would be willing to pay a dollar to see something, but they weren't willing to pay $2 to see something.

Now, the wonderful part of the story is that Terrence was very disappointed with the critical response to the play. But as he said many times, because of what Ted and I did to keep the play going, he decided instead of going into the advertising world, he was going to keep writing plays.

Terrence was, indeed, devastated by the response, and he thought that the play would close immediately, and even when Libin and Mann called him to say they were going on at the reduced prices, he didn't believe it could happen.

Perhaps shockingly, Taubman himself wrote to Terrence on May 3, just a week after the opening, "I am sorry I had to write as I did, but I am glad to hear that you mean to continue."

That would have been small compensation, but continue they did, and Terrence said,

> Suddenly, there was this line around the block, and of the 12 performances, every one was completely sold out, to my memory. And people loved it. People hated it. But it was lively, and it was a thing.
>
> There were pickets outside the theater, saying "This play must run!" and "It's a masterpiece." And the press wouldn't pick that up because they said that we had paid people to walk up and down with these signs. (They didn't.) If it had closed in one night, I doubt I would have ever written another play. I think the humiliation, the shame of running one performance would have just cut me off at the knees.

There were outpourings of support as well. John Steinbeck, who had attended the premiere in an opera cape, top hat, and silver-topped cane, to Terrence's embarrassment, wrote a letter supporting Terrence, saying: "My heart is sick today. There is no reason to anticipate or to expect fairness from critics, but I don't think they have the right of malicious mischief. Taubman and Kerr were not criticizing your play. They were punishing you for having written it." Steinbeck goes on, calling the critics and theater criticism into question and saying that his wife Elaine says that Terrence should fight back. Steinbeck, however, vilifies the critics as "sterile men" and reminds Terrence that Kerr's own play was "a stinker and his brother critics treated it as such." He does, ultimately have some advice: "There is no question about what you should do. You should go immediately to work. And as soon as you can. . . . As for the play's failing—remember the old Texas saying—'who ain't been thro'ed [sic] ain't rode.'"

Steinbeck's opinion was that they should close the show immediately and take their lumps rather than the indignity of limping along with a papered house, but for the play—and for Terrence—history shows the better course was to continue.

The play did ignite passions, and Terrence told the story of one performance where an audience member jumped up on the stage, grabbed Heckart, and pulled her off the stage.

> He said, "I hate that you're a great actress. Why are you contributing to this filth, this disgusting play?" And he pulled her off the stage, and she was on the floor of the theater. Then Bobby Drivas jumped off the stage, and they started pushing and shoving and cursing. It really upset people.

The most painful story for Terrence, however, didn't happen inside the theater. It's a story he told many, many times over the years, and even when he was eighty years old, the pain of an event fifty-four years earlier was still very much present, as if it still had the power to trigger old feelings.

On opening night, Terrence was standing under the marquee at the Royale and looking at the crowd. In 1965, it seemed like everyone smoked, and they smoked right up until the last minute when flashing lights meant that the performance was really going to start. Terrence would have been smoking as well, having whatever feelings attended his first opening night on Broadway.

As curtain time was approaching, Terrence saw the critic Walter Kerr and his wife Jean were finishing their cigarettes, and Jean turned to Walter and said, "Let's go see what the boyfriend has turned up." Fifty-four years later, he remembered the snide tone of the comment, and Jean's dismissive attitude.

As Terrence said, it became clear to him in that moment that he was being reviewed not as a playwright in his own right but as Edward's boyfriend. He was shocked and hurt, and besides, they had broken up a year or two before that night. He felt that she had nullified him and made him irrelevant, and he said, "I was sort of devastated before they had even seen the play." Walter Kerr was noted for being a harsh critic and for dismissing everyone from Beckett to Bernstein. And that's the thing about critics—which Steinbeck clearly knew—they are very present-focused. The people who moved the culture and shaped the future of theater often did not do well in Kerr's critcism.

It's likely, too, that Jean Kerr, a devout Roman Catholic, would have been threatened by the play, and her snide comment didn't reflect the popular image of the author of *Please Don't Eat the Daisies*, her book of humorous essays that had been a best-seller and made into a movie with Doris Day as the author's stand-in. (The book later became a TV series.) Jean's work was the very definition of Eisenhower gender stereotypes, what we might call now heteronormative hegemony. Her humor derived almost exclusively from her role as a long-suffering second banana— that as a woman and a mother, she had to deal with wacky children and doting on her husband, but her place was always subservient, even if long-suffering. The 1958 musical for which she had written the book and lyrics, *Goldilocks*, is a paean to traditional gender roles in which men who aren't aggressive are derided and women are incomplete without a man and need protection. Songs like "Where is the Beast in You?" and "Who's Been Sitting in My Chair?" celebrate that a functioning society depends on these roles. (Even with stars Don Ameche and Elaine Stritch above the title, and Margaret Hamilton in the company, the show lost its entire investment.) That the world was changing, and Jean Kerr's social hierarchy might be changing was threatening to her sensibilities . . . and her income stream. Far from being the long-suffering "little woman," she was the sophisticated wife of a *New York Times* critic, so the inherent hypocrisy of her life and writing, and her naked pandering to the market would sting, particularly to someone like Terrence who was always looking for the truth.

Jean Kerr, however, was only one of the people made uncomfortable. Terrence recalled that the response from the critical world to the play assumed that it was written by a gay man, and that he was reviewed as a gay man. He recalled that he was startled by it, never having actively hidden his sexuality. What disturbed people was that this was one of the first plays that presented a gay man who wasn't mentally ill, who wasn't unhappy, and who was comfortable being who he was, who actually thought he deserved to be loved as he was. Clarence meets a tragic end in *Bump*, but it's not because of his sexuality; it's because he has stood for a life free of fear, celebrating goodness and refusing to live in fear of the thing "out there," just as Terrence had.

In 2019, as Terrence recalled much of this experience, much of the pain, though mellowed with time, was still present. He said that he was still a bit surprised that he got so much credit for "coming out." Since from his first high-profile Broadway show he'd been known as a gay man; he felt that choosing how to express his identity was out of his hands. What he hated was being put in a pigeonhole, referred to—and even dismissed—because of his sexuality. With the perspective of years, Terrence also thought that *Bump* was written when he was trying to imitate Albee, and that when he wrote it, he had not yet found his own voice, but that insight would come decades later.

Nor was it completely accurate. While Terrence, in looking back, might have been trying to excuse a young writer—and certainly never stopped practicing his craft, as his penchant for ongoing rewriting of every play he worked on would illustrate—*Bump* also has elements in it that would always distinguish Terrence's work from Albee's. In Albee, the demons come from within his characters, whether in *Virginia Woolf* or *The Goat*; they ate at people from the inside. For Terrence the demons were almost always external, whether it was AIDS, the Vietnam War, or something completely unknown and unidentifiable. Whereas Albee's characters were almost always destroyed from the inside out, Terrence's characters had to struggle to accommodate situations not of their making and find love, connection, and, when needed, a kind of redemption from an often-hostile world that was on a very real level out to get them.

In the theater of the twenty-first century, a journey such as Terrence had had with *Bump* would be impossible. He knew that, and in later years often complained about the difficulty of getting work seen—one of the reasons he resisted writing musicals, though two of his four Tony Awards would come from the books of musicals.

He knew that what had happened with *Bump* could never be repeated: that it had gone from reading to regional theater to Broadway in around two years, and he often found the business of theater frustrating, certainly toward the end of his career. As he described it, the series of readings and workshops, which were deemed necessary, delayed the ability to get a play in front of an audience, if it ever could. At the same time, as a writer, he was always writing. As Mrs. Mac had said, "Nothing can substitute for writing." As noted, the published versions of his plays—and the ubiquitous "acting editions" from Samuel French—are often different from what was presented on stage.

Looking back in 2019, he said that he was still proud of *Bump*, though what he had learned mostly was what *not* to do. He said: "I was literally told to shut up and go away, and I'm glad I didn't. I've just had to persevere and be stubborn."

He had been chastened by the experience with *Bump*, to be sure, but he wasn't going to be silenced or hidden. He knew he had "rode," and he took strength from what Mann and Libin did in keeping the show running and in the positive responses from the people who saw *Bump* as groundbreaking and relevant.

They heard him.

They showed him he mattered.

4

The Next Chapter

I.

AFTER *BUMP* CLOSED, Terrence was at a loss creatively—and financially. Mann and Libin keeping *Bump* open for that extra time had given Terrence confidence that he could write—something he said that he had never doubted. He had a little bit of money from *Bump*, but not enough to live on.

About a month after *Bump* closed, he was hired by Twentieth Century Fox to write an adaptation of the Turkish novel *Memed, My Hawk*. He was paid $3,600 for that effort and turned in a script. However, production was dropped at the request of the Turkish government, which said that it was anti-Turkish propaganda. (The movie would finally be made in 1982 without Terrence's screenplay.)

Then, in August, he took a job as managing editor for the *Columbia College Today*, and the $9,000 a year salary was better than the $6,900 median family income in the United States in 1965, but it wasn't what he wanted to be doing. He was still writing plays, but he was spending all day editing other people's work and then spending nights trying to write his own was difficult. He was not happy with the job at Columbia:

> So, I was back at Columbia editing their alumni magazine, editing pieces by some of my former professors, which was really weird, correcting their grammar. But you know, they're like "Why the fuck

is he telling us this is a bad sentence?" And some of them wrote bad sentences. Mrs. McElroy had trained us very well.

When he had been in Minneapolis doing *Bump*, he had given an interview in which he said that this was a particularly good time to be a writer, since there were so many grants available for writers. That was true. Thanks in large part to the work of Edward Albee and the rise of the Off-Off Broadway movement, there was a cultural interest in American plays and playwrights. There was also a move away from traditional theater as Broadway musicals became less and less a source for popular music, and "youth culture" began to dominate all forms of art. In the simplest terms, the Baby Boomers, the largest generational cohort at the time of about 73 million, according to the U.S. Census bureau were coming of age, had financial autonomy, and were dictating tastes and styles across the culture.

Terrence received the first of his Guggenheim Foundation grants in 1966. It carried a stipend of $6,000 in the field of Drama and Performance Art, and he listed his various credits in the application and said that he wanted to use the grant to continue to write. This was not his first application, however; documents in his archives indicate that he had first applied in 1963. For that application, he had enlisted Steinbeck to write a recommendation and who—after months of being chased by the Guggenheim committee—wrote a glowing letter in which he said:

> I have read some of Mr. McNally's work, which I find excellent and provocative. His energy is enormous and matched by his curiosity.
>
> . . .
>
> All in all, I can't think of anyone I have met in recent years whom I could more enthusiastically recommend for a Guggenheim Fellowship.

It would, however, be three more years until the committee agreed.

II.

About the time that Terrence received the Guggenheim Fellowship, he met the first of many people who would become a McNally actor/muse. Though he wasn't having pieces produced, Terrence was going to the theater regularly, and he kept seeing an actor, and thought that no matter what he did, he was absolutely brilliant. That actor was James Coco.

> I'll always remember meeting him because Bobby Drivas who was his friend introduced us. And there was a coffee shop we used to meet at every day. Bobby introduced us, and I looked up from my *New York Times* and said hello and went back to my *Times*.
>
> Jimmy just ripped the paper out of my hand, saying "How dare you not even look at me when you're introduced to me." And it was not because he was James Coco. He was not the famous actor at the time, but his response made such an impression on me.
>
> So, I certainly looked at him, and I just said, "I think you're so great." And I named four plays I'd seen him in in the past. He worked all the time. I said, "I just think you're amazing."
>
> And he said, "Well, I'm going to die with my secret. No one writes leading roles for people who look like me." And so, I said, "I'll write something for you."

Coco was what's known as a "character actor," overweight, not conventionally handsome, but with a distinctive look. He was a versatile actor, but was always going to be relegated to supporting roles, at least where traditional casting is concerned. His concern and fear were justified, but as Terrence said, he saw something in Coco and was intrigued. As we've seen, Terrence liked writing for specific people; it fueled his imagination.

This was during the Vietnam conflict, and at the time there were, of course, a lot of protests of the draft, and New York City and, in particular, Greenwich Village were kind of an epicenter for these protests. (Terrence had registered for the draft as required and was classified as 1-Y,

"To be called up only in time of war or national emergency." Because Vietnam was never officially declared a war, Terrence would not have been required to serve, at least as Terrence related.)

Terrence described that one day he was in the Village, and there was a protest march, and there were a lot of people yelling at Terrence and his friends, saying, "You kids should serve." However, Terrence noticed that most of the people who were yelling were middle aged. He began to imagine what would happen if there were a glitch in the system and a middle-aged man was called up for his army physical. Terrence imagined Jimmy as that man caught up in a bureaucratic nightmare where even though the interviewer could agree that perhaps there was a mistake, she still had an order.

That play became *Next*, and he had written it specifically for Coco's talents. Coco plays Marion. It had its premiere at the White Barn Theater in Westport, Connecticut, in August of 1967 and had been produced for channel 13 in New York as part of their *New York Television Theater* series in March 1968. It was part of a three-play bill called *Apple Pie* that was among the first of Terrence's antiwar plays. In addition to *Next*, the bill also included *Tour*, a play about privileged tourists in Italy who can't grasp the horror of what their son is confronting in Vietnam, and *Botticelli*, a play about two men in a foxhole playing an intellectual game and casually killing an enemy. In *Next*, Coco was teamed with Elaine Shore, an actress noted in her native Chicago for her improvisational talent, and a good match for Coco. After it ended and the TV version had aired, as far as Terrence knew, that was that, and he went back to editing the writing of people who resented him for it.

As so often happened, however, Terrence believed he got very lucky one day. He continues the story:

> [The play] was funny. People liked it. But I was working at Columbia, and Jimmy was not famous. No one was saying, "Do you have a play written for Jimmy Coco by that writer who got the worst reviews I'd ever read for a play?"

And then one day I was at Columbia, and the phone rang. It was Jimmy. He said, "I'm up in Stockbridge, Massachusetts, working on *Adaptation*, a play by Elaine May. And the producer just came in very upset. The next play called *Lovers and Other Strangers* by Joe Bologna and Renee Taylor has just been cancelled. They've decided to bring it straight to Broadway, and they're canceling their slot at the Berkshire Theater festival. And they asked if anybody had a play. And I said, I have a play."

Jimmy gave the play to Elaine May. She read it, and said, "I'll direct it." Of course, by the time Terrence heard all of this, things were already in process, and they'd arranged to produce it, all without his permission, but it was all resolved in the end. The bill became *Adaptation*, which May had written, and *Next*. Terrence took an immediate leave of absence from the job at Columbia—he was not so brazen as to quit outright—and headed to Massachusetts that night. He met May. They clicked, and they went into two weeks of rehearsal; it was not just one night in Connecticut, or one shot on TV, which had been the play's previous life.

In 1968, when the play was presented at the Berkshire Theater Festival, Elaine May was a big deal. She had been part of the comedy team Nichols and May that from 1957 to 1961 had redefined standup comedy and improv, influencing a generation of comedians. In 1961, however, the team had split up. May wanted to try her hand at more daring work and so initially focused on playwriting and directing, and she and Nichols had found their improv material was getting stale. It was time for a change, although at the time she directed *Next*, Terrence remembered that while she could have made a lot of money touring for ten years or so, that wasn't how she wanted her life to be. He always respected her for putting her art and her growth as a theater artist over a pay day.

Next was presented at Berkshire on a double bill with *Adaptation*, a play written by May that was a kind of extended allegory in which people go through life as if it's a board game that follows players through Shakespeare's "Seven Ages of Man," a speech by the character Jaques from *As You Like It*. It's a satire that's a far more complicated play than *Next*, for all its comedy. Both plays were reviewed very strongly, with raves for Coco, and there was mounting enthusiasm for moving the play to New York. At that point, Terrence was both excited and nervous; it would be his first high profile appearance as a writer in New York since the bomb of *Bump*.

As happens from time to time, the stars align, and the show moved, opening in February of 1969 to sensational reviews. It was presented at Greenwich News Playhouse on 13th Street in what had been a former church (now a condominium). It was, Terrence said, a weird and unwieldy space. Nonetheless, it was a definite hit—and it made Coco a huge star. As Terrence remembered it, news spread around New York very quickly, and suddenly *Next* was the thing to see. He remembered being out in front of the theater and watching Noel Coward and Marlene Dietrich get out of a limousine. Off-Broadway, or at least a clumsy theater in the Village, was suddenly *the* place to be for the *cognoscenti*.

Terrence would never return to Columbia, and he said it never would have happened without having had the play already written, or the good fortune of having Coco call him at the last minute. For him, the experience of putting on *Next* went beyond just writing and getting the play on its feet. It taught him how important it is to have the right people in the room to do a play. For *Bump* he knew that it had been the wrong people in the room, but with *Next*, they got it right. He had written the play for Coco, and Coco had made it his own. Terrence said he'd seen other actors do the part, but they were never as successful because they didn't have Coco's unique gift to be able to go from hilarity to pathos in a split second. It couldn't be less naturalistic, and yet in the right hands it works because it delivers a solid emotional experience to the audience. Terrence wants them to say, "Wait a minute . . . we were just laughing!" The ability to achieve that level of theatricality while creating an authentic emotional experience for an audience was part of Terrence's genius, and it began to flower with *Next*.

Next would run for more than seven hundred performances over three years, with Coco staying for a long time and winning the Drama Desk Award for outstanding performance by an actor. Terrence always believed that the collaboration with May on that play was one of the most critical factors in his development as a playwright. It was through May he said that he learned that there has to be some kind of action or content; a play can't succeed on style or a concept alone. Even more importantly, he learned from May how to bring the audience into the play. It was, he said, a lesson that he had learned the hard way in *Bump*: always include the audience.

With the success of *Next*, Terrence was suddenly if not a darling of the press, at least on their radars. He gave great and playful interviews, talking about how "rotten" May was and proceeded to show how her rottenness was an attention to detail, demand for excellence, and commitment to the work. That piece first appeared in the Newark *Star-Leger* and was syndicated nationwide—not something that happens in the twenty-first century, least of all for an Off-Broadway play, though May's fame may have made it national fodder. For all the effort he put into sharing the limelight, Terrence ultimately wasn't successful at it. Since May was famously publicity shy, so Terrence stepped into the void, yet even late in life he felt that she may have resented all the attention he and *Next* got. He would never really know the answer to that, and May isn't talking.

III.

While *Next* raised Terrence's profile, he was working on much more than that play. The years 1967 and 1968 were very prolific times for him. It was also a great time to be a writer in New York, and he was constantly aware that at the time there was so much to write about.

As mentioned earlier, the Baby Boomers coming of age in the mid-1960s were having a profound effect on the culture. There were changes in music, style, and expression, to say nothing of the economic impact these young people were having in driving the culture.

Marco St. John as Clarence and Robert Drivas as Sigfrid in And Things That Go Bump in the Night *at the Royale Theater, 1965.*
PHOTO BY FRIEDMAN-ABELES / PHOTOFEST

The three plays of *Apple Pie* were part of the growing number of plays written in protest against the Vietnam war. *Hair* had opened at The Public Theater in 1967 and moved to Broadway in 1968, prompting shock at the nudity (always a bit obscure thanks to heavy backlighting but there nonetheless) and the antiwar message. *Hair* signaled a change in Broadway with an emphasis more on youth—as a profitable demographic as much as anything with Off-Broadway hits like *Your Own Thing*, an adaptation of Shakespeare's *Twelfth Night*, and outings by Beckett on Broadway, as well as the debut of Stoppard's *Rosencrantz and Guildenstern Are Dead*.

Vietnam would also inspire Terrence to write *Witness*, a one-act play about a would-be presidential assassin who has taken a prisoner and bound him to a chair to have him witness that the assassin is not crazy—and the window washer who stumbles into the scene and has his own issues with the war. It's a dark satire of government and the media.

Cuba Si! is a play about a would-be revolutionary and follower of Castro awaiting the revolution . . . in Central Park, where she encounters a conservative reporter. Although Terrence was adamantly against the conflict in Vietnam, his plays, even with the absurd situations, are well-argued on both sides of the issues. His growing ability to understand and present characters whose views he might not agree with but who have their own internal truth was steadily developing—and would only get more sophisticated with time.

Witness was first presented as part of the Playwright's Unit in June of 1968 with Coco in the role of the window washer. Between the closing of *Next* in the Berkshires and its opening in New York, *Witness* was presented at the Gramercy Arts Theater on 27th Street, in November on a double bill with *Sweet Eros*.

Sweet Eros dealt with the other issue that fascinated Terrence throughout his career: sex. And not just sex; power in relationships, what constitutes intimacy, cultural hypocrisy surrounding sex, and the nature of relationships. It's a topic about which he was never shy, nor was he ever anything other than direct when talking about sex. In *Sweet Eros*, a young man has kidnapped a woman, bound and gagged her, strips her and talks to her for forty-five minutes through a series of scenes, pouring out his heart and his observations on life to her. He wants to be heard. He wants to matter. He wants to be loved, and he wants her to submit to him, which after a fashion she eventually does, though to what extent is always unclear. It was possibly a cathartic play for Terrence as the character identified only as the Young Man after going through a litany of grievances and complaints about the world, like Ruby in *Bump* has to continue.

> **Young Man:** Something tells me not to stop trying. Maybe there's a chance I'll pull through. I've got to keep the legs going. A little longer, no matter how tired, if only for the chance of finding something better, finding my way out, my way back to love and lyricism and gentleness and accepting that it's strange, this life, and that's the point of it.

This echoes Clarence's speech from *Bump* where he holds out hope for "anything to make you want to live so much you'd die for it." Terrence, like his characters, had not yet found it.

Terrence wrote the play for his lover Robert Drivas, and Sally Kirkland played the girl in the original production. It caused a sensation. Not because of the subject matter, of course, but because of the nudity. For forty-five minutes of the fifty-minute play, Kirkland was completely nude. Cue the controversies.

Although *Hair* claimed to have been the first show to have full frontal nudity on the stage, as noted above, the scene was brief, and the actors were backlit so while the actors were, in fact, nude, the backlighting made it hard to make out genitals. (It's a trick that Terrence would use thirty-two years later with the end of *The Full Monty*.) *Sweet Eros*, on the other hand, had the naked Kirkland downstage, bound and gagged and very much in the altogether, allowing the play to claim that it was the first Off-Broadway play to have full frontal nudity. Even that was parsing it a bit close. The year before, Kirkland had appeared nude in a show called *Tom Paine*, as well as in other "experimental" works, but those were technically Off-Off Broadway. The next statement was that *Sweet Eros* had the *longest* nude scene ever staged Off-Broadway. And this is how legends are crafted because each permutation was reported, somewhat breathlessly, in the press.

Another legend quickly grew up around the show that the papers leapt at. As the story went, the producers said they had interviewed twenty-five girls for the part (sometimes that number grew to thirty-five), and they saw plenty of strippers and others who might not be considered serious actors. After narrowing the pool down to three, only Kirkland agreed to appear nude.

Here's where the fun part comes in. Kirkland did it because it was "art." The daughter of a Main Line Philadelphia family and herself a former art student, Kirkland maintained that nudity was artistic, stressing that there were directors and actors for whom she'd never disrobe, but *Sweet Eros* was art, and she was all in . . . or all off. The *New York Times* even did a feature on the issue of onstage nudity allowing Kirkland to make her case and even quoting her replacement Martha Whitehead who cited that age-old actor's defense, "I needed the job," but she continued asking, "What's the fuss?"

Well, the fuss was that Terrence was upset that what was being reviewed was the nudity and not the play. However, that's not completely accurate. Though the nudity was mentioned as distasteful to some of the mainstream critics—who were now regularly reviewing everything Terrence did—it wasn't the nudity that was as threatening as the dark thoughts of the Young Man, and his anger. Once again, though, Terrence broke the mold, or blazed the trail, or shook things up, because after *Sweet Eros*, the mantra of nudity on stage became, "What's the fuss?"

In addition to *Next*, *Sweet Eros*, and *Witness*, Terrence also had another show running at the end of 1968, leading critic Michael Feingold to refer to Terrence's work as "inescapable" in an article for *Plays and Players* in March of 1969. *Noon* is a one-act play about five people who arrive in a vacant apartment at noon after having answered a personal ad. Each of them is seeking some kind of sexual adventure, but none of them is the person who placed the ad, and suddenly they all have to deal with one another and their shared secret of stealing away at noon for sex with someone who is not their partner. The comedy is pure Terrence: the hypocrisy of people pretending that they don't want sex, or that sex is something to be hidden and ashamed of—times five. Since Terrence never hid his sexuality, he always found it both senseless and amusing the lengths people would go to seem "normal," that is avoiding talking about sex while secretly trying to get as much as they can. From his childhood, Terrence had never had that choice. Terrence wrote the play for Circle in the Square, and it was presented at the Henry Miller's Theatre on Broadway in November under the banner *Morning, Noon, and Night*, with *Morning* written by Israel Horowitz and *Night* by Leonard Melfi. The piece got lukewarm reviews, though Terrence came off best of the three, but the audiences stayed away. Producers Ted Mann and Paul Libin tried their *Bump* strategy again of lowering ticket prices to $2, and the audiences came for a while, but when the prices went back up again, sales tanked, and the show closed in January. At the time, and again later, Terrence speculated that it was the cost of attending theater that kept people away—an age-old problem.

The success of the *Apple Pie* trilogy on New York's Public Television encouraged them to create another omnibus evening in 1969 called *Foul!*, a series of short plays tackling the theme of pollution. Terrence's play is a series of blackout sketches, in which a teacher, nun, lovers, scientist, writer, all take their last breaths. They were warned that at 12:00 there would be no air, and each sketch starts at 11:59. Once again, Terrence returns to the threat "out there" and what it means for the destruction of humankind and all the things that make "life worth dying for": science, art, love, and just everyday living. PBS labeled Terrence as "avant-garde," but thanks in large part to Terrence's work and its visibility—even more than many of the other playwrights of the period—the avant-garde was establishing a significant beachhead in the mainstream.

His plays, other than *Next* of course, weren't getting lengthy productions at this time. A few weeks or even just a handful of performances was about the length of the runs. Some short plays like *Tour* were included in omnibus evenings of short plays at venues like Café Au Go Go in the Village. Despite their short runs, it was a time when journalistic coverage of theater thrived, and his plays were getting reviewed, visibility that's critical for a playwright trying to be heard. Even when the reviews were not raves, Terrence was consistently praised for his voice and his originality.

As Edith Oliver wrote in the *New Yorker*, in her review of *Whiskey*, a play about a carnival singing group all named for different alcohol brands, in 1973:

> Whether Mr. McNally's social comment is particularly penetrating or first-hand is open to question; he is more a ribber than a satirist. But his theatrical ideas are original and funny, invariably redeeming even the weakest of his plays—the soliloquy of that garrulous window-cleaner in *Witness*, for example—and he can write splendid parts.

The critics didn't always "get" Terrence—something that would be a constant throughout his career. Though critics may not deserve the unfettered drubbing they receive from William Goldman in his book *The Season*, theater critics are largely very much in the present. Their writing reflects contemporary audience tastes at the time, and Terrence, who consistently scored firsts and challenged current conventions, was often in their crosshairs. It's only in hindsight that some critics came around to understanding Terrence, but that didn't help ticket sales when plays were running, another issue that will come into play later on.

Case in point about critics: *Where Has Tommy Flowers Gone?* This 1971 play, an absurdist (almost Dadaist), picaresque farce, didn't sit well with the critics when it premiered at Yale Rep. in January that year, though Bobby Drivas got raves as the obsessed and marginally insane hero intent on setting off a bomb in the dressing room at Bloomingdale's, or another equally unlikely destination in New York. The play was criticized for being chaotic, and yet it's an accurate reflection of the time when the social order was upended, people were dying senselessly in Vietnam, and four students had been shot at Kent State in Ohio the previous year. Older critics—and they were all older—saw only the chaos and the threat to order the play embodied, and they pounced. Critics of art are always sounding the alarm that one piece or another represents the end of civilization, or something equally dramatic, only years later to acknowledge that the artist may have been on to something.

Terrence, who by this time was no stranger to criticism, kept writing. He said that after *Bump*, he stopped reading reviews. That's a popular trope among theater professionals especially—a means of polishing their *bona fides* as artists who exist in a plane above the vulgarity of criticism. It's seldom true, and even if it were, the people controlling the finances do read, and Terrence would have to confront the impact of a negative review on the bottom line many times in the decades. Again, like so many of the stories of *the theater*, the absolute truth is unknowable and—frankly—irrelevant. Whether Terrence read reviews or not, he listened to only one voice in what he wanted to say—his own.

And he was being supported where it mattered. He had received a second Guggenheim Fellowship in 1969, and he was able to write what interested him. And he was about to tackle a new style—and find something every artist needs: a home.

IV.

As the 1960s drew to a close, there was another major historic event that would shape Terrence's life and career. The Stonewall Riots that began on June 28, 1969, and ran for several nights, began as a police raid on the Stonewall Inn, a gay bar. Throughout the 1960s, gay bars were raided. Homosexuality wasn't illegal in New York, but serving liquor to gay patrons was ruled "disorderly" by the State Liquor Authority, so bars that weren't allegedly paying protection money to the mafia were often raided. The bars were often dirty, served watered-down liquor, and tried many ways to get around laws and regulations. Gay patrons were routinely harassed, and drag queens were especially targeted. The Stonewall Riots reportedly began when female officers raiding the bar were checking those dressed as female for their gender. Some violence erupted. It spilled out into the street, and chaos ensued. When the dust cleared, a movement had been born.

Terrence remembered going to gay bars in Manhattan during his time at Columbia. He recalled a place called Lenny's on 10th Street as a dark, narrow cellar. As opposed to the Stonewall, which attracted a more downscale crowd, Lenny's was a "hot spot" that attracted intellectual types, and Terrence went there with Albee. Albee, in fact, introduced Terrence to much of this world, including another place that attracted an artsy crowd, the Cedar Tavern. Terrence recalled meeting Samuel Beckett there when he was making a movie in the city with Buster Keaton, as well as Aaron Copland and Virgil Thompson, and others. A decade or more before AIDS would change the world, bars were a thriving gay community in Manhattan. They became a destination for a kind of "slumming" as well, and straight notables such as Ethel Merman and Tallulah Bankhead were also seen at Lenny's. Lenny's was joined by

Julius, the San Remo, Old Colony, and a host of bars. Cruising happened on Christopher Street—and pretty much any street in the Village.

There was another type of destination during this period as well that was hugely popular with gay men at the time: the baths. During the sixties and seventies, there were many of these establishments where men could go to hook up. Terrence was a regular at the Club Baths on First Avenue near Houston for many years. Probably the most famous of these, however, was the Continental Baths, opened in 1968 by Steve Ostrow, a former Metropolitan Opera singer and a showman. While most of the baths were dark, secretive places, Ostrow installed a stage and turned his into a showplace that attracted an almost mind-boggling list of entertainers. Of course, the most famous alumna of the Continental stage was Bette Midler, who was so popular she earned (or coined) the nickname "Bathhouse Betty," and she performed with pianist Barry Manilow, becoming a gay icon in relatively short order.

All of this, along with a growing gay liberation movement, was changing the visibility of LGBTQ+ people in the culture, and after the first protests in Washington Square Park in 1969, the Gay Rights Parade began in 1970. Terrence remembered appearing with Midler at the rally in Washington Square Park in 1973 at the end of the parade, and he recalled being nearly overwhelmed by the size of the crowd and the number of gay people who were willing to come out and be identified publicly as gay. It was a gathering of people facing the fear or whatever might be "out there" to challenge them but refusing to hide. The world had caught up to Terrence, once again, and he would use it to go further as an artist.

In 1966, director and teacher Robert Brustein arrived at Yale to head the theater school. He had, however, an even broader vision, which was to create a resident company of actors and designers with whom the students could collaborate and present professional productions, and many of these would move on to Broadway and other productions. Brustein had first brought Terrence to Yale for *Where Has Tommy Flowers Gone?* For the 1973–1974 season, Terrence was Playwright in Residence, working with students, including Christopher Durang and

Albert Innaurato, who collaborated that year on a freewheeling adaptation of *The Brothers Karamazov*. Terrence's contribution to the season was a three-act play called *The Tubs*, which he had begun working on the previous summer.

The Tubs was the only farce Terrence ever wrote, a tribute to Georges Feydeau whose farces gained worldwide fame at the end of the nineteenth century and into the twentieth. Characterized by stereotypical characters, mistaken identities, sex games, door slamming, manic behavior, threats of exposure, and, of course, a (usually implausible) happy ending.

Terrence loved the classics and classic forms, and it amused him to update the slamming doors of the boudoir into the doors of a sex club. The Ritz is a bathhouse that was inspired by the Continental Baths. Ohio-based garbage man and mobster Gaetano Proclo (whom everyone called "Gay" for short) is lost in New York and trying to hide from his mobster brother-in-law Carmen, ducks into The Ritz, not knowing the type of establishment it is. Carmine has put a hit out on Gaetano, to prevent him from inheriting the money from his dying father that should go to his sister Vivian, Gaetano's wife. Gaetano, on the lam, only wants to be in the last place Carmine would ever look for him—hence, a gay bathhouse. Hilarity ensues as the chase is on, chubby-chasing boys take a shine to Gaetano, and his wife Vivian tracks him down, only to think Gaetano has turned gay. There's also a private investigator sent by Carmen who finds himself in the mix. The most memorable character is Googie Gomez, a performer at The Ritz, who thinks Gaetano is a famous producer who will discover her, and her heavily accented rendition of "Everything's Coming Up Roses" from *Gypsy* is a comic highlight of the piece. The comedy comes from the pace, naturally, but also from the characters who arrive from outside the world of The Ritz, a farce trope that pretty much always lands. It's also significant that Terrence chose to make Carmine and Gaetano mobsters, since the mafia was believed to have owned and operated many of the gay establishments in New York, but never set foot in any of them. (Ironically, the mafia had no financial interest in the baths, allegedly.)

The show played twenty-two performances, opening in the first week of January to mixed reviews from the Connecticut papers, but a strong notice from Mel Gussow in the *New York Times*, enough to fulfill the Rep's desire to be a launching platform for larger productions. *The Tubs*, renamed *The Ritz*, was headed for the big time.

Adela Holzer, who would later declare bankruptcy and be convicted of fraud, was at the time the hottest producer working on Broadway. An original investor in *Hair*, she had a string of hits to her name, including work with the Royal Shakespeare Company in New York. At the time of *The Ritz*, she was also represented on Broadway by Murray Schisgal's *All Over Town*, starring Dustin Hoffman, which had a similar nontraditional (for Broadway) appeal. Holzer was also a woman at a time when the producing field was almost completely dominated by men. She signed on as lead producer with Robert Drivas directing.

The show was recast with Jack Weston as Gaetano, Jerry Stiller as Carmine, Rita Moreno as Googie, and F. Murray Abraham as Chris, a character whose running gag is that he is trying to get someone—anyone—to his room for a tryst. And the company headed to Washington.

There are three stories—one famous, two not-so—that Terrence loved to tell about *The Ritz*. The first was that he had always intended Googie to be played by Rita Moreno. It was her voice that he had heard when he was writing the part. More specifically, Googie was based on a character that Moreno had created and performed at parties. After having won the Oscar for Anita in *West Side Story* in 1962, she couldn't get cast as anything but an accented Latina, and this character, who had no name, would complain bitterly in broken English about how no one would see her as a great actress. Terrence ran with it. Though in the play Googie latches onto Gaetano, thinking he is Joseph Papp, she also has a lot of sharp lines about what a great star she is and how no one better get in her way—and that she is only waiting to be discovered.

The second story had to do with the casting of F. Murray Abraham as Chris, one of the gayest denizens of the club. Originally, the part had gone to an obviously gay actor, but it wasn't working. Terrence portrays Chris, a character who thought of "sex as just a way of saying hello."

Chris was flamboyant, but the actor they'd hired just didn't get it. Abraham, who was straight, managed it. In 1975, being out and gay could be the death knell of an actor's career, and actors who had spent their entire careers trying to hide their sexuality could be inhibited, or at least that was the concern in this case. Abraham had no such limitation, so he was free to go for it with a level of abandon that was part stereotype but a larger part a fairly accurate portrayal of a truly loving man seeking connection in one of the only places he felt safe to do so.

Abraham's success was certainly one factor that made Terrence resistant to saying that gay actors should play gay parts, which in 2018 had become an issue. He believed—and it was often proved—that good acting had nothing to do with who one slept with but with the inner resources and artistry of the actor. While Terrence appreciated the importance of providing opportunity and representation, he also always wanted the best actor in the role—a point of view that was somewhat controversial at the end of his career.

The third story had to do with the out-of-town tryout in Washington. No one was laughing. At first, they thought that F. Murray Abraham "played the gay off the gay man," as Terrence said. However, it was Holzer who got to the bottom of the issue: the set was the wrong color. Terrence said:

> She said, "I know what's wrong with the play." And we were all . . . what? She said, well, the set is three stories high. It was barely three levels of playing area, and she said, "It's so depressing to look at all that gray." But what would you do, Adela?
>
> "I think we should paint it warm. A warm, nice embracing color like Sardi's. You know when you eat at Sardi's, it's so warm, and it feels good to be there."
>
> We said you'd have to pay to have the set repainted. We shut down on the day off, and the day after that the actors got a free day off. The entire set was turned the color of Sardi's. And when the curtain went up, we got a laugh on the third line.

It wasn't just the color, Terrence was also quick to point out. He was, as he always did, working on the lines and the jokes, fine tuning them as he saw them play out in performance. Still, changing the set color from one of "prisons and battleships" to one that seemed more inviting was a theatrical stroke of genius. However, he always maintained that writing a farce was the hardest thing he'd ever done, but he added that they're so much fun. "You can have a character say, 'I'll just go in the other room,' and the audience is screaming because they know that what that character is going to find is the last thing they want or expect."

He likened writing—and staging—a farce to a 747 taking off from Kennedy Airport. "It's lumbering, lumbering down the runway, and you wonder if the pilot is ever going to take off, and you can see the Atlantic Ocean. That's what the first 20 minutes of the play always felt like to me."

Terrence learned something else about writing a farce. He had written the part of Gaetano for Jimmy Coco, and he was surprised—and a bit taken aback—when Coco turned it down.

> He said, "Thank you, but no." I said it's the lead, and he said it's the "workhorse" part. He [Gaetano] has 90 percent of the lines, and they have 90 percent of the laughs. I'm supporting Rita. And you know he was absolutely right. The show had many nominations and awards but not for Jack Weston in the workhorse part.

The Ritz opened on Broadway at the Longacre Theatre on January 20, 1975, and it ran for 498 performances, winning a Tony award for Moreno. The show was mostly well-reviewed, but reading the reviews with twenty-first-century sensibilities, there's still a lot of entrenched homophobia between the lines. Rex Reed in the *New York Daily News* described the setting as "a three-level tier of athlete's foot combined with hairdresser's heaven [code for gay]. But when the villains meet the violets and the underworld locks horns with the twilight world, all comic hell breaks loose." No critic could get away with that in 2022.

Clive Barnes, after praising the comedy, condescendingly wrote, "The straights (I assume we are still in the majority) will find this a hilarious tourist trip, and few people—not even the gay-libbers [*sic*] or the Mafia—will be offended." On balance, perhaps it's a long way for the critical establishment to come in the decade since *Bump*, but "the gays" were still on the margins, according to the mainstream critics . . . at least for a little while longer—the time it took for the world once again to catch up to Terrence.

There's yet one more story about *The Ritz* that Terrence loved to tell. During the time the play was on Broadway, Terrence was a big smoker, and he used to love to go the theater, wrap a towel around his hips, and smoke on the set with the other extras. He said he never came down from the third level, but friends would call him up the day after they'd seen the show and ask if he'd been in his own play the night before. He acknowledged that Equity, the actors' union, would never have allowed him to do that now but he said the cast was a lot of fun, and this is one way he got to hang out with them. It may also have been his reward for getting that plane off the runway. He said that *The Ritz* was about as much hard work as any other show he ever did, but it was worth it. The show closed the first week of January, 1976.

And the world changed.

Terrence would have a lot to say about AIDS, which first came into widespread cultural consciousness in 1981, but suddenly a play about a gay bathhouse would have been more scary than funny, particularly since in its early days, AIDS, initially identified as GRID (Gay-related Immune Deficiency) was thought to be exclusively among male homosexuals. Instead of flirting with an attractive stranger, the denizens of *The Ritz* would be seen as flirting with death. It was a no-go. There was a very short-lived, poorly reviewed revival at the Xenon discotheque in 1983, but it would be almost twenty years since the first revival closed that *The Ritz* would be revived on Broadway by Roundabout Theater Company. The script had to be updated somewhat to take out references to sexually transmitted diseases and essentially to downplay the realization that in the early days of the AIDS crisis, the baths were the home of unprotected, anonymous sex, and one of the chief spreaders of the virus among gay men.

Terrence wasn't very pleased with that production, which was directed by Joe Mantello. He felt that the farce fell flat, and, as he always did, wondered if the cause was the cast, the direction, or the play itself, but he didn't have a definitive answer, instead thinking, as so often happens in the theater, that it was a combination of things that just didn't click. More likely, however, in mounting the production, the producers saw only a rollicking farce and misread how the world had changed. The cultural awareness the audiences brought into the theater in 2007 was very different than it would have been in 1975. Ben Brantley, in his *New York Times* review of the revival, while praising some of the performances, sensed the manic nature a farce requires, and put the piece in historical context:

> Set in a gay bathhouse, *The Ritz* arrived on Broadway at a moment when gay culture seemed to embody the most advanced evolution of the sexual revolution. Heterosexual theatergoers who never made it to Plato's Retreat or wife-swapping parties could dip a vicarious toe into baths where you went to get dirty.

Well, yesterday's dirt, as is often the case, has become today's dust.

Even if the plane didn't quite get off the ground, Rosie Perez as Googie, however, got raves. The satirical view of the drive to become a star—and the naked ambition it requires—is a timeless trope that always scores. And the set was colorful.

Based on the original production, Terrence wrote the screenplay for the movie, which debuted in August of 1976 and was a modest success, with virtually all of the original Broadway cast appearing in it. The critics were lukewarm, though they had high praise for Rita Moreno. The problem, as film critic Roger Ebert said, was that the jokes were too gay.

The Ritz, however, had one more gift for Terrence. When he was in London for the filming, he would meet his next boyfriend, Dominic Cuskern, his relationship with Robert Drivas having fallen apart.

During this period, Terrence also worked on a musical, *Here's Where I Belong*, which began a lifelong love/hate relationship with writing musical books, and we'll get to that.

First, though, another event occurred that would shape Terrence's career as an artist. He had begun a relationship with the Manhattan Theatre Club, which had gotten him to Broadway a year before *The Ritz* with *Bad Habits*, and as the Angel declaims at the end of the first play of *Angels in America: Millennium Approaches*, "the great work begins."

5

Safe at Home

I.

IN FEBRUARY 1971, an article appeared in *Backstage*, announcing that New York City was going to get its first theater club. The article said:

> The aim of the Manhattan Theater [*sic*] Club is to provide a place where subscribers can have a moderately priced meal, see a play and mingle with professional theatre people in a relaxed, non-commercial environment.
>
> The Club is set up as a non-profit organization. Members of the producing board include William Gibson, Philip Barber, Eli Wallach, Harold Clurman and George Tabori.

The membership was $30 a year—"a husband and wife may join for $50 for the two." It had an altruistic bent as well, since $5 of each membership would go to provide tickets for school groups. The article continued saying that the enterprise had the support of Mayor Lindsay, who was a strong supporter of the arts.

Manhattan Theatre Club (MTC) had officially begun the previous September when it was incorporated as a nonprofit organization. MTC was the brainchild of PR executive A. E. Jeffcoat who had first experienced London's theater club scene when he was stationed there as a reporter for the *Wall Street Journal* in the 1950s. He was inspired by the London Arts Club, and it was designed around presenting serious theater, developing new playwrights, and presenting quality work. The emphasis of Jeffcoat, along with cofounder Margaret Kennedy, was on finding plays that might not get produced in New York—and in response to what they saw as the superficial and unsatisfying commercial work that was appearing on Broadway. In essence, a group of elite uptown non-theater professionals, who nonetheless loved the theater, were having exactly the same reaction that playwrights and small companies were having downtown at the end of the 1960s. Jeffcoat had recruited a lot of his friends to come in with him, including a fraternity brother from Williams, Stephen Sondheim.

As managing director since 1975, Barry Grove said, the theater clubs were formed to get around the censorship of the Lord Chamberlain in London who could shut down shows for covering sensitive topics, not just related to sex, or that the bureaucrats didn't like . . . for whatever reason. A lot of challenging work was being written in this period, and the censorship and government control of what was on stage was fairly common. The private theater club was a workaround that allowed producers to put whatever they wanted on the stage. Jeffcoat wasn't concerned about government censorship but being able to produce what he wanted outside of the challenges of critics determining the fate of shows. He had very specific ideas of what "quality theater" meant.

Jeffcoat and his board wanted to find a home and after a search landed at the National Bohemian Hall at 321 East 73rd Street. The building had been a theater, known as Stage 73, and it had also been a cultural center for Eastern Europeans in New York for several decades before, and MTC signed a ten-year lease. In addition to establishing some excellent playing spaces with theaters of three different sizes (65, 75, and 105 seats), the fledgling MTC was also able to rent out rehearsal space for Broadway shows to generate revenue. In the first year, MTC was supported by membership dues—and some board members and others reaching into their pockets. During the early days, a theater of 150 seats had to operate under a Broadway contract, and the fledgling MTC wasn't able to afford that. Many of their early productions were produced under the Equity Showcase Code, which allows union actors to work for little or no money (carfare always excepted), but put strict limits on audience size, rehearsals, and the number of performances.

It was not, however, successful. In fact, the organization was floundering, and the board knew that they would need a permanent artistic director, a vision, and very likely a complete overhaul if it was going to make it. It was not an easy task to find someone. It was a big job with uncertain budgets, a membership audience paying $200 a ticket in 1971, ensconced in a townhouse in need of serious maintenance, way outside the traditional Manhattan neighborhoods for theater. Who wouldn't leap at the chance? Enter Lynne Meadow.

Meadow arrived in New York fresh out of Yale Drama School, with an undergraduate degree from Bryn Mawr, with a passion for new work. She was twenty-five, a young woman who wanted to direct plays, and there weren't many opportunities for that at the time. She had directed a play at MTC in July of 1972, Anthony Scully's *All Through the House* and through that came to the attention of the board. However, Meadow remembers the board was highly skeptical about bringing on a woman as artistic director, and if a member of the board hadn't been willing to give her a chance, she never would have landed there. She was offered a three-month contract, and she leapt into the role for the 1972–1973 season.

Meadow adds that on her very first day, she wrote the mission statement for MTC. It's been updated many times over the years, but it largely has remained unchanged since that day, the current version reads, "MTC's mission is to produce theatrical works of the highest quality, most often by living playwrights. Equally important to us is the quality of artists who bring our shows to life." (MTC has since added language and programs supporting broad-based diversity.)

From day one, it was Meadow's taste, vision, diligence, and understanding of what made a good production for the group that helped propel MTC to its status as a leading theater company and a home for playwrights. Although she said there never was "an MTC play," she instinctively knew that diversity, new voices, and challenging the audiences would provide a foundation for growth. If anything, an intelligent eclecticism has guided the selection of work, ranging from daring and controversial plays to crowd-pleasing musicals. Throughout her career, while Meadow has collaborated with many people, what appears on MTC stages has always been her decision. It would be impossible to understate the impact Meadow had on American theater and playwriting in the last quarter of the twentieth century, in those she championed, the high stakes she embraced, and the chances she took. And after the first year, she never again had a contract.

Meadow says that shortly after she took the reins, she was visited by a group of downtown playwrights who were frustrated at not being able to get their plays produced and wanted her to help them. The group had organized under the name New York Theater Strategies, which in addition to Terrence included María Irene Fornés, Julie Bovasso, Sam Shepard, Lanford Wilson, and others. She distinctly remembers Terrence coming into her office in a button-down shirt with a Shetland sweater over his shoulders, a fashion statement at the time. Meadow had known Terrence previously as the writer of *Where Has Tommy Flowers Gone?* That had been produced at Yale when she was there, and she quickly got to know the other writers. She wanted to produce premieres, and here was her chance. At the time, she was an outsider, and she wanted to bring other outsiders into the fold.

As a result, her first project, which she agreed to out of what she remembered as "complete youth and enthusiasm," would be to fill the building with plays—twenty-three of them to be produced over six weeks.

The roster of playwrights who contributed to this effort includes many considered mainstream now and who had been part of the group eager to be seen: Wilson, Sam Shepard, Fornés and Terrence among them. Produced on a shoestring budget by a staff of four, including Meadow, over a seven-week period, "The festival filled every nook and cranny of MTC. It was a thrilling, if slightly insane idea, but we were also excited," Meadow said.

Terrence's contribution to the festival was a play called *Bad Habits*. It was produced on the mainstage in the building and could accommodate the largest audience of all the plays in the festival.

Bad Habits is a comic satire of the pop psychology movement that was gaining traction in the early 1970s. Books like the 1967 *I'm Ok, You're Ok* and the rise of Werner Erhard's EST trainings had begun to permeate the culture. Positing that everyone had problems and could get better with these methodologies—and of course investing their money in books and workshops—the self-help industry was exploding in the United States. Terrence, who at the time loved smoking and drinking, observed how otherwise normal people who also smoked and drank were suddenly becoming cultural pariahs, especially as the anti-smoking drumbeat grew ever louder during the 1960s and tobacco advertising on television was banned in 1971. The play asks, with tongue resolutely in cheek, whether we were actually better off with these so-called bad habits (among others, including promiscuity, homosexuality, and violence) than going through the arduous process of trying to get rid of them. Who are we without these so-called bad habits that give life meaning?

The play is divided into two acts. The first, *Ravenswood*, takes place in the eponymous sanatorium where couples come to work out their issues. They are encouraged to drink and smoke as much as they want while they engage in what is apparently some kind of transactional analysis with Dr. Pepper (yes that's the character's name). Bickering couples who may—or may not—have tried to kill one another, obsessive compulsives, and a gay couple (who don't publicly acknowledge their relationship though everyone sees it), are encouraged to indulge their bad habits—all in the quest for happiness. What that happiness is, however, is unknowable, so it's assumed the characters will keep banging on the way they have.

In the second act *Dunelawn*, nurses Benson and Hedges (yes, those are the characters' names) are perhaps in a lesbian relationship but perhaps not, and they are charged with treating the patients and injecting them with a serum that makes all their bad habits, urges, and lusts disappear—at least for a short time. Here Terrence is digging at the "magic bullet" notion that there is *one* answer to life's issues. Significantly, Dr. Toynbee who is the head of the institution is revered and admired as a great man and a quasi-savior to be revered, appears, but he speaks only in gibberish and indicates what the nurses are supposed to do. His power—and celebrity—is the direct result of the cult-like worship of him and those who arrive begging for a shot of the serum.

Bad Habits, according to Meadow, was the most successful of all the plays produced in that festival. The satire was unmistakable, and the sophisticated audiences who were likely fatigued with being browbeaten about *not* being okay and having many of their pleasures condemned as harmful, reveled in Terrence's take that all this "help" was probably bullshit and that people were never going to give up their bad habits.

Fun fact: *Bad Habits* was the first time an audience heard the name Googie Gomez, and one of Terrence's first digs at movie casting designed to appeal to a middle-of-the-road audience.

After the run at MTC, the play moved to the Astor Place Theatre where it opened in February of 1974, opening while *The Tubs* was still running in New Haven. Produced by Adela Holzer, it was directed by Robert Drivas and featured a cast that included F. Murray Abraham, Doris Robert, and Paul Benedict. Both the play and director Drivas won Obie Awards.

Mel Gussow, in his review in the *New York Times* on February 10, called Terrence a "social satirist" and a "writer of popular entertainment." The last comment was significant because Gussow admits in print that he would never have expected this level of incisive comedy from Terrence after having seen *Bump* nine years before, and he writes about Terrence's growth as an artist through other productions and Off-Off Broadway plays, saying, "He has steadily grown, refined his insights, and disciplined his comic talent." Gussow did acknowledge that with *Bump*, "Broadway was not ready for McNally and McNally wasn't ready for Broadway." Given—for better or worse—how often critics are the gatekeepers to broader awareness and cultural acceptance of artists, this was an important piece and a level of approbation that if it didn't silence the demons, at least it marginalized them.

The play subsequently moved to Broadway in May 1974, where it ran for 173 performances—Terrence's second Broadway outing where he fared much better than his first had just nine years earlier, and, more importantly, he was being hailed as a keen observer of culture with a unique talent for expressing it on stage.

MTC would revive *Bad Habits* in 1990 with Nathan Lane, Faith Prince, and Kate Nelligan in the cast and directed by Paul Benedict, who appeared in the original production. It was not as happily received. Frank Rich, in his review on March 21 of that year, called the play dated, saying, "However titillating this point of view was in 1974, it has long since lost its power to startle." The world had, indeed, moved on, and sixteen years after the satire had people rolling in the aisles, so to speak, the world had fully acknowledged the dangers of smoking, excessive drinking, and cholesterol. The voices decrying bad habits had moved from the fringes to the mainstream, so the power of using them as satirical subjects was blunted. All the same, with a strong subscriber base, MTC was able to risk a revival of what had been one of their earliest hits—and critics aside, the revival was well-received by the audiences.

II.

This is probably as good a place as any to pause for a moment and talk about Terrence as a writer of his times. His genius was in his ability to observe moments in culture as they were happening and create compelling or moving plays. He was always writing for his time, not for the ages. His gimlet-eyed view of the world around him often reflected what his audiences were experiencing outside the theater. To be a playwright—or at least support oneself being a playwright—one has to understand the points of view and outside experiences an audience brings into the theater. If they see themselves—or a heightened version of themselves—on the stage, they are going to be intellectually and emotionally engaged. Terrence consistently did that. If a play like *Bad Habits* doesn't age well, for example, it's not because it's not a good play; it's because the world has shifted and what at one time would have been biting and trenchant doesn't have the same effect on an audience encountering it years later.

This is precisely why revivals of *The Ritz*, *Bad Habits*, and later *Lips Together, Teeth Apart* were not well-received. At the same time, revivals

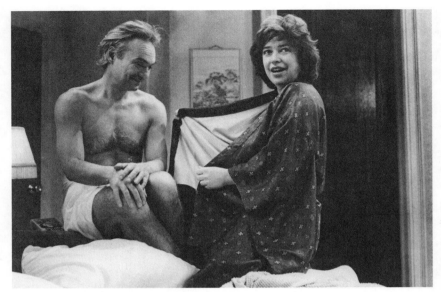

Kenneth Walsh and Kathy Bates in MTC's production of Frankie and Johnny in the Claire de Lune. *Bates was remembered as "fearless" in the role, and she said Terrence's seeing her as a sexual person was life-changing.*
PHOTOFEST

of *Frankie and Johnny in the Clair de Lune* can succeed, or a revamped *Broadway, Broadway* can become a hit as *It's Only a Play.* Playwrights don't set out to write plays "for the ages." They seek to entertain audiences in the here and now. If a play becomes "a classic," it's because its themes, characters, and situations reflect something essentially human and largely immutable over generations, whether it's the compelling exploration of what creates intimacy (as in *Frankie and Johnny*) or our appetite for dishy backstage tales (*It's Only a Play*).

Shakespeare survives because his plays speak to elemental human experiences that are unchanged—love, jealousy, power, revenge—over the centuries. (Though it's rare to see an uncut Shakespeare play, and canny directors excise such things as lengthy discussions of the Salique law governing royal succession in *Henry V* or other Elizabethan references a modern audience wouldn't get, to say nothing of shortening the plays to a palatable length for a modern audience.) On the other hand, plays that have languished in obscurity for hundreds of years such as

Michelle Pfeiffer and Al Pacino in the film of Frankie and Johnny *(1991). Terrence wrote the screenplay and expanded the story. He wasn't sure the piece worked as well when it wasn't a two-hander.*
PARAMOUNT PICTURES / PHOTOFEST ©PARAMOUNT PICTURES

Gammer Gurton's Needle, a "rollicking" comedy about an old woman who has lost the titular needle and which Terrence references in *And Away We Go!,* are so arcane as to have little or nothing to say to an audience today. They will probably never be seen outside an academic setting, where contemporary students will get something "good for them" while being bored to death. Terrence's life was lived in the present, and that's where his theater lived. Time will do what it does, but part of the magic of the theater is that it creates images and feelings that can last a lifetime. Frankie and Johnny brushing their teeth together at the end of the play, given all that has gone before, is arguably one of the most intimate moments a playwright has put on a stage, particularly in light of the graphic sex and conflict that has gone before. It is purely human, existing outside of cultural context, and every member of the audience will respond to that moment in relationship to their experiences, attitudes, and time of life in ways that are unique to them. That's what makes a so-called timeless classic.

Bad Habits was a success for MTC, but it would be a dozen years till Terrence worked with the company again.

III.

When Meadow arrived at MTC, there were nowhere near the number of Off-Broadway theaters and theater companies that there are fifty years later. Meadow describes the early years, saying, "Joe Papp was a model for us, and Joe had writers to whom he was very attached, and I think in response Andre Bishop who started production of Wendy Wasserstein's work."

In the mid-1970s, Meadow said that she would look at all the plays she read and see that the credits always included theaters and theater companies. She embraced wholeheartedly the idea that it was important for theaters like hers to have ongoing relationships with writers. Over the next years, in addition to attracting grants and subscribers, Meadow would develop producing relationships with such playwrights as Richard Wesley, John Guare, Athol Fugard, Brian Friel, Harold Pinter, Beth Henley, A. R. Gurney, among others, including English and American writers, all prior to establishing the relationship with Terrence.

Daring plays like David Rudkin's *Ashes*, a challenging examination of one couple's inability to conceive a child, would be MTC's first transfer to The Public Theater. In fact, it was done as a coproduction with The Public because the only way Meadow could get the rights for MTC was if she told Rodkin's agent it was a coproduction, which Papp was happy to do if it meant the play could get on. Henley's *Crimes of the Heart* would move to Broadway. MTC would launch *Ain't Misbehavin'* in the sixty-five-seat cabaret space before a Broadway transfer and a Tony for Best Musical . . . not to mention a great source of revenue for the not-for-profit company. Always depending on contracts, MTC can potentially have an interest in a production as it moves, develops, and grows, which any not-for-profit producer will readily acknowledge can be a little, a lot . . . or nothing.

Nathan Lane and Anthony Heald in The Lisbon Traviata. *Lane was initially considered too young for the part, and he was nervous about playing an openly gay character . . . but found he was good at it.*
PHOTOFEST

The company continued to grow in stature and importance to the theater communities, and in 1975, Barry Grove joined as managing director. Grove originally setting out to be a "math, pre-engineering, pre-med guy," as he said, he got cast in the freshman play, and his life changed course. In his sophomore year at Dartmouth, he found himself at the O'Neill Playwrights' conference, and then during his winter break got a call asking him if he wanted to come to New York to assistant direct *And Miss Reardon Drinks a Little*, the follow-up to Paul Zindel's previous play, *The Effect of Gamma Rays on Man in the Moon Marigolds*, which had won the Pulitzer and four Obies in 1970. Grove went on to stage-manage, be advance director for the tour of *And Miss Reardon*, work with Tina Packer on the launch of Shakespeare and Company in the Berkshires, finish Dartmouth, and teach in Rhode Island. Meadow found and hired him, saying she could offer a salary $150 a week; budgets were still tight, as they always are in the theater, but he took the job, managing a company with a $200,000 annual budget. Grove tells this story because he learned the theater business "by the seat of my pants," and having been surrounded by people doing new work, he was ready to take on the challenges of growing MTC.

In 1980, the lease on East 73rd Street was up, and MTC scrambled to purchase the building as a permanent home. They were also looking to purchase the East Side Playhouse on 74th Street, with that organization's backing. They were able to secure a $1.6 million grant from New York City to purchase the building, and it seemed like it was going ahead. At the last minute, however, the Bohemian Benevolent Society, the original owners, sued to block the sale on the grounds that it was a landmark, and they wanted it preserved. What followed was three years of legal wrangling, ultimately going against MTC, and in 1983, they had six months to a year to vacate.

Grove said that he immediately—and somewhat desperately—started looking for new spaces. Accompanied by the designer John Lee Beatty, he and Meadow began a search of many different potential theater spaces. Finally, they went to see Jerry Schoenfeld at the Shubert organization who asked him whether he had considered the basement of City Center.

It was, in a word, a wreck.

The building on 56th Street between 6th and 7th Avenues had been constructed in 1923 as a Masonic Temple, and was slated for demolition in the 1940s, but thanks to the intervention of Mayor La Guardia, it was preserved as a performing arts center. However, preservation had bypassed the basement. Grove says that it had rotting wooden floors over dirt, but MTC was able to secure the lease. Peter Solomon who was deputy mayor of New York, and later MTC chairman, was able to transfer the money from the other grant to City Center, and because there were other renovations going on at the time, they were able to marry all that money together and create the two performance spaces—Stage One a 299-seat theater that qualifies for an Off-Broadway contract and

Stage Two with approximately 160-seats that can be configured based on the needs of a production.

The theater opened in the fall of 1984. By this time MTC was established as a leading producer of new American playwrights and established European playwrights. Just over a year later at the end of December, Terrence's new version of *It's Only a Play* would open there. It was more than just "another openin' of another show," however. MTC—and particularly Meadow's championing Terrence's work—would be the event that would propel his career into his most productive period, supporting him as he matured as a writer, social critic, and activist and giving him the one thing he needed to thrive: an artistic home.

IV.

The period between *Bad Habits* and *It's Only a Play* wasn't easy for Terrence, personally or artistically. *Bad Habits* closed at the Booth Theater in October 1974. *The Ritz* opened the following January and would run until the first week of January 1976. During that time, Terrence went to London for the shooting of the movie of *The Ritz*.

Beyond that, however, there wasn't a lot of writing going on. Terrence had hit a block. It was not one he truly understood, though he said that he was drinking a lot during that period. His relationship with Robert Drivas was falling—or had fallen—apart. Though he loved Bobby, he was constantly aware that he was hidden, their relationship was widely known but never publicly acknowledged. Once again, Terrence was being asked to hide a significant part of himself, and it proved too much for the relationship to bear.

During the filming of *The Ritz* in 1975, as noted earlier, he had met Dominic Cuskern. It was not quite the "meet cute" of comedy, rather Dominic's favor for a friend. As Dominic explains:

> I had a friend Colin Hopkins who was one of the agents at William Morris. And Colin was chaperoning him around, going places. I guess after a week or ten days he says, "You know, I'm really bored.

I've got to take this guy around. And he likes opera and he likes theater, and, frankly, would you mind going out with him? Just like once? He just needs some company." I said sure, and was helping Colin out, so I said, "give him my number, tell him to call me, and we'll go to the opera."

Their first meeting was when Terrence came to Dominic's apartment at the end of a dinner party Dominic was giving, and they became intimate very quickly.

I had no intent of getting involved. I thought, he's leaving in six weeks, and that's it . . . right? As it happened, he was leaving after a month because of something that was going on in the States. And I realized that I loved him. He had an apartment [in London], and we spent a lot of time there, mostly at night. And when he told me he was leaving two weeks earlier than planned, I wasn't prepared for it, and I just burst into tears. I think he was surprised by this.

Anyway, he left me a book on his final day there, and the inscription said, "From your American friend who loves you." He didn't say "I love you," and I didn't say I loved him.

And then I called his number in New York while he was in flight and said your English friend who loves you. Hope you arrived safely. And that was the beginning of our relationship, and it was two years of flying back and forth, and then eventually it had to be, "I can't go on like this. What's going to happen?" Terrence said, "I can't live in England. I don't know the culture; it's not familiar to me. I'm a writer. I don't know what I would write about." And I said, "Maybe I could move to New York," and that's what we did. I flew over on August 23, 1977, landed and went to the apartment where I'm living now [2019].

Dominic had never been involved in theater prior to moving to New York. His first degree was in economics. He'd been a parliamentary assistant covering the automotive industry, been part owner of a deli.

When he came to the States, he volunteered for the Koch campaign because without a Green Card he couldn't work. (And while he didn't know much about Koch, he knew he was liberal and probably gay.) He ultimately decided that he wanted to go into social work and got his master's at Columbia. He'd be a social worker in New York until he answered the siren call of the stage, but that would be a few years later.

During these early years of the relationship, Terrence simply wasn't writing. Dominic would go out to do things and come home to find Terrence would be having a drink and not doing much of anything. He began to realize that as the days, weeks, and months passed, Terrence had stopped producing anything.

Dominic, not being a writer, didn't understand. One night after seeing an Albert Innaurato play *Ulysses in Traction* at Circle Repertory with William Hurt and Trish Hawkins, he was so moved by the piece that he ran home, collapsed on the sofa and cried. Terrence thought Dominic had been attacked or mugged on the three-block run home from the theater, but no. Dominic had simply been so moved by the experience of being in the theater that when he recovered, he said, "What you do is so important. You don't know how important it is, and you're not writing." Perhaps the stress on the relationship of Terrence's *not* writing had finally come home to Dominic. As he also said, "When he writes, it's nonstop. Nothing else exists. I would say, 'Do you want something to eat?' And and he would say 'yeah, yeah,' but he's not even noticing his food. I know he's thinking in terms of his characters when he's talking to you. He's so absorbed by it." Essentially, a whole part of the man with whom Dominic had fallen in love was missing.

A short time later, while Terrence was out in his house in Bridgehampton, Dominic was staying behind in the city to work for Ed Koch. He saw that a small theater was doing a revival of *Where Has Tommy Flowers Gone?*

I went to see it in this fourth-floor loft on 16th Street somewhere. Mercedes Ruhl was in it. She wasn't Mercedes Ruhl the way we know her now. She was just a young actress. I loved that play. It was a raw, bare production, but you heard the words. I called Terrence and said, "You have to come in and see this play. It's a simple, simple production, but you have to come in and see it. It's only got four more days to go."

"I'll come in and see it." So I got us two seats, and he came in, and when we got up to the fourth floor, there was this little hand-written sign that said, "Tickets for *Tommy Flowers* are sold out." And we saw the play and he loved it.

We went back to see the actors, and they had no idea Terrence was coming, that he was going to be there. And I remember that Terrence took that piece of paper down, and he framed it because those things were very important to him. Seeing an audience in that situation and responding to his play in that situation meant a lot to him.

Whether it was this experience that turned the tide or not, and neither Dominic nor any other close associates ever knew what caused the block, Terrence began to write again.

Perhaps encouraged by the positive response to the farcical nature of *The Ritz*, Terrence thought he'd try another comedy, and the only major theater project he embarked on in the next couple of years was *Broadway, Broadway*, a play that takes place in the bedroom of a townhouse of a first-time producer on the opening night of a new Broadway show, called *The Golden Egg*. Though not completely a farce, the play has a lot of stock characters—the first-time female producer, the drug-taking star, the TV star who turned down the role and is secretly happy when the reviews are ghastly, and various assorted other stock characters that circle around the fringes of the theater, including a person checking coats who aspires to a Broadway career. The plot of the play is minimal, and much of the fun came from the references to who was coming in to the party downstairs while all kinds of craziness was going on in the bedroom, supposedly a hideaway. There's a constant coming and going, all powered by Terrence's hilarious, fast-paced banter.

As he would so often in his career, Terrence turned to one of his actor muses. He wrote Jimmy Wicker, the part of the TV star reveling in his *schadenfreude*, for Jimmy Coco. He was also in his comfort zone, writing about the thing he loved most in the world—the theater—tossing off quick quips, incisive humor, taking on the critics, and even in the early versions, taking a shot at the vituperative, viperish Jean Kerr. There were a lot of demons to put to rest—and laser-like comedy was the weapon of choice.

The play found its way to Edgar Bronfman Jr. who had begun his career as a movie producer when he was seventeen, producing a movie called *Blockhouse*:

> It was a terrible movie with Peter Sellers and Charles Aznavour. I think it may have been the only "non-com" Peter Sellers ever did. It was pretty awful, but I decided to stay in the industry, and I did a TV show, and I was looking for plays to produce, and I produced a play that Paul Zindel had written called *Ladies at the Alamo*, which didn't do very well, and then someone sent me Terrence's script for *Broadway, Broadway*, and I loved it, and I thought: "Okay, I'm going to produce this one."

One of the reasons that Bronfman may have been so attracted to *Broadway, Broadway* was that the Zindel piece was also about the theater—in this case the backbiting backstage at a regional theater. He also said that he was twenty-two turning twenty-three, so he was really a kid, "I had no business doing what I was doing." However, he loved the play when he read it. He met Terrence, and they were off.

Bronfman recalls the rehearsal process:

> What struck me about Terrence was the degree to which he didn't come alive, and his script didn't really come alive until actors started to speak the words. I would have said the exact opposite of Paul Zindel who basically said "This is the line I wrote. This is what you

have to say," and he really wasn't very interested in what the actors thought of the lines or anything like that.

And Terrence was exactly the opposite. Sometimes, obviously, he would say, "No, that's not the way I want it." But mostly he was really interested in how he could help the actor better portray what it is the actor was trying to achieve.

There was a lot of work out of town, as Terrence was writing and rewriting. Some of it was because pieces of the play didn't work, but some if it was because the actor playing the role had a different take on it, and Terrence wanted to accommodate that.

Rehearsals continued, publicity was ramped up, and a piece in the *New York Times* on May 5, 1978, announced that the play—then called *Bye, Bye Broadway*—would be heading for Broadway in the fall. The piece listed a variety of places where the show would try out on its path.

On July 31, the play had its premiere in Guild Hall in East Hampton. Terrence was celebrated as a local, and anticipation was high that, as one gushing columnist wrote, this would be "AN EVENT" that would make the elite enclave a steppingstone for future productions.

It didn't go as planned.

The reviewer for the *East Hampton Star* wasn't having it:

> *Broadway, Broadway* as the title unambiguously proclaims is a play about the theater. Or rather—The Theater. As such it is just the latest in a long line of generally and deservedly unsuccessful exercises in the kind of literary incest which has given incest, and the theater, such a bad name. Usually of course such plays are basically narcissistic—actors, authors, the whole Thespian gang, being shown as lovable romantics emotionally sound and alone in a world of unlovably heartless cynics—but there is a variation on this one, which McNally has gone for with fearless passion. All of his characters, all connected with the theater, are either stupid, vain, nasty, thieving, vicious, jealous, greedy, et cetera, or more than one of all of these at once.

The play was lambasted for its "in-jokes" about the theater and calling it "an unloving travesty of the theatrical life." Nor did the actors get off easily:

> James Coco, as the unemployed actor does that old beseeching, bitchy homosexual routine. . . . From Miss Page, as from most of the cast, Robert Drivas, the director, has succeeded in getting performances the like of which I have not seen since Paris in the late '40s and had hoped never to see again. It is the kind of acting variously called camped-up, souped-up, doubled-up, or plain excruciating and clearly Geraldine Page for one is not really at home doing it.

The dig at Coco must have been especially painful—not that there was a single laurel hung on the production—because as Bronfman remembers Coco and Drivas who were both gay were closeted and terribly afraid of being exposed. That surprised Bronfman who acknowledged that Terrence was always very open about his sexuality and that Dominic was around throughout the whole process. Yet it was different for actors back then. A straight man could play gay, but an open or obvious gay man couldn't get arrested in the theater, in other words: would never be hired. As noted earlier with *The Ritz*, only an actor known to be straight and playing gay could carry off the excesses of the character without damaging his career.

Despite the scorched-earth reception, the next stop was Falmouth, Massachusetts, and then on to Philadelphia where the play opened at the Forrest Theater for a two-week tryout on September 4 with every intention of moving to Broadway immediately afterward.

It was not to be.

If the review in East Hampton was harsh, the uniformly negative reviews from the Philadelphia critics were savage . . . and then some. Called "a turkey" by the *Daily News*, a "failure" by the *Bulletin* and "a disaster" by the *Inquirer*, the only positive note was a mixed review by a second critic from the *Inquirer*. The critics took the play to task for the tiresome entertainment world focus, Emma the maid who was a Black transvestite, and the generally tiresome nature of the whole undertaking. There were some positives for Terrence, noting his ability with a comic line and his previous success with *The Ritz* and *Bad Habits* and for Drivas with his ability to direct the farcical nature of the play.

But it was bad.

Bad notices might go unnoticed from a small, family paper all the way out on Long Island (not entirely likely given the number of theater people who summered there and who could not have missed the hype around the premiere), and Falmouth might be another planet as far as New York City showbiz is concerned, but Philadelphia was a major tryout town. Still out of the glare of the New York critics, every producer looked to hedge their bets based on the responses of critics in the major out-of-town venues—Washington, D.C.; Wilmington, Delaware; Philadelphia; New Haven; and New York may be the *sine qua non* of theater, but for producers, these tryout towns were the coal mine canaries, and how they sang—or not—determined fate. *Broadway, Broadway* also had no way to counteract the bad reviews. It opened while there was a newspaper strike in Philadelphia, so there was no way to get the word out that this might be a fun evening of theater, despite the harsh reception.

Cuskern said that in leading up to the production, what made him happiest was that Terrence was writing again and writing about a topic he loved. Then, the play closed in Philadelphia . . . slammed shut, actually. As Cuskern recalls: "Edgar Bronfman, Jr., whose father was obviously the man sponsoring the money for the production came down and saw it and told his son to close it. He was not going to produce it, and it's not going to Broadway."

And that, it seemed, was that. Terrence was, naturally, devastated that his first attempt to get back on the theatrical horse was so roundly criticized and ultimately a failure. He took it hard, and said that the failure caused him to reconsider his career. He even, for the first time, went into psychoanalysis, though he didn't necessarily think it was all that productive and didn't like talking about it. Years later, it was still hard for him to understand why the play had failed so badly. He suggested that perhaps the set design had been the case—doors that slid open rather than opening, which killed the comedy of the party in the other room. When they were in Philadelphia, he was adamant that the set would have to be redesigned. But the problem was bigger than that. So, he put the play in a drawer and thought that was the end of it. What he didn't know was that this bomb was going to turn into his life preserver.

V.

The period after the implosion of *Broadway, Broadway* was particularly rough for Terrence creatively. It was during this period that he had the difficult time in Los Angeles, trying to write television, creating *Mama Malone,* and very much at loose ends as a playwright. He seemed to have lost his direction, or at least his drive, and he was continuing to drink.

It was during this period that Terrence got sober. It's a story that's been told many times, including by Terrence himself in the documentary *Every Act of Life.* It's significant, however, because sobriety changed the course of his life, as it has for many people who find relief from alcoholism.

Terrence's "sobriety date," as the first day without a drink is called in AA, as mentioned earlier, was April 25, 1982. What precipitated it was an event at a birthday party for Stephen Sondheim. Terrence attended and was quite drunk. He spilled a drink on Lauren Bacall who got incensed and told him that she was going to send him the dry cleaning bill for her dress.

He was still reeling from that encounter when he was approached by Angela Lansbury. He of course knew who she was, but they had never met. She was no stranger to the ravages wreaked by drugs and alcohol, however. Her daughter Deirdre and son Anthony had taken up with a bad crowd in Malibu in the 1960s and had gotten heavily into drugs and alcohol. Deirdre had even become associated with some of the kids who hung out with Charles Manson. Angela took a year off from all work, moved her family, including husband Peter, to County Cork in

James Coco and Geraldine Page in Broadway, Broadway *in 1978 in Philadelphia. It bombed. Eight years later, a rewritten version was a hit for MTC, and thirty-six years later it would be a smash on Broadway.*
PHOTOFEST

Ireland and spent the time helping her kids overcome their addictions, away from the temptations of Southern California.

Angela told Terrence that he didn't have to drink, that he was hurting himself and wasting his talent. He heard her, and while it didn't take immediately, within a few months, he was beginning to dry out. He attended AA meetings in Los Angeles and began the long process of becoming sober.

Who knows why someone is suddenly able to find sobriety after years of drinking and damage? Terrence didn't know specifically, but he remembered that it was Angela's kindness and gentleness more than anything that finally reached him and it would make them lifelong friends. Terrence's previous experience with alcoholism other than his own had been with his father who was belligerent and his mother who ignored him, and certainly it was central to his relationship with Edward Albee.

"What can you say about a relationship when both of you are drunk and fighting much of the time?" he reflected in 2019. Even the incident with Lauren Bacall had more in common with his past experiences. Like many alcoholics, Terrence hadn't really seen a way out until a higher power in the form of Angela Lansbury showed it to him.

Back living full-time in New York, newly sober, Terrence was still at a loss artistically, but that was about to change. In November 1982, *Broadway, Broadway*, rewritten somewhat and now titled *It's Only a Play*, opened at the Manhattan Punchline. Dominic couldn't recall how the company, which specialized in doing comedies, had gotten the script, but they asked if they could do it as an Equity Showcase production, and Terrence said yes.

The play was updated to include more current show business references, but possibly the most significant change was the title. "It's only a play" became a dismissive line in the script as characters tried to minimize how upset they were at the failure of the show they were working on. It also signaled to the audience that this was a comedy; the implication is that it's not having to do with something all that important, which gives the audience the permission and the freedom to laugh, revel in the over-the-top nature of theater people, and have a good time at the expense of this collection of people who are denizens of the theater. (As Tom Stoppard wrote in *Rosencrantz and Guildenstern Are Dead*, "We're actors. We're the opposite of people.") Though it was a bit more complex, it was like painting the set of *The Ritz* the color of Sardi's.

Small as it was, the production caught the eye of the usually acerbic *New York Magazine* critic John Simon. In his review in the December 6 issue, he praises many of the things that the critics in East Hampton and Philadelphia had castigated four years before: the in-jokes, the show-biz caricatures, digs at everything from Joseph Papp to the cast of *Annie*. Terrence had even added a reference to a playwright who sells out and goes to Hollywood. Perhaps it was sobriety, perhaps four years of perspective, but the updated script was more laughing at oneself and the theater than settling scores. It was a better, funnier, and more mature play overall.

Terrence was back, at least to himself, as a writer. In the next two years he would work on his second musical, *The Rink*, in 1984 and 1985, which will figure later in the story, and he would write a radio play for NPR called *The Lisbon Traviata*, which will also figure later on. (It never did air on NPR. According to Cuskern, the gay subject matter was too sensitive for the presumably liberal NPR.)

At the time, Meadow was looking for a play to produce, and the director John Tillinger gave her *It's Only a Play* to consider, with Tillinger at the helm. And now we circle back to Terrence's relationship with MTC. Meadow signed on to produce the play in the still-new Stage One at City Center where it began performances in December of 1985 as one of the theater's inaugural productions.

Once again Terrence updated the script for more current references, and the cast included James Coco, Christine Baranski, Joanna Gleason, Paul Benedict, Mark Blum, and Jihmi Kennedy as Gus. The character of Gus replaced the transvestite Emma in the previous version, a stage-struck wannabe actor, in awe of his surroundings as he shuttles coats and announces what celebrities are arriving.

This was the production that teamed up Terrence and Baranski for the first time—a relationship that would be personally and artistically important to both of them. As always, Meadow had a series of readings prior to putting the play into rehearsal. Stockard Channing was originally slated to play the first-time producer Julia Budder, but a scheduling conflict forced her to withdraw. Meadow told him there was "an actress he should meet," who was Baranski. Meadow said Terrence knew pretty much instantly that Baranski "got him," and that was that. Channing, as it turns out, would play the aging star Virginia Noyes in the 2014 Broadway production.

It took more than eight years for *It's Only a Play* to find itself, playing a major part in rescuing Terrence's career, and it was about to take off in a whole new direction.

In one of those stories about Terrence that has passed into legend because it has been told so often, and largely consistently in each telling, Meadow recalls what would be a defining moment for both of them.

By the way, these are the stories that we come back to again and again because they speak to the hope, heart, and hardship that come with a life in the theater; they can never be told too often.

> I treasure to this day the memory of Christine Baranski standing in John Lee Beatty's set of a luxurious bedroom playing the role of a first-time producer at her opening night party saying to Jimmy Coco, "I did it. I did it. I'm a real, live Broadway producer."

The cast of the film Love! Valour! Compassion! *Terrence insisted that Joe Mantello direct and the original cast appear. The only exception was Jason Alexander who played Buzz when Nathan Lane wasn't available.*
FINE LINE FEATURES / PHOTOFEST ©FINE LINE FEATURES

Tom and Terrence at the Broadway opening of Frankie and Johnny in the Clair de Lune.

Terrence had been working on the play for a long time and was understandably very nervous about the reviews. So, on a cold night in December, when the press was going to be attending, I stood backstage with him, and I sensed his anxiety.

And somehow, I spontaneously blurted, "I love this play, Terrence, and I don't care how the press responds—win, lose or draw I will produce your next play if you will write it." Terrence often said it was the best Christmas present he ever got.

The critical response was pretty much a draw. The reviews were mixed, though Terrence was praised for his ability to craft a joke. Frank Rich in the *New York Times* wrote, "Only a writer who loves the theater and has survived its bloodiest wars could write a comedy like this one." For the most part, though Baranski and Coco also got good notices, the critics took issue with the fact that the play didn't have much of a plot. One wonders if they had seen any of Terrence's previous works.

Ironically, John Simon, writing again for *New York Magazine*, criticized many of the things he had praised four years before, particularly the in-jokes. Still, it was not the extremely acerbic type of review Simon would become known for as he built his celebrity during the eighties on how acidic he could be. Perhaps he realized that he was on the pointed end of the satire aimed at critics.

Nonetheless, *It's Only a Play* was a hit for MTC and their subscription audience. And why wouldn't it be? It's a wacky love letter to the theater, and those who went to see it would likely pride themselves on their ability to get most of the references. It was a cavalcade of in-jokes for people who fancied themselves as the in-crowd, at least with respect to things theatrical.

More importantly, Meadow's promise meant that reviews would, if not completely eradicate, blunt the emotionally, artistically, and financially damaging power of reviews—the very things that could derail a playwright's career. Terrence could write what he wanted with the assurance that it would get produced.

He had finally found a loving and nurturing home.

6

A Growing Intimacy

I.

MEADOW WAS AS good as her word, and for the next fifteen years, virtually every season would have a new play from Terrence. She said that every year when she sat down with her notebook to map out the season, she would always slot in "New Terrence McNally play," even not knowing what it would be or what Terrence was thinking about.

Terrence was part of Meadow's "master plan," which was as personal as it was artistic. As she said of MTC:

> My vision for creating a theater was to create a home for writers, a home for artists. That's what I was trying for. I grew up in New Haven; I didn't grow up in New York. I wanted somewhere to hang my hat, and I was a woman director, and I couldn't get hired. So, in order for me to direct, I had to hire myself.
>
> I think great things happen in the theater when people who have the same hunger and passion and desire get together. And I longed to be in a home and to have an ongoing home.

The notion of creating a home for artists had been what drove Meadow for years. Even back to her original festival on 73rd Street, she was fostering relationships with writers. What she recalled was that the writers wanted more say in how their works were produced. While they could have that in places like Caffe Cino and at LaMama, Off-Off

Broadway for all its cachet was outside the mainstream. Although she had been only twenty-five when she started at MTC, Meadow was in a unique position as a female and running an organization that was committed to new voices and "quality" to make that happen. As a listener, collaborator, and producer, between *Bad Habits* and *It's Only a Play*, Meadow was accomplishing her mission of being (in twenty-first-century jargon) a "safe space" for writers and artists. While no theater anywhere is ever completely free of economic concerns, MTC was building a track record of success. Time and again, the market was validating Meadow's taste and ability to identify and support talent.

So, although she says she "blurted out" her offer to Terrence backstage at *It's Only a Play*, that blurt was based on a decade at the helm of MTC—and her own inherent talents.

As she recalled, several weeks after her promise, Terrence came to visit her with an idea for the next play. It was, as she recalled, going to be a nineteenth-century epic set on the coast of Maine and inspired by a Shakespeare play. (Most likely it would have been *The Tempest* that inspired the idea, but Meadow never said if Terrence had indicated which it was, and Terrence didn't recall either. He had so many ideas—notebooks and notepads full of them from a few words to a paragraph or two in his archives.) Whatever it was, Meadow gulped and said okay. However, she wondered how on earth they were going to be able to afford the sets, costumes, and company that the idea would have required. Bracing for a budgetary tempest, but committed to her promise, she waited to what would come her way.

What arrived was something completely different: *Frankie and Johnny in the Clair de Lune*, a play for two actors on a single set with both onstage the entire time. No crashing waves, no period clothes. Meadow heaved a sigh of relief:

> I didn't have any money, so I had envisioned a play with a ton of actors, a period set, period costumes, and I had no idea how we were going to do it. When he handed me a two-hander set in Hell's Kitchen, I thought I had died and gone to heaven.

"I had said 'whatever it is, I'll do your next play,'" she added but was grateful that fulfilling that promise was going to be a lot more cost-effective. And, as it turns out, a lot better for MTC and Terrence.

Frankie and Johnny represented a turning point in Terrence's career. Meadow remembered it as one of the "great leaps" he took as an artist. He had written many two-character plays in the past but stripped of the absurdist elements and propelled by an apparent new willingness to allow his characters to be emotionally naked and actively struggle with issues around intimacy, the play was unlike anything he had written before. Especially coming after the comedies *The Ritz* and *It's Only a Play*, such a comparatively quiet piece was not what was expected. It was possible for him to write it because of his home at MTC. He didn't have to write what the market may have expected from him; he could write what was in his heart.

II.

Another one of Terrence's favorite stories was how he came up with the idea for *Frankie and Johnny*. Whether apocryphal or polished up for popular consumption, Terrence never missed an opportunity to tell it in interviews. As discussed earlier, many of Terrence's stories were often polished for public consumption, but the truth may lie in what was going on in his life as he wrote the play.

As the story goes, Terrence was standing in line at a Blockbuster Video on a Friday night, getting ready to rent some movies for the weekend. As he looked around, he saw a throng of other people doing exactly the same thing. It suddenly struck him that there were so many people in the greatest place on earth—Manhattan—who were renting their videos and going home to be alone in their apartments. It got him thinking about intimacy, relationships, and trust.

These were top-of-mind for Terrence at the time because he was newly single. About eight years into his relationship with Dominic, Dominic met someone else:

I met my current partner whose name is Jorge Castillo, and I was just crazy out of control. I was besotted with this very beautiful Columbian man who could barely speak English, who lived in the Bronx.

I've loved people. I loved Terrence. I love him now, but it was a totally out of control thing that I kept trying to put under wraps. . . .

I told him [Terrence] again and again that I would stop, and then it just didn't happen. Eventually it became that I couldn't give him up, so we had to separate.

Terrence was, of course, devastated. He and Cuskern managed to remain friends, however. For several years he was Terrence's assistant because as Cuskern said, "I realized he needs someone to take care of him. I did not love him, having met Jorge. I knew we [Terrence and he] couldn't continue that relationship, but he needed someone to be there with him." Later, when Cuskern moved into acting, Terrence was quick to support him—and give him work. Just as Terrence had with Bobby Drivas, the relationship changed and kept going, but keeping a friend isn't the same as losing a lover, and having a friend didn't fill the emotional void that Cuskern's leaving him had created. Terrence realized that as he was approaching fifty, options were fewer than they had been. He added, "It was not a romantic time to be living in New York."

That, it certainly was not. The AIDS crisis was dominating gay life in New York. First identified in 1981, the "gay plague" had been growing steadily with cases in 1985 growing by 89 percent over 1984, according to the Centers for Disease Control. Culturally and politically, the gay community changed almost overnight from a kind of party atmosphere to one of seriousness and fear. This is a gross simplification, of course, but with the advent of AIDS, the rollicking, freewheeling seventies of *The Ritz* came to a screeching halt. Friends who had been dancing till dawn just months before were saying tearful goodbyes on the AIDS floor of St. Vincent's in the Village. The Reagan administration's non-response to the crisis and marginalizing the disease as gay-specific infuriated the gay community. The battles of Stonewall and the decade-long march to visibility seemed at risk of disappearing overnight. Anyone who was gay was assumed to have AIDS, or as it was known originally, GRID (for "gay-related immune deficiency"). Families were torn apart as lovers were kicked out of apartments by families when a son had died. A climate of fear hung over the city when casual sex could result in a death sentence. During the early years of AIDS, the creative community in New York was decimated. Phones rang like the tolling of bells announcing yet another death. Funerals of once-vibrant young men were the new gatherings. Someone who had been perfectly fine a week ago was suddenly at death's door, and men in the prime of life were being told to "get their affairs in order." Entrenched homophobia in mainstream journalism kept AIDS off the front pages, when it was mentioned at all, and obituaries needed to be parsed to see if the cause of death was from AIDS-related causes because it was assumed to be so shameful. Puritanical posturing throughout the culture suggested that gay people who fell sick were sinners and deserved what they got as punishment for their "chosen lifestyle." That fabulous gay friend became someone to be avoided because it was assumed they were sick and could transmit the disease easily, so little was known about it. Randy Shilts's *And the Band Played On* is the seminal book about the early days of the AIDS epidemic, the pathetic political response, and the rise of activism; it is essential reading to understand the impact—and implications—of AIDS on the community.

As the theater community was being decimated by AIDS, playwrights were starting to confront the disease head-on. Larry Kramer's *The Normal Heart* and William M. Hoffman's *As Is* both tackled the crisis, starting Off-Broadway in 1985 at The Public and Circle Repertory, respectively. Kramer's play was far more political and combative, and it reads now as a fair assessment of the fear in the LGBTQ+ community—and the controversies within it.

Some of Terrence's most famous works addressed AIDS directly, but they were yet to come when he wrote *Frankie and Johnny*. Notwithstanding, the specter of the plague hangs over the play without ever being mentioned. Whereas Kramer and Hoffman charged head-on into the political and cultural issues surrounding AIDS, Terrence instead mapped the emotional landscape that had been altered by the disease. (It would not be the last time he would use heterosexuals to contextualize grim, gay realities.)

The central theme of *Frankie and Johnny* is that sex is easy, but intimacy is challenging—nigh on impossible. The play opens with a couple in bed, under sheets having wild sex . . . *wild* sex. In his stage direction in the printed version of the play, Terrence wrote:

> Darkness. We hear the sounds of a man and a woman making love. They are getting ready to climax. The sounds they are making are noisy, ecstatic and familiar. Above all, they must be graphic. The intention is a portrait in sound of a passionate man and woman making love and reaching climax together.
>
> The real thing.
>
> They came.
>
> Silence. Heavy breathing. We become aware that the radio has been playing Bach's Goldberg Variations in the piano version.
>
> By this point, the curtain has been up for at least two minutes. No light. No dialogue, just the sounds of lovemaking and now the Bach.

What soon becomes evident is that these are not lovers; they are two people who barely know one another. They work together at a greasy spoon in New York. She's a waitress; he's the short-order cook. They've been on a date, and they came back to Frankie's place to fuck, and that will be that . . . your classic, one-time hookup. It doesn't play out that way, however. Johnny refuses to leave and instead begins a postcoital seduction, upending the typical way these things go, because he wants more than a hookup. Frankie is resistant, and most of the play is Johnny trying to overcome Frankie's pushing him away. We learn that both of them have been wounded, but Johnny still believes in romance, while Frankie is not so sure.

At one point, Frankie asks him, "Why are you doing this?" He responds, "I'm tired of looking. Everything I want is in this room." Johnny calls the radio station they've been listening to and convinces the DJ to play Debussy's "Clair de Lune." They make love again as the first act ends, though this time it is more connected: the dynamic has shifted. In the second act, Johnny tells Frankie he loves her, which comes as a surprise—and scares her. They talk. Johnny makes a sandwich. They talk more. Dawn is approaching, and Frankie is no longer insisting that Johnny leave. As the play ends, they are sitting on the edge of the bed brushing their teeth together as "Clair de Lune." comes through the radio again. It's unclear if this relationship will ever extend past this one night, but it's very clear that they have both begun to heal the past and, just perhaps, opened the door to a more authentic intimacy.

Frankie and Johnny was a new type of play for Terrence. It has none of the commentary of some of his previous work. He wasn't trying to defend smoking and drinking through satire, as he did in *Bad Habits*, or point out the absurdity of Vietnam, as he did in *Next*. Instead, he put two characters in a room and let them, as it were, go at it. Even in his earlier work, Terrence was never especially polemical, and in *Frankie and Johnny* he sets up a "fair fight" as the two struggle toward understanding one another. The nuance and complexity of his characters would be defining for all of them from this point forward.

Terrence loved to hear the voices of particular actors in his head as he wrote dialogue. In his *Memoir in Plays*, he writes that he had written *Frankie and Johnny* for Liza Minnelli to play Frankie. In subsequent interviews, he said that he had met Liza during *The Rink*, and was aware that she wanted to be taken seriously as an actor and had asked Terrence to write her a *real* play. *Frankie and Johnny* was that play, but ultimately it wasn't going to happen with Liza, and Terrence wondered if the nudity and onstage sex was too much for Liza, though she would never want to admit that. At the same time, as we'll see in talking about *The Rink*, once a star of the magnitude of Liza Minnelli is involved, the dynamics of production change—and not always for the better. A star vehicle is often more limited in what it can dare because of an audience's expectations of that star.

With Liza out of the picture, MTC staged readings with Stockard Channing as Frankie. Once again, she was unable to do the role. Finally, MTC and Terrence turned to Kathy Bates. Bates had made her Off-Broadway debut in 1975 in *Vanities* and appeared in several Broadway shows and on television and had established herself as an important American actress, though she always considered herself a character actress, rather than a leading lady. In 1983, she had gotten a Tony nomination as Best Actress for Marsha Norman's Pulitzer-winning *'night, Mother*, as Jessie Cates, a young woman who discusses her life with her mother before carrying out her plan to kill herself. Although grim, the play was praised for its honesty, and Bates's performance established her as "one of America's finest stage actresses," according to a *New York Times* article around the release of *Misery*, for which Bates won an Academy Award.

Bates remembers the rehearsal process as a lot of fun, and "I loved that he [Terrence] thought of me as a romantic character, and I'd never been cast like that, so I was very grateful for that." Pamela Singer, who stage-managed the production remembers her as "fiercely talented, and she cursed a lot." She also said that Bates took "big, big risks,"

> They're rolling around naked, and she's screaming, "fuck, shit, piss," and it wasn't as normal as it is today. It was out there and a little risqué, and it was a room in which there weren't a lot of women.
>
> Most of the other actresses who performed it after that, with the exception of Bonnie Franklin, who I think was really thrilled to take her clothes off onstage, were a little worried about how they looked and their bodies.
>
> At the time it was extraordinary on a literary level and on a social and sexual freedom level. One of the things about Terrence that I think is so important is that he is of his time, and time keeps changing. And so does he.

It wasn't always easy going, however; Bates and Terrence locked horns on several issues around the play, notably that Bates thought that it was really a one-act. She recalls that he wasn't offended, but he didn't agree.

The play premiered in June at Stage Two with Bates and F. Murray Abraham as Johnny. The two-week run was essentially a workshop. The play opened the new Stage Two space, and Terrence was thrilled to be able to open a theater with a new play of his. They had made the decision that plays in Stage Two wouldn't be reviewed, and that it would move to Stage One to be part of the next season. To make that happen, though, Meadow had to cajole Bates's agent into letting her do the play, and after a long conversation from a pay phone on Cape Cod where Meadow was on vacation, Bates was in, and the play moved into the larger Stage One in October for six weeks as part of the MTC season. By this time, Abraham wasn't available, and Kenneth Welsh stepped in as Johnny.

Bates adored working with Welsh and admits to having a "humongous crush" on him. Before the show, she used to write things on her stomach to amuse him, which apparently would have rubbed off by the end of the opening scene.

Bates recalled one night when Welsh was out, and the understudy was going to be playing Johnny. She recalls after "places" had been called, standing stark naked, looking across the set at the naked man she'd never met in her life, and that they were about to simulate sex. She remembered she could see the terror in his face, but he was also hopeful that it would go well. It did.

As did the production. It was a hit with audiences and critics, and after its run at City Center, the production moved to the Westside Arts Theatre where it ran from December 1987 to March of 1989. Bates won the 1988 Obie Award for her performance and was nominated for a Drama Desk Award, losing to Stockard Channing for *Woman in Mind*. Bates went with the show when it went to the Mark Taper Forum in Los Angeles. There, she caught the eye of director Rob Reiner, who cast her in the movie *Misery*, which firmly established her as a major star.

Bates didn't always have an easy relationship with Terrence. In addition to locking horns over the play, and some other projects which ultimately fell apart, like many actors before and after, Bates became a kind of muse for Terrence, though it was not a role she necessarily wanted to play. "I'm a gypsy, a magpie. I like to go. It wasn't something I wanted to do," she said. Terrence would write *Lips Together, Teeth Apart* for her, but she didn't want to do it. Instead, she wanted to head to LA, though *Frankie and Johnny* was the springboard to her film career. When she wasn't cast—or seriously considered—for the film *Frankie and Johnny*, she and Terrence parted ways . . . for a time. Bates remembered that Terrence wrote an article that said that Bates had a "mundane" voice, which made her sensitive about her voice from then on. Eventually, they healed their relationship. She said he told her, "I wish they'd never asked me to write that damn article," but she thought he was being a "mean queen." Years later Bates realized that what had upset her was not so much Terrence but the fact that Garry Marshall cast Michelle Pfeiffer and couldn't envision Bates in a romantic role and being kissed. She said that she didn't talk to Terrence for seventeen years after that but that at age seventy she couldn't fully remember why. Instead, she ended up being grateful to him:

> Somehow that play gave me tremendous confidence as a woman. And to be desired and thought of in that way. And I owe that to Terrence. If you want to be in this business, you have to get tough. You're not going to make it if you don't toughen up. I've been in this business for 50 years. You've got to have a head like a bullet and a heart like a baby.
>
> Everyone is suffering in some way. That's one of the layers of *Frankie and Johnny*. God brings us the right person for healing our wounds.

Frankie and Johnny would be one of Terrence's most enduring works. Singer, who worked on many professional productions of the show, said she felt no one ever got the role as much as Bates. A two-hander with one set and plum roles, it's done constantly in regional, community, and academic theaters.

It would also find its way to Broadway—twice.

In 2002, the play got its first Broadway production starring Edie Falco as Frankie. Falco was known for her role in *The Sopranos*, but also a stage actor known for a performance in *Side Man*, a memory play in which she played the alcoholic wife of a trumpeter. Falco was no stranger to playing complicated women. Stanley Tucci was Johnny. Tucci was largely known for his film work, having made his debut in *Prizzi's Honor*, but he had done stage work and was a graduate of the SUNY Purchase theater program. The production was directed by Joe Mantello, who remembered that it had come together quickly once the two lead actors were on board.

The production got a glowing review in the *New York Times*, and ran for 258 performances with Rosie Perez and Joe Pantoliano playing the roles for the last three months of the run before it closed in March of 2008.

The play was revived on Broadway in 2019 with Audra McDonald and Michael Shannon in the roles. Terrence had insisted that he would only consent to the production if McDonald was willing to play Frankie, and he stipulated that Arin Arbus was to direct.

Arbus was not an obvious choice. Known for her productions of Shakespeare and other classics, her work had come to Terrence's attention as an inveterate theatergoer. He loved her creativity and perspective, and he thought that in 2019, the play should, for the first time in a major production, have a woman as a director. Arbus had come to Shakespeare almost by accident during her time at Theater for a New Audience where she had started doing things like bagging costumes but eventually moved into directing. (We're skipping a lot here, obviously.) However, not having been a lifelong Shakespeare fan, some of her influences included Cicely Berry who ran the Royal Shakespeare Company in England and who insisted that Shakespeare was for everyone. Arbus immediately responded to the musicality in Terrence's language, but she still said that she was humbled by Terrence reaching out to her, and that he had supported her—as he had so many theater artists as they were beginning, or expanding, their careers.

The evolution of the sex scene in *Frankie and Johnny* is also a story of how theater—and culture—evolved over twenty-two years since its first production to the last Broadway revival. Whereas Kathy Bates described just going for it without much choreography or planning, Edie Falco said, "It's just something you do."

> Once you get over the initial horror of it, like anything you do, a bunch, it just becomes easier and less awkward. It was very hard in the beginning. We were in a small rehearsal room with giant windows and trying to figure out how to make this thing happen, and you just kind of embarrassed your way through it.

By 2019, however, the world had changed, sensibilities about how people interact onstage and off had changed radically. The revival was the first time an intimacy coach had been used on Broadway. McDonald said that rather than making the scene seem mechanical, it was liberating. As she said,

> It was very much in the same way how Terrence had always for me as an artist working with him, made the room a safe space. Because we knew we were safe, Michael and I were able to have a really deep level of intimacy as coworkers and colleagues. I have never felt safer on stage, and I've done a lot of interesting love scenes over the years, and that was the safest I've ever felt.

The world had also changed in relation to AIDS. The specter of infection as a death sentence had hung over the original production, though only slightly, as Frankie and Johnny struggle to find intimacy. The critics have always made more of that than Terrence had intended; he saw it as a background that was affecting everyone, something everyone should be aware of. By 2019, HIV had become, for many at least, a manageable, chronic infection, but still a concern. Jesse Green, in the

New York Times, suggested that what the passing years and treatments had done was open the door to the more comic elements of the play.

The production was well-reviewed, and Arbus especially was praised for the sensitivity of her work. However, Broadway had indeed changed, and a small, intimate play—even with star power—didn't find an audience. The limited run closed early, but that's more economics than art. The play is a staple of academic and small theaters, one of Terrence's most enduring, most universal, works.

(Fun Fact: *Frankie and Johnny* was also the name of a TV sitcom Terrence pitched during his Hollywood days. A typewritten page of the original concept is in his archives, and while the show was never produced, it does underscore that Terrence often liked to start with a title and work from there.)

III.

If one ever wanted to see how the course of getting a play produced "never did run smooth," one need look no further than *The Lisbon Traviata*. By the time it made its, for the most part, triumphant bow at MTC in 1989, it had endured about all the slings and arrows a simple play could stand over about nearly eight years. *Lisbon*'s progress could be a play in itself.

After NPR rejected the first act, the script went into a drawer. Once again, a producing organization was telling Terrence to hide and that what he was writing was inappropriate. It was not easy.

It's not clear why the play couldn't find a home. In fact gay plays were finding audiences. *The Normal Heart* debuted at The Public Theater in 1985 and *As Is* bowed a few weeks earlier and even moved to Broadway. Gay characters were no longer taboo, particularly if gay people and their friends were buying tickets.

The actor Michael Wager, nicknamed Mindy, was a friend of Terrence's, and the character in the play named Mendy was largely based on him. Terrence and Wager would get together and listen to opera records, another model for the relationship between Mendy and Stephen in the play. Wager, as it happens, was also acquainted with the director John Tillinger, known as Joey, an actor, director, and literary who had just had a big hit directing the 1981 revival of Joe Orton's *Entertaining Mr. Sloane*. It was through Wager that Joey met Terrence.

As Joey recalls, Terrence was at the time in a "fallow" period. This would have been around 1983 or 1984 before *It's Only a Play*. Joey was also known to Lynne Meadow, playing a variety of male roles in *Ashes*, a connection which will become important later. (If you feel about now like you're at the beginning of an Agatha Christie novel where all the characters are assembling at a country house or some such location, well, you wouldn't be that far off.)

Wager, thinking of course that there will be a part for him to play should the piece go anywhere, suggested that Terrence send Joey the play, and he did. Joey loved it, saying he thought it was a "brilliant" first act. It was, however, only a first act, and the idea was hatched to match it with Edward Albee's *Another Part of the Zoo*, which was a sequel to Albee's first hit *The Zoo Story*. In the new play, the two men were identified as gay, which they had not been in *The Zoo Story*, though audiences assumed they were . . . or at least bisexual. *Another Part of the Zoo* had only had one performance out in the Hamptons at a benefit Terrence had arranged; the plays were equally unknown outside a very select group of people. More than fifteen years after Terrence and Albee had ended their intimate relationship, the acrimony had healed, to some extent, and the two were at least cordial colleagues in the playwriting trenches, so to speak, and certainly game for doing a project together.

And so, they had a reading. Joey says that it was Terrence, Albee, Wager, and a few other people reading the other parts. What the reading showed them was that the two plays weren't compatible as an evening of theater; at least that was Albee's decision, Joey remembered.

It's not a surprising realization. Although there is only ten years between Terrence and Albee, they belong to different theatrical eras. Whereas Terrence was unabashedly open about his gay characters being gay—and positively so—Albee's work belonged to an era where gay people didn't appear on stage, and if they did, their sexuality was implied. An audience might infer that a character is gay, but it could not be stated. Terrence broke that implicit taboo with *Bump*, and he never looked back. (Despite accusations from critics and scholars, Albee always maintained that his heterosexual characters were not gay characters in straight drag. He wouldn't write another character who identified as gay until *The Goat, or Who Is Sylvia?* in 2002.)

With the two-play evening not going forward, Joey asked Terrence if he would write a second act for the play based on one of the characters— hoping it would be the Mendy character who was comically over-the-top and obsessed with Maria Callas (no surprise there), but Terrence was more interested in the other characters.

What emerged was a play with two very different acts. The first act takes place in Mendy's apartment where Mendy and his friend Stephen, former trick now best friend, are listening to opera. Stephen tells Mendy that there is a bootleg recording of Maria Callas singing "La Traviata" in, you guessed it, Lisbon, which he has acquired. Mendy, who worships all things Callas, insists that he *must* hear it. However, Stephen can't go home to get the record because his lover Mike has brought home a trick of his own, Paul. They have an eight-year relationship, which has recently been opened up, but Stephen isn't all that comfortable with it, despite giving it lip service. As it happens, Stephen himself is planning a hookup, but without a great deal of enthusiasm. Mendy gets on the phone to Michael, insists that he bring over the Lisbon *Traviata* recording and also talks to Paul, the trick. Michael does stop by, but it's the wrong *Traviata* recording; London not Lisbon. In and among all the discussion of opera trivia, we hear Mendy's disappointment at the lack of love in his life, his inability to have a relationship and see—and hear—all the energy he has channeled into his love of Callas. True to Terrence, there is high comedy in the references (one doesn't need to be an opera fanatic to laugh at the complexities of Mendy's passion), but at the same time, Mendy's bruised, hurting, and somewhat jealous heart is very evident as well. He is jealous of the seeming perfect relationship between Stephen, a successful editor, and Michael, a successful doctor, though Stephen is not so sure of the perfection. It's a poignant portrait of a certain sphere of gay men who haunted the opera and for whom their love of it gave them an identity that is all in all to them but would largely be meaningless in the outside world.

The actor Richard Thomas, who played Stephen in the later California productions, described the first act as *buffo* (comic), and the second act as *verissimo* (realistic). Indeed, the play turns dark in Act Two as the scene shifts to Michael and Stephen's apartment. Stephen, arriving home from sleeping on the couch at Mendy's—and not hooking up after all—finds Paul and Michael. Paul leaves, and Stephen and Michael are left to confront what it means that their relationship is falling apart. Stephen, still in love but finding he can't have the object of his affections, kills Michael in a tragic ending, reminiscent of *Tosca* where Tosca stabs Scarpia. (Callas famously sang the role with Tito Gobi at Covent Garden in London in 1964, which Stephen, Michael, and Mendy would all know.) Immediately prior to stabbing Michael with a pair of scissors, Michael, also an opera fan, had tried to leave Stephen to be with Paul, though Stephen blocks his exit. Michael echoes Carmen's final words from Bizet's *Carmen*, "Kill me or let me pass." ("*Frappe-moi donc, ou laisse passer*" in the original French.) In a huge, appropriately operatic gesture, Carmen, like Michael is stabbed and is bleeding out as the curtain falls.

Amid the fighting and the high drama in the play, there is also pointed conversation about AIDS, the fear it's causing in the community, and mentioning people who have died. While the mainstream culture was trying to avoid the disease, Terrence was, for the first time, placing the disease and a response to it at the center of the play, and making it very clear how the gay men whose community was being decimated were reacting to it.

Joey thought the play was brilliant, and they began to have several readings, but it got no traction:

> We had the devil of a time getting it on, but at that time, gay plays were accepted as long as they were covertly gay. *The Ritz* was obviously very gay, but it was a comedy.

The reading I remember most was for Andre Bishop at Playwrights Horizons, and he turned it down. I thought the reason was specious. He said he knew who all these characters were based on, which I don't think was true, but he obviously knew that Mindy was Mendy.

And then we did another reading at the Provincetown Playhouse, but no one picked up. I don't know who approached [producer] Sherwin Goldman, but he agreed to produce it on a shoestring in a space on 35th Street. It was very favorably reviewed, and we thought someone would surely pick it up. Well, of course no one did because people were truly nervous about gay plays.

Even with the promise of a production, it wasn't easy to get it going. Wager was initially cast to play Mendy, but as Joey remembered, he wasn't very good. While he was excellent in the readings, Joey thought he really couldn't play the part. He describes a dinner at Orso's where he, Terrence, and Sherwin were bemoaning that the production wasn't going well, and they really wanted to fire one of the actors.

He recounts that they were sitting trying to figure out a way forward when Elaine May came up to them and, clearly seeing there was a problem, asked what was wrong. They told her they were having a problem with an actor, and Joey says May immediately said, "Fire them. They never get any better. Just fire them."

After she left the table, Terrence said that the actor he really wanted to fire was Wager because he was so erratic in the part. Wager was fired, but it didn't go well as one might imagine given how instrumental he had been in getting the play to this point, but it had to be done. He was replaced by Seth Allen. The play opened in June 1985, and as Joey said it was very positively reviewed. And still no one picked it up.

At around the time the play was running on 35th Street, Joey remembers a conversation with Meadow that summer where she called him and said she'd heard he was directing now, and did he have anything for MTC, and what would he like to read.

Joey did two readings, *It's Only a Play* and Joe Orton's *Loot* later that year. He remembers that no one picked them up, which he said was terrible because the reading of *It's Only a Play* was a huge hit, Meadow did pick it up, and we've seen how it became a hit for MTC in December that year. MTC also produced the revival of *Loot*, which moved to Broadway in 1986.

Tillinger at this point was a very bankable director, and with the triple-threat combo of MTC, Tillinger, and Terrence; *The Lisbon Traviata* was greenlit for Stage One in 1989.

Now that he was getting a full-scale mounting, Terrence would have wanted Jimmy Coco to play Mendy, but Coco had died two years earlier in 1987 of a massive heart attack at age fifty-six, which was a tremendous blow to Terrence. Seth Allen and Terrence's former lover Robert Drivas had both died of AIDS in 1986. Combined with the breakup with Cuskern in 1985, Terrence's network was shrinking, so Mendy's retreat into opera may have had some autobiographical undertones, though Terrence never claimed that any of his plays were autobiographical . . . except one.

There are different versions of the story of how Nathan Lane became involved. As Tillinger tells it, while they were casting, he suggested that they see Nathan Lane for Mendy. Terrence, of course, had known of Lane, and in one of those oft-told theatrical "meet cute" stories, he said he had met Nathan on the stairs at City Center while they were both working at MTC. Terrence recalled having seen Lane in *Present Laughter* with George C. Scott in 1982. Although Lane had played a small part, Terrence remembered how funny he was—and what a good actor he was. "He managed to steal scenes from George C. Scott, which in my opinion is grand larceny," he said.

In May of 1987, Terrence was rehearsing *Frankie and Johnny* in Stage Two at MTC while Lane was rehearsing a parody of *Deathtrap* called *Claptrap* in Stage One. Although Lane would go on to get the best reviews of the play that was generally discounted, it was not going well, and Lane was upset. He said:

We were on a break, and I went into the lobby of the City Center theater and sat on the steps and put my head in my hands. And then I heard a voice say, "Hi, Nathan. I'm Terrence McNally," and he introduced himself and said he was a fan and mentioned having seen me in *Present Laughter*, which was my Broadway debut. "I know you're having a hard time with the play, but I wish you all the best, and I hope we get to work together someday." And I thought, wow, I wish we could work together right now.

Here's where fallible memories make for somewhat different stories. As Lane remembers it, they were looking for someone older to play Mendy, and at the time Lane was in his early thirties, but they were having such a difficult time finding someone that they agreed to see him. He also said that one of the dynamics of the play was that these were gay men at different stages of their lives—the older opera fans, the younger doctor who was a casual fan perhaps experiencing a midlife crisis, which made him want to trick with the college student. Since they couldn't find the right actor, however, they wanted to see Nathan.

Meadow remembers it differently. She said that after Coco had died and *Lisbon* was in the works, MTC casting director Donna Isaacson came into her office and suggested Nathan for Mendy. Though there was concern that Lane was too young, Meadow knew that he could do it "absolutely."

Joey's version is that he had just directed Lane in Jon Robin Baitz's play *The Film Society*, and they had become great friends.

He remembers that he asked Isaacson to call Nathan in for the part:

> She said, "Oh, no, he'll never accept this part." And I said, "Why not?" She said, "Well, he has problems with his sexuality." Well, I didn't know if Nathan was gay or not. It's not part of what I would consider, well, maybe if I were going to sleep with him. But the casting director said, "No, no, no, he would never come in on this."

> And so, I called Nathan, and I said, "You have to." He came in, and he started reading one of the long speeches, and he was on the fourth or fifth line, and Terrence leaned forward and said, "Jimmy's back," meaning Jimmy Coco.

Lane got the role, and the play went on, and what's important is that it was life-changing for all involved.

Singer, who also stage-managed this production, remembers a wonderful rehearsal period in which the play evolved even further.

> Nathan would launch into a monologue, and he would suddenly turn to Terrence, and say, "You know, I don't know how he gets from here to there." And they would sit down and talk about it.
>
> It was so extremely creative, and I didn't understand in those days that that wasn't always the way it happened. Not every playwright would want to think it through and talk about it, and explain, rewrite, and use the ideas coming from the heads of actors.

The play was a huge hit with audiences, though critics were somewhat mixed. The difference between the comedy of the first act and the seriousness of the second seemed to baffle them. John Simon in *New York Magazine*, of course, was especially vitriolic and homophobic, though that word wasn't in common usage then. By this time, Simon had established his "brand" as a negative critic, and people picked up *New York Magazine* as much to read what horrible things Simon wrote about people and plays, as to decide whether or not to go see a play. It was a corruption of criticism that sold magazines, but certainly didn't serve the theater, and a Simon review, though it could drip with acid, never had the life-or-death power of a review in the *New York Times*.

When the run finished at MTC, it moved uptown to the Promenade Theater where it ran for over a year. In response to some of the criticism and the controversy, Terrence rewrote the ending to take out the murder. Many "in the know" in showbiz had told Terrence that the violence was too much to handle.

Singer recalled that Mike Nichols had come in to a rehearsal and said, "This is never going to play." Mike Nichols being *Mike Nichols*, they changed the play.

Any opera fan would likely have disagreed, given the *grand guignol* attendant on the climax of many operas, but perhaps for an Upper West Side audience not versed in *Tosca, La Bohème, Carmen,* or *Don Giovanni,* it was enough that the relationship between the two men collapsed.

Whatever the ending, however, the play was a hit, and Lane received the Drama Desk and Lortel Awards. Joey won the Lortel award for direction, and Terrence was nominated for the Drama Desk Award for outstanding new play.

As for playing a gay, it proved to be no problem for Lane, and looking back, he said,

> I wasn't thinking, "Oh, God, how will this affect my career?" It made my career. It changed everything, and suddenly I was taken more seriously.
>
> I don't think I've ever told this story, but I was in a cab with an actor who I'm not going to mention because he's wonderful—and a well-known actor. I think he had auditioned for the play. And he said, "It's just so gay, and I don't know who's going to see this, and there was something about it that you would have to go out on a limb with a part like that, and how do you make it work?"
>
> And I just kept thinking I don't know anything about opera, but I thought it was screamingly funny. The first act is certainly as witty as anything that's ever been written for the theater, and I thought this is a gift of a part. I didn't really know that till we were in it, and Joey was encouraging the flamboyance, and I thought this is my debut as a flamboyant homosexual. It turns out I was good at it. It was the best thing that could've ever happened.

While *Lisbon* was playing in New York, Richard Thomas saw it, and immediately wanted to play Stephen. Thomas, who most audiences would have known from the television show *The Waltons*, was an accomplished stage actor with credits going back to his childhood. Thomas had first met Terrence when he was a kid and Terrence was working Albee's Playwrights Unit at the Cherry Lane in the mid-1960s:

> I must have been 14, 15, 16, and those plays [the Off-Off Broadway plays] were all in our heads in the 60s. There was a lot going on, a lot of theatrical shibboleths were being challenged. . . . I was one of the kids in the city who could come and do a reading or a one act play, and even much earlier when I was at the Playwrights Unit and the Actors Studio when they needed a child actor. I did a production of *Strange Interlude* in 1962.
>
> My memory of Terrence, and it's just an impression, was that he was very sweet to me and very supportive. Edward had a sort of hooded, darker, and more piercing energy and Terrence a very bright and open energy.

Thomas was drawn to *Lisbon* because as he says of Terrence's writing, "There's nothing coded in Terrence, nothing." He loved the inherent theatricality in the play and that Terrence's work could be acted, and that there is such a balance of comedy and tragedy.

Moreover, having grown up in the downtown theater scene, surrounded by gay people and gay sensibilities; it all felt familiar. Though Thomas was always straight, his response to the play went beyond sexuality into the pure theatricality of it. In many ways the size and scope of *Lisbon* is not much different than *Bump*. As Terrence himself would say about his characters, the world they inhabit is real, but they themselves are characters in a play, and for the play to have that dramatic impact, the audience has to know that as well. That's a technique inspired by opera.

Thomas saw the play and said, "Okay, I gotta do it." He called Terrence about it and asked if there were any plans for Los Angeles production because Thomas was living in LA at the time. Terrence said no, and Thomas said he was going to go talk to Gordon Davidson at the Mark Taper Forum. Davidson was concerned about the violence and how the gay community would respond. Thomas countered with an argument that to think that gay people can't have the level of emotions that could lead them to commit murder, was actually prejudicial against the gay community. Why, he asked, should they not be able to experience and express the full spectrum of human behavior? That was enough to convince Davidson, and the production debuted in November 1990, after a short run in San Francisco.

Still, as Joey recalls, Davidson had his reservations, and rather than planning for a full six- or eight-week run, he only booked the show for four weeks. The box office opened, and the line was around the block; the gay community was ready to see themselves—or a theatrical version of themselves—on stage. Finally.

What's more, they apparently wanted the whole operatic experience. Thomas remembers asking Terrence to restore the original ending, which he did, with revisions. Terrence felt that he had never gotten the ending exactly right, and as he had the chance to update the play, he took it. As Lane said,

> That impulse [to restore the violent ending] was right. And then he asked why since there was so much talk about Mendy, why didn't he make an appearance?
>
> And then I had visited him in Bridgehampton, and we were driving back to New York. He was driving, and Wendy Wasserstein was in the front, and I'm sitting in the back and we were just kibitzing and joking, and I said, "Well my idea is that when the young man [Paul] is struggling to get the door open to get out of this horrible situation he finds himself in, he opens the door, and I'm standing there about to knock, and I guarantee you that will bring the house down. And then I say, 'I hope I haven't come at a bad time.' And you figure out the rest."

Terrence did, and the brief scene with Mendy in the second third of the second act is absolute genius. Mendy has interrupted a verbally and physically violent scene, Paul is upset, and suddenly there is a clown. It is classic theater. It's the porter in *Macbeth*, the gravedigger in *Hamlet*, it's "By the Sea" in Sondheim's *Sweeney Todd*; it is a moment of levity before the play plunges into its dark and tragic ending. Just like the "bend and snap" in *Legally Blonde*, it works every time.

Looking back, *Lisbon* was life-changing for Lane. Far from being anxious about his sexuality, he embraced it, at least through the character.

> It was the beginning of a thirty-year collaboration, and it was a wonderful experience. It was the first time I was playing a gay man on stage, obviously a very flamboyant one, and so I remember thinking, "Oh, you don't want to go over the top. You want him to be a fully fleshed out human being." But Joey encouraged me to live up to the writing and to go far with it, and then when those small, vulnerable moments happened, it was very effective.
>
> Joey loved doing the play, and he would say, "It's too good. It's like a Fabergé egg, we should only show it to a few people who will really appreciate what it is."

Lane continues,

> And then we started performances, and I remember after the dress rehearsal I knew it was funny, and I knew it was a great part, and the audience reaction from the first day was spectacular, and when we ended, Tony [Heald playing Stephen] looked at me and said, "I'm glad you're not in the second act."

Of course, Lane knew it was a joke, and looking back given how revered the play is now, he said that people tend to forget the long history of the play—nearly a decade from the first, rejected radio play to the run in Los Angeles. Yet even though many people think *Lisbon* was a smash hit when it came out, it wasn't. Lane recalls that it was very controversial and the reviews across the board, in New York and Los Angeles, were not raves. But, Lane concludes, it was an incredibly theatrical piece of writing, and people wanted to see it.

And they wouldn't have had the chance, had it not been for MTC.

IV.

In 1988, AIDS was still ravaging New York. The city and the creative community continued to be destroyed, and deaths would not even peak in the United States for another six years. In 1987, AZT was finally approved for use in treating HIV, and although it was one of the fastest federal approvals of a drug up to that point, it could not stem the tide of death and loss that had cast a pall over the city.

AIDS, however, was just one of the many issues affecting city life. Life in New York has always been a balance of joy, fear, nuisance, inconvenience, frustration, and insistence that there is nowhere else on the planet to live. That admixture of emotions is endemic to city life—and part of what gives the city its character. People love to complain about living there . . . and they can't imagine living anywhere else.

Meadow knew all of this, and returning to her successful roots as the producer of an omnibus evening, sent out a call to writers for their take on life in New York in the late 1980s. The result was *Urban Blight*, an evening of twenty short pieces about contemporary life in the city. The ones that made it into the evening were selected from more than thirty that were submitted, and in addition to Terrence, the final show included pieces by Christopher Durang, A. R. Gurney, and Arthur Miller. There was music by Richard Maltby and David Shire, and the evening was directed by Tillinger. Though Meadow thought at the time that it was a bit of a risk, the show was a success. After all, the only thing New Yorkers love more than complaining about their lives in the city is watching others do exactly the same.

Terrence's contribution was a very short piece, called *Andre's Mother*. The published script is less than three full pages, perhaps eight minutes of stage time. Yet it is a powerful expression of the emotional impact of AIDS. The play is set in Central Park where Andre, his sister, his father, and mother (the only person in the play who doesn't have a name and who never speaks) have gathered to remember Andre and release balloons, a metaphoric way of letting Andre's soul soar away.

The center of the piece is a monologue by Cal, Andre's surviving lover, who, it becomes clear, has reached out to Andre's mother at Andre's request:

> I always had it in my mind that one day we would be friends, you
> and me. But if you didn't know about Andre and me . . . If this
> hadn't happened, I wonder if he would have ever told you. When
> he was so sick, if I asked him once, I asked him a thousand times,
> tell her. She's your mother. She won't mind. But he was so afraid
> of hurting you and of your disapproval. I don't know which was
> worse. *(No response. He sighs.)* God, how many of us live in this city
> because we don't want to hurt our mothers and live in mortal terror
> of their disapproval. We lose ourselves here. Our lives aren't furtive,
> just our feelings toward people like you are. A city of fugitives from
> our parent's scorn or heartbreak.

Andre's mother never responds, and Cal leaves, and Andre's mother can't release her balloon. The brilliance of this short speech is that it fully captures the experience of so many men in New York in the seventies and even after the AIDS crisis had infiltrated the city. The dramatic conflict was between the joy and liberation of finally being oneself juxtaposed against the ever-present fear of coming out to one's parents and needing to hide a full part of their life. As Cal makes so vividly clear with such simplicity, he had hoped that in time, he and Andre would be accepted by Andre's mother, that their lives would not have to exist on two planes.

For so many gay men, in particular at this time, this was their reality. As mentioned earlier, without marriage, there were no rights, and lovers struggling with the death of the person they most loved had to cope with vindictive families who denied them and the relationship so cruelly cut short. It may be hard to comprehend for people who came afterward, or who grew up in a world where AIDS is for many a chronic and controllable disease and not an automatic death sentence, where pills can prevent infection, or managing the viral load can ensure decades of life and that for those who are "undetectable," they are considered to be unable to transfer the virus to others during sex. Then, it was a time of cruelty and despair, of loss and fear, as men in the prime of life watched their chosen families suffer and die. That Terrence could capture all of that in thirty-six lines is yet another example of his genius. As always, he went to the heart of his character to illuminate the situation.

Andre's Mother was adapted by Terrence into a fifty-minute teleplay that starred Richard Thomas as Cal and Sada Thompson as Andre's Mother. Terrence won the Emmy for writing for the piece.

There's an interesting sidenote on the casting of the teleplay. Terrence always liked to write for people's voices. He said it always helped him if he could hear them in his head as he wrote. Early in 1977, he had reached out to Katharine Hepburn about an as-yet unwritten play to see if she would be interested in doing it, if he would write it for her. Her typewritten response in February was characteristically direct:

> Listen Terrence—
>
> Don't talk about it. Write it. You certainly are not silly enough to tell it. Fatal. And I don't know what to do until I see it—and read it.

She continued in her handwriting:

> I'm saying that you are the one to take the chance anyway. You wish to look at it [*sic*]. Not so? If you wish to talk. I will listen.

Ten years later, he sent her the teleplay for *Andre's Mother*, and she declined:

> I have read your script—and I really would not be interested in playing Andre's Mother—I am so busy writing myself that I can't imagine what would take me away from it—Good luck—and many thanks.

V.

By the end of the 1980s, Terrence was ubiquitously pegged as a "gay playwright," a term that always chafed him. Though he had been assumed to be gay ever since *Bump* and many of his plays had gay characters and references to gay relationships, and of course *The Ritz*, as his work matured and he continued to write about issues about which he was passionate, and as his work delved further into "rigorous honesty" (a term from Alcoholics Anonymous), *not* writing about gay themes would have been impossible.

As he said about why he wrote so much about AIDS, he thought how could he *not* write about it. Just as he had taken on Vietnam, the growing sexual revolution, and the fears of something "out there" in many of his early works, AIDS was very present to him. It was, after all, the thing that was "out there" for him and all gay men. Having lost Drivas and so many others to the disease, he wasn't just responding to the disease, he was responding to how it had permeated the culture. There was so much fear surrounding gay people, and because so little was known about the disease and since there was so much disinformation circulating in the culture, much of it spreading fear and demonizing gay men. Terrence had been directly affected by this as well. Cuskern tells a story of how Terrence had been at a meeting and there was confusion about whose drinking glass was whose and the person was afraid to touch the one that might have been Terrence's for fear of getting AIDS. He also told the story of a producer during this period who wanted a play that could be gay, but not *too* gay. This was a story Terrence told many times and also included it in more detail in his *Memoir in Plays.* So, yes, Terrence was angry.

He was also aware, though into middle age, that he was part of a new generation of playwrights who were willing to write about gay themes— and that the culture, or some of it, had evolved to the point where it had become acceptable. As he pointed out, prior to *The Goat,* Albee had written only one gay play, *Another Part of the Zoo,* mentioned earlier, which only ever had one public performance. Terrence said,

It was a companion to *The Zoo Story*. It was two gay men, and it was given one performance, and he never wanted it done.

A lot of writers of Edward's generation never spoke up during the AIDS crisis, and they wrote gay characters. I think it's generational, too, but Mrs. McElroy really influenced me to write what you know.

Terrence's next "gay play" was unique in that there wasn't a single gay character on stage. *Lips Together, Teeth Apart* takes place on Fire Island on one day of the Fourth of July weekend. Sally Truman has inherited the house from her gay brother David who has died from AIDS and has come for the weekend with her husband Sam, Sam's sister and brother-in-law, Chloe and John Haddock. The three acts are morning, noon, and night of the day in question. Not much happens in terms of plot. The play is nominally about homophobia—the characters are afraid to touch things, and they won't go in the pool, which was prominent in the set, for fear of getting HIV. As Sally says,

> One drop of water in your mouth or on an open sore and we'll be infected with my brother and his black lover and God knows who else was in here. Pissing, ejaculating. I think we're very brave to dangle our feet like this. They may fall off.

Each of the characters is damaged. John has cancer, "just the tiniest dot," as he says, and is confronting his mortality. He's also slept with Sally. Chloe is desperate that she'll lose her husband and spends the day talking about her roles in community theater, sprinkling bits of French into her conversation, and being manic and upbeat to keep her fears at bay. Sam worries about his finances, whether Sally has been unfaithful, and the bleak emptiness of his life. Sally is pregnant but is afraid to tell Sam after a series of miscarriages. Sally is also ultimately angry after a life of suppressing her emotions, as the speech above clearly indicates, and worries obsessively about a young swimmer she has seen walk out into the ocean and not return. For these characters, it's not just AIDS that is the harrowing threat out there; it's everything that is out there. As Chloe says at one point, "I think these are terrible times to be a kid in," to which Sally replies, "I think these are terrible times to be anything in." Though the play is realistic, the bumping music from the gay people at a party next door is as much a reminder of the unknown threats that Terrence was writing about in *Bump*.

The play is also easily the most Chekhovian of all of Terrence's work, dealing as it does with seemingly tiny disappointments and heartaches that come to dominate the characters' sensibilities. It has, arguably, one of the most Chekhovian lines Terrence ever wrote as Chloe says, "I talk too much because it's probably too horrible to look at what's really going on." She also observes late in the play as she talks to her brother about John's affair with Sally, and Sam suggests she face the truth, "That word has gotten more people into trouble than all the lies ever told. Fuck the truth, it's more trouble than it's worth." Coming as it does at the end of the play and its epigrammatic nature consistent with Chloe's earlier linguistic excesses, it's an example of how Terrence so often revealed characters in surprising ways.

Lips Together would prove to be a hit, though not all the critics were enthusiastic. Importantly, a rave from Frank Rich in the *New York Times* was enough to keep it running through the summer at MTC and move to the Lortel downtown. In all, the play ran for thirteen months, opening in May 1991 and closing at the end of June in 1992.

At the outset, it was anyone's guess whether the play would make it at all. Joey Tillinger remembers that Lynne Meadow had called him to see if he'd be interested in doing the play. He said of course. "However," she said, "I think you'd better read it first."

> The first act was a mess. I mean, it was horrendous. There were lines like "I know your hungry cunt wants my hungry cock," and I said to Terrence, "You can't say this."
>
> And he said, "Well, I've just read a book by John Updike where there's that kind of language." I told him it was different when you read it and so on. I gave him copious notes.

Christine Baranski remembered that she was asked by Meadow to do a reading. Baranski had adored Terrence after her work on *It's Only a Play*, and much of her Off-Broadway work had been done at MTC, and Baranski credits a lot of her early success to the support of Meadow and MTC.

The word was that Terrence had written a play for his "four favorite actors," so it was to be Baranski, Lane, Anthony Heald from *Lisbon*, and Kathy Bates from *Frankie and Johnny*.

Bates was unable to do the role, and it was offered to Swoosie Kurtz, who was a newcomer to the McNally pantheon of actors. Kurtz remembers that when the call had come in to offer her the role, she had also been offered a "trashy movie of the week." Her agents had told her she could choose the movie or "art." Kurtz chose art, and was grateful to have done so.

Meadow arranged a reading and sent out the scripts. As Baranski said,

> I remember I was in Buffalo visiting my mom and, I thought, "Wow, this play is a mess. Just a hot mess." And I called Lynne, and I gave her very specific notes, and I said I don't even know if it's worth having a reading until we get at least a second draft. There's just too much work to be done. It came time for us to do the reading, and shortly before the reading I got what I assumed was a revised draft, but it wasn't, it was the first draft. Wow.

"Wow" was pretty much Joey's response, and after the reading, which went ahead with the unedited script, he gave Terrence many of the same notes he had given him when he had first read it. Joey says he is not that great a note-taker, but he had four pages worth after the reading.

As Baranski recalls, weeks or months went by before the play was ready to go into rehearsal. The company gathered, and Baranski opened her script, "Oh, my gosh. It was the original draft."

Joey was keenly aware that nothing had changed in the script, either. None of it had been rewritten.

I was in despair, and Christine went ballistic. She doesn't ever lose her cool, but she went ballistic, and that prompted Nathan to go ballistic. And Swoozie was a stranger in the midst because she had never worked with any of them before, and she was looking around thinking, "What the fuck have I gotten into?"

The language was shocking without any important reason, and then Anthony Heald joined, and I tried to keep things quiet, but the next day was somewhat the same.

Baranski who at the time says she was emboldened by having just entered Jungian therapy and was speaking up for herself:

I had never done anything like it, but I confronted Terrence and I said, "Look, you have not done your work. We are now in a position where we as actors have to rehearse this, and we are going to be using precious rehearsal time [to work on the script]." That's our time to find the characters. There are parts that are just too salacious; it's as though Terrence put it all out there. The language of the characters was so explicit.

And I remember sitting there and my fellow actors were stunned, but I said you have put us in this terrible position, and I'm angry about that. I remember thinking that I might have to quit the play. I would have to back out, and I wanted the option of backing out. I wanted the option of backing out if it hadn't been rewritten for the first day of rehearsal.

I watched Terrence as he took this in. I don't think I raised my voice, but I was very angry and direct with him.

And I remember Joey saying, "All right, everybody, let's take a break." I went to the ladies' room and thought, "Whoa, what just happened?" And Terrence met me outside the rehearsal hall and said, "I thank you for your honesty; I appreciate that."

We went back in the rehearsal room, took our pencils up, and we started cutting the play. And I will always remember and be grateful to him because he could have reacted defensively. He could have been angry at me and held onto the anger, and not for a moment did he do that.

By the end of the day we started cutting the play, and everybody felt better. I felt that, honestly. I felt that I was speaking for my fellow actors and the director. I was at a place in my life where I just felt that I could do that. It was a lesson learned for me in the bravery it takes to be in an artistic collaboration.

She was glad she didn't leave, and in addition to excellent reviews, she won the Drama Desk Award for Outstanding Featured Actress in a play.

Crisis averted; however, it wasn't necessarily smooth sailing from that point. After those first two days, Joey remembers that Terrence disappeared while they continued rehearsals. He disappeared for ten days, and he came back with what Joey called, "A superb first act." He felt very privileged to be working on it and said that it was ultimately a very healthy experience in the rehearsal room, but he didn't really know what they had. He knew he had four very strong actors, and given all that, he thought his job was to "shut up a lot."

No play can exist in a vacuum, and though Joey loved what was happening, he wasn't sure.

He remembers that only when they did the run-through for Ken Billington, the lighting designer, did he know what he had: "At the end of the first act, Ken turned to me, and he said, 'Do you have any idea what you've got here?' I said No, but I do like it. He said, 'It's fabulous.' And so that was helpful."

As the play came together, finally, Lane noted that it was a chamber piece and each of the actors had what he called "mini nervous breakdowns" at different times wondering whether it was all going to come together, whether it was all going to work. He said that Terrence always liked to write something that would embarrass him.

So, he had me get into a shower. Just take a shower on stage, and then my sister asks to see how I turned out. I remember when that came up and we were rehearsing and Christine and Tony were, like, it's a little vulgar, isn't it? I don't know if we need this. And he's [Terrence] just doing these things if just to see . . . just to provoke me really. 'Cause he's really five years old. So, he would write things, and it turns out to be one of the best scenes ever. And I said, we have to try this in front of an audience. And it's to a brother and sister. He quickly opens the door and closes it, and she just says, "My compliments to our parents."

Difficult as it must have been—and it wouldn't be the last time Terrence would retreat from the fray only to come back with problems solved beautifully—the process of *Lips* underscores the collaborative nature of theater, and Terrence as a man of the theater was always a collaborator. Sure, he would fight for what he believed in and wanted, but as Kurtz said, of the process, he was always open to hear what actors had to say. Unlike other writers, his words were to be honored, but they weren't sacrosanct. What mattered was what was on stage—and what the audience experienced. In her review in the *New Yorker*, Edith Oliver wrote that, "No modern dramatist that I can think of writes better parts for actors than Terrence McNally, and in this case he has had the luck to have all four of them performed with style and skill." Ultimately, the actors were all grateful for the play.

Nathan Lane's opening night note to Terrence, which comically speaks to their deep love for one another, read:

> Dear big Sister—
> I'm sick to death of thanking you. Kiss my ass butthead.
> Fuck you.
> PS: Thanks for the great part in the great play and for being my friend.
> Love, Nathan.

(The relationship between Lane and Terrence was always jocular. When Lane left *Lisbon* to take a real paying job, Terrence was annoyed and for years sent Lane a card with a one-dollar bill in it on his openings.)

On opening night of *Lips Together* when the reviews finally came in and, as mentioned, the *Times* gave it a rave, Lane remembered that Terrence was "tickled" because it wasn't an easy process for any of them. That it came together in the end and became such a positive experience for all is one of the miracles of the theater.

In the ensuing years, the play became a period piece. Enough is known about AIDS so no one would think that a pool could poison you, though the underlying anxieties of the characters are timeless. It has never been successfully revived in New York. A planned 2010 revival at Roundabout that was supposed to be directed by Joe Mantello was cancelled when Megan Mullally, who had been cast as Chloe, abruptly withdrew. Mullally had become a huge star playing Karen Walker, an acerbic assistant on the sitcom *Will and Grace*. The reason for her withdrawal was said to be "artistic differences," but beyond that no one was talking, at least not for the record. A second revival by Second Stage in 2014 got mixed reviews. Charles Isherwood in the *Times* called it "middling." Terrence wasn't involved in it, but he wasn't happy with it, and thought that the tension that he, Joey, and the cast had worked so hard to find in the original production was missing, as was the sense of fear and foreboding that hung over each of the characters in the original production.

The title of the play, by the way, came, as the legend goes, from Terrence's dentist, Dr. John Roston, who told him to repeat the mantra as he fell asleep to reduce grinding. Apparently, it worked, and Terrence told Dr Roston that the line would make a good title for a play. He gives that line to Sam who, stressed out about life, is grinding his teeth. MTC got a lot of positive response from the dental community as the play went on, with many letters arriving from dentists praising the advice, including Dr. Roston, who was flattered at being immortalized.

VI.

In the late 1980s, Terrence would not have described himself as particularly spiritual. He was still sober—as he would be for the rest of his life—and there is a spiritual component to sobriety through Alcoholics Anonymous, but that is very much guided by the individual and adheres to no particular set of dogma. A trip to India would, if not change his perspective, at least open him up to more spiritual considerations. As much as his sobriety, responding to AIDS, and the losses he experienced, the trip would change his writing and expand his exploration of the inner life of characters.

In 1987, according to Cuskern, Terrence was invited to go on a several-week trip to India. Cuskern couldn't recall the name of the person or the organization behind the trip, but the idea was that several high-profile people including artists and museum curators, a very bright group, would travel around the country and hopefully be inspired to do something that would promote Indian tourism to the United States, England, and Western Europe. Terrence asked Cuskern, who at that time his assistant and no longer his lover, to go, and Cuskern jumped at the chance.

The trip started in Bombay and was mainly concentrated in Rajastahn, a state in the northern part of India. Of course, they went to the Taj Mahal and New Delhi, and out into the desert. They also took a trip on a luxury train known as the Palace on Wheels, which at the time was relatively new and designed for tourists to get around in luxury reminiscent of the Raj.

On the train, Terrence and Cuskern met two women from Connecticut who had wanted to get away, to see something different and had decided to come to India because it was unlike anything they knew. Their husbands, however, were somewhat dull. Cuskern recalls:

> They were looking for spiritual renewal, I think, though I don't think they ever said those words. They were women of a certain age who had a certain wealth and a certain background.
>
> We loved them, and they loved us. We spent as much time as we could together, and I think one of those women came up with the idea of a perfect Ganesh.

Ganesha is one of the most widely worshipped of the Indian gods. With a chubby body and an elephant head, images of Ganesha are everywhere in India. Ganesha is the patron of the arts and sciences and believed to be the remover of obstacles. Ganesha is also the saint of beginnings, so a natural god with which to start a spiritual journey.

As they traveled around India, Cuskern became intent on finding a figurine of Ganesha that spoke to him:

> So, Terrence said, keep your eye out for one. We had this guy who was the rickshaw man pulling us everywhere, and we told him that we were talking about gods, and we just loved this man. He seemed so simple and pure, and hardworking. I don't really know what the hell he was like. Maybe he was a murderer. Who knows? We just totally loved this man. I don't know if I caught a tear in Terrence's eyes. He's not inclined to tears, but he was very moved by this man.

The driver told them he knew exactly the place to take them to find an image of Ganesha, and he took them there. Cuskern picked one out of the many statues that were there, and it was all white. However, the proprietor said he couldn't take it; it had to be painted. Cuskern was happy with it being white, but the proprietor wouldn't hear of it. When they came back the next day, Cuskern realized why it had to be painted; it was so delicate and beautifully painted.

The trip was very healing for Terrence coming shortly after the deaths of Jimmy Coco and Robert Drivas, a lukewarm reception of *The Rink*, as well as the continuing tragedy and toll of AIDS and the changing climate of New York. Cuskern believed that something was sparked within Terrence as a result of the trip, much of which had to do with understanding loss and perhaps putting some of his grief in perspective.

That spark would remain an ember for a few years, however; though it would stay within him and inform the characters of the two plays that immediately followed: *Frankie and Johnny* and *Lisbon*. The influence of his trip can be felt in those scripts; the characters are more human, more complex, and written with more compassion than earlier works. Even in *Lisbon*, despite its operatic scope, as Lane mentioned earlier, that excess served to amplify the quieter, more heartfelt and human elements of characters.

Playwriting is never a linear process, and it most certainly wasn't for Terrence, who had ideas bouncing around all the time, and his archives have notes, scraps of paper, endless lists of titles, and situations, most of which would never see the light of day.

The trip to India got a much more literal representation in *A Perfect Ganesh*. Terrence said that it had taken that long for the lessons of Ganesha to filter into his thoughts and writing.

The plot, as in most of Terrence's plays, is simple and concerns two women from Connecticut, Katharine and Margaret, who are traveling to India for enlightenment, or at least something different. They have left their husbands, who aren't interested in any vacation so exotic, at home. As Katharine says, "We're going to India for two weeks. I told my husband, 'Enjoy TNT, AMC and canned tuna fish. I'm out of here.'" It's as if the initial situation had been handed to Terrence on that deluxe train trip.

That was merely the jumping off place. Katharine and Margaret have deeper motives than just going to an exotic locale. Katharine is haunted by the ghost of her son, Walter, who appears from time to time, and her own guilt because she rejected Walter for being gay, and he was murdered in a violent gay bashing by a gang of Black men. Margaret, who has also tragically lost a son who was run over by a car at age four driven by a Black woman, has just discovered a lump in her breast, but has yet to tell anyone. The scenes take them through India exposing them to the Taj Mahal, and a trip down a river where they encounter dead humans and animals as well as interacting with many people they meet, including two hotel neighbors suffering with AIDS. There is some ongoing mourning, tempered with homophobia and racism, and some scenes are not easy to watch . . . or hear. Katharine hopes to assuage her guilt about Walter by kissing a leper on the mouth, for example. It is a constant juxtaposition of horror and beauty as they slowly awaken from their protected lives and clouded souls. The god Ganesha appears throughout, taking on different roles and narrating the play, and one actor, billed only as "Man" plays all the other male characters. Ganesha is virtually always present, and in an opening monologue explains that Ganesha is everywhere in everything.

The show opened at MTC Stage One in June of 1993. The production was directed by Joey Tillinger, with sets by Ming Cho Lee and costumes by Santo Loquasto, two major designers of the mid-to-late twentieth century in New York.

The cast included Cuskern as Ganesha, Frances Sternhagen as Margaret, Zoe Caldwell as Katharine, and Fisher Stevens as Man. The casting of Cuskern was an important milestone in his career, and one that Terrence helped to facilitate.

Not surprisingly, after getting his Green Card, his MSW, and starting a career in social work, Cuskern ultimately got burnt out with the pressures of the job. Being a social worker in New York City can be as challenging as being an actor. Cuskern had naturally been cast into theatrical circles through his relationship with Terrence and had begun to get the acting bug. At one point, Michael Wager (Mindy/Mendy from *Lisbon*) was doing a two-week non-paying showcase job, and Terrence suggested that Cuskern go see him about getting a role: "What have you got to lose, right?" Cuskern said:

> It was an all-male version of *The Women* called *City Men*, and they were looking for someone to play the Norma Shearer role. Terrence had said "Dominic could do that."
>
> I went and auditioned. I came directly from work. I had no headshot, no resume no nothing. I'd never been on stage. I just assumed because Michael was in the production, I'd just assumed he told him that this novice was coming. Anyway, he didn't, and they asked me when was the last time I was on stage? What was the last thing you did? I told them I was one of the three Wise Men in the Christmas pageant in second grade.

They laughed, of course, but Cuskern got the part after walking through rehearsals for three days.

After that, he did showcases at night and went to classes and HB Studios. Terrence would come see him, and when they did readings of Terrence's plays, Cuskern would read the stage directions.

He got involved with Brooklyn-based Gallery Players and got cast in another play. He said a lot of celebrities came, but after taking his final bow at the end of the run, he thought it was all over.

> I thought this wonderful thing is never going to be part of my life. And Terrence came back to congratulate me, and he was standing at the door watching me weep. He came up to me and asked if I was okay. I said yes. He asked me what was wrong, and I said I just loved this so much. I love acting.
>
> I'll never forget this. He said, "Well, if you like it that much, you have to keep doing it, but it's going to break your heart."

Cuskern remembers that he wasn't the first choice for the role of Ganesha:

> Lynne was always on the lookout for someone to play Ganesha because she knew I'd never acted professionally, and I think she wanted a "name" to go with the other names. I think they were flying in B.D. Wong and God knows who else to audition, trying to see if they were available.
>
> Eventually, at one final reading Lynne said, "We're still looking for Ganesha," and I'll never forget this. She leaned forward and said, "I think I have our Ganesha." I got the role.

Once again, Meadow went with her gut, and Cuskern's career was off and running . . . even though he wore a mask the entire time, and "the best costume anyone ever wore for anything." Cuskern only took off the mask at the end of the play, and his face was gilded—a man after all.

Casting Zoe Caldwell was an entirely different experience. Terrence had loved her since he had first seen her as Helena in *All's Well That Ends Well* at the Royal Shakespeare Company on a trip to London while he was a student at Columbia. The Australian-born actress had moved to the United States and appeared in leading roles at the Guthrie in Minneapolis and was a member of the Actors Studio. Terrence had also seen her in many plays on Broadway, including her Tony-winning role in the title role of *The Prime of Miss Jean Brodie*. As he usually did, he wrote the part of Katharine with Caldwell's voice in his head, never knowing if she would be available to play it. At the time she took on the role, Joey Tillinger said it was difficult to get into it. Caldwell assured him that "the muscle is not atrophied." She asked for three or weeks, and, as Joey said, "In the third or fourth week, it began to gel, and she was tremendous."

Frances Sternhagen was perfectly matched to Caldwell, and Fisher Stevens was known from films. Joey said that *Ganesh* was almost his favorite of Terrence's plays:

> It's a transitional play for me. He was writing one kind of play when I did *It's Only a Play*, but by the time he got to *Lips Together*, he was trying new ground, a new take on plays and people.
>
> I wasn't initially asked to direct it, and then Lynne called and asked would I do it, and I said yes in a heartbeat.
>
> I didn't know the play, but they did a reading, and I burst into tears at the end of the first act. We had Franny Sternhagen and Zoe Caldwell do the reading. And I thought, why bother to bring me in?

Once again, Terrence's voice heard through the ideal actors was an almost magical combination. The play—and the production—were not without their problems, however. Joey worked with Ming Cho Lee who told him that the problem was that the stage at MTC Stage One was "low and fat," he said. They decided to amplify the structure of the stage, and as Joey remembers, making it longer and using the depth of the stage in ways that it often was not.

The play opened to mixed reviews. Frank Rich in the *New York Times* wrote in summary: "With death everywhere, Mr. McNally cannot be blamed for fighting against helplessness and hopelessness by searching for faith. When he fails to make a convincing case that he has found it, his audience, its own hopes dashed, cannot be blamed for going home with a very heavy heart."

Two weeks later, David Richards published a more positive review in the *Sunday Times*, but by then whatever damage was done could not be undone, though Cuskern speculated that if the two columns had been switched the play might have fared better in the long run. As it always seems to, a critical review in the *Times* tends to scare away money.

Although the MTC box office was strong, and the run was extended. *Ganesh* ultimately did not make a move to Broadway. Joey always assumed it would, given the stars that were in it. Still, the play has not vanished, and it's been revived in various small theaters and gets generally positive reviews. Many of those programs and clippings have been saved in Terrence's archives, more of them than for any other his plays except *Master Class*.

For Terrence, though, the play was an artistic success. As he would say about other shows he worked on, "We accomplished everything we wanted to do with it." And it opened the door to what would arguably be one of his most celebrated plays.

VII.

Among Meadow's wonderful memories of Terrence is that he once gave her son a book of Greek myths, noting in an inscription that these have been around for such a long time because they tell great stories. As Meadow said, what drove Terrence was telling stories.

Terrence was in residence with MTC for at least twelve years, Meadow says, and she was always eager to see what he was going to do next.

Shortly after *Ganesh* opened, Terrence was in Meadows's office, and she asked him, "What are we going to do this year?"

I said, "What play are you going to do?" And he said, "Give me a piece of paper." So I gave him a piece of paper and he wrote down Love (period), Valour (period), Compassion (period).

I said, "That sounds interesting," and he said, "I think it will be."

True to Terrence's style, he had the title, and a lot of ideas, but writing the title in Meadow's office was an important step in getting the entire play down on paper.

Even as Terrence was working on crafting his story about eight gay men on three weekends over a summer, the world inside and outside the theater was changing.

Angels in America had been working its way to Broadway through regional and London productions since 1991. The first of two plays, *Millennium Approaches* finally opened in May 1993 at the Walter Kerr Theatre about a month before *A Perfect Ganesh* bowed at MTC. The second play *Perestroika* opened that December, and the two parts subsequently ran in repertory until December 1994. It was the hottest ticket on Broadway.

Subtitled *A Gay Fantasia on American Themes*, Tony Kushner's sprawling, passionate work was written in response to the AIDS crisis. It is lyrical, harsh, and an often in-your-face condemnation of a political system that allowed an entire generation to suffer. Mixing myths, political figures, and the story of a young man dying of AIDS, it created a sensation and in many respects put an end to delineating plays as "gay theater," at least for much of the culture. Terrence certainly felt that and was glad it had done so. Highly intellectual, argumentative, and tremendous in scale, the two plays of *Angels* became the Broadway event of the season. (This is, of course, a simplification of the play and its impact on the culture, and there are many fine works about *Angels* and its impact on late twentieth-century theater.) Significantly, though *Angels* would walk off with Tony Awards for actors, play, and director, it began its life in the nonprofit world as a commission for the nonprofit Center Theater Group in Los Angeles and would premiere in San Francisco. As with

MTC, the vision and passion of an art-centered theater would propel the form in ways that the commercial theater simply isn't set up to do.

Angels was the very antithesis of Terrence's work. He called the work "high art," as a means of distinguishing it from his own work, and he appreciated historic context. However, it was not the kind of play he wrote, or the stories he liked to tell. Where Kushner reached for global scope, Terrence kept things closer to home—expressing his inherent operatic impulses in the development of his characters. As *Love! Valour! Compassion!* (now with exclamation points instead of periods) developed, obviously the characters were gay. What Terrence explored, however, was the unique bonds that developed among gay men in the years before marriage, in the chosen family so many created—out of both love and necessity—and how they responded to the AIDS crisis. Terrence said he hadn't set out to write a play about AIDS, but to avoid the impact it was having, the fear it engendered and the existential questions around the disease would have been impossible. Whereas Kushner cast his play against a cultural backdrop and challenged audiences intellectually, Terrence cast *L!V!C!* against the hearts of his characters and along the way opening the hearts of his audiences.

The play was a logical next step after *Ganesh*. Underneath the bitchiness, musical comedy quotes, zingers, and laughs was an existential examination of what it meant to be a gay man at this time in history. There is the same sense of coming to terms with tragedy and loss and the inevitable sorrows of life—as well as its joys and laughs along the way as in the previous play. There is no Ganesha to guide the way or clear obstacles, that the eight gay men have to do for themselves—or not. Yet just as Ganesha talked to the audience in the previous play, here the characters speak for themselves as Terrence continued to explore what it meant to experience theater, where the inherent falseness of the form can still tell truths. It was one of the most constant themes of his career.

It was also a time of great personal happiness for Terrence. In 1993, he had begun a relationship with Gary Bonasorte, a playwright and one of the founders of the Rattlestick Theater Company, an Off-Broadway troupe that was dedicated to developing new writers. Terrence knew that Gary was HIV-positive from the time they met, which surely influenced some of the meditations on mortality in *L!V!C!* and the persistent theme of the possibility of deep love in the face of inescapable death.

There isn't much plot to *L!V!C!*, but there's a lot of character. The three acts of the play take place in an upstate New York house, Dutchess County, a gay enclave two hours from Manhattan. The house belongs to Gregory, a choreographer who lives there with his young, blind lover, Bobby. They are joined for the weekends by Perry and Arthur, who have been a couple for many years, the twins John and James Jeckyll, John's young boyfriend Ramon, and Buzz, a single man and musical theater fan, though "fan" is an understatement. Buzz is the kind of character whose identity and worldview wasn't just inspired by musicals; it was shaped by them. Like Terrence's wishing that Gertrude Lawrence from *The King and I* could have been his own mother, Buzz's longing for happiness that seems just beyond his grasp and the resulting heartbreak that he knows it's fiction is instantly relatable. There is a kind of cruel realization that life is never like a musical, and particularly for gay men who grew up in homes where they either had to hide or were rejected for being "different" in an era before the world allowed them to be themselves, there is an anger that's never quite resolved. At least, that's the case for Buzz.

Over the course of the three weekends, infidelities happen, fights break out, illness is revealed, and yet beneath it all there is a deep bond between these men as they grapple with their individual hopes, disappointments, and struggle to get through life and cope with AIDS. It is on some levels a bleak play, but it's also one where the characters have grabbed joy from a world not overly inclined to give it to them. In the writing, Terrence grapples with the realities of long-term friendships, expectations, whether gay men can—or should—lead heteronormative lives, and what it means to love platonically confronted by the specter of inevitable loss. In a world where same-sex marriage is (at least for a time) a given, where there is broader acceptance by parents of queer kids, where for many being gay is as unremarkable as one's eye color; the idea of a tight community of gay men may seem distant. At the time of

L!V!C!, however, it wasn't just a gang of pals, it was a social structure that allowed people to be themselves, yet always with the knowledge that they were different, outsiders from the main event. Terrence was keenly aware of this. After all, he had lived it.

The structure of the play intersperses scenes with the characters speaking directly to the audience, including at the end as we learn how each character dies. There are a lot of funny lines, and a speech by Buzz about how he'd like to see musicals reflect the way the world really is— bleak and depressing. However, as often happens with Terrence's work, the most powerful line is the simplest. As the character Gregory says at the end as each talks about what happened to them, "I. Um. Bury every one of you. Um. It got. Um Awfully lonely out there."

For gay men whose chosen families were decimated by AIDS, that halting line carried in it more than a decade of fear, hope, and loss. It may now be difficult to remember that expressing one's love could also be signing one's death warrant. Terrence knew. Perhaps the most remembered image from the play is the cast in tutus. Gregory has convinced his friends to perform an excerpt from *Swan Lake* for an AIDS benefit, and while they may complain, they do it. It's more than just camp, however, it is the culmination of everything that has gone before: the insistence on being seen, which is what had driven Terrence from the time he was twirling to musical records in his parents' living room.

Although Nathan Lane would be nominated for a Tony for his performance and win the Drama Desk Award for it, the part of Buzz wasn't written for him, though Terrence said everyone always assumed that. He had actually written the part for Charles Busch who he said had called him up and asked if he would write a part for him. Busch was known and loved by New York audiences for his over-the-top pieces in which he played the leading lady celebrating camp sensitivity. He had most recently, however, played Solange in a production of *The Maids* at Classic Stage. By the mid-nineties, however, his brand of camp was no longer the draw it had been, and he wanted to play a man. He was tired of being in drag all the time. Terrence thought that Buzz would be an ideal transition, as Buzz had just enough camp to be funny and just enough soul to be real.

As the play was in development, Meadow arranged a first reading that lasted nearly three and a half hours ("at least," she said). Charles Busch read the part of Buzz, and Nathan read the parts of the twins. Terrence was always enrolling actors he loved to do readings, whether or not they would ultimately play the parts. Lane had done the reading as a friend because Terrence wanted to hear the characters.

After some edits, a second, formal reading was staged for industry people, which was in the Stage Two space at City Center. Nathan Lane, who attended only to be in the audience, recalls that there were about 125 people there, and he was there to support his friends—and Jerry Zaks, the director with a string of Tonys and a reputation for comedy was directing. Lane had suggested Zaks to Meadow as the director:

> They were having trouble finding a director, I don't know why. I was doing *Laughter on the 23rd Floor*, the Neil Simon play, and Jerry was directing it. He was complaining that he was only considered for comedy, and he had done *Six Degrees of Separation* and other kinds of plays. I said, I know a play that would be interesting to you.

Zaks met with Meadow, and he was directing the reading. It seemed like all systems were go, and Lane continues the story:

> We're waiting for about 25 minutes and nothing's happening. I see Terrence and Jerry walking up the aisle to me, and they say, "David Drake was supposed to play Buzz and is stuck in traffic. He can't get here, and we don't want to keep these people waiting much longer. Would you read the part?"
>
> And I had played the other part [John and James Jeckyll] before, but I had a vague memory of the play, and I said, "Yeah, sure if it will help." So I go down, and of course Jerry had already worked on the script for three days. So we start, and it's a great part. I'm

killing, and it's like I've done it for years. I'm having a grand time. Then in the middle of the first act, I look over and David Drake has arrived and he's sitting in a chair in the corner and I'm thinking, "Oh, this is awkward." And then I figured he'll take over, and I can sit down. Jerry and Terrence come over and said we think it would be too upsetting to switch actors in the middle of the reading. And I said, "Oh, man, David Drake will never talk to me again," but I said, "Okay, whatever helps."

The reading was a huge success. John Glover, who won a Tony for playing the twins, said missing the reading "was the biggest mistake of his [Drake's] career." Lane was sure that Zaks would sign on as the director, but ultimately he declined. Charles Busch called Terrence and was upset that he wanted to withdraw from playing Buzz. He had been offered the chance to develop his first mainstream play *The Tale of the Allergist's Wife* for MTC, and he thought his future might be more in playwriting—in fact, saying that he wanted to be a playwright "more than anything." Though Terrence could take it very personally when people abandoned him—or at least he felt abandoned—he let Busch off the hook, wishing him the best in a difficult career. Terrence recalled saying, "It's so hard to get a play on these days, you have my blessing. I won't be mad at you." (Busch's play would have a successful run at MTC in 1990 and transfer to Broadway where it would get three Tony nominations.) Now, there was only one option for Buzz . . . Nathan.

Lane agreed to do the part, but there was one more hitch:

Terrence called me and said, you're going to have to sign a nudity clause. And I said, "No, I won't be signing a nudity clause because I won't be doing any nudity." I said I had read the part of the script where it says he comes in naked serving drinks. I said, "That's not going to happen. No one needs to see that; it'll only be traumatic for the subscribers."

And also, by the way and more importantly, it's not funny. So I said here's what I'll do. The character is a costume designer. He goes off and improvises an amusing costume to serve drinks. So I said I'll wear an apron, high heels, sweat socks, a big picture hat, and sunglasses. I won't have anything on underneath. That was amusing to me.

Lane proved again to an ideal collaborator who knew how to make a moment land—as he had done bringing Mendy back in the second act of *Lisbon*. When he came on in that getup at an invited dress rehearsal, he remembers he got the longest laugh he'd ever received on stage. He would bend over to serve drinks, and the audience would see his ass, and the laugh would go back up again. He said that Stephen Spinella as Perry, who had the next line, kept trying to cut off the laugh. Every time he did, however, Nathan would stick his ass in Spinella's face again, and the laugh just continued.

Before they got to that point, however, they would have to find a director. Zaks ultimately withdrew, but Meadow was committed to doing the play. She had read it and loved it, though she remembered that given the scope and the subject matter, "*Love! Valour! Compassion!* was a giant leap, and people said I was crazy to do it, but I knew what Terrence was trying to do, and I embraced what he was trying to do." The show, as they say, went on.

It was about this time that Meadow was diagnosed with breast cancer, and she would have to address that, which would take her away from the rehearsal process. She had called the producer Rocco Landesman and given him the play. He said to Meadow, "What happens in this play, Lynne?"

"And I said, 'What happens in *Uncle Vanya*?' And he said, 'okay.'"

While she was in the hospital, she got a call from Michael Bush, the associate artistic director who had gone to see the work of another director they had been considering. Bush suggested instead that they seriously consider a young director Joe Mantello who had been an actor who had appeared in the original cast of *Angels* and been nominated for a Tony—and who had recently directed a successful production of a play by Jon Robin Baitz, Mantello's life partner at the time.

The problem with the play everyone acknowledged was that it was supposed to take place in a sprawling summer house, and the challenge of putting that on the stage was monumental. Mantello envisioned that the play would be done with a model of a house on the stage and the rest on a green carpet, with set pieces when necessary for each scene. The inherent theatricality of that appealed to Terrence, and Mantello got the job. Loy Arcenas designed the final set.

Mantello said that the inspiration for the set came from his work with Circle Repertory and Naked Angels where they didn't have a lot of money.

> So the idea of being inside a house, and then in canoes and underwater would be prohibitive. I thought we'll just figure out a way to do it, and I think Terrence responded to that sense of playfulness, and it aligned with his sense of simplicity.
>
> I think the things that Terrence always loved about his work and in other people's work was when you didn't throw money at something and you relied on a kind of theatrical imagination. Because that was something I'd always done up to that point, it never occurred to me to approach it any other way.

The cast gathered around the house model, clearly showing that the lives and hearts of the men were bigger than the house.

Those who were there remember the five-week rehearsal process as one of the most joyful they had experienced. There was an immediate camaraderie among the cast, and they all knew they were involved in something that was very special.

It was a longer-than-usual process, Mantello recalls, and he thought that was perhaps because Meadow was familiar with the way Terrence worked, that he did a lot of rewriting in rehearsal.

> Terrence felt very confident—in a blind confidence kind of way with my ability to direct it. I'm not so sure that the power that be at the Manhattan Theatre Club were as enthusiastic.

It was pure bliss. We worked really hard, but I have to say—and I think it may have been my naiveté—but I was just not intimidated by it. Honestly, if I were approaching the same material now, I would, I think, be paralyzed.

Terrence did some really great writing toward the end, and the underwater scenes were jettisoned.

Like other Terrence scripts, Mantello thought that the script had been pretty unwieldy through workshops and drafts, but by the time he got it, the shape of it was pretty well established.

John Glover remembers that "everyone was there for the play to serve the play." The only tensions came from serving the play. Glover remembers that at one point he thought Lane was mad at him, finally asking him about it. As it turned out Lane thought Glover was stepping on one of his laughs, though Glover thought he should be getting a laugh at the same time. They worked it out. Both got the laughs, and as Glover recalled, "I don't know if maybe there were two smaller ones as opposed to his big one. I don't know." These are the things that happen in rehearsals, and Lane and Glover were very close.

Glover wasn't always slated to play the twins. At one point Terrence called him and said they were having trouble casting Gregory, the choreographer. Glover, of course, said okay, but then, he says, they found Stephen Bogardus, who was, he said, brilliant.

He's a black belt in jujitsu and his wife Dana was a Fosse dancer, and after we were doing previews, I would see Dana and Bogey down on the 50th Street subway waiting for the train and she was giving him pointers on the station platform, such as how to point your toe better and stuff like that.

It was a big deal for Glover to play a gay man, two gay men, as well. Several years earlier he had withdrawn from another MTC production because as his TV career was taking off he couldn't risk being seen as gay. It was only during *L!V!C!* that Glover and Meadow talked about the issue; she had thought he didn't like her as a director, he said. It was a big deal.

> I pulled out my contract one night when I couldn't sleep, and I was reading through it. And there's this morality clause—moral turpitude—and I called my agent. I don't know how late it was at night. I called her up in a panic saying, "What if they found out I'm gay?" And she just laughed and said this is all left over from the Fatty Arbuckle days.

Arbuckle was a silent film star, who in 1920 was arrested for murder, and though he was ultimately acquitted, the scandal surrounding the death of actress Victoria Rappe electrified Hollywood—and the nation. Something had happened in a private hotel room, and Rappe died several days later. Arbuckle's alleged tryst came to symbolize casual morality of the post–World War I world, particularly among show people—an age-old presumption. In response, Hollywood executives afraid they would be tarred with the same brush, instituted "moral turpitude" clauses in contracts to protect themselves. Turpitude has been interpreted many ways, however, so even in 1994, being gay might qualify for a dismissal. Thus, it was a relief to Glover that he could participate without precipitating in a potential scandal. He loved doing the play, the company, and the writing. Terrence, he said, believes in passion, and passionate characters are always fun for an actor to play.

Billy Barnes, who was the production stage manager, remembered that there were lots and lots of rewrites as the play was developing, and said he was always coming to rehearsals with excitement and love and joy, and he believed in the production so much and he loved the stage managers and the crew.

Barnes remembered specifically two scenes that were added in rehearsal. In one, James exposes one of his Karposi Sarcoma lesions to Buzz, and Buzz kisses it. Both characters have been told they have AIDS—and that they probably should have already died. It is so potent because it asserted the power and possibility of love in the face of inevitable death. Terrence was deeply aware of this, knowing that his lover Gary was HIV-positive, and at the same time it addressed the reality that was a constant in the lives of young, gay men, an entire generation of men who could finally be themselves only to find they were untimely doomed.

The second was when Terrence added what is probably the most-often cited speech from the play. John Benjamin Hickey, who played Arthur, says that one day during rehearsals Nathan said, "There needs to be something for this character here." He says that Terrence went away for a day or two and came back with the speech for Buzz. Lane read it cold, and everyone was thrilled—and a bit in awe. Hickey said, "The first time Nathan did it, all of us just sat there with our mouths on the floor at how perfect it was. It was truly an 11 o'clock number." It's very near the end. In it Buzz is challenged by Perry that "musicals don't always have happy endings."

> Yes, they do. That's why I like them, even the sad ones. The orchestra plays, the characters die, the audience cries, the curtain falls, the actors get up off the floor, the audience puts on their coats, and everyone goes home feeling better. That's a happy ending, Perry.

He goes on to imagine a series of classic musicals where truly awful things happen to the characters. It's both screamingly funny and a *cri de coeur* of a man who has been betrayed by the very thing that made his life possible, and a realization that he is going to die, "Soon. Sooner than I thought, actually," which is how he sums up his life at the end of the play. Buzz is, understandably angry, and the character Perry thinks that Buzz is angry at him because he's not infected, and it's unfair. Buzz responds, saying:

> I can't afford to be fair. Fair's a luxury. Fair is for healthy people with healthy lovers in nice apartments with lots of health insurance, which of course, they don't need. But God forbid someone like me or James should have it.

In the boldness and honesty of these speeches, Terrence once again gives voice to things that aren't spoken about. AIDS, of course and as noted, is the thing "out there" that permeates the lives of every one of the characters. It was a constant for Terrence as well as he had to go through his life, write, get plays on, and know that the man he loved was facing his early curtain.

Though Lane refused to appear nude, there was nudity in the piece. As Hickey remembers,

> We were all so vain, not to mention young, and there was just endless talk about being naked and how we felt about ourselves and our bodies and whether or not we had, you know, achieved the perfect look.
>
> The cast was about half and half gay and straight. I don't remember. That was back at a time when people would come back after and ask who was gay and who's straight. You don't really get those questions any more.
>
> But by the end of the run, we were so familiar and intimate with each other that you could walk up to one of your castmates stark naked and be like, "Does my penis look okay tonight? I don't know. I've got to go out there in front of 800 people, and I feel weird about my dick tonight."
>
> You really did have these discussions based on the fact that you were about to parade yourself [in front of an audience]. It was all very quick, but you achieve a kind of intimacy with people you otherwise wouldn't achieve, whether it's stage management or the backstage crew.
>
> And that water. It was important for the water to be very warm. I will leave it to your readers to understand why you would want that.
>
> There was a scene where Ramon and my character come up out of the water, and we lie on this raft naked. We had to get wet backstage, so we would stand in a bucket of water, and the stage management would dump water on us. There was a ladder that took

us right up onto the stage from the basement of the Walter Kerr. I barely even remember how we did it at MTC.

The play had a lot of logistical challenges for designers and stage managers. Barnes remembers the pool in both locations, and how it had to be treated like a regular pool with balancing chemicals and making sure that the water was not, as Hickey put it, "funky." It became a running joke.

Barnes also remembered that there were many other challenges at MTC. In a scene where Hickey as Arthur joined Ramon on a raft in the middle of the lake, in order to make that work on the shallow MTC stage, Hickey had to lie down on a dolly, which on a cue was pulled to center stage, where Hickey could pop up on the raft.

The play opened at MTC in October 1994, and it was an immediate hit. The ensemble was praised unilaterally, and Lane in particular was singled out for his performance as Buzz. Far from being the "workhorse" part, Buzz is the pithy, snarky character every gay man of a certain age was trying to be at the time, battling over more obscure references to old musicals. The difference, of course, is that at the end of all the delicious excesses, what Buzz fears most is dying alone. He spoke for a generation of men.

Hickey, Glover, and even Terrence were a bit surprised that the play was such a hit. They thought that it would play its run at MTC, and that would be that. What they hadn't, perhaps, counted on was that the universal theme of love, finding love, and facing mortality is present to all people. That the characters were gay was becoming incidental, somewhat, at least to a presumably liberal, sophisticated New York audience. Nonetheless, the critics lagged behind as they do, and Mantello remembered feeling that some of the reviews said the play was good, even though it was about gay people, something he quickly added would not happen in 2022.

The upshot, though, was that Terrence was finally moving away from tagged as a "gay playwright" to being understood as an observer of human condition, of the big issues of survival, love, and death. The irony, of course, is that Terrence hadn't changed in how he was approaching these issues. That he was considered a pioneer in this and that his early vision had been daring, exotic, or controversial were labels that perhaps helped critics contextualize what Terrence was doing, but they were unable to grasp his vision, see beyond their biases (while pandering to conventional cultural thinking to sell papers), or understand that the zeitgeist was evolving. Terrence had arrived there first, and with the response to *L!V!C!*, it became apparent that the world had caught up to the artist's vision, and, not completely, was able to hear him in new ways.

In a word, what Terrence did with *L!V!C!* was monumental. Here, for the first time, were gay characters who could not be played solely for comedy, who were real human beings and who were not symbols. They were not political statements, nor were they the picture of a marginalized subculture outside the mainstream, as the characters in Mart Crowley's 1968 play *The Boys in the Band* were. As Meadow said, Terrence's great skill was as a storyteller who told stories from the heart. In this big and emotional play that moved so many people, he did as much for equality and acceptance of gay people as any parade or protest; he wrote people who could not be dismissed.

The play transferred to Broadway the following January, and it was a huge hit. Mantello, and others, remembered the opening night party at the Russian Tea Room, an elegant, old-school haunt of New York theater folks. Indeed, Mantello described it as the end of an era—the last of the parties where reviews from the early editions of the papers were read aloud to the people present. Meadow was back from her cancer treatment for the Broadway opening, having missed the opening at MTC, and she was obviously excited to have yet another McNally hit on her hands.

Vincent Canby's review was pretty much a rave, hailing the Broadway transfer and openly stating that he would not have thought it was fare for Broadway (a powerful statement):

> This is not the sort of thing you might expect to draw Broadway's
> usual big spenders. Yet *Love! Valour! Compassion!* is written, directed

and acted with such theatrical skill and emotional range that it's as broadly entertaining as it is moving. . . . Would *Love! Valour! Compassion!* have the same impact if it were about heterosexuals instead of homosexuals? Of course not. Mr. McNally hasn't written a play about gay people living straight lives. It's a comedy about some comparatively privileged gay people in a world whose problems are ultimately shared by everyone. Though particular, as all good plays are, it's not parochial.

The language is very much of its time, but it was a time that was changing. The play would run at the Walter Kerr for 276 performances, with Mario Cantone stepping in for Lane after about three months, and Stephen Spinella, who had played the role of Perry at MTC but wasn't available for the Broadway run, was taken over by Anthony Heald.

The transfer is significant from a show *business* perspective as well because it was the first play produced under the Broadway Alliance to recoup its investment. The Broadway Alliance was a program that was founded in 1990 and was designed to limit costs. A show had to be produced for $400,000 or less (a great deal less than the capitalization of a typical show at the time), tickets were capped at $45, and everyone agreed to take reduced salaries until such time as the show recouped.

Without this program, it's unlikely that *L!V!C!* would have been able to move, or it would have strained Meadow and her team to attract investors. It turned out to be a great move all around. Terrence won his first Tony for best play. John Glover won for featured actor, and Joe Mantello, Anthony Heald, and Stephen Bogardus all received nominations.

VIII.

In the intervening years between *L!V!C!* and his next outing with MTC, Terrence had been anything but lazy. Indeed, it was one of his most prolific—and acclaimed—periods. After *Frankie and Johnny*, in 1992, he wrote the book for *Kiss of the Spider Woman*, for which he won the

Tony, saw a successful production of *It's Only a Play* in Los Angeles, had written *Master Class*, for which he won his third Tony, and won his fourth Tony for the book of *Ragtime*. We'll talk about all of these in due course.

However, he still had a home at MTC, and Meadow had slotted him in for a new play in 1995. It would be a play that would rack up another string of firsts for Terrence, MTC, and the New York theater community, but they would not be happy ones.

With four Tony Awards, commercial success, and an ever-growing number of other awards and tributes bestowed upon him, Terrence by this time was at the top of his game, easily one of the most prominent American playwrights of the latter half of the twentieth century. His works were being taught in schools, staged around the world, and he had watched LGBTQ+ people become more visible and more accepted in the culture, in part thanks to Terrence "normalizing" gay relationships—or showing them as fraught and funny as straight ones. He was still being pigeonholed as a "gay playwright," but there wasn't much he could do about that. Well, except keep writing.

As Terrence approached sixty, he became more and more concerned about his productivity and began writing even more. He told his friend Edgar Bronfman Jr. that he was terrified of slowing down, and that he was determined to write a script a year . . . at least. He didn't want a life where he was reliving older plays, and that he wanted to continue to write plays that were fresh and remain engaged.

There certainly was enough going on in the culture. In 1996, President Bill Clinton had signed the Defense of Marriage Act, which defined marriage for federal purposes as between one man and one woman, something which upset him terribly. It was another way that people were being marginalized—and forced to hide. It had followed the policy of "Don't Ask, Don't Tell" implemented in 1993 and that allowed gay people to serve in the military—if they hid. At the same time, anti-gay rhetoric was becoming the *lingua franca* of the Evangelical Right in the United States, and in addition to heightened language was a surefire way to rake in donations. Many a megachurch, and quasi-religious social action organization, not to say grift, was built on the rock of the mite of people terrified that "the gays" were coming for them and their children. It was not only the Protestants, however, who were annoying Terrence; the Catholic Church was experiencing its own sex abuse scandals, which would only grow in later years. Terrence clipped and saved articles from the *New York Times* that detailed these horrors, and the callous defenses mounted by the church.

He was appalled by the hypocrisy of the church to a certain degree, but he was also increasingly aware that in the climate at that time, the doors of traditional religion were barred to gay people. They were not welcome, and if they wanted to participate in a community of faith, they could not do so wholly; they would have to hide their true natures.

At a time in his career when he could have written virtually anything, could have used his talents to write another comedy, another starry two-hander, he instead chose—as he had done with *Next* two decades earlier—to address what he saw as a gross injustice and cultural blindness to suffering.

Terrence being Terrence, as we've said, he didn't shout his politics from the rafters, he made the issue personal. Rather than taking up arms against a sea of Pharisees, he created a world where everyone was welcome, where a life of the spirit was not barred to people because of who they were, but rather it was a kind of spiritual come as you are, and you will be embraced.

The result was *Corpus Christi*, a sometimes gentle, sometimes confrontational, sometimes funny, yet always contemporary retelling of the Gospel story of Christ. Well, if not quite contemporary, many of the references are to the culture of the 1950s when Terrence was in high school, so let's just say "modern." Terrence places Joshua (the Hebrew name for Jesus is Yeshua, which translates to Joshua in English) in Corpus Christi, Texas. There are some autobiographical asides, such as digs at football being the center of life in town and that "all boys in Corpus Christi play football," mentions of Mrs. McElroy, and an appearance by Peggy Dobbins (née Powell). Joshua marries two men, and the recurring theme throughout is that Joshua asks each person to see and respect the divinity in one another. It is a story of love and acceptance. It is not unlike Terrence's response to AIDS, where ignorance and intolerance had a catastrophic effect on individual lives. Though an indifferent Catholic in practice, what apparently baffled Terrence was the hypocrisy of organized religions. For all his artistry (as Alfie Byrne says in *A Man of No Importance*, "We take the crude clay of reality and shape it into art"), Terrence was quite literal in starting from a scriptural base, looking to no less a source than the Gospel of Matthew in the Bible (chapter 22: 33–40, KJV).

> Then one of them, which was a lawyer, asked him a question, tempting him, and saying, Master, which is the great commandment in the law? Jesus said unto him, Thou shalt love the Lord thy God with all thy heart, and with all thy soul, and with all thy mind. This is the first and great commandment. And the second is like unto it, Thou shalt love thy neighbour as thyself. On these two commandments hang all the law and the prophets.

(The phrase "Corpus Christi," for those who don't know Latin, translates into "body of Christ." In the Latin Mass, the prayer of consecration includes Jesus saying, "hoc est corpus meum quod pro vobis datur," which many Christians recognize as what Christ is supposed to have said at the Last Supper, "This is my body, which is given for you.")

As he saw how religion was being used as a weapon against gay people, and that Christianity was being corrupted for political posturing, writing the play was thus a deeply personal mission for him, based in his own journey from the dogma of the church to the more spiritual life he discovered in India.

> I grew up more as a Christian more than a Roman Catholic, and I think most of what Christ tried to teach us is valuable. I'm glad I have that in my DNA, but I never took a lot of the mythology of the church seriously.
>
>   I guess everybody was an altar boy, but I wanted to be an altar boy because I loved the costume, and I loved to show off, frankly.

I was the generation where we still did the Mass in Latin, so I did it phonetically. I didn't know what I was saying, and I could speed through the mass really fast. I didn't know what I was saying. And serving communion.

Of course you're taught that if the sacrament, even the tiniest fragment of it, falls, it's like atomic. But I never believed any of that stuff. If I ate meat on Friday and got hit by a car, I'm not going to hell. And I'm not even sure if I ever believed in hell like that. And the nuns made it pretty graphic . . . put your hand in a candle and hold it for five seconds, and that's what your whole body feels like forever and ever.

Terrence's take on the Gospel, inevitably, would be consistent with how he approached all his work—from a deeply personal standpoint. Consistent with his other work, something "out there" is inescapable, unknown, and dangerous. Joshua is aware of this and that will ultimately take his earthly life. It is a constant hammering offstage as the cross on which he will be crucified is constructed.

> **Joshua:** All My life I've heard hammering. Like someone is build-
> ing something and they never stop. Something for Me. And they're
> waiting for Me to what? I don't know.

It is also a play that is conscious that it is a play. The actors at the beginning introduce themselves by their own names. According to the stage directions, they are on stage from the beginning, and the play starts with three thumps (as is the French tradition from the time of Molière).

It is not overtly political. Perhaps the most political it gets is in Judas's first speech:

> No one has ever told this story right. Even when they get the facts
> right, the feeling is wrong. One and one are two. So what? What
> does that tell you about anything? This is what matters. *(Judas hits
> his right hand onto his chest.)* The only thing. Nothing else. People

can't stand the truth. They want their Joshua, seen through their eyes, told through their lies. Truth is brutal. It scalds. It stings.

That comment aside, most of the play is about the desire to belong, to fit, to be validated. It would, however, be naïve to think that it would not be controversial. Religion is a "lightning rod" issue. It attracts controversy, and anything that challenges a specific cohort's orthodoxy is a target for criticism and the easy outrage that was becoming more and more a part of all public discourse in these years—any topic that could generate headlines and sell papers. Just ten years earlier, photographer Andres Serrano had created international controversy over a photograph of a crucifix in the photographer's urine. The "Piss Christ" sparked outrage around the world. A year later, the film *The Last Temptation of Christ* had protesters marching around movie theaters. Organizations like the Catholic League ramped up their vociferous outrage to decry what they saw as attacks on Roman Catholics—and raise funds.

Of all the plays Meadow and Terrence worked on together—fourteen premieres in all—*Corpus Christi*, she said, this is the one that took the longest. She wasn't completely sure why, but she said the time was a measure of the thinking and personal investment he had in the piece. She added that the slot for the play in the MTC schedule started in 1995, and it wasn't ready, and then it was announced for both 1996 and 1997. Finally, it was ready for the 1998 season.

Meadow said that she never commented on a play until she had heard it read. As she had always done with Terrence's work, she knew that they needed to work on it and have readings. When the play was finally set for the 1998 season, they had a reading. After the reading, she, Terrence, and Joe Mantello went to discuss the play in a conference room at MTC. According to Meadow,

> I said we need to work on the play, and this play is going to create a firestorm, but we need to be able to work on the play, too. We have to make sure that we can really stand up because we're going to take flack for doing it, but I believe in it. So, let's go in knowing.

We agreed. The play was just a draft, and Terrence is an incredible re-writer—and an incredible writer.

Meadow's concern—with which she says Terrence and Mantello agreed—was that the play needed to be more developed, "put more flesh and bones into the characters, so it wasn't just a statement or a protest. It needed more depth than just the assertion that Jesus was gay." She didn't want the play to be a protest or an assertion of an idea the public had not—and most likely would not—embrace or even accept.

Looking back, Mantello felt that it was a pretty benign play that if anything is incredibly earnest and about someone struggling to find their place in spirituality and personalize their own kind of spirituality. And so it came from what he called "a really delicate place" in Terrence.

Mantello said that he believed that at that point in the process, Terrence was on to something important in the play but that it needed to "cook a bit more." After that meeting, he said MTC was on the brink of postponing the play for purely creative reasons. Meadow even said that had it been a "normal" situation, they would have simply postponed the production, which would have given them the time to work on it . . . and then all hell broke loose.

As Meadow recalled, "We left that room with the intention of going our separate ways to do work on the piece, and in a matter of hours after we got out of the room, the Catholic League somehow got ahold of a script.

We gave actors the script [at the reading]. We didn't say, "You have to leave the script here." We didn't know what they would do.

Suddenly, as Mantello recalled, it became a tabloid story:

> I hesitate to call him a journalist, but this man Ward Morehouse stumbled onto the story. As I remember he overheard two actors. We had done a workshop of it. He overheard two actors discussing the workshop, and he published something in the *Post*, about a gay Jesus play and Jesus has sex with his apostles. And he started this firestorm.

It quickly got blown up—as scandals in New York, and especially about Jesus tend to do. Worse, the *Post* story relied on an "unnamed source" who had attended a reading and described the play as it was at the time.

In addition to Morehouse continuing to batter the play in the *Post*, which of course sold papers, the Catholic League jumped into the fray. And, Mantello said, due to the controversy, the play, ready or not, was fast-tracked for production.

The Catholic League is a lay Catholic organization, which is not sanctioned by the Vatican. Founded in 1973, its mission has been to defend the Catholic Church from any criticism or denigration. It was also a big business. At the time, the organization's president Bill Donahue pulled down a salary approaching half a million dollars, and in 2022 the group reported taking in more than a million in donations. Terrence was very much aware of Donahue, "His father was a yellow journalist and takes full credit for getting Mae West and the cast of her play *Sex* arrested." As it turned out, West was able to leverage her arrest and ten-day sentence for maximum publicity value, which only enhanced her career.

MTC was not so lucky. Donahue began a program of what can only be described as stochastic terrorism against Terrence and MTC, inciting protests and outrage and death threats against Terrence and the company. The Catholic League went even further, as reported by *Playbill* at the time. Though they claimed not to have read the script (here recollections vary as to whether they indeed had a copy or not), according to people involved in the production, the Catholic League demanded rewrites, and press releases from the time say that Donahue had personally written to every government official to demand that they cut off any government support for MTC. They were looking to fill their own coffers as well. Mantello remembered that flyers protesting the play also had a call for donations. The postcard said, "Terrence McNally or Manhattan Theatre Club is doing a play where Jesus is a homosexual having sex on stage with his apostles. Would you like to donate $1, $5, $10? Please send your check to . . . ," he said.

The controversy confused Terrence. The Catholic League's "job was to go out and defend the Catholic Church, which I found so strange.

Where's it ever been written that Jesus Christ was Roman Catholic? None of the other churches said a word."

Faced with all of this, Meadow felt she had no choice but to postpone the production. She had hoped to wait for the "hullabaloo" to die down. She had even suggested moving the play to Stage Two where it would not attract so much attention, but Mantello felt the space was not right, for a very practical reason. The smaller stage in that theater could not accommodate thirteen men ranged across it. In other words, it would be impossible to portray the Last Supper on that stage.

Meadow was essentially caught. After all, given the rage that Morehouse and Donahue had fomented—and the flames of it they continued to fan—Meadow's priority had to be protecting her audience. On May 22, MTC announced that they were withdrawing the play from production, citing security concerns. Meadow was roundly criticized for making safety their concern, but she thought, "what if one person gets hurt?" It wasn't an option.

Contemporary readers may think that was a sound decision. After all, in 2022, attendees at Broadway shows routinely go through metal detectors and have their bags searched. A whole generation has been born and come of age in a world where security screenings in virtually any public situation are the norm. In a world where mass shootings are a regular occurrence, where an author can be stabbed on stage by a religious zealot, erring on the side of caution makes sense.

However, in New York nearly three years before 9/11, Donahue and his ilk were considered "crackpots," as Mantello called them. The fear, however, was real. A few years earlier, MTC had invited Salman Rushdie to read in their "Writers in Performance" series. A fatwa had been issued against the author by Ayatollah Khomeni accusing him of blasphemy against Islam and offering a bounty for killing him of $3 million, and MTC had gone to great lengths to provide security. Rushdie ultimately decided not to come, and Meadow recalls that MTC was "vilified" for going to extremes in providing the security. (It turns out, however, that in 2022, Rushdie was stabbed multiple times before giving a lecture in upstate New York.)

In withdrawing *Corpus Christi*, MTC was immediately accused of censorship, that they were silencing the voice of one of the theater's most admired playwrights and reliable moneymakers. As loud as the Catholic League was in damning the play and its supposed blasphemy (with no citations ever provided, which lends credence to the idea that the protestors had not read the script), theater people were just as loud in castigating MTC for censorship. Athol Fugard withdrew his play from MTC, and there were public statements from playwrights Larry Kramer, Tony Kushner, Craig Lucas, Marsha Norman, Lanford Wilson, Wendy Wasserstein, and actors and other theater people. Terrence, too, felt that he was being censored, just as he had with *Bump* during its production at the University of Minnesota, thirty-four years previously. A May 28 op-ed in the *New York Times* accused Meadow of "capitulating" to the critics, validating, at least in the public mind, that MTC was engaged in censorship.

Meadow was in that proverbial dilemma—damned if you do, damned if you don't—but she says at the time, her only thought was for the safety and security of her subscribers, the MTC staff, production personnel, and audiences. There had already been protests, and she feared for more. They consulted with the police department, and then-commissioner Howard Safir. They hired security, including checking Terrence's and Meadow's apartments for potential vulnerabilities. They provided security for the actors, all of which was extremely expensive, and Meadow says that MTC's board stepped up to fund it all, and as Meadow said, was in favor of taking every measure possible.

Having arranged for unprecedented levels of security, however, on May 28, the same day the *Times* op-ed appeared, Meadow announced that the play would go on, and she pointedly added that in her twenty-five years at the helm of MTC, the organization had never censored a play because of content. (There would never have been a need to; if she was the final say on plays produced by MTC, the notion of censorship would never enter into consideration. Plays she felt were not appropriate for MTC simply wouldn't be produced.)

The announcement that the production would go ahead did not kill the story. Instead, it ignited a six-day battle for headlines between condemnations and ongoing howls of censorship. What's remarkable, nearly a quarter of a century later, is that no one spoke up for MTC, even after Meadow played tapes of some of the threats they received. Even the office of Mayor Giuliani released a tepid statement saying, "Although the Mayor doesn't agree with the tone of the play, threats of violence in New York City will not be tolerated." There is no evidence that the mayor's office ever reviewed the play. There was a lot of axe-grinding, indignation, and, frankly, noise, in the media, among people, and on message boards, but the production was back on.

Mantello remembers that there were security guards present during the rehearsal period—something that had never happened before. He also remembers that he wanted to rehearse the play in an unorthodox way (pun only partially intended), which he had discussed with Terrence:

> These guys are going to come to work under a lot of pressure. I want them to have real ownership of the play. And the play had a kind of improvisatory feeling to it. So, what we would do is we would take a chunk of the play, either five pages or a parable or something where there was a natural beginning or ending to a section. We would read it. We would talk about it a little bit. And I said, "Terrence and I are going to sit outside now; call us when you're ready."
>
> When we got to the end of that process, they had such ownership of the play because it had emerged from them, and they had formed into this ensemble because of them.
>
> It wasn't as if we kept everything they came up with. We'd refine from there. One thing they found, which I never ever would have thought of—and I thought was absolutely brilliant—is there's an opening speech of the play that a character gives, which is like a welcome and a benediction. I walked in, and they did a kind of spin the bottle, and the person it landed on read the speech. They

did that every night, so they were all responsible for knowing the speech. It was exciting and unpredictable, and the audience knew it was happening in real time, and it was in the spirit of the play, which was playful. It was saying, "We're all in this room together," and it's one of the most brilliant things I ever saw a company of actors do.

If the rehearsal room was a safe place for discovery, the world still was not. The actors were told to take different routes home at night, and not travel together. Terrence had personal security for a short time, provided by MTC, and MTC was mum on the script, protecting the rehearsal process, and members of the company did no press ahead of the opening. MTC, which had been barraged with letters and postcards both against and in favor of the play, offered to refund any tickets for people who were offended by the subject matter and established a phone number people could call to express their views.

Mantello remembers that when previews began there were bomb-sniffing dogs in the theater. There were also protestors outside at every performance, and MTC apologized in advance to ticketholders for the "inconvenience" of getting through the metal detectors.

The play was presented simply, on a bare stage with a platform, the actors dressed in khakis and white shirts. They took on the different characters without changing anything, often announcing who they were. As Mantello recalled, "It's a wonderful, earnest little exploration of spirituality done by these wonderful young actors."

Despite the controversy, the metal detectors, the police presence, and the protestors, Terrence and MTC had been able to put on the play. Meadow knew that the narrative had been taken over by outside forces, but ultimately, MTC stood by Terrence's right to write whatever he wanted, and MTC produced a play that Meadow says Terrence had been wanting to write for a while.

However, by the time the play opened, the controversy was so beyond the scale of the play itself, with audiences anticipating all kinds of shocking blasphemy, that it was impossible to see the play for what it was—Terrence's intention to explore spirituality in an intimate way and say that spoke to anyone, but particularly gay people who have been traditionally marginalized in religion and spirituality. Scandal is always good for business, and the production quickly sold out. Painful, hateful, and irrational as it was, once again controversy put butts in seats.

Ben Brantley in the *New York Times* gave *Corpus Christi* a lukewarm review, saying it was "a minor play from a major playwright," yet he also saw the inherent innocence and simplicity of the piece and that Terrence was trying to reach for his themes of the difficulty of connection and "that no one should be persecuted for being different." The review ran two days after Matthew Shephard had been tortured and beaten in Laramie, Wyoming. He would die six days later.

There were those who "got" the play, and it had a passionate following. Terrence's high school friend Peggy Dobbins said that after seeing *Corpus Christi*, she began to consider his work in a new way. "I thought for a long time that he was just pandering to Broadway and wanted to grow up and be famous. *Corpus Christi* made me begin to realize what he'd done with his life." She later reconsidered many of his plays in light of what they were saying and the avenues of communication they opened up. She admits that she finally heard Terrence.

Early on, there had been rumors of a Broadway transfer for *Corpus Christi*, but many productions are whispered about as they are in development. The show ran its course and closed. It has been produced in various places around the country, sometime with controversy, sometimes not. A revival in 2008 at Rattlestick Playwrights Theater added women to the cast. It still got a middling review in the *Times*, but the play was finally seen for what it was, a thoughtful exploration of spiritual searching, even if imperfect.

The play continues to be done occasionally, with more or less controversy, which is probably to be expected. Though in 1998 the Catholic League pledged to "wage a war that no one will forget" on subsequent productions, they've moved on to other targets over which to, metaphorically, foam at the mouth. Protests, such as they are, remain localized. In 2019, Terrence still considered *Corpus Christi* one of his major works but acknowledged that when it got done (and not often enough that he could live on the royalties), there were protests. He recalled one college production that went so far as to cast a Black actor as Joshua was cancelled. In his opinion so many years later, he felt the protests always arose because the play does challenge myths—as the text says right up front. "But who," he asked, "has the exclusive rights to myths?" Nonetheless, the climate of the 2020s is that outrage is a default emotion for many people and organizations, and anything that potentially challenges an individual's idea of Jesus—as Terrence clearly stated—is often seen as anathema. What Terrence bridled at, and tried to address, was that we need to find our own path to spiritual enlightenment and growth—and, most importantly, that all are welcome at the table.

Ironically, in 2011, *The Book of Mormon* opened on Broadway, set in AIDS-ravaged Uganda, with a song "Hasa Diga Ebowai," ("Fuck you, God"), and while there were some protests, the show was a hit and quasi-scholarly pieces dismissed the piece as comedy in its excessive offensiveness—and open blasphemy. The show would win nine Tony Awards, including Best Musical. Once again, Terrence, who examined the Christ story from a place of love rather than looking for laughs, was ahead of his time.

In another bit of irony, less than a month after *Corpus Christi* opened at MTC, Morehouse "resigned" from the *Post*. The paper's explanation was the typical public relations non-statement: "We've decided to take our Broadway coverage in a new direction," as reported by *Playbill*. The article also stated, "From the time of his hiring, many New York theatre professionals accused Ward Morehouse . . . of inaccuracy and fabrication." As Meadow observed in hindsight, it was terrible, the damage that rumor and inaccuracy had done.

As for MTC, they kept going. The play Athol Fugard withdrew was produced in 1999. Ironically, in 2018, MTC mounted *Ink*, a play about the rise of Rupert Murdoch whose *New York Post* had done such damage to *Corpus Christi*. In his review of that play, Ben Brantley referred to Murdoch as "Mephistopheles." After all the *tsuris* dished out by the

Murdoch-owned *Post*, it may, perhaps, have been gratifying to see this comment served up cold.

IX.

MTC and Terrence both emerged from this storm bruised but pressing onward. MTC had kept all its people safe, and Terrence's voice had not been silenced—or even altered. As noted, it would have been impossible for critics or audiences to appreciate the play on its merits alone. For many, scoring a ticket became a *cause celèbre* or some kind of status, rather than appreciating the play for what it was, though as mentioned above, many people were moved by it, and while Terrence maintained that he was no theologian, he was happy to have reached people. The run came and went, and like so many of these publicity-seeking tempests, the instigators were on to other targets.

There was, however, a storm on the horizon, that would shake the relationship between MTC and Terrence in a more significant and permanent way.

In the 1990s, MTC was focused on the future. They had initiated a long-range plan to help ensure sustainability. One of their missions was to have their own Broadway theater.

The Biltmore Theater on 47th Street was first opened in 1925, and it had been a Broadway house as the Times Square area was becoming the center of Broadway, a showcase for the WPA Federal Theater Project in the Great Depression, and even at one time a TV studio, and again a legit house into the early 1980s. Over time, though, it had fallen into disrepair, and despite having been granted landmark status, by 1988, the building was designated as "unsafe." Through a series of deals that involved the building of apartments, the renovation of the theater, and approvals that seemed to stretch on for months, by 2000 MTC had acquired the theater and begun what would end up, when it was all totaled up, a $35 million renovation.

In addition to being expensive, it was an involved process that required draining water out of the basement, ripping out and rebuilding the orchestra section, and resolving all the headaches to put a modern theater in an antique building. Set to open for the 2003 season, the theater itself had become a Broadway gem with some of the best sightlines on Broadway but still maintaining the intimate feel of MTC.

The opening of the Biltmore had one more advantage for MTC. Productions produced there would be Broadway shows and eligible for Tony Awards. Previously, MTC shows were only eligible when they were transferred to Broadway houses, essentially creating a new production. Of these transfers, Terrence's plays had been among the most successful, but the move is significant in that just as Meadow and MTC had brought Off-Off Broadway to Off-Broadway, now Off-Broadway would expand to be part of what *Variety* call "the main stem." Having their own Broadway house was a significant move for the organization and the playwrights they nurtured and produced. In essence, it was a kind of coming of age. As Meadow said, "They wanted to write for the Broadway stage, and Terrence was a leader of that group of writers who all had an artistic home [with MTC]. Now, original MTC productions could be on Broadway without having to mount additional productions.

With the Biltmore, MTC had, to use the showbiz colloquialism, hit "the big time." Given the importance of opening a new Broadway house—the most recent previous ones being the Marquis in the Times Square Hotel in 1986 and the Ford Center (now the Lyric) in 1998—Meadow was aware that her first production needed to be big. Naturally, she turned to Terrence. "I wanted Terrence to write the first play to open the Broadway theater," Meadow said. The opening was slated for November 2003.

For the play, Terrence returned to one of his favorite topics—the theater. *Dedication, or the Stuff of Dreams* is a wry love letter to the theater, or at least the possibility of theater. Lou Nuncle, who runs a children's theater in Upstate New York out of an abandoned shoe store, has the opportunity to take over a decrepit Vaudeville house nearby and transform it into the stuff of those proverbial theatrical dreams, if he can get the okay of the aging, and dying, Anabelle Ward, who owns the theater—and hates children and children's theater, which she calls, "Grownups desperately trying to hold the attention of a hostile audience."

Lou can have the theater free and clear, if he will do one thing: kill Anabelle. It's the classic Faustian deal (and one which will come up again in *The Visit*). The play is replete with classic Terrence jibes at the theater, such as "Shakespeare has too many words," and "Comps killed the theater. No one ever asked Aeschylus for comps." There is also an autobiographical detail in that Lou liked to put on his mother's skirt and twirl, which leads to the idea that Lou, whose sexuality is ill-defined though he is married to a woman, is gay.

The play is sprawling and filled with other characters as well, but it's easy to understand his inspiration and motivation in writing it. After all, it's a play about fixing a decrepit theater that would play in a theater reclaimed and rehabilitated that celebrates the passionate love for theater and the desire to create it and a need for it, metaphorically a life or death situation. It seemed tailor-made for the opening of the restored Biltmore.

Terrence, as he had done before, gave Meadow the first act of *Dedication*. As Meadow recalls they had a director who talked with Terrence after the reading. Terrence went away and came back with the second act. She recalled:

> I guess, maybe for one of the first times, I didn't really understand what Terrence was actually trying to say. I understood the themes that he was dealing with about death, but it was the second act that really confused me.
>
> I didn't know how I could stand at the back of the theater on the opening night, and if someone said to me, "Why did you do this play?" I didn't know how to answer the question, for the first time ever.
>
> I understood every other play of Terrence's. If someone criticized us for *Lisbon Traviata* or for *Lips Together, Teeth Apart*, I embraced and understood what Terrence had written. What was unusual about that period for Terrence was that he was writing about things

he cared about and avoided repeating himself, just to have another
hit.

With *Dedication*, as presented to her, however, Meadow was at a loss.
She didn't feel she would be able to tell an audience member that she
was sorry they didn't like it, "but here's what I believe Terrence is talking
about."

She talks about the decision not to produce the play as a "dark night
of the soul" for her, and "I have stood up for many plays that many people did not like." At this point in her life and as the artistic director, she
said, "You keep learning about being truthful to yourself, and I couldn't
do the play. I just couldn't do it."

It was a devastating decision for Meadow, and she knew that it would
be difficult—"agony," she said—for both her and Terrence. "I couldn't
respond simply to my loyalty to him. We had a relationship of so many
years of me saying yes, and I knew he never wanted to hear no, and
I understood the decision would be painful. It certainly wasn't a cold
decision but was made with reflection and integrity."

In practical terms, Meadow was up against the reality of scheduling;
the theater needed to open.

> We undertook a $35 million renovation to create a Broadway the-
> ater for Terrence McNally, and Donald Margulies, Richard Green-
> berg, and so many of the playwrights with whom we had worked,
> and there was Terrence at the forefront of them.

Under other circumstances, Meadow would have given the play time
to develop through workshops and readings, and see what they have,
but she didn't have that luxury. She had heard Act One of the play,
and knew that it wasn't ready, and she couldn't do it. MTC had not
announced *Dedication*, she says, so MTC simply withdrew it.

The play that MTC chose to open the Biltmore was Richard Greenberg's *The Violet Hour*. Greenberg, who had written *Take Me Out* about
gay baseball players, had had four plays premiered at MTC. The play

got largely positive reviews as well as Robert Sean Leonard in the leading role but there were quibbles with the production.

Terrence was, of course, both upset and quite angry by the cancellation. His version of the story is somewhat different than Meadow's:

> I had a home [at MTC] and in the twelve years I was there, I wrote, like, ten plays. And a lot of my best work, my most successful work . . . I consider central to my body of work, and she produced some pretty much sight unseen.
>
> They asked me to write a play immediately. She [Meadow] disputes it and says this is Terrence's memory, but they asked me to write a play to open their new theater on Broadway. I said I would be upset you'd asked anyone else to write it.
>
> I wrote this play, and the reading had not gone particularly well. It was a cold reading. And Lynne called the next day or two days later and said, "I think the play's not ready to be done, and we're going to do something else." And I did say, "Lynne, I think you should count to ten before you call the next playwright, or sleep on this. This would be the end of a 12-year very, very successful relationship."
>
> I hung up, and the phone rang like a minute later, and it was my agent saying that Lynne doesn't want to do your play, but she wants to do a play of another writer I represent.
>
> And that created a big divide between us.

"Big divide" is probably an understatement. Terrence was deeply hurt, and the rift never fully healed.

Dedication was presented at Williamstown in 2004 and got its New York premiere at Primary Stages in 2005. The company was founded in 1984 and was dedicated to producing new American plays. The company had celebrated their move to the 199-seat theater at 59E59 Theaters the previous year, from a 99-seat theater, with Terrence's *The Stendhal Syndrome*, two short plays starring Richard Thomas and Isabella Rossellini, and the production of *Dedication*, starring Nathan Lane and Marian Seldes. Though it was largely warmly received, many of the critics echoed Meadows's concerns.

The Primary Stages production was problematic. Lane recalled that Marian Seldes was having a very difficult time remembering her lines. Her character was dying of cancer and spent much of the time in a wing chair. They rigged a small speaker into the wing chair, and whenever Seldes went up, she would writhe in pain and lean back in the chair at which point the stage manager would give her the cue. As Lane said, she became so comfortable with that arrangement that during one performance when she didn't hear the line, she turned and looked at the chair and said, "What?"

It wasn't all that easy for Lane, either. Terrence had written a part where Lou would put on a Mexican dress and twirl—a callback from Terrence's childhood, you'll recall. However, Lane wasn't having it. He felt it didn't make any sense. Instead, he came out in a rabbit suit, which for those who saw it, didn't make that much dramatic sense, either, but there it was.

Lane was also supposed to suffocate Seldes in the play by putting a pillow over her head. They had worked it out so that Seldes would turn her head when that happened . . . so she could still breathe. Seldes, however, was a very committed actor, and Lane remembered her turning her head toward the pillow one night as he acted suffocating her. The acting must have been especially effective that night, as he heard a man in the audience say, "Well, that's the end of Marian Seldes."

Terrence did work with MTC eight years later when they staged a well-received revival of *Master Class* starring Tyne Daly, a production that had begun in Washington, D.C. As Meadow reflected on that production several years later: "It made me so happy when Terrence was back on that stage at the Friedman Theater (the Biltmore had been renamed in 2008), which had been created with so much of him in my heart."

For her part, Meadow never gave up on Terrence, and there are many of the notes Meadow wrote supporting him and expressing her affection for him in the archives, some of them, perhaps, are tinged with a bit of

Terrence in New York in his early twenties.
COURTESY TERRENCE MCNALLY ESTATE

ALL SEATS FOR ALL PERFORMANCES $1.00
Fri. & Sat. $2.00

Original sign posted at the box office for And Things That Go Bump in the Night.
Reducing the seats to $1 allowed the show to run an extra week.
PHOTO BY CHRISTOPHER BYRNE

Terrence in front of the Mark Hellinger during rehearsals for The Rink.
COURTESY TERRENCE MCNALLY ESTATE

Terrence on his first trip to India where his spiritual journey was transformed (1987).
PHOTO BY GARY BONASORTE / COURTESY TERRENCE MCNALLY ESTATE

Roger Rees (standing) and the cast of A Man of No Importance *at Lincoln Center, 2002.*
PHOTO BY PAUL KOLNIK

Terrence in front of the Prince of Wales Theater for the opening of The Full Monty, *2002.*
COURTESY TERRENCE MCNALLY ESTATE

Zoe Caldwell and Audra McDonald in Master Class. *With this play, Terrence felt he'd finally written the play he promised Caldwell, and he called it his most autobiographical.*
PHOTO BY JOAN MARCUS

Anthony Roth Costanzo, Joyce DiDonato, and Federica von Stade in Great Scott *premier. Dallas Opera, 2015. Terrence always hoped to revisit the libretto, but never got the chance.*

PHOTO BY KAREN ALMOND / COURTESY DALLAS OPERA

Terrence, Frederica Von Stade (left), and Joyce DiDonato (center) backstage during Great Scott.

PHOTO BY JAKE HEGGIE

Joyce DiDonata, Philip Cutlip, and the company in Dead Man Walking *at the Houston Opera, 2011.*
PHOTO BY FELIX SANCHEZ

Sister Helen Prejean (left) Fredericka von Stade (center), and Terrence at the opening of Dead Man Walking *at San Francisco Opera.*
PHOTO BY JANNA WALDINGER, ART & CLARITY

Terrence with the cast of Mothers and Sons *on Broadway, 2014: (left to right) Bobby Steggert, Grayson Taylor, Fred Weller, Terrence, Tyne Daly. With this play, Terrence felt he had finally arrived on Broadway.*
PHOTO BY JOAN MARCUS

Chita Rivera (center) and the cast of The Visit *on Broadway, 2015.*
PHOTO BY JOAN MARCUS

(Left to right) Rupert Grint, F. Murray Abraham, Stockard Channing, and Nathan Lane in It's Only a Play, *which finally became a hit on Broadway in 2014, thirty-six years after its first production.*
PHOTO BY JOAN MARCUS

Anastasia *on Broadway, 2017. After swearing off writing musicals, Terrence jumped at the chance to do this one because of his love of Russian history . . . and the production team.*
PHOTO BY JOAN MARCUS

Curtain call for Frankie and Johnny in the Clair de Lune *Revival; (left to right) Director Arin Arbus, Terrence, Audra McDonald, and Michael Shannon, 2019.*
WENN / ALAMY STOCK PHOTO

Peter McNally (left) with Terrence and Terry the Terrier.
COURTESY TERRENCE MCNALLY ESTATE

Terrence and Tom reaffirm their wedding vows with Mayor Bill DeBlasio at New York City Hall the day same-sex marriage is legalized nationwide.
ZUMA PRESS / ALAMY
STOCK PHOTO

Terrence and Tom walking in Hartford. Terrence loved being able to hold his husband's hand in public.
COURTESY JEFF KAUFMAN

sadness if one reads between the lines, but it's clear she never stopped believing in his talent.

For his part, Terrence, too, became more sanguine about the relationship, saying, "I have the gratitude I feel towards Manhattan Theatre Club, which is enormous, inexpressible."

X.

Terrence would have one final play with MTC: *Golden Age*. It was staged at the Philadelphia Theater Company in 2009, later moved to Washington, D.C., in 2010, and finally landed at City Center on Stage One in 2012. The play takes place backstage at the premiere of the Bellini opera *i Puritani* in 1835 and is considered part of an unofficial "opera trilogy" that also includes *Lisbon Traviata* and *Master Class*, at least that's how it was presented at the Kennedy Center under the title *Nights at the Opera*.

The play received mixed critical reaction, filled as it was with Terrence's inside knowledge of opera and lots of fast-flying jokes and cattiness. It's another backstage play, and while it seems to have been intended as at least, in part, a kind of boulevard comedy, there is a serious side to it as well.

Bellini himself may have been gay, and Terrence ran with that. The play shows Bellini in love with his friend and patron Francesco Florimo. What is the nature of love? What is the nature of opera? How do they affect us as humans? These are all questions that were always on Terrence's mind, and if he doesn't necessarily break new ground with this play, it is both funny and thoughtful.

The play got a sumptuous production in New York with stars F. Murray Abraham, Bebe Neuwirth, and Lee Pace. However, Charles Isherwood in the *New York Times* was dismissive, faulting Terrence for taking artistic license with facts. The irony, of course, being that the "facts" are not necessarily accurate. For people who write about theater, the inconsistencies of the *New York Times* critics are sometimes glaring, and the dismissal of Terrence's "poetic realism," which is consistent through all his work, is a flaw in the critical process. Notwithstanding, the production extended. At least the audiences appreciated it, which is what mattered.

Golden Age and the revival of *Master Class* represented a mostly happy ending as a final act, and though Terrence acknowledged "all arrangements eventually come to an end," the relationship between Terrence and MTC was the very definition of a "good run."

It was a partnership—and an artistic journey. Meadow asked how many playwrights write the number of plays he did? Or how many careers were made and defined by Terrence's work at MTC, including actors like Nathan Lane, Christine Baranski, and many others. There was a time, Meadow adds, when the only way one could see shows at MTC was by being a subscriber, and that Terrence was a major part of that. She adds that without Terrence and his work—and all it did for MTC—they might not have been able to create a Broadway theater.

The relationship between Terrence and MTC was, finally, perhaps one of the most important in the modern theater, where art and commerce are necessary bedfellows. From Off-Off Broadway, to Off-Broadway, to Broadway, the girl who wanted to direct and do theater (as Meadow calls herself) and the guy who wanted to be heard found one another. Their work changed the theater and the culture and helped expand the art form in ways that are still being felt.

7

. . . And Then When You Have to Collaborate

I.

THE SECOND ACT of Sondheim's *Sunday in the Park with George* opens with a song, "Putting it Together." In it a group of contemporary artists complain about the difficulty and challenges of having their work seen. They bemoan their state saying, "Art isn't easy," saving the apparently worst challenge for the end: "And then when you have to collaborate . . ."

There is no theater form more dependent on effective collaboration than a musical. Book, lyrics, music are only the beginning. Then there's the director's vision, and often the ideas of a producer, and so on through all the design elements, right down to the poster and where to have the opening night party. Perhaps this last bit is an exaggeration, but there is virtually no area on the production of a musical that doesn't require the input and expertise of a team. The same could be said of a play, to some extent, but the creation of the actual work, the show, is not the province of a playwright, it is an essential collaboration. The Lionel Barts and Meredith Willsons who write books, music, and lyrics for *Oliver* and *The Music Man* are anomalies in the business of musicals.

The collaboration process wasn't always easy for Terrence, but he loved musicals, and the end products earned him two Tony Awards for Best Book of a Musical, and, most importantly to him at least, a chance to work with people with whom he truly enjoyed working—and loved—however tense the process might become.

Terrence's lifelong love of musicals began, as we've seen, in his childhood. Whether listening to his parents'—and later his own—albums or in a Broadway theater at age ten or so, they gave him entrée into a world very different from his own. For many young people, and especially closeted, gay young people, the images of a perfect world with a happy ending is a tonic and a respite from complicated home lives. As Terrence had said about Gertrude Lawrence in *The King and I*, he had wanted her to be his mother—someone who loved and paid attention to the children in her life.

Then there's the trope of gay men and musicals. It's the convention that Terrence so thoroughly illuminates with Buzz in *L!V!C!*, but many of his other characters make references to musicals, and sprinkle conversations with lyrics and ephemera about shows and performers, diva actresses mostly.

Still, while slightly tangential, the role of musicals in gay culture, particularly in the mid-twentieth century, deserves a quick look. For men, primarily, who could lose their livelihoods, families, freedom, and even lives for being openly gay, musicals, for a certain sector of the population, created an identity and a means of bonding—and signaling to one another. Terrence remembered how closeted so much of New York still was when he started going to bars in the Village. Even when it was nominatively a "gay bar," a patron could get in trouble just by touching another man on the arm. Singing at a piano bar like the famous Five Oaks or Marie's Crisis in the Village, notorious as being "boy bars" since World War II, and before, provided a release, and particularly at Five Oaks, it was not uncommon to see Broadway stars after their shows, or even legends like Judy Garland or Shirley MacLaine. Coupled with the fantasy of a more perfect world as seen in so many musicals—*Camelot, Brigadoon, My Fair Lady*—the sense of community and belonging that grew up around musical theater became a center of gay culture, at a time when it still lurked in the shadows. *La Cage aux Folles* would burst all of that open in 1983, and its hit song, "I Am What I Am" would become a *de facto* gay anthem, but that was still many years away.

Terrence grew up in the culture of musicals, and he loved the escape they provided. He also would have loved the scale and storytelling—as well as challenging himself and pursuing a new artistic outlet.

II.

Terrence's first musical book, as seen earlier, was for the Columbia Varsity Show, *A Little Bit Different.* Still, despite the attention it got, it was an intramural activity. Basking in the reception of *Next* and with the pain of *Bump* receding into the past, he was about to get his first shot at a "great big, Broadway show."

The impact of *East of Eden* on Terrence's high school generation was monumental. John Steinbeck's 1952 novel got lukewarm reviews, but it became a popular hit with readers. At just over seven hundred pages, it was a challenge for many readers, and it was criticized for its lack of focus.

It was, however, the 1955 movie directed by Elia Kazan and starring James Dean that resonated with Terrence and his peers. (The characters

Liza Minnelli and Chita Rivera in The Rink *(1984). Terrence, John Kander, and Fred Ebb achieved exactly what they wanted with this show . . . even if critics didn't agree.*
PHOTOFEST

mention having seen it multiple times in *Corpus Christi*.) The movie focuses on the fourth and final part of the novel, and it's essentially a retelling of the Cain and Abel story from the Bible, set in California in the years right before World War II. The movie got mixed reviews, but it was Dean's performance that made him an icon of youthful angst. It was his screen debut, and his style of acting shaped by the Actors Studio seemed to capture the spirit of the time. The inter-generational conflict with his father, played by Raymond Massey, spoke to teenage audiences. It's important to remember that after World War II, greater leisure time for young people and the move away from an agrarian society was creating the adolescent/teenager as a population cohort. In *East of Eden* and later that year *Rebel without a Cause*, Dean became the tortured emblem of that generation.

By the early 1960s, record producer Mitch Miller had become a household name with his popular TV show, *Sing Along with Mitch*. His weekly show on NBC featured music artists and lyrics at the bottom of the screen so, presumably, families could sing along.

Miller acquired the musical rights to the novel *East of Eden*, and *Here's Where I Belong* began development with United Artists providing the capital—estimated at anywhere from $500,000 to $700,000 as its reported in various sources. Terrence was hired to write the book. Robert Waldman signed on to write the music, and Alfred Uhry would contribute the lyrics. It was a first time out for all of them in those roles. Michael Kahn was the director, and, at least at the outset Hanya Holm, one of the choreographers credited with the creation of modern dance, would stage the musical numbers. As William Goldman writes in *The Season*, having first-timers in so many key roles is often a recipe for disaster.

Kahn assumed that Terrence got the gig because of his relationship with Steinbeck and that Kahn was hired on the recommendation of Terrence. By this time Kahn had begun to make a name for himself in the Off-Broadway world with major successes like Adrienne Kennedy's Obie-winning *The Funnyhouse of a Negro* and Lanford Wilson's *The Rimers of Eldritch*. However, he had never done a Broadway musical; he'd never directed a musical except in summer stock.

The final cast included Ken Kercheval as Adam Trask, Heather Mac-Rae, Walter McGinn, and James Coco. Coco was cast as Lee, a native Chinese man who served as a kind of narrator for the piece and cook for to the family. The choreographer Graciela Daniele made one of her first appearances as a dancer, credited simply as one of the "Whores" in the cast list in Philadelphia, but she got a name, "Faith," by the time the show opened in New York.

Set in Salinas, California, the intricate plot includes the Trask family trying to make a business out of shipping lettuce to the East Coast (always something to sing about), but when that business fails, the bad son, Cal, tries to establish a new business growing beans. Meanwhile, his brother Aron has fallen in love with Abra, who actually has the hots for Cal. Cal and Aron are trying to get along with dad, Adam, since their mom died. Surprise: mom is alive, and runs a nearby brothel, which Cal found out and subsequently went to her for the money for the bean business. The bean business grows, and Cal tries to give the money he made to Adam, but Adam says the money is tainted because it's from war profiteering. Cal's upset and decides to introduce Aron to their mom. Aron can't cope and runs away. Adam has a heart attack, and Lee convinces Adam to forgive Cal, which he does before he dies. Cal is left alone on stage as the curtain falls. That's a plot that Oscar Wilde would call "crowded with incident."

There was trouble almost from the outset. There was ongoing conflict between Terrence, Waldman, and Uhry. In May of 1967, as they began writing the show, there were evidently disputes about the script and how the characters were to be portrayed. Waldman and Uhry kept asking for rewrites, and there appears to be persistent conflict about the tone of the romantic relationship. In a letter to Terrence dated May 5, 1967, Uhry wrote, "I'm sorry you take our criticisms of the script so badly. Our *only* intention is to have a successful show." Uhry and Waldman had already invested years in the project before Terrence came on, and they had specific ideas of how it should be. Uhry continues that he knows Terrence can fix the script "because you are very talented." However, he gets his digs in, writing, cruelly, "I wouldn't tell you all this if I didn't think you could fix it. Better that you should be irritated with me than come in with a flop. Face it, you can't afford to be a three-time loser." The working relationships didn't improve, not surprisingly. In a letter about two weeks later, Uhry tried to patch things up, saying, "Any criticism I have is absolutely criticism of the show—not of you, or your life. You said once that you and I are very different, but we like each other." It's hard to read this without thinking it's a dig at Terrence's being gay.

The script finally got at least to a point where it could go into rehearsal, but reading between the lines of notes and letters, it appears that the relationship between the collaborators was conscientiously cordial but cool. As the show came together, the strained relationships proved too much, and not to put too fine a point on it, *Here's Where I Belong* was a disaster, almost from start to finish, despite how hard Kahn said they all worked on it. The original novel had also been one of Kahn's favorite books, and he identified with the two brothers, and that only added to his frustration in trying to realize the material as a musical.

Case in point: as they entered rehearsals, Kahn said Holm was in one room with the cast working on choreography. He remembers that the room had a large sign on the door that said, "keep out," and that that was clearly directed at Kahn and Terrence. While his memory wasn't precise more than fifty years later, Kahn recalls that at one point Hanya was fired, and Tony Mordente was brought in to stage the numbers. Kahn and Mordente had gone to high school together so they at least knew one another and could work together.

The show lumbered along, and finally got on its feet in a three-week tryout at the Shubert in Philadelphia. Steinbeck had written Terrence a note of encouragement, saying he had made "a good start," but the show just wasn't working. Kahn said that the opening scene was a mess with Coco as Lee introducing each of the characters as they came on stage, but the show—and the music—didn't really start until the second scene, the kiss of death for a musical. So, he says, they decided to cut the first scene. All well and good, but in cutting it, they got rid of all the exposition, so the audience had no idea who was who or what was going on. He recalled:

I remember how desperate we were, and how naïve. There was one reviewer who said "*Here's Where I Belong* doesn't," the producers got scared. They would have been, sure. Then they brought in a joke writer, somebody who had written jokes for Mitch's television show. It was a friend of his, Alex Gordon. They felt the show needed laughs.

This proved to be too much for Terrence. He was, to put it mildly, irate. He felt that he was being disrespected, as was his work, as he had with *Bump*. People on a production team routinely write one another notes during rehearsal, so as not to disrupt the process. On one sheet of yellow paper, Terrence, who had clearly had a conversation with the person with whom he was communicating the day before, had written, among what appears to be rehearsal notes, "Everything I said the night before in spades."

The person writing back had responded:

> It would be the *supreme compliment* to be fired from this show—
> You are a major writer—write major.
> You are potentially one of the most interesting talents to come out of the theater—now make whats [*sic*] interesting—into a greatness—which only you can do.
> No matter how good the book for a musical is, it is second rate writing—great writer [*sic*] are never *second rate.* They starve first.

Supportive as this might have felt, it didn't solve the problem, and as the production moved back to New York, it still wasn't working. The producers pushed the opening date from February 20 to March 2. (It would finally open March 3.)

Terrence, outraged at new material that devalued all he was trying to do dramatically, wanted to have his name taken off the book. For him, it was a question of integrity; he didn't want another person's writing to be presented as his own, particularly when he didn't think it was good. A call to Miller on February 6 was followed up with a handwritten note:

I simply cannot allow someone else's work to be presented under my name. It is dishonesty on both our parts and that is a word neither of us are in the habit of using about the other. As a friend and admirer who wishes you every success possible with the project, I ask that you remove my name from all advertising and programs beginning with the Feb. 8 Thursday preview.

If you won't do this (and I can't imagine what reasons are holding you back) I will call Sam Zolotow and ask that he run an item to this effect in his column. This is not a threat, Mitch, but simply a plan of logical action on the part of someone who feels very strongly about how and where his name is used.

For whatever reason, Miller declined, and a minor battle in the press ensued. A headline in the *Times* stated "Libbretist Disowns Work on Musical." Miller's response as appeared in a headline was, "It's 85% His Script, I Won't Erase His Name: Mitch Says to McNally." The *Times* piece also mentioned the failure of *Bump*, which had to sting as well. Miller's argument was that since Terrence was still receiving royalties, he could not take his name off the show. A letter from Terrence's agent to Miller on February 29, sought $1,171.88 in unpaid royalties for the Philadelphia tryout.

Terrence's name, however, was ultimately taken off the show, replaced by Alex Gordon, the gag writer, and it opened at the Billy Rose Theatre (now the Nederlander on 41st Street) to terrible reviews. Kahn recalls that in the final previews and up to the opening, the house was mostly "papered," seats given away. The reviews killed the show, and it closed in one night. Of course, it had had about twenty preview performances leading up to that opening, but it was still considered a one-night flop.

The reviews had some nice things to say about some of the music and Ming Cho Lee's sets. It may have been this production that inspired Clive Barnes in the *Times* to coin the now-common observation, "No one ever left the theater humming the scenery." Mostly, the response was that the book and the story, though representing only a fraction of the source material as the movie did, was unwieldy. Walter Kerr, in a follow-up piece for the *Times* suggested that the material should never have been adapted for a musical, given its dark subject matter and complexity. He praised the comparative simplicity of shows like *My Fair Lady* and *Oklahoma*, which gave characters "something to sing about." He was especially snarky about a dance in *Here's Where I Belong* that centered on getting heads of lettuce into a boxcar before they wilted. (A dozen years earlier, *The Most Happy Fella* had a number about picking grapes, so one might say produce-laden production numbers had precedence.)

The morning after the disastrous opening, Kahn recalled that there was a meeting at the advertising agency, and the conversation turned to whether or not they could pull it out—and survive the reviews. They realized, he said, "there's nobody left to come. Every USO officer had already seen it, and we closed. It was the most heartbreaking thing."

An item on page one of the *Variety* on March 6, called the show "The costliest 1-Night Stand on Broadway." William Goldman in *The Season* breaks down the economics of the show in detail. Ghastly as it was, however, it doesn't even make the list in a 2019 of the *100 Biggest Musical Flops.*

Looking back, Kahn added that as everyone left the show, the producers put a box around his name in all printed materials, so by the time the show opened, he was, with the exception of Waldman and Uhry, the last person standing from the original production team—and the only name that might have had any recognition in the theater and sold tickets.

There was one other issue that affected the show. A group of Asian American actors protested Coco's portrayal of Lee—an early comment about "yellow-facing," hiring Caucasian actors to play Asians. Kahn remembered that the part had been written for Coco, so they'd seen no one else. He also remembered that he had confronted the three protestors in front of the theater, all of whom had to leave for their curtains because they were working. It was not the kind of organized protest that would impact *Corpus Christi*, but it did prefigure it.

Kahn added that after the show tanked, he and Terrence stopped being close, though it seems to be one of those relationships that faded away more than abruptly ended. Terrence and Kahn didn't work together again.

Waldman and Uhry would go on to have a success with *The Robber Bridegroom*, and Terrence, of course, would continue writing for the theater—and continue to push it forward. The material ultimately may have been impossible, and the production spoiled like Trask's undelivered lettuce, but the question that was never asked through all of this was, Why does a musical have to adhere to a specific formula? Can audiences be challenged with something darker and more human? Terrence was taking a chance on the form. He was willing to look at the family story and classic issues that had made the book and movie of *East of Eden* so popular, though he was ultimately forced by the producers into trying to fit conventional molds, which in this case doomed the project. As some reviews suggested, it might have been more palatable to an audience in 1968 as an opera, given its scale. *Here's Where I Belong* didn't shy away from pushing the form. Once again, Terrence was ahead of the culture.

III.

It would be fifteen years till Terrence tackled the book of a musical again. It was that somewhat lost period in the early 1980s where *Mama Malone* was shot but not released and he'd had the early disaster with *Broadway, Broadway*. In 1983, he began one of his most successful—and happy—collaborations with the team Kander and Ebb.

John Kander and Fred Ebb were a powerhouse score-writing team. They had arrived on Broadway in 1965 with *Flora, The Red Menace*, the tale of a would-be graphic designer who gets inadvertently recruited into the Communist party. It wasn't a hit, though the album remains a favorite among musical fans, and the song "A Quiet Thing" has become a cabaret standard. *Flora* lasted only eighty-seven performances, but it introduced Broadway to the nineteen-year-old Liza Minnelli, who went on to win the Tony Award for her performance.

The next year, however, *Cabaret* established Kander and Ebb as Broadway royalty. *Cabaret* opened in November, 1966, and ran for 1,661 performances. Though audiences were initially wary—and resistant to—the immorality of lead character Sally Bowles, cabaret performer and occasional "working girl," the score, including the title number, eventually won people over. Perhaps, as the sexual revolution was in full swing and conventional morality was questioned, the character of Sally began to seem like a woman in charge of her own life, however tragically, and not so immoral. Whatever the reason, younger audiences warmed to her, and Kander and Ebb took the Tony for their score. The 1970 movie directed by Bob Fosse, made an international superstar of Liza Minnelli, garnering Academy Awards for both Minnelli and Fosse.

Kander and Ebb continued producing nonstop, at least by Broadway standards, creating hits and misses—*The Happy Time, Zorba, Chicago, 70 Girls 70, The Act* (also starring Minnelli and making history with a new top ticket price of $25), and *Woman of the Year*—before starting on *The Rink*.

By the time Terrence was brought into *The Rink*, it was not going well. Albert Innaurato (who had had a major hit with the play *Gemini*) had originally been hired to write the book, and Arthur Laurents was slated to direct. They left, citing that perennial reason for something falling apart, "artistic differences." (It was a line that Kander and Ebb had used in "The Cellblock Tango" in *Chicago*: "I guess you could say we broke up / Because of artistic differences / He saw himself as alive / And I saw him dead.")

Neither John Kander nor Terrence remembered how they were first put together, but there was an immediate bond between Kander, Ebb, and Terrence. As Kander said, they would go on to "three glorious collaborations," and *The Rink* was the beginning of an enduring, artistic intimacy.

The Rink had had its genesis when Kander went to Ebb suggesting a musical adaption of *Peer Gynt*, a five-act Norwegian drama by Henrik Ibsen. The drama is a kind of hero's quest mixed with a tale of the Prodigal Son, combined with the enduring, healing power of love. Once again, we are relying on gross simplification, but one of the central relationships in the piece is between Peer and his mother, who after all his selfishness and wandering ends up at home with her, healed by her love.

As Kander said, "No one who sees *The Rink* today would guess that." Not surprisingly, they couldn't make the Ibsen musical work, noble though the effort might have been. They remained, however, fascinated by the relationship between Peer and his mother and the idea of coming home as redemption, and when Terrence came in, they jettisoned the *Peer Gynt* story for a much simpler storyline about the relationship between a mother and a daughter, how it was broken and how it could be fixed. It ended up being a very simple story—at least from a plot standpoint. Anna, who owns a dilapidated roller rink at an unspecified seaside resort, wants to sell up and get out. Her plans are scotched, however, when her long-alienated daughter, Angel, returns, now with a child of her own. Old resentments are hashed out, and a loving resolution is finally achieved.

It's a small and intimate tale, and Terrence was excited to undertake it, remembering that he believed that while there were endless books and plays about the relationships between fathers and sons, there were few, if any, modern examinations of mother/daughter relationships. He felt it was timely.

One of the first things Terrence did as the new book writer was cut the references to Vietnam. Angel was a hippie who had run away from home, had a child with her boyfriend who ultimately went to Vietnam. The creative team wanted to remove those references, which would have seem dated in 1984—and well-worn topics by that time, particularly for Terrence who had dealt with Vietnam in the 1960s with *Next* and *Where Has Tommy Flowers Gone?*

Kander remembers how easy it was to collaborate with Terrence:

> We would talk and talk, and then knock out an outline and begin
> to talk about the characters, and then all start to write at the same
> time in different places. Terrence would bring in some pages, and
> we would talk about them. And he was so musical, he would reach
> a point in the pages that he gave us that would be an aria. He would

write a speech that he knew was going to be a song, and we almost
felt guilty for stealing it, or writing from his inspiration. That was
the part of Terrence, the writer, the poet . . . I don't know how to
explain it exactly. His words would really inspire us.

We would say, "we're going to steal you blind." The point is that
it leads to better work, that kind of collaborating is the best time
in the world.

As the show evolved, it was to be played by Angel and Anna with a
little girl as Angel's daughter, and six men playing all the other parts,
male and female. The original idea was that it should be a smaller, chamber musical, that the story and themes would work in a smaller venue,
but when name-above-the-title stars get involved, the dynamics change,
and Broadway becomes the only option.

Chita Rivera, who had been nominated for a Best Actress Tony for
her performance as Velma Kelly in *Chicago* was signed to play Anna, and
Liza Minnelli, last appearing on Broadway in *The Act* seven years earlier,
was signed to play Angel.

Virtually everyone involved in the production was excited during the
rehearsal process. Rivera especially loved working with Terrence:

> He's very collaborative, but he also was very clear about what he
> wanted. One of the great things about Terrence is that he knows
> who he's working with, and he writes according to what he feels the
> person is like, and that's what he did with me. He made me realize
> things that I didn't know about myself that were absolutely true. So
> we really got to know one another.
>
> She's a very strong woman, Anna. I look at it now in the light
> of 1984, and it was a very daring part. It seems to me that Terrence
> was always really ahead of his time in what he was writing. He knew
> with all his heart, and he wasn't afraid to write it.

No question Rivera was a star. She'd become an international star
playing Anita in *West Side Story*, and she would go on to win the Tony

for her performance in *The Rink*, the only one the show would receive, but she was—and considered herself—a working actor. Liza Minnelli, on the other hand, had become, as a result of *Cabaret*, not just a star, but a personality, and the creative team of *The Rink* had to confront that. Liza was known for showbiz razzamatazz, to put it mildly, so to have her play Angel as a disaffected, angry, young woman who dressed in jeans, a t-shirt, and a jean jacket was not the image that people buying tickets to see Liza would expect. Minnelli, however, was intent on being taken seriously as an actress, and Terrence loved writing for her and appreciated what she was trying to do as an actress. He was always advocating for artists to do theater.

The conflict between Liza the superstar and Liza the actress was never successfully resolved. The fault may lie with the producers who never really communicated to a potential audience what the show was about or what they could expect. It didn't help that the TV commercial was a high-energy thirty seconds, which though it included the slap between Angel and Anna; if you blinked, you missed it. What people saw was two Broadway legends having a good old fashioned Broadway blast. Not exactly truth in advertising.

Chita, with a reputation for knowing what works and being one of the most generous actors to work with, loved rehearsing with Liza and was very sensitive to what she was going through, and she said,

> It was a big chance because—God love the gift and brilliance of Liza—but people have not really allowed her to be herself. People have always said she was Judy Garland's daughter. And I know that when we did *The Rink*, that was about her mother and herself . . . if the audience wanted to think about that. Halston [Liza's favorite designer at the time] had to make two sequin dresses to please the audience because they were disappointed to see Liza in overalls when she was being an actress.

Dealing with audience expectations is always a challenge when stars are involved. Can one, in a mere two and a half hours overcome those?

Hard to say. In the case of Liza and *The Rink*, the pressure on her was enormous.

Rehearsal pianist Paul Ford who sat in on rehearsals from the workshops forward saw the impact that the stress was having on Liza as she tried to find the truth of her character. It was hard work, and because she was *Liza*, there were almost daily rumors about her in the theater community and sometimes in the press.

Jason Alexander, who played one of the six guys in the ensemble, had been in the original production of *Merrily We Roll Along* and would go on to win a Tony for *Jerome Robbins Broadway*, play Buzz in the movie of *L!V!C!*, as the only one not from the original company and the only straight man, and gain worldwide fame as George Costanza in *Seinfeld*; loved the rehearsal process. He'd lied about his ability to roller-skate in the auditions, and quickly learned with the help of some kids in his neighborhood, but he said that it was an ensemble unlike any he had ever been in.

> *The Rink* remains probably the happiest time that I can recall in my
> 40-year career. Consistently from day one, from the day we all met
> to do the workshop till the day we closed. Every day of that show
> was joyous because we all believed in the material. We all believed
> in the show. Chita and Liza were a gift that just kept giving. They
> were funny and generous and ensemble players, when they had no
> reason to be ensemble players.

Of course, as the show developed, rewrites kept coming, and director A. J. Antoon kept tinkering with it and giving notes and new ideas. Alexander has a favorite story from the show about Terrence that happened during rehearsals. One night during previews, Alexander was standing backstage and Antoon came up to him and said he wanted him to play Uncle Fausto (one of the several characters Alexander played in the ensemble) as gay.

> And I must have been just walking around in a daze going, "How
> the fuck do I do this?" And I see Terrence backstage, and he goes

"What's going on?" And I said "AJ just told me he wants me to play Fausto gay," and Terrence, of all people went, "Oh, fuck that." I mean he just went "I forbid you."

I went "Okay, all right. So you'll take the heat." And he said "I'll take the heat." I thought of all people, the frontline banner waver and supreme god of the gay movement, he's the first one that went, "Oh, please, for God's sake."

He was always looking for the integrity of the character.

That was pure Terrence—to put the integrity of the character first. Later in rehearsals, there were some conflicts about script changes coming from the director, and it was the only time the cast saw Terrence put his foot down and insist that not one word would be changed without his say-so. Still, he was very generous, as Kander noted, in seeing words he'd written as lines turn into songs. As Alexander would observe, whatever Terrence did was always about what's best for the piece.

Kander and Terrence both would later say that they accomplished everything they wanted to do with the show. They were proud of it, and hopes were high going into the opening. Alexander recalls that the preview audiences were loving it.

The critics, however, weren't having it. Alexander said,

> It's the only time that I can remember actually being completely blindsided on opening night. Usually, I have some inkling about this is on the positive or negative side . . . And then we got those devastating reviews. And it wasn't that audiences didn't love it afterwards, but we had to earn it every night. The curtain would go up on folded arms, and people were sitting back and going, "Show me. Show me."

Frank Rich's review in the *Times* on February 10 was lacerating. He said, "the running time is forever and a day" and criticized it for being "turgid, sour" and a "curious affair." He called parts of Terrence's book "psychobabble," and accused him of pandering to the audience with the resolution of the relationship between Anna and Angel. Naturally, as Kander recounts, Liza was upset by the *Times* review.

Terrence said he was backstage with Liza who was in tears. "He dismissed me in one sentence." "You're lucky," he said. "He dismissed me in two paragraphs."

So much for artists not reading their reviews.

Terrence's brother Peter was so outraged at Rich's review that he wrote a letter to the editor, saying that he was "puzzled," saying in part:

> Mr. Rich seemed so critical of almost everyone and everything it made me (us—there were 33 in our party) feel as if this man was trying to make the Broadway theatre self-destructive. Most people don't have the opportunity to see Broadway productions of enough to be "expert" critics. However, when an audience is obviously entertained and moved by a production then to read one man's critical opinion the next day—the aftershock is too much to take.

Throughout his career, Rich was often referred to as "the butcher of Broadway."

Looking back, it's easy to focus on the bad notices, from virtually everyone, and all the gossip surrounding Liza during the rehearsal and the run, especially after all that had dogged her during *The Act*. "She literally went from the stage door [of *The Rink*] to the Betty Ford Clinic," Ford said.

However, what is easily missed in such casual dismissal is that once again Terrence and his collaborators were breaking new ground. *The Rink* was a musical that dared to have working class heroes—strong, if flawed, women at the center of the story. No one left *The Rink* wishing that Anna of *The Rink* (unlike Anna Leonowens, the heroine of *The King and I* was their mother). Moreover, all the reviewers who castigated the show, saying that the women were distasteful were white, middle-aged men. Not a single major reviewer—even Liz Smith, more a columnist and a gushing promoter of the show—identified the women's issues at play.

And a flashback to a gang rape of Anna was, though beautifully staged, a challenge. It wasn't what audiences wanted from these stars.

"Who wants to see Chita Rivera get raped?" Ford asked, though Anita's attackers are stopped just short of rape in *West Side Story.*

The show did find an audience. It ran for 233 performances, including previews, and Stockard Channing would take over for Liza in July.

There have been a few attempts to revive the show. It had a brief run in London's West End in 1988, and a complete reading in 1995 for MTC featured Dorothy Loudon (the original Miss Hannagan in *Annie*) as Anna and Julie Johnson (who in addition to appearing in the award-winning *a capella* cabaret group RSVP had been the voice of Baby Bop for the *Barney* preschool franchise) playing Angel. The cast also included John Benjamin Hickey and Stephen Bogardus.

Johnson remembered it as a wonderful rehearsal process. She remembered how kind and supportive Terrence was to her, even introducing her to perform at an MTC gala, saying he'd found someone people would want to hear. Johnson also had a chance to talk directly to Chita about the role, and said Chita told her that she's always wished they had had the chance to go back and visit the more intimate nature of the piece.

MTC decided not to do a revival, saying, as Johnson recalled, that they were going to focus on new works.

The show hasn't completely disappeared, however. The opening number "Colored Lights" sung by Liza and "Marry Me" introduced by Alexander live on in cabaret.

Mostly, however, the show exists only in memory, and in a grainy bootleg video shot from the mezzanine one can find online . . . if they're lucky. It was a noble effort, to be sure, and as Terrence said in a Sunday *Times* review four days before the opening, "We're asking a lot of our audiences." Only the naïve would expect anything less from him.

IV.

One of the things Terrence hated about musicals was how long they took to produce—if they ever got produced at all. As he had said about plays, no one gets paid in the development process, so the many years, at times, spent in creating and fine tuning, and getting seen and revising, and raising money, and all that goes into it, can be agonizing and heart-breaking. It can also be exhilarating as a piece comes together.

Fortunately for Terrence, after *The Rink*, he had a lot in the works to keep him very busy. He was at the beginning of his relationship with MTC, he'd written at least the first act of *Lisbon*, and *Broadway, Broadway* was stirring again downtown.

During this time, he also worked on another musical that pretty much died aborning and stands as an object lesson about how these things fall apart.

George Bernard Shaw's *The Shewing Up of Blanco Posnet* is another unlikely bit of source material for a musical. Subtitled, *A Sermon in Crude Melodrama*, it's play set in the American West. The 1909 play became a bit of a *cause cèlebre* as public performance was blocked by the censors in London because of what were interpreted to be blasphe-mous statements in the arguments about morality and divinity. Like a lot of Shaw, it was more polemical than theatrical, and reading it with twenty-first-century eyes, it's tough to imagine how well it would play. The play was ultimately produced in Ireland and later in private clubs in London, but American critics took exception to the cartoonish interpre-tation and language supposed to indicate the American West.

According to Michael Korie, who wrote the lyrics for the show, many years before *Grey Gardens* and *Flying Over Sunset*, the entire process in 1986 and 1987 was "a lunatic asylum." Vincent Dowling, head of the Great Lakes Shakespeare Festival decided he wanted to make a musi-cal out of the play. He didn't have the rights, and was having a hard time getting them from the Shaw estate, so he decided to rename the show but change as little of the original dialogue as possible. Korie was teamed up with music industry veteran Skip Kennon to write the music in what he called "a shotgun wedding."

They had six weeks to write the score, and Dowling also wanted to do things like eliminate the pit orchestra and have the actors play the music (a crazy idea till director John Doyle made it a signature of much of his musical directing). They didn't do that.

The show didn't come together, though it got on its feet in Cleveland. Korie says there even was a live horse who would neigh every time it heard a certain note in the audience, and since it got a laugh, it stayed in. Korie thought that production finished the show off, but no.

It later got a reading in New York as part of a showcase for regional theaters to see if they wanted to do the shows. Korie said they threw out some of the stuff they had done in Cleveland, and wrote some new stuff, which still didn't work, but revived the show . . . a bit. It was still a mess, according to Korie, the new material not matching the Shaw and so forth.

Kennon had done another one-act musical with Terrence according to Korie (though it's lost), and he convinced Terrence to come on, but it took a very long time to write the book. Terrence didn't care much for the Shaw, and particularly for the argument of divinity and morality—which was the centerpiece of the original—and wanted to rewrite it more like the 1959 show *Destry Rides Again* with Dolores Gray, which Terrence loved, but which had been a complete flop. Moreover, Terrence's book was filled with ethnic and racial stereotypes to which there was already a level of cultural sensitivity and that wouldn't play.

Korie says all the time Kennon was thinking that a book by Terrence McNally was his ticket to Broadway, and Korie was thinking it was a mess. Terrence had changed the name of the main character to Bingo, so that when he had his final revelation he could shout, "Bingo," which Korie and Kennon thought was terrible. Meanwhile Korie thought Kennon's music was terrible, "His version of pop. It wasn't pop."

And so it went with meeting after meeting and argument after argument. At one point, someone said they didn't like the name Bingo and it would have to change. That was the breaking point for Terrence, Korie said, saying that if everyone felt that way, then he didn't want to do it. From there, the whole project fell apart. Korie was left relieved that he had escaped—and went on to do his own work, much of it avant-garde.

The point of this story is that collaborations can be amazing . . . and they can go terribly, terribly wrong, as this one did.

Blanco! (note the added exclamation point), with a new book by Willy Holzman, finally got produced at the first National Alliance of Musical Theatre festival in 1989 and was picked up for a "world premiere" at Goodspeed Musicals in 1990. It's since retreated into obscurity. Kennon and Terrence did work together on another one-act musical *Plaisir d'Amour*, which was part of the Summer Shorts series at 59E59 in 2008. Once again, it was always about the work—and the opportunity to do something that was an artistic challenge was always greater than the personalities involved.

When collaborations work, however, the result can be pure theatrical magic.

V.

Creative people in the theater are always working on—and chasing— "the next one." A bit after *The Rink*, John Kander says that he and partner Fred Ebb were working in the studio one day, "and out of the blue, Fred said, 'Kiss of the Spider Woman.' And I said yes. He said yes. We called Hal Prince, and he said yes.

"And everyone else we talked to thought it was the worst idea they had ever heard."

Still, they moved ahead. Prince was eager to have Manuel Puig, who wrote the original novel and had adapted it into a stage play, write the book. All Kander would say was that "that didn't really work out," and so coming off the successful collaboration on *The Rink*, they invited Terrence to write the book—and he jumped at the chance.

Why wouldn't he? The novel was a perfect match for Terrence's sensibilities—a gay character searching for love and connection as he is thrown together with a stranger in a prison cell, movies as an escape from a dark and difficult life, a threat of further, undefined torment "out there," multi-layered intrigue, and an unexpected intimacy. Operatic in its scope, with a character who essentially dies for love, it has both the scale of opera and the intimacy of what is largely a two-character play.

The original novel published in 1976 is written largely in dialogue. It was initially banned in Puig's native Argentina, where the story is set, but ultimately was permitted in 1983. An English translation followed shortly after the initial publication, but the novel got mixed reviews.

It was the 1985 movie version, which won William Hurt an Academy Award as Molina, the gay hairdresser, jailed for "corrupting a minor" that brought the film to the attention of Kander and Ebb. It was nominated for Academy Awards for picture, director, and adapted screenplay as well as many other film awards, elevating its profile. It was still only a modest success grossing slightly over $17 million worldwide at the box office.

To reimagine the story for the stage, Kander knew it would require more theater and less politics. True to Terrence's style, it was clear that the fascistic repression in Brazil that had landed two men in prison would have been difficult to convey dramatically—to say nothing of being a bit of a slog for audiences. Terrence opted to focus on the growing relationship between the two men and the escape into fantasy that made the horrors of daily life behind bars marginally tolerable. In the way that Buzz in *L!V!C!* turned to musicals, escape and fantasy would become a necessary, if imperfect, salve to their souls. Of course, Terrence didn't abandon that political situation altogether. How could he? It's the backdrop against which an impossible, tragic love develops. Ironically, given that so much of the violence is offstage in the musical, the brutality becomes even more effective dramatically. The constant threat of torture is the thing "out there" that is controlling the lives of the characters. Terrence focused on the two men and their dreams of a better life, against seemingly insurmountable odds.

At rise, Molina is already in the cell, having been there for three years. Valentin, a Marxist revolutionary is brought in bloody and beaten. Molina's method of coping with the daily cruelty and terror of the prison has been to conjure up in his mind the movies of Aurora, a glamorous movie star, in the vein of Rita Hayworth in *Gilda*, the classic *femme fatale*. Molina loves all of Aurora's movies, except the one in which she plays the Spider Woman, because her kiss means death. Molina is manipulated by the warden of the prison to try to extract information from Valentin about his fellow revolutionaries. In exchange, Molina will get his freedom. The torture of both men continues, and Molina continues to tell stories from the movies, as images of those appear around him. Valentin talks about his girlfriend Marta, who it turns out is middle class and not a revolutionary, and Molina talks about the "fellow" for whom he has feelings. Slowly, the bond grows between the two men as Molina tells the stories of more movies. Molina protects Valentin from more torture as the act ends.

In the second act, Valentin tells Molina his dream of a world where oppression has ended, and people are free. As it looks like Molina is going to be released, Valentin asks Molina to make some calls for him on the outside, seducing him into sex. Molina willingly acquiesces, since he has now fallen in love with Valentin. Molina on the verge of his release gives the warden some names and leaves. On the outside, Molina finds the world has changed, that the love he counted on was an illusion, and so decides, against his better judgment to make the phone calls Valentin wanted. He is apprehended by the secret police and thrown back into jail where he is brought into a cell where Valentin is being tortured. Molina confesses his love for Valentin and is shot, dying for his love. In the final moments, Molina appears in a cinematic dream sequence, as the Spider Woman kisses him, bringing death, as the curtain falls.

Well, that's quite a lot, and to make it a bit more complicated, much of the musical happens in the minds of Valentin and Molina—a technicolor complement to the bleakness of the jail cell. The notion of sacrificing oneself for love is, of course, a classic. Perhaps in that sense, *Spider Woman* has more in common with an opera like *Rigoletto* where Rigoletto's daughter sacrifices herself for the love of a Duke.

Yet the scope would not have been inconsistent with the work of Prince who signed on to direct. Prince was no stranger to scope and showmanship. He had directed both Sondheim's *Sweeney Todd* in 1979 and Andrew Lloyd Webber's *The Phantom of the Opera* in 1986, both of which won the Tony Award for Best Musical in their respective years.

By 1992, it was becoming increasingly expensive to mount a musical on Broadway. Producers were looking at $5 million plus to walk through the door, and a year earlier *Miss Saigon* had shattered records with a nearly $11 million capitalization. That only meant the risks were getting greater with each passing season—and raising that capital even more difficult. Terrence recalled that when he was newly arrived in New York, one would see a single name, or two, above the title of the play in the Playbill. "It would be David Merrick presents . . . Or Kermit Bloomgarden presents . . . Today, you're likely to see twenty or thirty names above the title." And those would only be those who had raised sufficient revenue to merit inclusion in the program. Many of those names are aggregators who put together their own packages of even smaller investors. Moreover, everyone putting money into a show has to attest that they can afford to lose the money they are investing. (That's a story for another day—or another book.)

In 1990, a group of producers developed a program designed to mitigate financial risk and allow shows to be developed in front of an audience. A column in *Time* magazine in February announced the program to be called New Musicals and that the first musical to be staged would be *Spider Woman*. The program would allow everyone to work at reduced compensation—unions included—and should a show transfer, fees would return to "normal levels," whatever that might be. The idea was similar to the Broadway Alliance, the program that allowed *L!V!C!* to transfer to Broadway. The shows would be mounted at SUNY in Purchase, New York, which had a strong professional theater program as well as the kind of facility that would allow a full production.

As Kander said,

> The program was a very good idea. A musical could go to Purchase and perform. You could really do a production with a set and a full orchestra. You could change it every night, and you could have discussions with the audience. After a certain number of weeks, you could take what you learned, write a full production, and produce it.

One of the key elements of the program was that it was a laboratory, and while tickets were going to be sold, the productions were never intended to be reviewed. This might harken back to Terrence's experience with the University of Minnesota with *Bump*, but since the audience was going to be self-selecting and anyone could buy a ticket, there was no objection. Moreover, Terrence never fully knew what he had until he got it in front of an audience—a real one that had *chosen* to be there.

The process of putting together *Spider Woman* was joyful for everyone. Kander called it a "very genial" experience. One of the reasons he said that he, Ebb, and Terrence were such strong collaborators was because they "didn't give a shit." Now, that doesn't mean that they didn't care about what they were writing; they did very much. However, in the creative process, they focused on the piece *they* wanted to create. He acknowledged that naturally there would be disagreements or issues with a producer as the piece was developing or out of town, but, he adds, that's all part of the process. What he said was most important, was that "the three of us were satisfied." It was the complete antithesis of the experience on *Blanco!* because, at least for Terrence's peace of mind, it was built into the process that he would be heard.

In May, the team took up residence, and went to work, ready to perform from May 1 to June 24. The show was changing daily, but there was a sense of excitement about it. And then the worst thing happened: the *New York Times* decided to review it.

Kander said:

> All the papers agreed not to review it, except the *New York Times*. Seventeen of us, including the president of the Dramatists' Guild went down to the *Times* to beg them not to review, saying it was like "reviewing childbirth," but they did anyway. Frank Rich came with his wife right in the middle of the process at a performance where we put in a lot of stuff, and the audience was going to see it for the first time.

Rich's review published on June 1 was scathing. His rationale for reviewing the show was that since it was open to the public, and they were charging money, then it was fair game for review. Ironically, one of his primary criticisms is that the musical was not allowed to develop in a workshop setting like *A Chorus Line* or *Sunday in the Park with George.* He objected to the fact that the production was fully mounted, and glancingly noted that the New Musicals was presenting "works in progress. The review was interpreted as a hit piece on Harold Prince, and Terrence isn't even mentioned. It does, however, beg the issue that if an audience is asked to purchase tickets, can producers stop reviews from appearing because those audiences look to publications like the *Times* in deciding whether or not to spend their money on a show. It is almost irrelevant that the show was in development because that's what people were being asked to pay for. Moreover, the New Musicals program was newsworthy, having been widely promoted as an innovation in production and development, so critical coverage was justified—at least from an editorial perspective.

The result, however, was cataclysmic. Nothing frightens away investors as powerfully as negative press, and potential money for a "real" production of *Spider Woman* dried up, and even worse, the entire program was scuttled. Ironically again, it would be *Times* writer Alex Witchel, who would marry Rich in 1991, who would write the obituary for the scuttled New Musicals program. One of the reasons cited for the program being shuttered was that ticket sales fell 40 percent short of projections—but as Roxie says in *Chicago*, "that's showbiz, kid."

Kander says, that review "ruined the program," and one of the other shows that was supposed to be part of it was *The Secret Garden*, which found another route to Broadway where it opened in 1991 and ran for 709 performances.

It looked for just over a year thereafter that this would be the final curtain for *Spider Woman*. Enter Garth Drabinsky. Kander didn't know exactly how, but he knew that Prince was connected to Drabinsky. They would have connected in 1989 when Drabinsky raised the money to buy the Canadian rights to *Phantom of the Opera*, which Prince had directed.

Drabinsky came out of the movie theater business, having cofounded Cineplex Odeon and getting a reputation for being a risk-taker and a visionary. He was eventually bought out of the company, and he formed his company Livent, short for "Live Entertainment," of Canada, for the *Phantom* rights in 1989. Drabinsky's business model was unique in the theater, and his was the only publicly traded, exclusively live theater producing enterprise in North America. Rather than putting together a bunch of investors for each show and producing under a production-specific LLC, Livent put all its productions under the corporate banner, allowing greater fluidity of where to put revenues against multiple projects—and to move them around as needed. Actors, designers, and technicians were employees of Livent, which meant that actors, especially, were in arrangements like the old studio contracts of Hollywood and could be used as the employer saw fit. Drabinsky took a very corporate approach to the whole undertaking, and at the same time invested more time and energy in developing pieces, though one might call it "product development" rather than an artistic enterprise.

At that point, however, much of this strategy that would contribute to Drabinsky's success—and ultimate controversy and downfall—was still untested, as the company was just over a year old. However, he was making a lot of noise in the press and generating a lot of admiration, and a bit of skepticism, in the Broadway community.

Working with Prince, Drabinsky took on *Spider Woman*, and the development process began in earnest. Brent Carver was brought in to play Molina, Anthony Crivello was cast as Valentin, and, most importantly, Chita was cast as the Spider Woman. Again, irony rules, as Frank Rich in that damaging review had written:

> What is needed in this role is not, perhaps, a mysterious reincarnation of Rita Hayworth (which is what Sonia Braga brought to the film version) but a dazzling musical-comedy presence of the Chita Rivera sort who has always ignited the flashiest Kander-Ebb songs.

Chita, who had seen the show at Purchase and had had reservations, didn't know that she had been considered and passed over for the part originally. Though they loved her, the creators thought they needed a younger actress in the title role. However, as Chita remembers, she went to see it, and while the actor in the role could sing, she couldn't dance, and when the role was revised, well, she knew she could be the perfect embodiment of the Spider Woman. It was a relief to the creators as well when she accepted the role, and they set about expanding the role to take full advantage of her talents.

Brent Carver almost didn't get the role, either. Terrence had wanted Richard Thomas to play Molina originally. Thomas had done a reading with Chita after the Purchase debacle, and Kander remembered that both he and Chita thought Thomas was perfect for the part. "We were trying so hard not to break down; it was so moving and touching."

Thomas, however, was in his first marriage, and he thought that if he took the time away, it would give his marriage no hope of surviving. The marriage ultimately dissolved, and Thomas said, mordantly, "I should have done the show." Terrence, however, let him off the hook, saying, "You still owe me a musical."

True to his word, Drabinsky encouraged the show to be workshopped and developed in Toronto. Chita remembered Terrence constantly working on the book throughout the rehearsal process. She described that they would be working on a scene, and he would always sit in the same place in the room, and she would hear the *click, tick tick* on the typewriter.

"He would create and write and write from there, and we would get what we needed right immediately from Terrence. We never had to wait till the next day, so it was really, really exciting," she remembered.

It wasn't always easy, and Chita's recollection is only one perspective on the situation. The rewrites came fast and furious as the company was working on scenes. At one point Hal Prince reportedly didn't want Terrence in the room and banished him from rehearsals so they could focus on getting what they had up and running. Terrence couldn't stop, and he ended up slipping rewrites under the door of the rehearsal studio.

Kander remembers the process well and that they were able to fix the show after the hard lessons of Purchase. For instance, they had to figure out how not to have the sets and the dream sequences overwhelm the actors. There were a lot of extraneous moments that were eliminated. "We had the benefit of learning everything that we did wrong, and you don't always have that if you don't go out of town. And if you stay in New York, you don't learn." Perhaps the biggest change they made was fixing the focus of the piece, and Kander added, "We also went out of town with Chita, and that never hurts anybody."

The Toronto run was successful, and Drabinsky had another idea: take it London and make it a hit there before bringing it to Broadway. In 2022, that's a common practice, as the Tony-winning 2020 revival of Sondheim's *Company* demonstrated, but in 1992, it didn't seem like a very good idea.

Kander explains,

> London is always a surprise, I think, even for those of us who have been going there for decades. We speak the same language, but audiences are different. *Cabaret* opened on Broadway, and it was a big hit. Then we opened in London with exactly the same production—and in addition we had Judi Dench—and the critics didn't like it. The audiences were okay, but it was that funny difference, and while a lot of people talked about it, that difference is real.

Garth's idea of coming to London and then New York was a gamble, and it worked out. *Spider Woman* opened in the West End at the Shaftesbury Theater on October 20, 1992. It would run for 390 performances and take the Evening Standard Award for Best Musical a month later.

Spider Woman opened on Broadway at the Broadhurst on May 3, 1993. Unlike the reviews from Purchase, where he was ignored, Terrence's book was both recognized and praised. In particular, several reviews noted that the piece had adapted the magical realism that is part of Latin-American literature, reflecting Puig's original book.

The *New York Times* didn't run a weekday review of the show, but Sunday reviewer David Richards wrote a piece that borders on gushing, praising every aspect of the show. Given what a hit it had become, *Spider Woman* was big news, and the paper ran several other features on the show during its run.

Spider Woman was nominated for ten Tony Awards and took home seven, including musical, actress, actor, supporting actor. Kander and Ebb won in a tie with the score from *Tommy*, and Terrence won best book of a musical. It was a rough journey that paid off, and though it's not had a major Broadway revival, at the end of his life Terrence was talking about the possibility that it might happen—and it still may.

VI.

When Terrence was going through the arduous, and draining, process of doing a musical—and dealing with the fact that he was only one part of the creative process, at least in the initial stages, he could work on other things . . . and he was always working on other things. Just stop and think about all he had going on artistically as *Spider Woman* opened: *Ganesh* would open a month later at MTC. He was working on *Love! Valour! Compassion!*, *Master Class* was gestating, and now he was part of Livent.

Nor had Drabinsky been idle. In 1993, Livent would open its most successful show yet, a revival of *Showboat* that would play in Toronto, open on Broadway the following October, snagging five Tony Awards, and run for 959 performances, including previews. It was a huge success, and as touring companies went out, cash poured into Livent. Many productions were planned, and Drabinsky seemed like the impresario who would redefine the business of Broadway.

Drabinsky had acquired the rights to E. L. Doctorow's novel *Ragtime*, and he wanted to turn it into a musical—a big musical. Doctorow's 1975 novel had been well-received when it was published, and turned into a movie in 1981, one that the author wasn't very pleased with.

It's a sprawling story starting in 1902, and in order to win over Doctorow and convince him that it could be turned into a musical,

Terrence, working with Drabinsky, wrote an initial treatment that ran about fifty pages. Doctorow was evidently satisfied with how Terrence was approaching his material, and the production was set in motion. The book would go through inevitable changes as the show was developed over the next three years, and not much of the original treatment remained in the show, though there are a few lines that survived.

The story was virtually unchanged from the novel and mingles fact and real-life characters with fiction. A family in suburban New Rochelle—Father, Mother, Mother's Younger Brother, Grandfather, and the Little Boy, Edgar—live in relative comfort. Father, who has made his money in fireworks and patriotic products, goes off on expedition with Admiral Peary, leaving Mother alone, and getting her first taste of independence. Tateh and his daughter, The Little Girl, have arrived as refugees from Eastern Europe and live in the tenements of lower Manhattan. Mother's Younger Brother, a young man in search of a purpose and not content to enter the family business, is in love with vaudeville star Evelyn Nesbit, who became notorious after her husband the architect was murdered by her lover, the "eccentric millionaire" Harry K. Thaw.

Mother finds a Black newborn baby buried in her yard, and the police have Mother meet the child's mother, Sarah, prior to taking Sarah into custody. Mother, however, takes in Sarah and the child.

Musician Coalhouse Walker, father of the baby, searches for Sarah, finding her and wooing her. Sarah is initially resistant but finally yields and rides with him in his Model T, a symbol of his success and accomplishment in the white man's world. They are stopped by a racist volunteer fireman who demands a toll to pass. When Coalhouse refuses, they destroy his car. Coalhouse seeks justice but to no avail as the judicial system is stacked against a Black man. He refuses to marry Sarah until his car is restored. Sarah then goes to seek help from the vice presidential candidate appearing in New Rochelle, but she is mistaken for an assassin and killed. Coalhouse is devastated and swears revenge. And that's just Act One.

Act Two follows Coalhouse as he seeks justice. Father has returned, but Mother, having tasted liberation, can't return to her subservient role.

Instead the family travels to Atlantic City, where they meet Tateh who has reinvented himself as a filmmaker. He has discovered flip books—early animation—and is shooting in Atlantic City. Mother and Tateh meet as their children become friends, and they watch them play freely in the sand. Meanwhile Coalhouse has escalated his attacks, and joined by Mother's Younger Brother, they take over the Morgan Library. "I know how to blow things up." Father eventually negotiates an end to the occupation, and Coalhouse convinces Mother's Younger Brother that violence ultimately is not the solution. However, as he tries to leave the library peacefully, Coalhouse is shot and killed by the police. Many real historic figures of the time, who create the world around the family, Coalhouse and Sarah, include Emma Goldman, Booker T. Washington, Harry Houdini, and others. The show ends as Edgar tells what happens to everyone, notably that after Father is killed in the sinking of the Lusitania in 1915, Mother and Tateh marry and adopt each other's children, and Sarah's surviving daughter. And that's just the high points. It is, to say the least, a plot-heavy piece. Terrence, however, loved the scope and was eager to bring it to the stage. With Drabinsky's commitment, the show—on what clearly was going to be an enormous scale—was going to happen.

With Terrence on board, and Doctorow having given his blessing, the next job was to find a director. At the time, Terrence's agent was Gilbert Parker at William Morris. Parker had represented many playwrights, including A. R. Gurney, Richard Wilbur, Paul Zindel, and others. He also represented director Frank Galati. Galati met Terrence over lunch, and they hit it off. Next stop, Toronto, where Galati met with Drabinsky, and after a daylong interview was signed to the project. What convinced Galati that he wanted to direct it, he said, was that he read the first line of the treatment was the first line of the novel: "In 1902, Father built a house at the crest of the Broad View Avenue Hill in New Rochelle, New York, and it seemed for some years thereafter that all the family's days would be warm and fair." He says that he knew instantly that Terrence was going to preserve the original novel, and it was a story he was keen to tell.

The search for writers for the score began immediately. Above all, what Terrence didn't want was a repeat of the *Blanco!* experience. What he adamantly did not want was to embark on a project where a few months—or even years—into the process he would be unhappy with the direction it was taking, or have his authority taken away. As a result, prospective score writers were sent the treatment with a opportunity to submit four songs, blind. Drabinsky and Terrence would pick the composer and lyricist without knowing anything more about them than what they submitted. In a business of egos, personalities, and the importance of bankable names to secure investment, it was a big risk, but Drabinsky certainly wasn't averse to risk, and, as we'll see, it paid off beautifully.

Lynne Ahrens and Stephen Flaherty were the ultimate winners. They had met during the BMI Workshop in New York, a training ground for musical writers. Prior to *Ragtime,* they had written three shows together that had been produced—*Lucky Stiff* (1988), *Once on This Island* (1990) and *My Favorite Year* (1992). Even so, they were still fairly young in the game.

They immediately focused on the theme of the show—upheaval. As Ahrens said,

> I always found it interesting that ragtime music is a combination
> of white and black keys, and there's this John Phillip Sousa thing
> going on in the left hand. But then there's this very sly and tricky
> and syncopated right hand, which the African American composers
> brought to it.

Ahrens and Flaherty were both excited—and a little scared—at writing the songs. They knew Terrence's work, of course, and that he was one of the go-to guys for musical books. Flaherty says that he had admired him for years, but he didn't meet him till after he and Ahrens got the job:

> Lynne and I had our first show on Broadway, *Once on This Island.*
> We were at the Booth Theater, and it was into the run of the play.
> I got a little note delivered to me at the stage door. I opened it,

and it was this amazing charming and positive note from Terrence McNally, who I'd never met. Basically, the content was congratulations, welcome to Broadway. What a wonderful evening we had. And it was just full of compliments from someone I admired but had never met.

At the time in my little studio apartment, I had a corkboard, and I put the note up on it. The show closed. The tour closed. We had been working on a film that had not worked out. It was the first time after I had had a big success that it felt like a fallow time. I was feeling very vulnerable. The thing that kept me going through that vulnerable time for me as a young writer was Terrence's note on that corkboard. I would look at it and say, "Well, Terrence McNally sees something in me, so there must be something there."

The assignment was to write four songs based on the treatment, and Flaherty says that he and Lynne were doing a variety of things, and he was in London at the time for part of that. They counted the working days and realized they had eleven days. Ahrens said they divided up the work with her writing two lyrics and Flaherty writing two melodies, and then they'd switch. Perhaps it wasn't how they would work optimally . . . but they had eleven days. They got the songs done, went into the recording studio, did the vocal arrangements, and handed them in.

Of the four songs that they submitted three stayed in the show: the opening number "Ragtime"; the end of Act One, "Till We Reach This Day"; and "Gilding," the song Tateh sings to his daughter. The other song they wrote was for Evelyn Nesbitt to sing to Mother's Younger Brother, but the affair between those characters was cut, so that song wouldn't have survived anyway. They were hired, and they were off.

With the team in place—and Galati finding the designers and other staff—they began writing. Flaherty remembers that they worked on the show for about six months. He said the show was a pleasure and that "it wrote itself, really, very, very quickly." He described the process as "running a long-distance course . . . but sprinting," and he said that they were all energized by knowing that what they were writing was going to get produced. As noted previously, it's far more the norm for creators to toil for years with only the faintest hope that there work will ever make it to a stage.

He said that he'd met a young singer, Brian Mitchell (the middle name Stokes would come later) who was singing a song of his from *The Glorious Ones*. Once he heard that voice, he started writing for it. Originally, he thought that Coalhouse was going to be a tenor, but when he heard Mitchell's baritone, he knew that was the voice it should be. They had started writing for Audra McDonald's voice as well, thinking that she would be the ideal Sarah. McDonald had won the Tony for Terrence's *Master Class*, which we'll get to in a bit.

Given how well they worked together, it's not surprising that Ahrens and Flaherty, like Terrence, were inspired to write for particular voices. One of those had been Broadway star Donna Murphy, who had been in an early reading of *Ragtime* but who ultimately wasn't cast. As Flaherty said of Murphy,

> There's something about having an actor of that intelligence and who comes to the table with so many ideas about the character that even if that actor winds up not being in the show, there's something about that interaction that makes the piece richer.

As development progressed, Terrence was very excited about how it was shaping up. His favorite character, he said, was Mother's Younger Brother because he shows up and is passionate and goes through so much in the course of the story. It was also a story about political change and the transition from the nineteenth century to the twentieth century. It's something Terrence felt as they were approaching the twenty-first century, and as Ahrens said later, at the time they were writing it, they hadn't anticipated that the show would have such ongoing relevance, and yet many of the themes are timeless and, for better or worse, are still at play in the twenty-first century.

It's not that there weren't challenges in putting the show together. As she reflected in 2020,

We've done three shows with Terrence. Every show is a joyous experience and also a battlefield. He and I particularly [argued] because we're both, I think, control freaks about our work. He's a stickler for punctuation and a stickler for the way people read his lines based on the punctuation. I'm not so much like that, but I'm very aware of the sounds of words, and when words get repeated it's a little death for the ear. I don't want to say a word in the lead into a song that's then going to appear in the song.

Those are the kinds of discussions we had. Terrance is a playwright who writes from the soul. He writes these lyrical, poetic passages that leap into lyrics, and he doesn't censor or edit himself.

On the other hand, I'm a lyricist, and lyrics are all about the economy of writing, of words and how tight everything has to be. So, when I would edit him—*suggest* something—he would say no, and we'd have a fight. So I had to become a little, delicate drip of water for quite some time to accomplish what needs to be accomplished in terms of editing.

The fights, as Ahrens calls them, were only about art, and it would become emotional because they were both so connected emotionally to the material, and it was a wonderful collaboration.

How one song in particular found its way into the show is a perfect example of how Ahrens, Flaherty, and Terrence went from conflict to consensus—and even excitement. "What A Game" in the second act comes when Father takes Edward to a ballgame to take their minds off all the difficulty at home. As Flaherty tells it, he and Ahrens wrote the song and played it for Terrence, who hated it. In the plot, Father is surprised that the gentleman's game he played in college has become low-class, swearing, racist, epithet-heavy, and rowdy, another symbol of how times were changing. The upbeat number is comic, and Terrence objected because he felt that this was a darker, dramatic moment and was expecting a different kind of song altogether. Flaherty argued that the happy-go-lucky melody actually dramatized everything they wanted to convey at this moment. Eventually, Galati was brought in, and he loved the song. He thought that coming where it did in the act was that last moment of levity before the plot turns, and the audience needed the release. As discussed earlier, it was like Buzz's last speech about musicals in *L!V!C!*, giving the audience a chance to exhale and laugh before things got dark. Terrence acquiesced and later even said that the song had grown on him.

Ahrens also tells the story of how that collaboration resulted in one of the defining moments of the show, one which would crystallize the focus for the entire piece as well. At one point, Father is going to New York to offer himself as a hostage of Coalhouse who has taken over the Morgan Library. Saying goodbye to Mother, he says that once this whole thing is over, he'll come back, and they'll find someone to adopt Sarah's baby, and then everything will be like it was before. And Mother says, "We can never go back to before."

> I remember reading that scene and thinking, "Oh, my God. I've been trying to think of what mother would say or sing at the end of the show to make a statement for herself. She's the one character that didn't have that kind of a song, and she deserved it. At the time we wrote it, it was really a statement of a woman stepping from the nineteenth century into the twentieth century and taking her power.

Clearly, it was a statement for Mother in the context of the show, but it was also a statement by Terrence and his response to what was going on in the world. While they were working on *Ragtime*, the "Don't Ask, Don't Tell" policy had been implemented to tell members of the American armed forces that they had to hide, and he was increasingly upset by the anti-gay sentiment that policy represented, no matter how it was spun. Giving those words to Mother was a statement about her time, and about Terrence's time as well. The thing that was "out there" was the inevitable, unknowable changes that were happening in the world.

For his part, Flaherty built drama into the music. Though one could go through the score—or listen to the recordings—there are two in

particular that emphasize the strength of collaboration. Edward's opening speech, "In 1902 . . . " begins in the middle of a ragged phrase off
the beat. It's not where an ear accustomed to traditional musical comedy structure would expect it, so right from the outset, Flaherty sets up
a feeling of disquiet, that something isn't right, though Edward says,
"It seemed for some years thereafter that all the family's days would be
warm and fair." Second, in the song that came out of the scene Terrence wrote that became Mother's anthem, "Back to Before," until that
point, Mother has been a light soprano, but as she progresses through
the song, her voice opens up to a full-throated sob, the vocal equiva-
lent of acknowledging that she's in crisis, what this change means on a
deeply personal level, and finally seizing her power. As Ahrens said, that
made Mother the central character in the piece. Marin Mazzie who
originated the role in Toronto and on Broadway consistently moved
audiences to tears. In the opening sequence, Flaherty's chords don't
resolve to the tonic for about ten minutes, the ten minutes in which all
the characters—the family, immigrants, the marginalized Black citizens
are introduced. What this would mean to someone not versed in music
theory is that our ears are attuned to specific chord progressions that
indicate a phrase or a song is complete, particularly in musical comedy.
By not resolving those chords, it keeps the audience on edge, perhaps
subliminally understanding that this is not going to be a piece of nos-
talgia but a serious work, until there's finally a release.

As Terrence, Flaherty, and Ahrens worked together, the show took
shape through constant give-and-take, negotiation, and argument.

Then there was Drabinsky. He was used to giving notes—and he
did, extensively. He would write lengthy and highly detailed notes and
expect them to be implemented immediately. This did not sit well with
Terrence, who wrote:

> Dear Garth:
>   I'm not used to working this way: pages on demand. And you
> know what? I don't want to get used to it.

I think it's best I withdraw from the project at this point. All my alarm systems are sounding loudly: "This is just the beginning. Get out while you can."

So, I wish you and Lynne and Stephen gread [*sic*] good luck on the project. It was very dear to me, but I really don't want to work for someone who has so little understanding of my creative process, so little respect for my feelings and so little confidence in my work.

I'm sure you're thinking "Terrence, you completely misunderstand me." I'm afraid, Garth, I understand you very well. You want things when you want them. I can appreciate that. Trouble is, I'm not the person to fit into your scenario at this point in my life.

My feelings for you remain cordial. I don't think we were meant to do RAGTIME together, that's all.

Yours,

Terrence

The note is undated, and an original typed version is in the archives, but in fact, there's no evidence that Terrence ever sent it. Whether he did or not, he didn't leave the production, and as he had happened with *Bump* and *Here's Where I Belong*, he took strenuous objection to what he felt was his craft and artistry being disrespected.

The first production of *Ragtime* opened in Toronto on December 8, 1996, and the team continued to work on it. The U.S. premiere opened at the Shubert Theatre in Los Angeles in June 1997, where it got supportive reviews, particularly from John Lahr in the *New Yorker*. Throughout this process both Ahrens and Flaherty said they continued to work on the show, cutting, trimming, revising. Flaherty recalled that in Toronto the show ran over three hours.

While the show was getting ready, Drabinsky was building a home for it in New York. Livent had capitalized the show at about $10 million each for separate productions in Toronto, Los Angeles, and New York, with the New York production growing to $12 million by the time it was running. In addition, Livent had spent $30 million to create the Ford Center for the Performing Arts on 42nd Street, a combination of two theaters as part of a Times Square renewal project. Livent intended it to be the home for many other productions in the years ahead.

Drabinsky was also a micromanager, unlike many other producers, weighing in on the script, of course, and everything from songs to light cues. On one hand, it's understandable. As CEO of Livent, he was looking out for his "product," and was doing everything to ensure that it was on budget and profitable. On the other hand, that kind of management style was anathema to creative teams, as Terrence's response to script changes made clear. As a manager, he did one more thing that enraged Terrence. He hired a polling company to gauge audience reaction as a way of knowing how to "tweak" the product. Terrence felt, as any artist would, that focus group testing would kill the ability of an artist to respond creatively to the perception of a theater piece based on his own creativity and taste.

On March 1, 1998, the *New York Times* published an article by Michiko Kakutani that called focus groups or polling in the arts "shameless second-guessing," and she quoted Drabinsky as defending polling audiences, a practice from his days in the movie business, as necessary. He also said that as a result of polling, Terrence's book went through "some 20 drafts." Kakutani also reported that Drabinski required writers to create a treatment to ensure that the writer is not "going off on a tangent and doing something that is incongruous to the philosophy or ideas of the producer."

Terrence was livid. In an angry letter to the editors, which was sent but never published, he refutes Kakutani's statements, clarifying that he had written the treatment to get Doctorow's appraisal. He said that their initial draft which "we revised hundreds upon hundreds of times over the course of several readings, workshops, and out of town productions." He says that while they were aware that there were researchers present, neither he nor his collaborators ever saw the research. What he objected to most was the implication that his art was subject to random opinions. He wrote:

It never entered into our creative process or influence our writing. If
that had ever been requested by Mr. Drabinsky or anyone else, we
would have all immediately resigned from the project. To suggest
anything else verges on libel.

In the letter, Terrence goes on to say that Kakutani never spoke to
the writers, and that the article was an insult to their integrity, ending
with, "We would be happy to accept her apology." As happened with
his "Statement" during the process of *Bump* in Minnesota, once again
Terrence's prose, which veers decidedly toward the purple when he is
outraged, was an attempt on his part to express how deeply hurt he was
by his honor as an artist being impugned.

For their part, *Times* editorial director at the time Adam Moss wrote
back to Terrence saying that the facts Terrence was disputing came from
an on-the-record conversation Kakutani had with Drabinsky, as well as
refuting Terrence's other claims. "If you have issues with these points,
you'd best take them up with Mr. Drabinsky," Moss wrote.

Ragtime had opened at the Ford Center on January 18, 1988, to
mixed-to-negative reviews. Ben Brantley at the *New York Times*, despite
praising many elements of the production, called it "utterly resistible."
The show, however, found an audience and was nominated for thirteen
Tony Awards. It lost Best Musical to *The Lion King* but picked up the
prizes for Ahrens and Flaherty for the score, and Terrence for the book.
It ran an impressive 861 performances, but due to high running costs, it
never recouped its investment.

As Livent continued to grow, they also opened "sit downs" (i.e., resi-
dential fully mounted productions rather than tours) of *Ragtime* in Chicago and Washington, D.C. Drabinsky was hailed as a genius by some
on Wall Street, and the phrase "corporate theater" began showing up in
news reports, which as things looked rosy heaped praise on Drabinsky's
risk-taking bravado. Drabinsky would be lauded as a showman, bor-
rowed heavily, and attracted lots of money, to the envy of other producers. The showman, however, would turn out to be more P. T. Barnum
than J. P. Morgan.

Ragtime would have several international productions, including two revivals in London and was revived on Broadway in 2009, after a run at Kennedy Center in Washington, D.C., but it would prove too expensive to run, lasting only ninety-three performances. The revival did, however, get seven Tony nominations.

Terrence would work on one more project for Livent, a revival of *Pal Joey*. It was a project that he was excited about perhaps because of his early experience of the show and his love of the Rodgers and Hart score. He wrote an updated book that tried to solve the problems of the original, and his archives are full of pages of notes and character analyses, but his adaptation got only one public production, at the City Center Encores! series in 1995, starring Patti LuPone and Peter Gallagher. While the Encores! concerts are often a test for a Broadway run, this one never went further. A 2008 revival of *Pal Joey* by Roundabout Theatre featured a new book by Richard Greenberg.

Livent may have already been feeling the heat that would take it down. Finances were strained because there was no new "product" to continue funding the company. In a *New Yorker* article published in June 1997, Terrence said he "recently took a strong stock position in Livent," thinking it would go up after *Ragtime* opened. He perhaps should have followed the advice of Max Bialystock from *The Producers*, "Don't put your own money in the show."

Livent declared bankruptcy in the United States and Canada the following November, and Drabinsky was convicted of fraud and forgery for the period between 1993 and 1998. It was speculated at the time that his business model wasn't quite what it had been cracked up to be, and the high running costs of *Ragtime* contributed to his falsifying financial statements. After serving a prison term, Drabinsky tried to return to Broadway in 2022 with a new musical *Paradise Square*. It didn't find an audience, and Drabinsky was put on the Actors' Equity "Do Not Work List," as a result of his not paying the company and poor working conditions. No union actor can work with him, ending his career as a Broadway producer. (At this writing, Drabinsky is contesting that.)

When Livent collapsed, some more traditional producers felt vindicated, though they did not want to comment for attribution, and the buzz was that Livent's problems would spell the end of so-called corporate theater, but Disney would prove that wrong as it thrived on Broadway. The difference, naturally, is that Disney's theatrical division is protected somewhat against the challenges of the theater because of the parent company's diverse businesses. A loss in theater can be buffered by revenues in other divisions, such as theme parks, movies, and now a streaming channel, all of which are somewhat more dependable revenue producers than theater. Livent went all in on theater, and demonstrated that a lack of diverse enterprises and trying to make commerce out of art can be a risky business.

Terrence, however, would thrive—and keep working.

VII.

When collaborations work, it's almost seamless. There are no angry letters in the archives, no reports of fights or arguments, no threats to quit. It's not very dramatic, but better the drama should be on the stage.

That was the case with *The Full Monty*. The 1997 film had been a huge international hit. The story centered on six unemployed men in Sheffield, Yorkshire, who create a Chippendale's-like act to raise money so the main character, Gaz, can pay his child support obligations. In promoting their act, they promise to go "the full monty" (i.e., take it all off). Through a series of twists and turns, the men's lives are exposed— as they are literally in the finale. Part buddy movie, part human comedy, part "bromance," the film was a mega hit, grossing more than $250 million worldwide on a budget of only $3.5 million.

It was a goldmine for Fox Searchlight pictures, and it was the first project that new president Lindsay Law put into production. Five years later, itching to return to the legit theater, where he'd worked previously for decades, Law moved back to the East Coast to begin producing theater. His first project was based on his biggest hit, and Fox Searchlight signed on as a producer.

Law's first call was to his friend Jack O'Brien, artistic director of the San Diego Old Globe. They were interested—and in fact had considered that the movie was perfect to adapt as a musical. They were in.

O'Brien in turn reached out to Terrence who said yes immediately. It became one of the legends of the show that Terrence said, "I would have killed you if you asked anyone else." Previously, Producer Elizabeth McCann introduced O'Brien and Terrence, and they worked together on a play Terrence wrote called *Up in Saratoga*. It was an adaptation of an 1870 play *Saratoga*, which combined melodrama and farce. It was McCann's idea to update it, and Terrence did. The Old Globe had mounted it under O'Brien's direction in 1989. It bombed. Sprawling and apparently deeply in need of editing and focus, the *Los Angeles Times* called it a "frenzied three-hour-plus white elephant."

Nonetheless, O'Brien and Terrence loved working together and created a bond that would last through the rest of Terrence's life. O'Brien and Law wanted to use *The Full Monty* as an opportunity to launch a new musical talent, and they approached Adam Guettel, who, as O'Brien recalled, screened the movie and thought it was one of the best books for a musical he'd ever seen. However, he turned them down because at the time he was working on *The Light in the Piazza*. However, Guettel said he had a friend, David Yazbek who was "dying to do a musical."

As O'Brien remembered:

> I called David up and asked if he was interested. And he said he was. And then we said, would you send us some of your materials so we would know what your things are like and would you consider writing a couple songs on spec?
>
> And he said he would be happy to do so. He sent a couple of albums. There were things that we thought this could go right into the show, although they didn't, but they were clearly wonderfully raw, blue collar, original modern stuff. And when he sent his three songs on spec, two of them went straight into the score. So, we knew we had the right guy.

Yazbeck was hired and work began. However, he said that when he went to the Old Globe for the first meetings, there wasn't even a first draft.

Jack O'Brien looked at his schedule for the Globe and pointed to a date a year from the date we were there and said we're going to start rehearsing here. That's unheard of for a musical.

Yazbek remembered that for the first draft of the script, Terrence hadn't indicated where any songs would go, which wasn't typical for Terrence, but the entire team, which now included Jerry Mitchell as the choreographer and Ted Sperling as music director, would look to see where songs would fit in the script. The show really developed as a collaboration.

For the musical, the story was relocated to Buffalo, New York. The basic premise of the story remained unchanged from the movie. Six men either out of work or without prospects decide to put on their own strip act after their wives see a tour of Chippendale's. They ultimately pull it off (pun intended) but not without going through many challenges, heartbreaks, and questioning themselves and their relationships, and their manhood. The story was ideal for Terrence. The themes of self-doubt, body image, gay impulses, and insecurities about being male all figure into the story, giving it depth and complexity.

The production moved ahead easily. As O'Brien said, it's not always that a show comes together with such relative ease. "Relative" being the operative word in that sentence. O'Brien noted that it wasn't always easy working with Terrence:

> In spite of his incredible wit and his charm, he was very uncomfortable in rehearsal. He was grumpy. He was teeth-grindingly angry most of the time, but the anger was pretty much directed at himself. How could he get this righter? How could he make this more specific, clearer, better? That is not a sunny disposition. And if he gives you a good paragraph and you're chewing it up, he's enraged.

It was, though, ultimately all about the work. Yazbek, who was in his late thirties at the time, found Terrence to be a great collaborator. As he had with Ahrens and Flaherty, Terrence's speeches were often transformed into lyrics. Yazbek remembers working with Terrence to shape it, even cutting numbers that everyone liked because they didn't serve the story. It was, Yazbek said, a tremendous learning experience for him.

When deep in the development of a show, it's sometimes easy to forget that life outside goes on. Terrence's mother died during the process, and Terrence was diagnosed with lung cancer, but he never faltered. Yazbek said,

> It tells you something about him, that he was able to work at such a high level. And have a hit show. I do remember him telling me, "well, I was a journalist, and you don't have any choice. You have got to make the deadline."
>
> But here's the thing, he was also, he'd put in his 10,000 hours and then some, so that's what I'm learning these days is at, at the age I'm at, which is almost the age he was at when he did *Full Monty*. You've learned a lot; you have your talent, you've hopefully empowered it as much as you can. You've acquired lots of knowledge and you can, that can help you get through hard times while you're working.

Yazbek added that watching Terrence and O'Brien working on scenes again and again to get them right was inspiring. He would say that Terrence would willingly rewrite scenes, but at the same time, he would never feel he had to defend his work to Yazbek, or anyone when it was questioned. It was always about finding the best possible way to express something.

Challenges and the usual difficulties notwithstanding, *The Full Monty* went up at the Old Globe, and it was a huge hit. Yazbek remembers that it was the biggest hit the theater had had. It kept extending.

The move to New York was comparatively easy, which means it wasn't agony and complications from day one. After the run at the Old Globe, the piece was about 90 percent complete. There were cuts for running time, and minor changes, but the ability to work everything out at the

Old Globe put them ahead of the game. The production closed in California in July 2000 and opened the following October in New York. It would run 805 performances total, and be nominated for every major award, but it was up against *The Producers*, which won twelve Tonys out of fifteen nominations. Yazbek would win the Drama Desk award for Outstanding Music.

Ben Brantley in the *New York Times* was harshly critical of Terrence's book, while calling it "that rare aggressive crowd pleaser that you don't have to apologize for liking." How the show could have been a "crowd pleaser" *without* the book is unknowable, and one of the reasons Terrence would so often be frustrated by critics.

VIII.

Terrence would contribute the books for five more musicals during his career.

Chita Rivera: A Dancer's Life in 2003 was a love letter to a performer he adored and who he said taught him so much about being a professional in the theater.

Catch Me If You Can, based on the Spielberg movie of the same name, was a modest success that landed on Broadway in 2011, after more than six years in development. It was a tough go for Terrence, and he never had much to say about it. The reviews, which were mostly mixed, weren't kind to him. Once again, Terrence was adapting a movie, and there were issues in trying to fit the source material into a musical. Jack O'Brien, who directed, thought the score by Marc Shaiman and Scott Wittman was better than their score for *Hairspray*, but the critics didn't agree. Terrence's assistant, Logan Reed, referred to *Catch Me If You Can* as "the one we don't talk about."

A Man of No Importance (2002) was near and dear to Terrence's heart and reunited him with Ahrens and Flaherty.

The Visit (2015) took fifteen years to get to Broadway, one of the longest gestation periods of Terrence's career—or of many musicals that eventually get to Broadway.

Anastasia (2017), again with Ahrens and Flaherty, was Terrence's final Broadway musical.

For all of these, the creative processes were challenging as musicals are, but Terrence proved himself to be the consummate collaborator, though always quick to speak up for his own work and at times adamant about what should be in the show. At times he would disappear, particularly during *A Man of No Importance*, which would frustrate his colleagues. Lynne Ahrens often delivered the complaints with affection and gentleness. It was a process.

During *A Man of No Importance*, Terrence had undergone his first cancer surgery, and he'd met Tom Kirdahy, the man who would become his husband—and the love of his life. (More on that in a bit.) He certainly was changed by it, and the book of *A Man of No Importance* is one of his most poetical, heartfelt, and simple. For a man who had always started from a place of overwriting (something he would still do from time to time), he was finding a new economy and simplicity in his language.

A Man of No Importance is based on the movie of the same name. It tells the story of Alfie Byrne, a bus conductor in Dublin in 1964 who elevates his prosaic life by reciting Oscar Wilde's poetry to his passengers and directing the local theater troupe. A deeply closeted gay man, he is secretly in love with his driver, Robbie Fay, who claims he is not "poetical," though he is kind to Alfie. Alfie's sister Lily is desperate for him to marry and be settled so she can marry Mr. Carney, the butcher, and get on with her life. When Alfie wants to produce Wilde's *Salome*, the monsignor who allows the troupe in the church is outraged at the play's presumed immoratily, and shuts down the production, killing Alfie's spirit. Alfie is revealed as being gay, Robbie runs off, and Alfie realizes that he can no longer hide. The show ends with the members of the community rallying around Alfie, including Robbie who has come to join the new acting troupe.

One of the important tropes of the play, not mentioned in the above synopsis, is that Oscar Wilde is a character in the play. Alfie is largely alone and isolated with no one to talk to. Wilde appears in Alfie's dreams and tells him how to express his hidden self, as Wilde did. It didn't go well for Wilde, and it doesn't go well for Alfie, but it gave the musical an important dramatic element.

Flaherty says that the idea for the show came from Terrence when he brought Ahrens and him a VHS copy of the movie. "I thought it was beautiful," Flaherty said, "and I like what it had to say. I like that it was Dublin in the sixties, and I loved that it was all about Catholic stuff because I really know this stuff." In writing the one song, "Confession," he said the feeling he was trying to capture was that of being in that booth as a child. He said it took several drafts to get it right, particularly since Alfie knows he's not telling the truth.

There was one other problem—a big one—in trying to dramatize the story. If you've got a musical, the main character has to sing . . . and usually a lot. Since Alfie spends most of his time in the bus or in his room alone, it's a challenge. Flaherty wondered; How would the audience get to know him?

And so, Terrence came up with the idea that Oscar Wilde would appear as a character in the musical. He was not a character in the flim. Flaherty said:

> Once we did that, it was easy to write for Alfie because he and Wilde could be having a conversation. It's a fantasy conversation, but it really helped the character to come out, as it were.
>
> So we wrote the song "Man in the Mirror," and we play it for him. He [Terrence] hears it once and never asks to hear it again. He goes, "Oh, okay" and takes it in. It was not until we assembled the actors in a reading that he heard it again.
>
> He got really excited, and he said, "There, that's the sound right there. That's the sound of the show. That's who this person is."
>
> I couldn't have done it without Terrence being able to open that door for me.

Flaherty remembered that during the process of creating the show Terrence kept mentioning The Gallery Players, Dominic Cuskern's company in Brooklyn and where Cuskern got his start acting, as an inspiration for Alfie's theater group.

The show was staged at the Mitzi Newhouse Theater at Lincoln Center, the smaller of the two houses (Lynne Meadow had reached out in a letter to Terrence to see if MTC could coproduce, but that went nowhere), and it was directed by Joe Mantello. It was his first musical, and he said that he did it because it was Terrence pushing him in that direction. Mantello was approached about directing *Wicked* at the same time, but he insisted that they change the date so he could do *A Man of No Importance*. After a lot of back-and-forth during which Mantello continually expressed that he would honor his commitment to Terrence and the production team, the *Wicked* dates were moved, and Mantello would get to do both, picking up the Tony Award for *Wicked*.

A Man of No Importance could not have been a more different piece than *Wicked*. It was small, intimate, and heartfelt as opposed to large and lavish. As Mantello said,

> It was an unorthodox idea for a musical. We were just coming out of a time of the British big mega musicals. I think only Terrence would have seen the potential for a musical in that story because it was about everything he loved, and Stephen and Lynne were the people to write it.
>
> It was a really charmed experience. It was infused with all of Terrence's passion for the theater and what he thinks theater can do.
>
> We were all in shock that it didn't have a better reception from, I think, primarily the *New York Times*.

That was an understatement. Ben Brantley attacked the show for its sentiment and simplicity, the very things that to many gave the show its heart. Though he didn't mention the book, other than to say that all the creators were "immensely gifted," he called the show "treacly." Other than mentioning that Alfie is exposed as gay, he doesn't mention, or perhaps perceive, that the show is about something larger, about finding oneself, and finally, as Terrence himself had done many years ago, refusing to hide, no matter the consequences. It was the kind of review that Terrence hated. He was open, well as open as he could be, to real criticism, but it bothered him when a critic basically said, "I like it," or "I don't like it" and made no argument.

The tepid critical reception was frustrating and damaging. The anticipation was that the show was going to move to Broadway. Terrence and others said that they were ready to go into the Booth Theater, one of the smaller Broadway houses on 45th Street. They said that once Brantley's bad review came out, the financing dried up. Andre Bishop, the producer at Lincoln Center called the show "the one that got away," but he disputed the idea that the show was headed to Broadway:

> There was never any plan to move the show to Broadway, though that thought always exists in the hearts of the creators and is always discussed around new musicals. The audience warmed to the show and liked it a lot, and the proof is that it is done all over the country. But the critics were almost universally bad about the show. The *New York Times* critic did not like it because he felt Roger Rees who played Alfie [and who had become a major star playing the title role in *The Life and Adventures of Nicholas Nickleby* on Broadway in 1982, and earning the Tony for best actor], was miscast and simply too good looking to play a lonely gay man. What he was forgetting was that this was the 1960s and in a rigidly Catholic country. People were not "out" yet. I called the show "the one that got away" because we all truly felt it was good and beautifully done (if a tad overlong), and that sometimes there are shows that have all the talent and goodness and somehow get overlooked or criticized for reasons you cannot quite fathom. I have no doubt that if the show were to be revived now in a first rate production, it would be a success.

What's not in question was that *A Man of No Importance* helped to open the door to the intimate musical as both viable and able to attract an audience. Bishop had certainly championed smaller musicals both at Lincoln Center and when he was running Playwrights Horizons. *A Man of No Importance* demonstrated that difficult subject matter can make effective theater when it's in the right hands.

As for a first-rate revival, the first major revival of the show was mounted at Classic Stage Company (CSC) in Manhattan in the fall of 2022. Working with Tom Kirdahy, director John Doyle cut the piece down to one act, running an hour and forty-five minutes. It was a deeply personal production for Doyle, and though Terrence had died, Doyle felt that it was nonetheless a powerful collaboration. Doyle, who worked with Terrence on *The Visit* felt a deep connection to Alfie. Both Doyle and Terrence had grown up in an era when it was dangerous to be gay, though Doyle had grown up in Scotland.

He said, "I'm a gay man, a gay man who was exploring my sexuality while it was still an imprisonable act. I know what it felt like. I can remember when living in a small community where you daren't express who you were—long before the days when terms like 'coming out' came into our vocabulary."

In addition to simplifying the story, Doyle wanted the music to be more Celtic, and Flaherty and Ahrens were on board. Bruce Coughlin created new orchestrations as well with an emphasis on Irish pipes, violins, and percussion.

When it had its Broadway premiere in 2018, Jim Parsons, a star from the TV sitcom *The Big Bang Theory* and had had a huge hit as Michael in *The Boys in the Band*, was Alfie. The production was a hit, extended, and finally received the critical praise it deserved.

IX.

The process of getting *The Visit* to Broadway is a story in itself. Probably its most likely literary model is the case of *Jarndyce v. Jarndyce* in Dickens's *Bleak House*, though not quite so long and without the tragic ending. Still, the stop-start nature of the process and the feeling that it would *never* get on stage lingered for many years.

The Visit was based on a 1956 German play by Friedrich Dürrenmatt. Terrence had first encountered it when he was at Columbia and loved it; it had premiered on Broadway in 1958, directed by Peter Brook. The idea of updating it or doing it as a musical had been in Terrence's mind for years. Finally in the late 1990s, Terrence began to work on it with Kander and Ebb. The piece would go through many revisions in the process—and three completely realized versions—before it would land on Broadway.

The story is about the world's richest woman, Claire Zachanassian, who returns to the town she left as a girl. As a result of the war, the town is bereft and on its last legs. Claire offers to solve all their financial problems, if they'll do one small thing for her: murder Anton Schell, the man who jilted her many years ago and who continues to live in the town. The play is a biting satire about the ends to which people will go for wealth, but it's also a dark reflection on mortality and lost love. That it would be appealing to Terrence at this time in his life isn't surprising. His lover Gary Bonasorte was suffering with AIDS and would die from complications of it in November of 2000. Though the work on the show had started previously, by early 2000, it was evident that Gary was severely ill. Notes to Terrence at the time are trying to be as optimistic as possible, celebrating rallies in Gary's health, but it was clear that Gary was seriously ill and dying.

Angela Lansbury, who had grown close to Terrence over the years, had signed on to play Claire, and they were preparing for a 2001 run at the Goodman in Chicago with Frank Galati slated to direct and choreography by Ann Reinking. Tony-winner Philip Bosco was set to play Anton.

In March of 2000, Galati sent Terrence lengthy notes, as he had done on *Ragtime*, suggesting cuts and changes, and it's evident that Galati was having ongoing conversations with Lansbury and doing his best to address her concerns about the piece. However, in his notes, Galati was careful to let Terrence know that what he was sending were only suggestions, and that while Angela was eager to see the revisions, Galati acknowledged that Terrence would have the final word on the next version. He also added that they had looked at the Broadway theater as a possible home for the show when the show arrived in 2002 on Broadway.

Sadly, Lansbury's husband became very ill, and Lansbury withdrew from the production. In an earlier note to Terrence, she had said that her husband Peter Shaw was ill—and refusing treatment. By July of 2000, the situation was dire, and Lansbury felt that she needed to be with her husband. Finally, she sent a letter to the producing team, withdrawing entirely:

> The kind of commitment required of an artist carrying a multi-million dollar production has to be 100%, and in fairness to you, and incidentally, myself, I realize I simply couldn't manage being available to you of the company, and fulfill my desire & need to care for Peter. . . .
>
> To have come this far with you for naught seems so sad & unfair. The infinite joy of being with you, Frank, John, Fred & Terrence & Ann hammering out our ideas & feelings about the play will be forever a memory of my time in the theater to cherish.

John Kander remembered, "it was a lovely experience, but a short one. And then came Chita." Chita Rivera stepped in for Angela Lansbury, and John McMartin stepped in for Philip Bosco. The show opened in Chicago to rave reviews . . . on September 11, 2001.

Galati remembers that no one from New York could fly out to see it.

> Nobody would fly, and some people who were involved in the production were stuck. We had the finale of the first act called "Yellow Shoes," it's where the villagers all on credit get themselves shiny, new yellow shoes [In anticipation of Claire's bailout]. And the yellow shoes were somewhere in Pennsylvania. We'd had a fitting, and they were sent away to be finished. So we had to drive. We had a kind of relay system driving from New York to pick up the shoes to go the next rest stop to deliver the shoes to another car who was going to take the shoes finally to Chicago.

The shoes got there, but no potential producing partners did, and so the show closed after its run at the Goodman.

It would be seven years till the show was staged again. Terrence had rewritten the script, and according to Kander it was much improved. "It's about the art," he said, of Terrence's writing process with the book. "People who do it long enough learn to do less. Verdi had a long career, and his last piece was *Falstaff* where he could do in one phrase what it previously took him an entire aria to do." Signature Theater in Virginia produced the show, again with Chita. Three years later in 2011, a concert version was staged in New York with Chita and John Cullum in the lead roles, but other announced productions had fallen through. By this time there was a joke among actors in New York that if the show ever got to Broadway, actors who would have been seen as one of the Eunuchs, part of the young, male chorus, would be right for Anton.

Logan Reed, Terrence's assistant, said that *The Visit* had become a passion project for Terrence's partner Tom Kirdahy who had become a producer, and who arranged for it to be produced at Williamstown in 2014. Terrence wrote another version, this time shortening the piece to one act. Once again, Chita stepped into the role of Claire, joined by Roger Rees as Anton. Also in the cast was Judy Kuhn, from the original cast of *Ragtime*.

John Doyle had signed on to direct. By this time, Doyle had become a kind of wunderkind in musical theater. He had pioneered revolutionary—and less expensive, let's be honest—productions of Sondheim musicals where actors also played the instruments, beginning with *Sweeney Todd*, which he had debuted at the Watermill Theatre in England and subsequently brought to Broadway with Patti LuPone and Michael Cerveris in the leads. A subsequent revival of *Company* starring Raúl Esparaza began in Cincinnati and moved to Broadway. He was very much an actor's director, and LuPone recalled how he had worked with her to find the role of Mrs. Lovett. He also took home the Tony Award as best director for that production. Doyle is an enthusiastic director, who for all his sophistication and experience loves actors and loves the process. He would be a perfect fit with Terrence.

How he got involved is one of those showbiz stories of opportunity and serendipity:

> I was going to (or coming from) London, and I was flying across the Atlantic somewhere. I was walking down the aisle of the plane, and there was Tom. And he said, "How lovely to see you. Would you take a look at *The Visit*?" I cannot believe I'm being asked about a job on an airplane. I said, "yeah, yeah."
>
> So, I looked at it, and how would you say no to something that involved John Kander and Terrence McNally? And then, eventually, Chita Rivera and Roger Rees. I mean, it was extraordinary.

Fred Ebb had died ten years before in 2004, and Logan Reed remembered that throughout the entire rehearsal process, Kander and Terrence kept talking about how they wished Fred was with them.

The Williamstown production was successful enough to move to Broadway, but they were having trouble getting the financing. Edgar Bronfman Jr. said that Tom had come to him late in the day and asked if he would coproduce. Bronfman thought it was a risk. He acknowledged that it was something very special, but it was also a tremendous risk.

> I thought the odds were low to be honest because with that kind of show if you don't get a rave from *The New York Times*, you're probably not going to survive. It's kind of crazy to throw $10 million or whatever it was all for the opinion of one guy who can make or break your show.

It was not a rave, so it broke the show. Though Ben Brantley loved Chita, he called Terrence's book "tartly didactic." The show opened at the end of April and closed just under a month later. What's remarkable looking back at it, however, is that Terrence continued to be fearless as an artist, that he was willing to go to the dark places. Kander, Bronfman, Galati, and others thought the darkness of the story gave it its power, but audiences weren't ready for that level of social commentary, however beautifully expressed it was.

Chita perhaps expressed it best, saying that she wasn't sure that audiences understood *The Visit*. While it was on the surface a story of revenge, the way Terrence wrote it, it was a love story at its heart.

> It's a conundrum—original musicals and original stories. They're not the stories people know, but it can take you somewhere dark, and it's kind of delicious to go there at times.
>
> It's a journey. That's all life is—a journey. The mere fact that she takes him back after he has admitted he was wrong and he ruined her life. But she took him back, and to this very day, those two people are in their caskets overlooking the Mediterranean, Positano you know. They're overlooking the water and being with each other. That's the love story.

John Kander said that of the three shows he and Ebb and Terrence did together, none of them got great reviews, and yet it was the artistic collaboration of a lifetime and all a theater artist could wish for.

X.

After *The Visit*, Terrence swore he'd never do another musical. (He really meant it this time.) Aside from the time it took, he felt limited creatively, though he invested wholeheartedly; the collaboration was demanding even when it was good, and it was just too stressful. Famous last words, as they say.

When he was approached about writing the book for *Anastasia*, he said yes. Asked why he agreed to after so publicly saying he didn't want to go down that long road again, his husband Tom said Terrence loved Russian history, was fascinated by the story, and he would be working with people he loved. He said that he and Terrence were in London at the time, and either Ahrens or Flaherty called and said they had an idea and an opportunity, and would he be interested? He was, and more to the point, as Terrence was getting older, he only wanted to work with people he loved.

That was reason enough to dive in again. However, to hyper-extend the metaphor, the waters would be choppy. At this point, however, would he expect anything else?

One of the things that Terrence was adamant about going into the project was that it wouldn't just be a rehashing of the 1997 animated version that had grossed more than $80 million worldwide. He had no interest in doing that. He loved the 1956 movie starring Ingrid Bergman with a screenplay by Arthur Laurents, but Terrence wanted to go even further. He wanted to go deeper and write the story of a young, strong woman.

It was, however, a requirement that musical's book be based on the two movies, both from Fox, and they would be required to list that it was inspired by both those movies.

Flaherty says that it was a little different going into this production because he and Ahrens had already written songs for the animated version, which would be included in the staged musical, so the project didn't quite belong to the three of them at the outset as *Ragtime* and *A Man of No Importance* had. But they soon hit their stride. As they began work, they had help from Dimitry Bogachev from Stage Entertainment Russia who helped them with details of how Russian culture could be accurately portrayed, particularly the love of country for people of the Romanov era who had been forced to flee. He wrote a lengthy justification for why the piece should be set in 1922 instead of 1927, largely having to do with the different regimes in power at those times and how they would have been perceived. However, he acknowledged that they were not writing a documentary; the setting stayed in 1927, which makes sense because Anastasia would be twenty-six and more believable as a young adult, than had she been about twenty.

Darko Tresnjak, the director, had won the Tony and Drama Desk Awards for *A Gentleman's Guide to Love and Murder* in 2014, and he was the newbie to this team. He described being in the room when Ahrens, Flaherty, and Terrence were going at it:

Oh, my God, I never saw people fight like that, like those three when they got into it. And it was just amazing to watch Terrence McNally and Lynne Ahrens go at each other. There was one night were it was just like, "Oh, this is crazy."

And then we went out to dinner that night, and Terrence is like, "How are you, Lynne? What's happening in your life?" and "How are you, Terrence?" And I was like "I guess they really love each other and that's why they can fight like that. It's just not my style; I don't work that way."

I thought these three would never agree on anything.

But then there were moments like the moment when Christy Altomar walked in and auditioned. I looked around, and all three of them were leaning in, and I was leaning in. And I thought, we're not even going to have to discuss this. She just cast herself. So, there were moments of grace like that right in between the other moments.

Christy Altomar was a find for them as Anastasia. Tresnjak likened the search to the search for Scarlett O'Hara for the movie of *Gone With the Wind* in the 1930s, when the producers saw virtually every actress in Hollywood and beyond before finding Vivien Leigh. For *Anastasia*, Tresnjak said he had seen every actress in New York and beyond (or so it seemed), and they were almost despairing when Altomar came in to the audition room.

Terrence had written the role of the Empress Maria, Anastasia's grandmother for Angela Lansbury, but though she appeared in a workshop of the piece, Mary Beth Peil played the role on Broadway.

Still, there were times in the process when Tresnjak thought he couldn't handle it, or couldn't manage it, but he was aware that everyone thought he was the right director. He said the only argument he ever had with his agent was when he wanted to quit and was convinced to stay. He was glad he stuck it out. The show would go on to run for two years on Broadway and establish companies all over the world.

The show premiered in May 2016 at Hartford Stage where Tresnjak was the artistic director. Rehearsals were mostly successful, though Flaherty recalls one night walking with Tresnjak after rehearsal and asking if for just one day he could have the rehearsal room without the authors in it. Flaherty responded, "You're the boss." As Harold Prince had done on *Spider Woman*, the director needed a break from the constant rewriting to get the show on the stage.

Fifty-one years after *Bump*, Terrence was still pushing the envelope and working to stay contemporary, while other playwrights had rested on their laurels or simply faded away. He was still trying to reach audiences, to be heard. He had seen audiences change and evolve—and catch up with him—for more than five decades, but *Anastasia* also represented another shift in a Broadway audience.

Though *Anastasia* wasn't designed or written to be a kids' musical, or even a family musical, a large portion of the audience was young women. Moreover, these were women who had not, as Terrence had, been raised on theater. For them with Broadway prices being what they were, going to a Broadway show wasn't a regular thing; it was an event. A lucky child might see two or three shows as they were growing. As such, this audience had not developed the understanding of styles of conventions that would have been common to Terrence's peers—both playwrights and audiences. This new audience has been raised on movies and television. They had a very different understanding of entertainment. Tresnjak tells the story of how Terrence came to understand that:

> There was one really hard day during previews on Broadway, and I didn't think it could get any harder. I decided not to go to the theater that night to the preview. I needed to get away.
>
> But there were things that I had been thinking about in the show that were off. Terrence had not been coming to every preview, and I texted him, "are you coming tonight?" He said no, and I asked if he was doing anything because we needed to talk. He told me to come over, and I went to his apartment and went upstairs.

I think I chose that day because I was thinking the day couldn't get any worse. And if he's mad at me, who cares? Everybody is mad at everybody. So, I sat down with him and I said this is the youngest audience you've ever had. Their hearts and minds move at a rate that's so much faster than what we have on the stage; we're losing them. We're behind the beat and I'm worried.

He pushed the script towards me, and said, "show me."

Tresnjak says they cut about ten minutes of running time, and it was interesting because Terrence still wanted sentence structure in a certain way, but he was also willing to take pages of cuts. It was a meeting of two artists, working for the best result for the piece, two generations of theater artists working in a dynamic climate. Tresnjak also describes what it's like for a director in previews: "You're seeing the audience with tentacles for a musical." It's not scientific, it's a feeling, "a pre-conscious feeling," he said.

That was one of the most interesting moments working with Terrence, Tresnjak said, understanding where the exposition needed to be and the perceptions and perspectives they would bring to the show. For *Anastasia*, if their young audience didn't understand royalty and succession, they would never get the conflict in the piece, but they worked it out, and at seventy-eight, Terrence was relearning what he had learned from Elaine May half a century earlier: always include the audience. He was still as passionate as ever about being heard, and when that changed, he was still willing and excited to grow as an artist.

And Terrence's writing was beautiful. As Tresnjak says, the eleven o'clock number in *Anastasia* isn't a song, it's Terrence's scene, a beautiful encounter between the Empress Maria and Anastasia. They were all adamant that that had to be a scene, rather than a song.

Towards the end [of the scene] the line that breaks my heart every time is, "We never know which goodbye is the last." And that to me is my favorite line in the show because that has happened to so many of us. We don't always know when we're seeing somebody for the last time, and it takes Terrence to write a line like that.

For Terrence, his characters, and his collaborators, it was always about finding that new music.

8

Bel Canto

I.

TERRENCE LOVED OPERA. Beyond his fame as a playwright, he was known for his love of the opera. Since that first experience of hearing a record in middle school, opera spoke to him. The scale, the passion, the drama, all ignited his heart in ways that would shape his entire life.

Though Terrence wasn't much given to analyzing his emotions, he did say that the grandeur and the intensity of opera was what drew him to it—as well as the larger-than-life stories. It could be, too, that as a young gay man in a repressive time, opera gave voice to emotions that he was at a loss to express. He didn't speak of it in that way but rather talked about how he came to love opera in more practical ways. It opened a new world for him, a world of imagination, narrative, and passion so beyond his daily life. It was part of what convinced him that as soon as he graduated from high school he would be "on the first plane out of Corpus Christi." He needed a bigger world.

Terrence grew up listening to the Met radio broadcasts, which were live broadcasts of the Saturday matinee performances from New York. He took over the living room of his home, even as noted earlier, relegating his parents to listen to their football game in the car. Like every fan, he became immersed in the details, and as we've seen, amassed a collection of opera records before he graduated from high school. There is in the dedicated fan—no matter what they're fans of—the identity and pleasure that comes from intimate knowledge of a topic; it becomes a defining part of one's personality. In Texas, Terrence also had an inherent sense that opera was sophisticated and was a way to distinguish himself in his sleepy oil town whose aspirations were so much different than his own. After all, he had said that he liked to show off, and he wanted to be seen and heard.

All that pales, however, compared to the dramatic impact on Terrence as a young writer and storyteller. As we've also discussed earlier, Terrence was fascinated by the artistry of the theater, and opera in particular, that something as inherently false—sitting in a dark room surrounded by strangers watching people on a platform talk or sing—about the theater could speak so much truth and have such an emotional impact on people. He understood how an aria could move one to tears and the feeling of goosebumps that rise automatically in response to a certain wave of sound and how it affects the body and the spirit. It is that pre-conscious response that Darko Tresnjak talks about in an audience, and when it works, that feeling is amplified by sharing it with hundreds of strangers in the dark. In that way, it's no different than a crowd leaping to its feet and screaming when a batter hits a homerun. These experiences speak to something elemental. Though, Terrence, at his trenchant best observed in a column for *Horizon* in 1985, "An opera isn't a football game, although it's often staged and sung like one."

This feeling, this common experience, has seldom been expressed more simply—and more effectively—than by the Stage Manager in Act Three of Thornton Wilder's *Our Town*:

> We all know that something is eternal. And it ain't houses and it ain't names, and it ain't earth, and it ain't even the stars . . . everybody knows in their bones that something is eternal, and that something has to do with human beings. All the greatest people ever lived have been telling us that for five thousand years and yet you'd be surprised how people are always losing hold of it. There's something way down deep that's eternal about every human being.

Terrence knew this, and you have an inkling of it, too, or you probably wouldn't be reading this book. If you've ever sat in a theater and had
a transporting experience that takes you out of yourself, you know this.
Suddenly, it doesn't matter that you're sitting in a dark room and that
what's unfolding before you isn't real. You're not worried about remembering where you parked the car, or if you left the oven on, or any of the
myriad things that clutter our minds on a daily basis. You are heart and
soul in that moment, and the heightened, poetic, reality takes us out of
ourselves. Whether it's at a baseball game or the Metropolitan Opera,
these are moments when we feel fully alive and suffused with joy—and
they make life bearable. This is what Terrence understood from his earliest days as he saved his money to buy opera records so he could sit
in his room in the humidity of Corpus Christi and be transported to
someplace magical and magnificent.

It's also what Stephen Sondheim was writing about in *Into the Woods*
when the Baker's Wife, after having a fast tryst with a prince that is the
opposite of her quotidian life, sings:

> Who can live in the woods?
> And to get what you wish
> Only just for a moment
> These are dangerous woods
> Let the moment go
> Don't forget it for a moment, though
> Just remembering you've had an "and"
> When you're back to "or"
> Makes the "or" mean more
> Than it did before
> Now I understand
> And it's time to leave the woods.

Throughout his life, Terrence always had that "and." He insisted on
it, and he fought for it. In Terrence's work that scale, those moments

exist in Ruby in *Bump*, in Mendy in *Lisbon Traviata*, in Buzz in *L!V!C!*, in Chloe in *Lips Together*, in Sister Helen Prejean and Joseph De Rocher in *Dead Man Walking*, and even in Googie Gomez in *The Ritz*. All of them experience through art something that soars beyond the quotidian, makes life livable, provides an outlet and a coping mechanism. It is what makes it possible to go on, even always knowing that there is something dangerous "out there."

II.

Through his own education, study, and interest, Terrence became an expert on opera. Nights of standing room at the Met, hearing Maria Callas and many of the stars of the so-called Old Met on 39th Street (beloved for its acoustics and demolished in 1967 after being denied landmark status) broadened his experience and refined his taste, which over the years became more and more specific.

In an undated note he wrote that he "made a resolution to stop seeing operas I hate twice. We all see the performances we *want* to see."

He loved hearing opera live, but he was also grateful for "Mr. Edison's recording machine," which had allowed him to experience the great singers who had gone before. Earlier, in high school, he wrote an Italian sonnet celebrating Enrico Caruso, very much in the style of the Romantics like Shelley:

> Now gone is the titan of opera's art;
> His clarion notes will sound no more for men
> To hear. Now fair angles in God's heaven
> Alone hear him sing with impassioned heart.

And it goes on in the same vein. Though perhaps overly effusive, he captures the nineteenth-century linguistic style and he nails the rhyme scheme and meter. He would have been a stickler for the form even back then thanks to Mrs. Mac.

As Terrence became more known for his expertise in opera, he was asked to write notes for programs, liner notes for recordings, recording reviews, and published articles on opera in various journals including *Ovation* magazine and *Horizon*, for which he wrote a monthly column in the mid-1980s called "The Prompter's Box." His pointed observations, good humor, and obvious love of opera radiate through all of these. He also published lists, such as "Terrence McNally's 10 Favorite Opera Recordings," and the significance of that is that in each case, what he responds to is the humanity in the performances of the singers and what sets them apart from more traditional performances. For the Metropolitan Opera Guild, he wrote and recorded a piece on *Wozzek*, often considered the first avant-garde opera of the twentieth century, dating from the 1920s, which intrigued Terrence.

Most famously, Terrence appeared on the Texaco Opera Quiz from 1979–2008, one of the intermission features on the Met Opera broadcasts. Once again, he drew on his knowledge, appreciation, and sense of humor about the operas. He became a popular regular on the show for nineteen years. In the midst of a period when he was having difficulty writing in the late seventies and early eighties, he credited that show with getting him writing again.

In the oft-told story—one of those that has taken on legend status in Terrence's biography—he said that he was in a store buying an opera recording when someone asked if he was Terrence McNally. When he asked the person if they knew his plays, they said they recognized his voice from the Met broadcasts. Terrence, then in his early forties, thought that he didn't want to be remembered for being on the radio opining on opera; he wanted to be remembered as a playwright. So, he got back to work.

Over the years, as his knowledge, appreciation, and fandom continued to grow, he became increasingly convinced that more playwrights should be writing the libretti for operas. Particularly in the latter quarter of the twentieth century and early twenty-first century as more new operas were being written—and more American operas—he felt that only playwrights could adequately create the drama that was needed on stage. He didn't want operas to have boring parts, such as those during which he did his reading on the steps to standing room when he was at Columbia. Naturally, he acknowledged that in opera, music is the dominant element, but he also knew that people wanted the full theatrical experience, and that meant strong narrative, and well-expressed.

In the mid-nineties, he had, of course, had a major hit with his paean to Maria Callas, *Master Class*, his teleplay *The Last Mile* about a singer about to make her Met debut had aired on PBS. Terrence, however, had never written a libretto himself.

But that was about to change.

III.

In 1996, Jake Heggie was working in the PR department of the San Francisco Opera. Previously, he'd been a pianist and a composer, but he developed a focal dystonia in his right hand, which caused involuntary muscle spasms and his hand started to curl up. Not able to play music, he also stopped writing because, as he says, he went into "a dark place." Coming out of it, he realized that he could write, so he was writing press releases, annual reports, speeches, basic corporate PR writing.

He was also meeting all kinds of people—artists, administrators, journalists, and it was a very effective way to learn the opera business from the inside out. Then, after five years of physical therapy, he was able to start playing again.

He also started writing songs for some of the amazing singers that he'd met. When they found out he was a composer, they were curious to see what he had. He ended up writing music for Renee Fleming, Frederica von Stade, Brynn Terfel, and others, all well-known and established opera stars. Suddenly, his songs were getting done internationally, and he won the annual G. Schirmer American Art Song competition, which resulted in 1995 with many of his works being published.

Heggie, in his role as PR guy, was escorting Patrick Summers, artistic director of the Houston Grand Opera and principal guest conductor of the San Francsico Opera to an interview, a year earlier. Heggie and Summers got talking about Heggie's music. Summers asked to listen to some, and Heggie sent it. As Summers recalled, "I thought Jake was an extraordinary songwriter. I mean, they were so orchestral and so operatic and so narrative-driven, he seemed to be a natural opera composer."

Summers said that he and San Francisco Opera director Lotfi Mansouri discussed having Jake write the opera, but they would need a seasoned playwright to complement Heggie's debut opera.

This was obviously all happening behind the scenes because as Heggie tells it, one day "out of the blue," the opera director Lotfi Mansouri asked him if he had ever thought about writing an opera. It can hardly have been "out of the blue," even if Heggie wasn't expecting it. He had previously written a piece commissioned by the San Francisco Opera for their 75th Anniversary Gala, called *Too Many Notes*. Though Heggie downplays it somewhat, he and his talent were well known to Mansouri and the Opera—and to Summers.

> And my first response when he asked that question was, no, I haven't ever thought about writing an opera. I've seen how difficult it is and how much goes into it. I just can't imagine taking it on.
>
> He said, "Well, I think you're a theater composer. Look at the people who are championing your songs and doing them all over the world to great effect." He said that that kind of ability is something that's missing in a lot of new operas. We talked at length, and finally he said to me, "Look, I have been trying to get Terrence McNally to write a libretto for ages—everyone has. Everyone's been after Terrence to write an opera libretto for a very long time because of his famous passion for opera and his great knowledge of the art form of the singers."

Mansouri had been among those who had been "after Terrence," and had asked him to write a libretto for an opera based on *A Streetcar Named Desire*. Terrence didn't want to go through the process of trying to adapt Tennessee Williams, possibly because at the time he was already knee-deep in adapting E. L. Doctorow and was eager to do something original. (Summers said that no one wanted to touch the Williams play, though it was ultimately written by Philip Littell. That opera, which debuted in 1995, got mixed reviews, though the creators were restricted by the demands of the Williams estate, which allowed very little variation from the original script.)

And so began what could easily be described as an artistic courtship between Terrence and Heggie. Heggie wasn't sure it was going to go anywhere, but he brought the general director of the San Francisco Opera with him to their first meeting just in case. The idea was that they would come up with a comic opera for the millennium season celebration, what Heggie called something "bubbly and sparkly and fun and witty," something, they felt Terrence could do very well.

At the time, Terrence was immersed in preparing for the movie shoot of *L!V!C!* and had little time for a meeting, though Heggie recalls he couldn't have been more welcoming and said he'd liked Heggie's music that he'd heard. He told Heggie that the story would be critical—50 percent of the work would be the story.

Heggie was pleased to have gotten Terrence's perspective, but he was increasingly discouraged that it wasn't going to happen, that Terrence was no longer interested, and Heggie's big dream was just going to fall apart—and by that time it had become a big dream.

He decided, however, to give it one last try:

> At the end of '96 and early '97 I had had a big premiere with a great singer name Frederica von Stade, who he [Terrence] loves. I sent him one final tape cassette and one final plea to ask him if he would consider this, even though I really thought he had probably made up his mind not to do it.
>
> He called me almost instantly after he had received it and he said it was just the weirdest serendipity. He had received my tape and my letter just after he had heard a concert at Carnegie Hall of American music sung by Renee Fleming, and he was all excited about American music. He went backstage and he saw Renee and

he said he had been thinking about writing an opera and she pulled him aside and said, there's only one composer you should think of working with. And that's Jake Heggie. And then her manager came over and said, yes, you have to work with Jake. You need to write an opera with Jake. And then he went home, and my package was there. Then he listened to it and he said, he called me and he said, "I believe in serendipity."

The working relationship began with Terrence coming to San Francisco in June of 1997 with a list of ten possible operas. Terrence also said that it was important for them to get to know one another since they were going to be spending a lot of time together. Terrence gave Heggie the list, and said he was only going to do one, but he wasn't going to tell him which one was his favorite.

First on the list was *Dead Man Walking*:

And I just remember every hair on my body standing on it. And I felt this immense shiver of music, drama, theater all coming together, that this was exactly the right project. And I said, that's it. You don't have to read anything else. That's the one. And he said, well, I did write this whole list, so do you mind if I read the whole list? And I said, fine. And he read, and I, I seem to remember they were two other ideas. That's what jumped out at me. One was *Moby Dick*, which I eventually did later, and the other was, *Sunset Boulevard*, which I thought that was interesting. I thought that was kind of bold. And then, uh, but the only thing I was really interested in was *Dead Man Walking*. It just kept going over and over in my head, even when he was reading the names of the other options. And he said that's the one I really want to do, too.

In order to do the opera, they had to get the rights from Sister Helen Prejean who had written the original book and on which the 1995 film had been based. The book was a nonfiction account of Sister Helen's (as she was known) working in the Louisiana Penitentiary system, counseling men on death row. Through her ministry, she became convinced that the death penalty was wrong, but in a larger sense, her mission was to get the convicted to acknowledge their crimes and understand the moral issues attached to them to achieve a kind spiritual awakening.

Shortly after he started trying to get the rights, Jake got a call from Sister Helen:

> She said to me on the phone, "Jake this is Sister Helen Prejean, and they tell me that you and Terrence McNally and the San Francisco Opera wanna write an opera of *Dead Man Walking*. Do you know what I said to that, Jake?" I said no. She said, "Set it up 'cause we're gonna do an opera of *Dead Man Walking*. I don't know boo-scat about opera, so you're going to have to educate me. But one thing I want to ask you. You don't write this atonal stuff, do you? I mean, we're going to have a tune we can hum, right?"

Heggie says there was amazing goodwill around the project from the beginning, and he and Terrence started working almost immediately, talking about characters and how they were going to tell the story. He said that Terrence told him to read the book, underline and put notes in the margin to point out the parts that were particularly meaningful or that spoke to him musically.

Terrence insisted throughout that he was not a *librettist*; he was a *playwright*, and he was approaching the piece in that way. Unlike previous projects, he was also approaching it that his words wouldn't be gospel or unchangeable but rather that they would inspire the music. He kept telling Heggie that his words should make him "feel the music," and if he didn't, then he'd do them another way.

This was also a significant time for Terrence. He was doing something he loved and had wanted to do while still being inspired, in part, by his spiritual journey with *A Perfect Ganesh*. The theme of that play— finding redemption—was an ideal complement to the work of Sister Helen. *Master Class*, about Maria Callas, was currently running and a huge hit, with its message about the essential nature of art, and he was in the middle of developing *Ragtime*, which was not a spiritual experience, to say the least. Working on *Dead Man Walking* was feeding and inspiring him on many levels.

None of this happens quickly, however, but the development kept going. In March of 1998, just eight weeks before the controversy over *Corpus Christi* would erupt, Heggie flew to New York for a press conference announcing the project and then on to Key West with Terrence to work on the piece.

> He wrote the first act in about five days. He just wanted me there to ask me questions. And I remember at the end of that week, he sat down and read me the whole first act, and I just dissolved in tears. I was so moved and inspired. Then I took six months to write the music for the first act and I went to meet him in Bridgehampton so he could write the second act libretto, and the same thing happened. He wrote it in a matter of a few days, I had played him all the music I had written, and then it took four or five months to write the next act.

Writing the second act would have been in the middle of all the fracas regarding *Corpus Christi*, just a month before the play would finally open.

What Heggie remembered was how, when they were writing, Terrence was very collaborative and happy to move elements of the script around. Heggie remembers that if something they were working on didn't ring true to him, he would stare off into the distance, move his lips and begin to inhabit the character. It was almost mystical as Terrence began to bring the characters to life right in front of Heggie. For Heggie, this was exciting because it was much the same way he worked. "I want to be inside a character's head, and I want *them* to tell me how it goes." The two men working in very similar ways loved spending time together, and they grew very close.

The timing for this could not have been better for Terrence—the artist dodging the slings and arrows of people perverting the nature of his work for publicity—or for the opera world. A few years before the beginning of this project, Mansouri had initiated a project at the San Francisco Opera called *Pacific Visions*, with the goal of adding a new, American opera to the season every year, to complement the older repertoire. Among the pieces produced under the program were *The Death of Klinghoffer* by John Adams, which was well-received, and the aforementioned adaptation of *Streetcar*. *Dead Man Walking* was going to be the fifth commission.

Heggie, working at the San Francisco Opera, would have been very aware of these, of course, and he knew that if there was going to be a new opera created it would have to be very current and very alive, which was the direction in which *Dead Man Walking* was going.

Once the opera was complete, the company began a series of workshops, and Joe Mantello was brought in to direct. Mantello said that he'd never done an opera before, but as had happened throughout his career, Terrence was pushing him to expand creatively—just as Terrence was pushing himself. Mantello recalls it was an exciting time. Why wouldn't it be: first-time composer, first-time librettist. As Mantello said, it was "written in a way because it was Terrence."

Terrence was truly in opera heaven. As Summers said,

> Terrence was the father figure for all of us. *Master Class* was new at that time, and we were all just I think in awe of Terrence. But once you got down to work, Terrence was all work and just a thrilling energy to work with. I found—and have always found—Terrence very inspiring. As a musician, you want to make those words as clear as you can as a conductor.
>
> Director and conductors are "re-creators." What we're supposed to do is illuminate what a composer and librettist put there.
>
> What I found so miraculous about the libretto for *Dead Man Walking* was that it was quite unlike the stories that had been told in American opera before, with some exceptions. They suffered from a lot of cultural cringe, and it always had to nod to Europe. So we did a lot of operas in extreme vernacular. If operas were set in America,

then they had to be set in Appalachia or some place that had a vernacular built in.

What Terrence did with *Dead Man Walking* was to break that mode, to create something that was authentically American but embraced a story told in the tradition of grand operas, no matter where they came from. It was another first for redefining the form.

Dead Man Walking deals with huge, archetypal issues, but what Terrence did—as he had and would continue to do in his plays—was to take huge issues and humanize them, bring them down to a scale where they can resonate with the heart. Nor is *Dead Man Walking* polemical. Though Sister Helen would ultimately be opposed to the death penalty, there is nothing political in *Dead Man Walking*; that's not its purpose.

The plot of the opera stays close to the book and the movie. Sister Helen Prejean of the Sisters of St. Joseph of Medaille has been corresponding with a death row inmate, Joseph De Rocher, who has been convicted of the brutal murder of two teenagers. When Joseph asks Sister Helen to be his spiritual advisor as he faces death, she agrees, against the advice of her colleagues. Arriving at the prison, the chaplain tries to dissuade Sister Helen from meeting with De Rocher, but she perseveres, convinced that she can reach him. De Rocher hopes to get his death sentence commuted to life in prison, but he is denied, and only an intervention from the governor could save him now. De Rocher's execution date is set, and while he and Sister Helen have some disagreements, they develop a deep bond—and a realization that they both love Elvis Presley. Finally, the night before he is to die, De Rocher finally admits what he has done to Sister Helen, though he is afraid she will condemn him, Sister Helen forgives him and puts his mind at ease, somewhat, as he is walked to the execution chamber—in prison slang, "a dead man walking."

While *Dead Man Walking* would never be confused with musical theater, Terrence's fluid structure as the scenes move from one to another, balancing comedy—Sister Helen gets a traffic ticket on the way to the prison for the first time and the shared love of Elvis—with a believable grappling with spiritual issues. In that way, Terrence's libretto recalls

Poulenc's *Dialogues of the Carmelites*, a powerful tale of a group of nuns martyred during the French Revolution for refusing to renounce their faith. Yet it is what Sister Helen calls "the conflict of the human heart" that is at the center of the piece.

The structure is classical, inspired by the *bel canto* tradition—duets, trios, and even a sextet, but Heggie's sound is distinctly American. The sextet in Act Two is also dramatically important rather than a bunch of people standing around singing. It comes when Sister Helen has appeared at De Rocher's commutation hearing and is confronted by the parents of the teenagers who were murdered. It is a heartbreaking expression of the sorrow, frustration, and loss the families feel at Joseph's violent act. Yet the point is not to make a political statement. Dramatically it's to move Sister Helen further on her spiritual journey. In that way, Terrence echoes his own work in *A Perfect Ganesh* where horrors and violence provide an opening for the spirit. It's the opening his characters in *Lips Together, Teeth Apart* are looking for, but never quite find.

The debut was set for October 7, 2000, and rehearsals proceeded well. Mantello was figuring it out as he went along, realizing that the opera process was quite different than what he was used to from theater:

> No one talked me through the process. You tech the whole opera before you go into rehearsal. And they neglected to tell me this. So, you're in an empty theater with designers and they're saying, where is she going to be? What's going to happen? And I had to think very quickly on my feet and you know, and sort of give it a shape. Then, three or four months later, we went into rehearsals. And then there's a way in which you have to rehearse. You have the principals, you have the chorus, and you have the supers, and they all have a different kind of rehearsal process and they generally only come together a very few times. So you sort of . . . you're putting them all together . . . but you're rehearsing them in discreet rehearsal rooms. I had very, very little time to put it all together. It was not more than two days, and we just didn't get through it. And I went to the artistic director of the opera and I said, I'm just, I'm not through.

And he said, well, the rest of the rehearsals are for the Maestro and I can't give those to you. And I said, I'm going to have to take my name off of it because I can't put something on the stage that I haven't teched. Fortunately, the Maestro [Summers] gave me another day to work and we were able to get it done. And I think because, because it was a new, 'cause it was a contemporary opera and, and it was written in a way that, you know, it's not like *La Bohème* and where the curtain comes up and that's that. We had moving pieces; the set moves. And it was, it was . . . it was huge.

When he wrote it, Terrence had envisioned that Frederica von Stade would sing Sister Helen. He had met her when he had organized a major AIDS benefit concert at Carnegie Hall and was a huge fan—in the way only Terrence could be. When it came time to do the opera, however, von Stade declined:

> I just didn't feel it was right to do Sister Helen, even though they asked me. There are so many young great singers around, but I did want to be in it.
> And they said, "Well, who would you play?" And I wanted to do the mother of the convict. So, Terrence wrote two fabulous arias, the most touching and beautiful words you could imagine.

At the time, the piece had personal importance for von Stade. She was working with a group called Young Musicians Choral Orchestra (YMCO), which worked to get at-risk kids out of bad situations, where often one parent is in prison, and into college through music. She said her own experience as a mother and sometimes being unable to completely protect her children gave the role of Mrs. De Rocher special meaning to her. Von Stade loved the piece as an artist as well.

As an American singer, the best thing that could possibly happened, she said, was to be able to sing not just in English, but in American English.

Susan Graham, who had made her international debut at Covent Garden in 1994, was tapped to play Sister Helen and was released from the Paris Opera to do the role, Heggie said. Graham is a mezzo soprano, and while Heggie had initially thought that he would write Sister Helen as a soprano, he said he liked the texture of the mezzo voice better, particularly to serve Terrence's words; the mezzo voice he said, allows more accurate speech, important since it would be in English.

As the opening approached, Terrence's partner Gary Bonasorte was declining rapidly. Terrence flew back to the East Coast, but Heggie remembers that Terrence was always available to talk, saying that his primary concern was making sure that the music happened.

The opening night was a sold-out house, full of celebrities. Julie Andrews and Gary Marshall who were in town filming *The Princess Diaries* were there. Susan Sarandon and Sean Penn from the movie version were there, as well as Tim Robbins, Woody Harrelson, and Robin Williams. Sister Helen was there, as well, naturally.

As Heggie recalls, "It was surreal. I mean I went from being the PR guy to writing this massive opera and being the first composer in residence. It went really, really well."

The opening was a major success, and the vast majority of the reviews were positive. Summers, too, thought that it was "perfect." He said,

> There wasn't a single thing in it that didn't need to be there, and it's set Jake into a course of being a musical dramatist. Of course, he's worked on several other librettos now, but it really set Jake on a course to do what he's doing, which is to really alter the forward movement of American opera. Terrence had a lot to do with that.

Dead Man Walking has become the most-produced American opera with more than seventy international productions, and proceeds from the production have gone to benefit Sister Helen's order. Her royalties from the opera went to benefit their fund, and that was something of which Terrence was especially proud.

The next major production by Summers at the Houston Grand Opera in 2011 featured Joyce DiDonato as Sister Helen. Given the chance to revisit it, of course Terrence wanted to make changes. At that time in his life, Gary had died, Terrence had met and married Tom Kirdahy, and he was continuing to battle his cancer, but DiDonato remembers how engaged he was:

> I didn't think "Oh, there's the famous Terrence McNally," but it was really clear he was a strong presence in the room, even though he was very discreet, not drawing attention to himself at all.
>
> He came up to me one time. He had a yellow notepad, and he said, "I've been thinking I want to change one word." I said, "okay." And he made one change from the word "cold" to "cool."
>
> My first instinct was, "Oh, okay, whatever. We have fun. Cold, cool, whatever." Then I started thinking about the context, and that slight change changes the meaning. It's about temperature, but it's very different if you talk about something being cold or cool. And this may sound naïve, but I thought he was really thinking about every word. It was really formative in how I now prepare pieces. It's the importance of the text and each word and the clarity and inflection and syntax of it. I remember that encounter quite strongly.

It was the kind of attention to the words and what they meant that made Terrence fall in love with actors, singers, those who would bring his writing to life.

IV.

A short time after the Houston production of *Dead Man Walking*, Terrence and Heggie began developing their idea for their next opera. It was commissioned by Dallas Opera to debut in 2015. They decided that they wanted it to be a contemporary, story, an original story. The result was *Great Scott*, a tale of opera . . . and football. One of Terrence's first list of notes—a scene rundown—are on a notepad printed with "The Composer Is God," a line that he gives to Maria Callas in *Master Class*. Terrence certainly believed that, though he would write and overwrite as he worked on his librettos, knowing that only a portion of what he wrote would make it into the final piece. He was eager to do another opera.

In the intervening years, Heggie had written a musical scene *At the Statue of Venus*, with a libretto by Terrence for the 2005 opening of the new opera house for Colorado Opera, and in 2008, Heggie had written *Three Decembers*, based on an unpublished play by Terrence, though Terrence did not write the libretto. It had its premiere at the Houston Grand Opera. *Three Decembers* is a series of three Christmas letters written by an aging star to her children during the AIDS crisis in 1986, 1996, and 2006, and it's been performed at several opera companies since.

As the idea for *Great Scott* developed, Heggie and Terrence had immediately approached DiDonato since both Terrence and Heggie were eager to write for her again. She had said to them that whatever they wrote, she wanted to have a mad scene:

> I said, "Please let's do something where you give me a mad scene. Usually in opera the sopranos get all the mad scenes, and I want a proper, real on mad scene. I mean, if I'm going to have input, let me ask for the world and see what you get."
>
> I think I wrote Jake back a little later and said to forget the mad scene. I think we need to do a comedy. I mean, there's not enough comic opera, and the world needs a laugh. Somehow the genius of Jake and Terrence found a way to give me both. So, it's a proper mad scene, but it's the funniest opera ever written.

That's not to say DiDonato didn't need convincing. When Terrence told her the story, she said it sounded very much like her story—from the Midwest, specializing in *bel canto* and so forth. Terrence, however, assured her that it wasn't biographical. He was trying to write an "everywoman" or certainly talk about what every woman artist goes through at a latter point in their careers. DiDonato did agree, finally, that the theme was universal, though it struck pretty close to home. Terrence and director Jack O'Brien worked with her because, as she said, "I didn't want to be Joyce up on that stage."

The story is about as complicated, and hilarious, as anything Terrence ever wrote. Arden Scott, a world-famous mezzo, has discovered a long-forgotten *bel canto* opera: *Rosa Dolorsa: Figlia de Pompei* ("Daughter of Pompei") by a forgotten Italian composer named Vittorio Bazzetti. Arden has come home to perform its modern debut at the small opera company where she got her start. The problem is that the opera is set to open on the night of the Super Bowl, and the husband of Winnie Flato, who is producing the opera, is the owner of the city's football team, which has made it to the Super Bowl. "Who schedules these things?" is a constant refrain in Act One.

The first act is also set backstage and is about Arden's mid-career crisis. She gave up traditional home and family to have her career. At the same time the other artists are questioning if they're good enough, and what does it all matter anyway? If *The Last Mile* had a follow up, Arden Scott would be that singer about to make her Met debut in *Tosca* several years later. The cast also includes Tatyana, an Eastern European, social media obsessed soprano who is on the rise and performs (hilariously mangles) "The Star-Spangled Banner" at the start of the Super Bowl, a countertenor (almost de rigueur for a *bel canto* opera), the hyper-masculine owners of the team, and more. (Fun fact: the name Arden Scott was one that Terrence had used before in a musical that he had attempted to write with Stephen Sondheim, called *All Together Now*, which never was completed, and the process caused a rift between Terrence and Sondheim over whose ideas were whose. What scraps of the musical exist seem a bit like it was shaping up to be *Company 2*. Despite sending occasional friendly notes and birthday greetings, the two remained cordial, yet distant. "Don't bother trying to talk to Steve," Terrence had said while both men were still alive, "you never know what you're going to get.")

The second act is the opera within the opera. Musically, it's more an homage than a parody, though Rosa as the slave girl who saves Pompei walks a fine line in that department. Heggie's music uses forms and harmonics from *bel canto*, but it's original and contemporary. One of the best examples of his talent is Rosa's prayer, beautifully and delicately sung . . . right before Vesuvius erupts. It was written for DiDonato and perfectly showcases her magnificent voice.

The opera went into rehearsal with von Stade taking on the role of Winnie, and Summers conducting. Deb Skinner who was in the Dallas Opera Chorus remembered a joyful rehearsal period, and that both DiDonato and von Stade were wonderful to work with and seemed to revel in connecting with everyone in the cast. Skinner also said that when Terrence was there, he seemed to be having a wonderful time, and the show was so much fun because it was highly theatrical, and the leads really had to act, "There were no 'park-and-bark' performances," Skinner said. Everything was moving all the time.

It wasn't all smooth sailing, however; O'Brien said that Terrence kept wanting to change the libretto. O'Brien thought that because Terrence hadn't been able to be present for the final stages of *Dead Man Walking*, and Heggie had had to do some of the final edits, which is not common in opera. So, when it came to *Great Scott*, Terrence was asserting himself in ways he had not during *Dead Man Walking*:

> He wanted every word to be his and he wanted total control over it. As he started to write it, it became more and more and more dense and began to reveal itself more. Typical of Terrence, which he did all his life, he wanted to rewrite it [on the fly as the show developed]. Well, Jake couldn't do it because he had to take the libretto, then set it to music, edit it properly, then orchestrate it and then put it in other people's hands so they can learn it. So everything took five times the amount of time. And so when Terrence would say, "I want to change this in the second act," Jake was fit to be tied. He called me in despair asking, What am I going to do? And I said, You just have to write the music that you hear that makes you happy. You can't make him happy because he's going to want to be changing till the night before the first general or orchestra rehearsal.
>
> What we put up with was amazing, but it was a grand plan for one of the most original pieces I think I've ever known in my life

because it was hilarious. And it was, it was moving. It was very much the kind of theater magic that make Terrence who he is. It was all about the wonder of opera and the theater and creativity and discovery and collaboration and the accidents, all the things that he was profoundly gifted at.

Inevitable challenges aside, O'Brien and Heggie in the end said they had a wonderful time doing *Great Scott*. Both thought that it would need another set of rewrites and some more productions to be fully realized. While they were pleased—and the audiences loved it, too—artistically, they and Terrence could see where it needed to go. In one of Terrence's notepads, he had written, "*Great Scott*, not a great triumph. Makes people think it's better than it is." He would have been happy to keep working on it. After Terrence's death, O'Brien was especially disappointed that it was unlikely that *Great Scott* would ever get the attention it deserved. After the debut in Dallas, it got one more production in San Diego in 2016, which proved to be a crowd-pleaser, even if it got a somewhat dyspeptic review in the *Los Angeles Times*. The recording of the Dallas production featuring DiDonato and von Stade was nominated for a Grammy.

That was the last collaboration between Terrence and Heggie. The one that got away was *Moby Dick*. Although it had been one of Terrence's original ideas and he wanted to work on it, when the Dallas Opera commissioned it in 2005 for debut in 2010, Terrence was having a particularly bad time with the lung cancer that he'd been dealing with for five years, and he had to withdraw.

Looking back in 2019, he was proud of the operas he'd written—and still a bit in awe that he had had the chance to write them. He was particularly pleased that if there was going to be a biography of him that it would include his operas. Having had so much of his art influenced by opera, he was always so pleased that he had been able to create his own—and that his work was now part of the canon.

9

The Voice Matures
Master Class and the Later Plays

I.

ONE OF TERRENCE'S most famous plays—and the one for which he won his fourth Tony Award—*Master Class* began as a simple handwritten list on a piece of lined paper, torn from a spiral notebook. It's not certain, but it appears to be from 1992.

As always, there was much going on in Terrence's artistic life. The movie of *Frankie and Johnny* had come out. *Spider Woman* was finishing its development in Toronto and ready to go to London, the screenplay for Barbra Streisand was, well, going nowhere; *It's Only a Play* was having a well-received run in Los Angeles; *The Last Mile* aired on PBS, and *A Perfect Ganesh* was coming together.

He knew at the time he was going to write about Maria Callas, but the play had not yet taken shape in his mind. Callas, of course, had been an important part of the plot of *The Lisbon Traviata*, and, as we've seen again and again, opera informed so much of Terrence's artistic sensibility. Terrence was also a tireless worker who often had many projects going at once. Given the inherent challenges of the theater, it was anyone's guess what might get off the ground—and what might work, artistically or financially. Terrence was also unique in that he is one of the only playwrights who wrote for so many different forms—opera, musicals, plays—and also wrote for both the commercial and nonprofit theater. His artistic home at MTC gave him the freedom to write what he wanted to . . . and so he did.

The list he wrote that would become *Master Class* was this:

Macbeth with tape at La Scala–She was the ambitious one.
abortion
o mio babbino
Farewell to students
The last class
She can't do it anymore
Difficulty of teaching
The line of tradition

To read this scratched-out list alongside the script is to see how much of those initial ideas found their way in one form or another into the script. Callas performed Lady Macbeth in Verdi's opera only five times in 1952, but it was considered the definitive performance of the role. The scene the play refers to is in Act One, Scene Two, in the opera. Known as "the letter scene," the aria is "nell di a Vittorio," or "They met me in the day of success," the first line from the scene in Shakespeare where Lady Macbeth realizes that murdering Duncan will be their ticket to the throne. It is Lady Macbeth who is ambitious for her husband, but it was also Callas who was ambitious for her life and her career. Like Lady Macbeth, like Callas, and, yes, like Terrence, it is that drive to have an effect on the world, to be heard that is, and this is not too excessive to say, a driving passion. Neither Callas nor Terrence were driven to homicide to get what they wanted, but you get the idea.

The reference to "abortion" stems from a supposed miscarriage Callas experienced when she was romantically involved with Aristotle Onassis in 1960, but Terrence will raise the question whether it was truly a miscarriage or if Callas had an abortion so Onassis wouldn't leave her. In the play it becomes a metaphor for the sacrifices that are required to have a career in the arts. There may be some regrets, but it's not as if it was ever really a choice.

"O mio babbino" is a beautiful *bel canto* aria from Puccini's *Gianni Schicchi*. (A video of Callas singing it at the Paris Opera in 1965 is available on YouTube.) Arguably one of the most beautiful operas in the canon—it is also one that would be familiar to an audience not fully versed in opera from other popular performances.

The next three items have to do with the character of Callas's emotional state as she teaches, and the final, "the line of tradition" suffuses the play as Callas looks back at her life and tries to pass on what she knows to the students in the master class.

Terrence was fond of saying that *Master Class* was his most autobiographical play. He said it a lot—and he meant it. If Terrence was unwilling to plunder the literal story of his family because that would be a well soon drained, though he would pick and choose specific events and memories, he had no such compunction about plundering his artistic life and sensibilities because that, to quote Shakespeare's Juliet, "is all as boundless as the sea."

Terrence tells the story—or a slightly romanticized version—of how the play came to be in his *Memoir in Plays*. In it he says that he had the first line, "No applause, please." And the last line, "Well, that's that." and was simply left to fill in the middle parts. He writes about how he had written *A Perfect Ganesh* for Zoe Caldwell but realized that it was not the play he wanted to write for her. *Master Class* was.

He also writes that the idea for the play was inspired by master classes at Julliard given by Leontyne Price that Terrence stumbled into during the brief time he taught playwriting there with John Guare at the request of Michael Kahn who was running the program. Callas, too, had taught master classes at Julliard in 1971 and 1972, and Frederica von Stade remembered attending them. There are videos of these also available on YouTube, and they show that Callas was demanding, and though she had last performed on stage in 1965, could still exhibit that dazzling power that had made her the world-famous diva she was.

Terrence also writes about a reading of a draft of the play in Big Fork, Montana, where he discovered that a non-opera audience could still relate to his fictionalized Callas and her struggle with art.

The script is a gentle but not-so-subtle manifesto about art, and in places sounds exactly like Terrence and the way he would fight for the work and clarity throughout the process, though he seldom expressed it with quite the full-throttled approach he gives his Callas. (Fights with Ahrens and Flaherty apparently to the contrary.) Terrence is once again using the character of Callas as his puppet to say what he wants, reveling in the security of being behind the stage to get what he wants to say front and center—not so different from Ollie the dragon who inspired Terrence so many years before with his iconoclastic comedy.

When early on in the play, the First Soprano says, "this is hard," Maria answers sharply:

> Of course it's hard. That's why it's so important we do it right. "This is hard." Where am I? I thought I was somewhere where people were serious. This is not a film studio where anyone can get up there and act. I hate that word. Act! No! Feel. Be. That's what we're doing here. "This is hard." I'll tell you what's hard. What's hard is listening to you make a mockery of this work of art.

The structure of the play is Callas teaching and holding forth with the students. There is also one monologue in each act—spoken arias, really—where Callas gives an insight into some of the facts of her life but also the emotional toll her career took on her and her grief at being abandoned by Onassis so he could marry Jackie Kennedy. These speeches are essential to the fabric of the play in that they create the dichotomy between the public persona and the interior life of the artist.

It's particularly poignant with Callas because her antics, her "temperament" were discussed so publicly—and she denies, or clarifies, the stories in an interview on *60 Minutes* in 1974 (also available on YouTube) three years before her death. YouTube was still ten years away when *Master Class* debuted, so Callas would have been as much an abstract idea and a memory of some in the audience as she was a real person, which worked for Terrence's theatricality.

Terrence also said, and wrote, that *Master Class* had the fewest rewrites of any play that he wrote. It seemed to have just poured out of him, based on years of fandom around Callas, naturally, but also by this time of thirty years of being in the playwriting trenches, dealing with fame, frustration, failure, and a life where his work—if not he himself— was constantly in the public eye, for better or worse.

As many said of Terrence, what was remarkable about him was not just the work he produced, the boundaries he pushed, or the fearlessness with which he wrote, but the fact that he kept going. By the time of *Master Class*, the challenges he faced—to say nothing of what would come—had informed him, and he simply could not stop. He had things to say, and he wanted to be heard. In Maria's final speech to the audience, Terrence puts a life in art in perspective. She says, "The sun will not fall down from the sky if there are no more *Traviatas*." There is also advice for everyone: "What matters is that you use whatever you have learned wisely. Think of the expression of words, of good diction, and of your own deep feelings. The only thanks I ask is that you sing properly and honestly. If you do this, I will feel repaid." That, in their most reductive terms, is all Terrence asked of anyone.

Master Class was initially commissioned by Circle Repertory Company, which explains why it wasn't done at MTC because at the time Terrence was still very deeply involved with them on *Perfect Ganesh* and *L!V!C!*. After Big Fork, it went to Philadelphia where it was produced by the Philadelphia Theatre Company (PTC) at the Plays and Players Theater, a 290-seat house at 17th and Delancey Streets in Philadelphia. It would be the first of four of Terrence's plays to get their premieres there. PTC had been founded in 1974 to promote the new work of American playwrights—very much like MTC.

Leonard Foglia directed, and of course Caldwell was Maria—after her triumph in Big Fork, she was tied to the show—Karen Kay Cody was cast as the First Soprano, Sophie; Jay Hunter Morris was the Tenor; and Audra McDonald, who the year before had won the Tony for her performance as Carrie Pipperidge in the Lincoln Center revival of *Carousel*, was the Second Soprano, Sharon Graham. David Loud was the Accompanist, Manny; and the small, but at one point important, role of the Stagehand was played by Michael Friedl.

The show was further refined, though not substantially altered, during the Philadelphia run. McDonald, who would win her second Tony Award for the performance, said it would not have been possible for her to find the role without Terrence's attention to the smallest detail of the words as the key to unlocking the emotion—just as the music was.

Sharon's final speech is a kind of indictment of Callas:

> You can't sing anymore and you're envious of anyone younger who can. You just want us to sing like you, recklessly, and lose our voices in ten years like you did. Well I won't do it. I don't want to. I don't want to sing like you. I hate people like you. You want to make the world dangerous for everyone just because it was for you.

The speech has a lot to say both about Maria and Sharon. Maria flew without a net and crashed and burned dramatically, never acknowledging her limitations, which was her tragedy. Sharon is more workmanlike in this and just wants to sing and have a career. She doesn't see the need for the grand passion. It's obvious which side Terrence came down on in this. As he had said, he had first fallen in love with Callas because her voice was like no one else's, and that's what always intrigued and thrilled him about performers that they were authentically themselves, come hell or high water. Neither Callas nor Terrence were ever content to play it safe.

In rehearsal, McDonald knew the emotional place Sharon had to get to be able to confront and accuse a woman who was internationally revered, and she just couldn't get there emotionally.

> I've done theater my entire life, but I didn't really have good technique, but Terrence and Zoe, and Lenny just believed in me, and they never made me feel like I didn't know what I was doing. Terrence was so very collaborative, so for him it was always about making sure I found the character, and he was doing everything he could to help me find it.

Maria was saying things to Sharon like you don't have it in you to be a Lady Macbeth; you'll probably be a Mimi, and it was hard for me to find the anger and pull up the vitriol and deliver that blistering indictment.

Terrence came to me after one preview and said, "It's not devastating enough, is it?" I guess I was too afraid at the point to say, "Dearest Terrence, you superstar, *you* fix this, but he opened the door for me. I was thinking that Mirella Freni did Mimi and had a really great career among other roles or a *Traviata*. That's not a terrible thing."

And so, he says I need to make it more devastating for Sharon so that she can get to that place to deliver what needs to be delivered to Maria, so Maria can have the ending she needs in the show.

Instead of him saying, you're a bad actor, or figure it out, or Lenny, help her to get to this emotional place, he realized my work is not done here, and we can make this better.

As happened when he was working with actors whom he trusted, hearing the words in their mouths opened the door to finding the characters, which is why Terrence often said, "A script is not a play."

Master Class moved to the Golden Theater where it opened November 5, 1995, to an enthusiastic response from audiences, critics, and especially Vincent Canby in that all-important *New York Times* review. He lavished praise on Caldwell and the play, though he mentioned the other members of the cast only in passing. Canby understood Terrence's poetic realism and acknowledged that audiences wanted to see the extravagant personality of Callas embodied by Caldwell. It was the rave a show needs, and *Master Class* became one of the hottest tickets on Broadway. In addition to McDonald, Caldwell and the play took home Tony Awards, and it played to packed houses.

The sold-out houses kept going in July of the following year when Patti LuPone took over the role, with almost an entirely new cast. LuPone remembered that she was still at Julliard when Callas was giving the Master Classes there, and she didn't go because she was in the acting program, but of course years later she wished she had, having seen the recordings of the classes.

At first, however, she wasn't sure she wanted to take on the role when producer Robert Whitehead, also Caldwell's husband, called her:

> I remember saying "you'd have to be a fool to replace Zoe Caldwell."
> I found out later that she was on the line. But I said no because there was no way I could any way measure up to Zoe's performance, I was so intimidated by her performance, I didn't think it was a wise decision.
>
> They said, well please read the play again and get back to us. I read it, and in my head I said, I would have to be a fool to replace Zoe. And I would be a fool not to play this part. So, I accepted Robert Whitehead's offer.

It was a short rehearsal period with Foglia and the new cast. Still, it was challenging to LuPone because it was the only time she'd ever been a replacement. She felt tremendous pressure because Caldwell's performance was still fresh in audience's minds—and those of the theater community. A replacement has minimal rehearsal time, but LuPone was true to her reputation in the theater as a diligent worker who always shows up prepared and ready to work. She said that Terrence was around though she didn't interact with him that much, but she described him as an "extremely happy leprechaun with an ebullient personality."

LuPone also made the role her own, and Canby re-reviewing the piece loved her vulnerability as Callas and wrote that, "It's now clear that the McNally text is a good deal more complex and difficult than it first seemed."

LuPone recalled one performance that would have been opera-worthy in itself.

> I was doing the first act speech, and I had timed it to the music, I'm speaking the speech in the Greek accent, listening to the music and I see someone house left aisle get up and go up the aisle. And

in my head while I am speaking in the Greek accent and listening to the music, I went "well, we lost one." And it's funny how the mind works.

And then he came down the center aisle and started screaming, "This is shit. Fuck you. Terrence McNally," coming down the center aisle and in my head again went, "Don't shoot the messenger" while I was doing the speech. And I think the audience thought it was part of the show.

LuPone went with the show to London, but she said it was a flop. According to her, she was promised that the American cast would go, but they didn't, and she said the London cast wasn't up to the demands of the play. "It was hard to do the show in London with that cast where the soprano went, 'I'm not hitting the high note tonight,' and I was, like, excuse me. That's the purpose. That's the reason we're doing this."

They lost their voices, and they couldn't handle eight shows a week, she said.

LuPone also said that Robert Fox, the London producer was "ineffectual," and that the "the Brits don't like Terrence, and the Brits also own unconditionally Maria Callas, so they didn't like what I did with her."

Despite that, the play still ignited passions in the audience, as happened one night:

> We were in previews, and I was describing the aria to the first student. I was on my knees, and then I heard an American voice go, "If you don't shut up, I'm going to strangle you." And there was a kerfuffle. In the intermission, the Bobbies came and took the guy away. The next day we find out the American voice was Lenny Foglia, and the guy they arrested was wanted for murder.

The production lasted about a month in the West End, and by the end of it, LuPone said, the audiences were back after the drubbing the play took in the press, but it didn't run.

Meanwhile, back in New York, Dixie Carter replaced LuPone and played the role till it closed in June 1997. Faye Dunaway played the role on tour in 1996.

Master Class was revived in 2010 by MTC, a happy return for Lynne Meadow and Terrence, with Tyne Daly playing Maria.

Daly for her part loved working on the play, and said that Terrence was "very proprietary" about the script. "And why not? He's the guy who wrote it. I think it must be awful for writers to turn their plays over to other sounds and other voices."

The production was a success for Daly, MTC, and Terrence, though Ben Brantley in the *New York Times* felt compelled to snipe that "*Master Class* is not, by even a generous reckoning, a very good play, though it can be an entertaining one." The things Brantley called "pulpy" are many of the things that had charmed Canby in the same paper six years earlier, such as the scenes when Callas speaks of her memories. Brantley praises Daly's performance and other elements of the production. He then goes on to compare the production to the original, which is both odious and unfortunate criticism for a daily paper because audiences

Dewar's ad featuring Terrence, 1972, an indication, at the time, that he had become someone.

can't see the original production, and many won't have that frame of reference. Nonetheless, it's a common technique, but it's one that Terrence felt was unfair because he didn't feel it served the piece or the audience trying to determine whether to spend their hard-earned cash on a ticket.

The play has become a modern classic. It's been done around the world—and often. Terrence's archives are full of glowing letters of thanks from actresses at all levels of the profession who have had the chance to play Maria and what's it's meant to them as artists and women.

If *Ganesh* was the way Terrence explored his spirituality, *Master Class* arguably expanded his soul as an artist, and opened the door to one of his most prolific times with the plays, musicals, and operas we've seen—and there was more to come.

II.

Terrence had been working on *Some Men* for many years. The play is a series of scenes about gay men and their culture in the United States over eight decades. It begins and ends with a same-sex wedding, and it has scenes in a tentative courtship in 1922, a Harlem nightclub in 1932, the Stonewall riot in 1969, a gay bathhouse in 1975, an AIDS ward in 1989, an online chat room in 2004, a support group and wedding finale in present day.

In Terrence's archives, there are notes of characters and situations, many of which are undated, but some seem to go back as early as the 1970s.

In 2004, the topic would have been very present to Terrence. He had had a civil union ceremony with Tom Kirdahy in Vermont in 2003, and the first gay marriage had occurred in San Francisco the following year. In 2004, same-sex marriage had become legal in Massachusetts, and the trend was moving toward more and more acceptance, though the opposition was heating up as well.

Terrence, who at sixty-five had lived through a great deal of that history, knew both its comedy and its heartbreak, but in 2005, though he had a lot of notes and a lifetime of immersion in the subject matter, it had never gelled into a play.

Producer Susie Dietz, who described herself as a "tagalong" producer on other projects had been working with Peter Schneider, a producer who had had a powerful career with Disney where he had overseen the revival of the animation studio. Schneider had approached Dietz with an idea for a show to be called *Café Verboten* (*Forbidden Café*). The concept was an anthology (aka "jukebox") musical that was the soundtrack for the gay experience in the twentieth century—Judy Garland, Barbra Streisand, and so forth.

Dietz said she didn't think it was a musical, but that it could be used as music in a play about gay life. Dietz took it to Philip Himberg at the Sundance Institute, and he liked it. He wanted to produce it for the Sundance winter workshop, known as White Oak project in Yulee, Florida. According to Dietz, the compound in Florida had been built by Howard Gillman who loved the arts and whose family owned a paper mill, and built an arts facility on his property . . . as one does.

Dietz and Schneider knew they needed a playwright, and there was only one person they both thought of: Terrence. So, they all decamped to Florida . . . for a week. Dietz figured that Terrence had had commissions before, "but I'm not sure that he had ever been through that sort of intense development project." The facility, however, Dietz says, was beautiful, and very state-of-the art at the time. They were sharing it with the musical *Grey Gardens*, which was also in development.

They took a bunch of great actors down to Florida including Michael Rupert and John Glover, and they decided that the way to introduce the music was to have a Black Diva and a White Diva sing the songs between the scenes. Dietz said:

> We got it to a point where it was kind of a mess. It had crazy scenes
> in it that would never see the light of day. It was incredibly long,
> but it was kind of wonderful, too. And my husband who was not a
> professionally theater person—he's a music business guy—was just
> absolutely mesmerized.

Mess or not, Dietz, who was from Bala Cynwyd, Pennsylvania, a suburb of Philadelphia, knew Sara Garonzik at PTC, and so they agreed to do the world premiere of *Some Men* in the same theater where *Master Class* had first bowed a couple of years earlier. (And *Frankie and Johnny* and *Lips Together* before that.) It was PTC's thirtieth anniversary season. Philip Himberg was set to direct, and the opening was set for May 2006. But the play was still overly long—and a mess. It got lukewarm reviews and, in Dietz's words was "overwrought." Nevertheless, even though it was still a work in progress. Carole Rothman had agreed to produce it in New York at Second Stage. Dietz said that deal was done before the Philadelphia premiere; PTC would present it as a coproduction with Second Stage.

However, for New York, Rothman insisted that she would have the right to change the director and ask for other changes in the production. The updating began. Dietz remembers that Terrence dove in: "Terrence decided that the women were superfluous. Why did we have them? He was calling the play *Some Men*," she said.

A scene that had featured a mother became a father, and there was one scene where a husband left his wife, and as they looked at it, Dietz said, they realized that it was a scene that had been done in "a million movies." What Dietz remembers most of all was that Terrence was very clear-eyed about what worked and what didn't. As with *Lips Together*, he had had to go far out to come back in closer to what he wanted to accomplish.

The play was simplified and edited down. It opened at Second Stage, and the *Philadelphia Inquirer* came back to review it, and said it was "much improved." Ben Brantley, once again, delivered a lukewarm review for the *New York Times*, but since Second Stage is a subscription-based theater, an audience was assured, and it was popular with gay theatergoers as they saw their history portrayed—and honored. (Subscriptions are invaluable for theaters and playwrights that want to take chances.)

Terrence never intended *Some Men* to be political, but given the subject matter and what was going on in the country, it was almost unavoidable that it would be seen that way. Instead, he had wanted the play to be his *Our Town*, Thornton Wilder's play quoted earlier, about Grover's Corners, New Hampshire, set in 1901 and 1913, that talked about everyday life, marriage, and death and was lyrical in its simplicity. He saw the potential for *Some Men* to do for gay men what Wilder had done for America at large. However, in 2004, eleven states passed constitutional amendments defining marriage as the union of one man and one woman and in 2006 nine more states did the same, and the LGBTQ+ populations were still oppressed by the ten-year-old Defense of Marriage Act (DOMA). Given this climate, the play did evolve somewhat between Philadelphia and New York. Prior to AIDS, Terrence said, many gay men defined themselves—and certainly identified themselves—through sex. Later that turned to activism for health care and later for marriage equality.

Terrence himself would become an ever-more vocal supporter of marriage equality. As his relationship with Tom Kirdahy, who had previously been a public-interest lawyer helping people with HIV and AIDS, deepened over six years, Terrence insisted that all people deserved equality, and it would continue to be a major fight for him for the rest of his life. We'll talk more about this in a bit, but in addition to being merely a play, *Some Men* came at a time in Terrence's life when his perception—and the culture's perception—of what it meant to be gay was changing. It was no longer okay—though it always was amusing—for characters like Buzz and Mendy to be on the outside looking in, and by the time *Some Men* premiered in New York, Terrence knew that he and Tom had a rightful place on the inside. As always, it was what he was driven to write about.

III.

Not every play of Terrence's was a smash hit, but very few, after *Bump* were total disasters. Even the ones that were less successful still managed to incorporate wit, and intriguing characters, and creative situations, even if they weren't well realized and if critics couldn't fully appreciate what Terrence was going for. At least he was always going for something.

Deuce, in 2007, was a play that was a disappointment, even if it did manage to run for 148 performances. Hopes were high going into the production. It was to be Angela Lansbury's return to the Broadway stage for the first time in twenty-five years (it was really twenty-four, but promotional folks weren't counting that closely), matched with Marian Seldes, a beloved Broadway veteran, muse for Edward Albee, and known for her precise acting work . . . and never missing a performance. (She appeared in every one of *Deathtrap*'s 1,793 performances, earning her a spot in *The Guinness Book of World Records*.) The play was about two retired tennis stars watching a match. Midge (Seldes) is a sophisticated woman while Leona (Lansbury) is more working class and earthy. They are watching a match as part of an event where they are being honored for their careers in tennis, and the play is largely their conversation, memories, and somewhat scathing comments to one another. On an emotional level, it's about aging, facing mortality, and looking back at careers in the spotlight and a relationship that was not closely but deeply intertwined. It's a much better play than it ever got credit for being, probably because it's quiet and reflective, and not much happens. Midge and Leona represent the passing of an era, and whether it's tennis or the theater, eras do pass and at some point everyone finds themselves between the old and the new. On many levels, that's where Terrence spent his entire career, breaking boundaries, pushing the art form and then as the world changes, looking to find themselves again, or still. It was something Terrence was concerned about in his own life as he was aging and he wondered whether he would be relevant to a new generation, wanted, or able to be heard.

The last line of the play says it all. The admirer who idolizes Midge and Leona says, "Look at them. This time really look. You will not see their likes again."

The staging was simple. Midge and Leona are seated through the entire play, looking out, as if they are watching the tennis match. So much for complicated blocking.

The production was challenging, however, and Terrence was unable to do rewrites once they started rehearsals because it was too much for Lansbury who was eighty-three at the time of the show or Seldes who was seventy-nine to put in the inevitable changes Terrence would have wanted. In the end, both actresses wore earpieces so they could be prompted.

Terrence had been eager to write for Lansbury since she had had to pull out of *The Visit*. Terrence and Tom had become very close to Angela as well, and the pressure was on everyone to make it good.

Between Lansbury's return to Broadway and what that meant in the theater community and as a national news story, given how beloved she had been in the TV series *Murder, She Wrote*. (Lord knows, she wouldn't want to be remembered just for that. From *Mame* to *Sweeney Todd*, to a sparkling revival of *Blithe Spirit* two years later, Lansbury was the quintessential Broadway star.) The show was being watched from all corners, and the stakes were high. Kirdahy said the production was "put on a fast track," and they didn't have the chance to work on the play to the extent that Terrence—and all involved—would have wanted.

Tom Kirdahy describes what happened on opening night:

> It had been a very difficult preview process. Opening night came, and the curtain went up, and the applause went on forever. It just didn't stop because it was Angela's return to the stage. Marian's name was above the title in a Broadway show.
>
> It didn't go well that night. Marian got to page two in the script, and she just jumped. She just went up; just forget where she was in the telling of the story. So she asked Angela a question that didn't come till page sixteen. Angela was completely thrown, and it was a difficult night. It's the first time I just walked out the theater and said, "I'm gonna take a deep breath."

What happens when the show goes so far out of bounds is that everyone backstage just holds on. Veteran stage manager Liz Reddick said that you keep flipping through the script trying to figure out where people are, and hoping they'll get back on track. In this case they eventually did, and the play righted itself—and that never happened again during the run.

Terrence, however, stayed through the entire performance, rocky though it was, and he remembered Tom's upset with great affection, noting that it was one of Tom's early efforts at producing and that this was a kind of baptism by fire.

In the end, Lansbury's return to the stage overshadowed the play—and the reviews. While Terrence was taken to task for the script, Seldes and Lansbury were praised to the rafters, as much for their star power and history as their performances in the play. Kirdahy says that since it was the "new Broadway," the critics had not waited to come till opening night, and all seen earlier performances where there had been no problems. (Today, "first night" critics, from major outlets and Tony voters, tend to be invited to cover a show in its final previews so there's time to write a review. Gone are the romanticized days when critics would race up the aisle as the final curtain fell, sprint to their typewriters and bang out a review to make the morning papers.)

With his characteristic grace, Kirdahy says, Terrence was very loyal to everyone involved in the production. "Terrence never complained, and he really took the bullets for that production, and, frankly, I think we as producers should have."

That was pure Terrence. He knew how to get up when he got knocked down, which he did once more, and Lansbury was nominated for a Tony for her performance.

IV.

After *Deuce*, Terrence wrote *Golden Age*, which returned him backstage at the opera—a place of comfort for him. He stayed backstage for *And Away We Go*, another play about the theater, or more accurately, THE THEATRE. The play is a hilarious survey course of the theater, covering two thousand years from backstage at the theater at Epidaurus to the present day—along the way taking us from the theater of Aeschylus to

Opening night curtain call for It's Only a Play *on Broadway.*
WENN / ALAMY STOCK PHOTO

Shakespeare to Molière to Chekhov, for the first reading of *The Seagull*, to Samuel Beckett's *Waiting for Godot* at the Coconut Grove Playhouse in 1956 to the present day. Interspersed among these scenes are messages from contemporary theater board member Anne Tedesco-Boyle about the perilous state of the theater. It is an unabashed Valentine to the "theatre" (Terrence insisted on that spelling), and while that's a cliché to be sure, Terrence was happy to dabble in clichés to make his larger theatrical point—and amuse his audience.

The play was commissioned by the Pearl Theatre, a small Off-Broadway company that specialized in the classics. The Pearl was the only resident theater in New York with an established company, and Dominic Cuskern at the time had been a member of the company and a teacher there. When the company wanted a new play, Terrence was a natural choice. In writing it, Terrence wanted to respect the tradition of the company and write something new. The result was *And Away We Go*, a six-actor, thirty-six-character romp through the history of the theater. In each of the scenes, people complain about a life in the theater, for huge comic effect, but Terrence's *leitmotif* is that no matter where, no matter when, producing plays is hard and more a labor of love than an act of commerce, though commerce will inevitably rear its ugly head because no matter the period or the continent, somebody has to pay for all of this. A running plot point in the play is that the contemporary company is threatened with having to cancel its production of *King Lear* due to lack of funds. Just at the last minute, however, the board member who wants to be "in the theatre" even if it's only saving the day comes with a big check. (In case you hadn't noticed, we're back to a play as crammed with plot as *Dedication* or *The Ritz*.)

Jack Cummings III, director of The Transport Group in New York, an Off-Broadway company that stages both new works and "radical-ly-reimagined revivals," signed on to direct. In fall of 2012, he and Terrence sat down to work on the play, and Cummings said, "It was definitely rough, but wasn't a mess." So, they had a year.

Cummings, however, never felt that Terrence was "crazy about devel-opment" in terms of reviewing a script and doing rewrites from a more academic perspective. He always wanted to get a play on its feet and work from there, once he could see actors doing it. It was nonethe-less a productive time, even if there were stylistic differences in how to approach the material. As Cummings said,

> He would say, "Why do you have to do all this? You learn in front of the audience," and so forth. He hated [table] readings, which I don't blame him for necessarily.
>
> Transport Group, though, has a real strict policy. I just won't do anything without a couple of readings, and I won't do something new without a full four-week workshop on your feet. And I really prefer that after the workshop there's a full year to maybe do one more reading to work on it and learn from it.

They took the show in one of its early versions to a play festival in Ojai, California. Cummings remembered that Terrence and his play were the centerpiece of the festival, and they did a lot of the develop-ment there—of both kinds. They had a presentation in a big theater, and it was packed. It was done as a reading with the actors on book at music stands. After the presentation, there was a talk back, and Cummings remembered it clearly:

> Someone asked, rightly, "How's this going to work? How's it going to look?" And Terrence said, "I have no idea. When I work with my design team, hopefully we'll figure it out, but right now, I have no idea."
>
> And I remember falling in love with Terrence a little bit more that day because he didn't flinch, and he didn't say anything like "What do you mean?" At least with me, he was very process oriented. A lot of people hate that because they don't want to suffer through the bad parts, and every process is going to have bad parts.

After Ojai, however, Cummings insisted that the Pearl do a workshop of the piece. He said that Terrence didn't want it, but he was supportive. Cummings thought that Terrence wouldn't have thought of it, and certainly wouldn't have insisted upon it, thinking that perhaps it was a generational difference between Terrence and him as to how to approach material. "It was a blind spot for him," Cummings said of Terrence. "He seemed to think that if it was on the page, what else did you need?"

Cummings remembered that during the workshop, *Golden Age* had opened, and the reviews for that were not good. Terrence came to rehearsal at the Pearl anyway, and while everyone was trying to avoid mentioning the bad reviews, Terrence preempted any awkwardness saying that being in rehearsal for a new play was exactly where he wanted to be. Again, having been knocked down, he had no choice but to get up and keep going.

They did a final workshop presentation of *And Away We Go*, and Cummings remembered it didn't go well. In fact, Cummings said it was "pretty bad," but Terrence didn't panic. That, Cummings said, was unusual because typically if a presentation doesn't go well, people panic, and producers head for the hills, but that wasn't the case here.

The play went into rehearsal, and it was complicated. There were pages and pages of notes created by Cummings in the process, trying to figure out how all the pieces of this complicated, but comic, play all fit together. Donna Lynne Champlin and Micah Stock were the only members of the cast who weren't members of the Pearl company. Champlin, who had worked with Cummings before, ended up explaining his process very often. Because the Pearl had always focused on classics, the actors, except Cuskern presumably, were not used to working on a new play that was constantly changing. Micah Stock had joined the cast after Ojai, and while Terrence had felt abandoned by the actor who had originally played his parts, he and Stock grew close, and Stock would walk away with a Tony nomination for the Broadway production of *It's Only a Play* a year later.

Staging the play wasn't easy, but Cummings said it was exciting, "Terrence really is playing with form and time and place. It's the shifting and colliding of all these eras." For example, the scene in the Greek theater is interrupted by a canon shot, and the actors have no idea of what's going on, but suddenly we're in Elizabethan England, and the canon announces a play is about to begin. This group in turn is interrupted by three knocks on the floor, which announces the start of a French play. It's meta and manic all at the same time. As Cummings said, "It was risky and adventurous."

The play opened at the Pearl in November 2013, and one event that everyone remembers from the production was that after the show was open, Terrence decided he wanted to put in changes. As Cummings said, it had been complicated to do in the first place, but with a couple of weeks of playing left to go, Terrence had reworked the script:

> I remember one night, I was in my office, and he sent me the script, and the changes were in red, and I had mistakenly forwarded it to the actors thinking the changes were not going to be a lot. By the time we opened, they were barely getting through it, but they were, like, "Okay, we finally opened."

Then I had to break the news to them that there were going to be changes. So I had sent the script to the actors without looking at it first, which is a huge mistake. I just wanted to get it to them, and then I was going to look at it.

Donna Lynne emailed me back, and said, "I love you to death, Jack," but absolutely not.

Champlin remembered there were about fifty changes, and it was worse because they were all in red. She thought they could go back to Terrence and have him pick his top five, which they could spend an hour on each. They wanted to do something because they loved Terrence, but the structure of the play was "like a house of cards," as Champlin said. "But it also made me sad," she said, "to see so many changes that close to the end. We're going to close this show, and it's not going to be what he wants." Even years later, Champlin regretted that he wouldn't see the play he wanted it to be. "He was an artist, and he never let it alone. He never wanted it set." Champlin, who appeared in the revival of *Sweeney Todd* with Patti LuPone in 2005, said Stephen Sondheim was the same way; they had to demand that he stop making changes. But that's the artist—always trying to make it better.

They put in a few changes and finished the run. The play was well-reviewed and for once, the critics appreciated the play for what it was. Incidentally, as both Stock and Cummings point out, Terrence had the last word: the printed version of the play—and the acting edition for other productions—feature all the edits he wanted. So, perhaps the play he wanted finally will be getting seen somewhere where people love the theater as much as Terrence always did.

V.

Away from the theater Terrence was ever more deeply involved in the push for marriage equality. In June of 2013, the Supreme Court ruled that DOMA was unconstitutional, and states—California, Delaware, New Jersey, Rhode Island, Hawaii, and others—were using the concept of "equal protection" to allow same-sex marriages to move forward. Terrence and Tom, who had been joined as a civil partnership in 2003 had been married in Washington in 2010, and the country was inching closer to national recognition of same-sex marriages.

Tyne Daly had been doing a charity event at the Buck's County Playhouse—where she had earned half her Equity card at age fifteen and where her parents had performed—and she was asked if she would consider doing a play there. "I [Tyne] said, 'give me a play,' and he [Earl Jones] said, 'I'm talking to Terrence McNally about *Andre's Mother* now.'"

Not long after, Daly says, she was having dinner with Tom and Terrence:

> I said, I can't get excited about redoing what was done then, but I'd be real interested to see what happened to these people in the last 25 years. And then we were off to the races about telling another part of the story with the growth of a quarter of a century.
>
> Then it began to be really interesting to try to talk about the present and recall the past. That's a play about forgiveness and moving on from grief and not just lying there like a rag.
>
> Katharine is so stricken and stalled by grief.

When Daly looked back at the play from the vantage point of 2020, she said that she had just begun to deal with grief in her own life, and said, "and, boy, do I get it now. I get it much better than when I played the play."

Terrence wrote the play for Daly, and it was a *tour de force* for her, but in a quiet way, perfectly suited to Daly's ability to fully inhabit a character, bottling up for this play all the power and complexity that made her such a ferocious Mama Rose in the 1989 revival of *Gypsy*.

Katharine is Andre's Mother—she has a name now. She has come unannounced from Dallas to the apartment overlooking Central Park West where Cal, Andre's surviving lover, lives with his husband Will and their son Bud. It is twenty years since they saw one another. At rise, she and Cal are standing in his apartment overlooking Central Park West.

Cal has a good job in finance, and Will, fifteen years younger, is an aspiring writer. Katharine is wearing an enormous fur coat that almost dwarfs her. It was, Terrence said, "her armor."

Katharine has come by to drop off Andre's unopened journal, and she soon realizes that Cal, despite mourning Andre, has moved on with his life. What follows is Katharine trying to resolve her own feelings, looking for redemption, dealing with the thing "out there," which for her is the grief that has left her life and her heart frozen for twenty years. Katharine never accepted that Andre was gay, or that he died from AIDS, or that he died, period.

Over the course of the play, Katharine and Cal struggle to come to terms with the past. It's not easy, and it often gets emotionally messy, as Katharine remembers how she was and Cal remembers how hurt Andre was by her. All Andre ever really wanted was love and acceptance, but unable to get that from his mother, he sought it in his life in his chosen family, and in Cal—and in New York, Terrence returning to that theme again.

One of the more remarkable aspects of the play is that it presents the marriage of Cal and Will as a simple fact, two years before the Obergefell Supreme Court decision that made same-sex marriage legal nationwide—and ten years after Terrence and Tom had a civil marriage in Vermont. The play isn't about that, though there are some observations from Cal about how he had to get used to the word "husband," which directly reflects Terrence's own journey. To track the course of gay love from Clarence in *Bump*, literally dying because he believed in the possibility of love to Cal and Will married and living in an apartment overlooking Central Park—and so many in between—is to see the nearly fifty-year evolution of gay relationships in the United States. It is to see how gay men in particular evolved from the outlaws to the ordinary, and while it comes with fewer fireworks, the "ordinary" is the thing to rejoice in.

This is also an Easter egg from Terrence in the play. In an interview before the play opened with *Gay City News*, Terrence, in commenting on what it meant to be married to Tom, said that his favorite sentence was, "The reservations are in my husband's name." Cal has that line in the play.

(As it turns out, this was one of Terrence's "curated" interview lines, and he used it repeatedly. That doesn't make the feelings any less authentic. Terrence was overjoyed to be married to Tom.) Cal is also concerned about the age difference between Will and him, something that was initially a concern of Terrence's in his relationship with Tom, though he makes the difference in the play fifteen years, while in his life that difference was twenty-five.

> **Cal:** At first I was embarrassed about Will. Not his age. I worry about the difference more than he does. He knows what he's getting into. But it felt like a betrayal of Andre. Of us. Even after 8 years. How much could I have loved Andre if I can love Will the way I do now?
>
> **Katharine:** Yes, how can you?
>
> **Cal:** I don't know. I don't pretend to understand these things. I honestly think Andre sent Will to me.

After Gary Bonasorte died in 2000 and Terrence met Tom in 2001, he became fond of saying that he felt Gary had sent Tom to him. Moreover, Cal, like Terrence, reflects on what marriage means, as he thinks back to his relationship with Andre more than two decades earlier:

> Of course we'd never taken marriage vows. We weren't allowed to. Relationships like mine and Andre's weren't supposed to last. We didn't deserve the dignity of marriage.

The play is steely in its honesty—about AIDS, about marriage, about the struggles of gay men in the latter half of the twentieth century, about what it means to follow one's heart, and about Katharine and her grief and a whole generation of parents unprepared for loss, and the deep regret she feels for merely being Andre's Mother. That she finally speaks up for herself at the end, in a speech that is "Rose's Turn" from *Gypsy* but in prose and acknowledges her role in what happened by the end of the play, she has opened, slightly cracked to be honest, the door to healing. It's one of the marks of Terrence's genius that he allows Katharine her rage, her grief, her guilt, her flaws, and ultimately her inability—or willingness—to understand Andre. Katharine embodies the loss of a generation of parents, particularly mothers, who were forever alienated from their gay sons because they were trapped in emotional prisons. Terrence doesn't forgive her, but he does understand.

Because the play was so deeply personal, from that initial conversation with Daly, the play pretty much flowed out of Terrence. Well, as much as the process of writing ever "flows" smoothly. Bobby Steggert, who played Will, his last role before becoming a therapist specializing in issues related to gay men, said that the script arrived almost fully formed:

> And from the moment we started rehearsal to the moment we opened, there were only minor adjustments to the script. For some reason with that play, Terrence knew what it was and structurally it never changed a bit. Sometimes there is a different kind of freedom in that because you're not constantly adjusting to the new parameters. You know what your parameters are and because of the safety in that structure, you can expand into it.

The play opened in June of 2013 at the Bucks County Playhouse, while *And Away We Go* was still in development. As with *Deuce*, *Mothers and Sons* was performed without an intermission. Terrence wasn't thrilled about that format, but he was fully cognizant of the new realities of Broadway, as he would be later with *Anastasia*. "How long is it?" he said is one of the first questions people asked ushers when they came into the theater. He didn't love that, but with *Mothers and Sons*, he accepted it. He always preferred the longer form, but he also found the powerful emotional payoff in the compression of what he had considered a full-length play into ninety minutes. Of course, he could do it.

After all, *Andre's Mother* had originally begun as an eight-minute piece, and for many years, he had been a master of the one-act format.

The play, which had always been announced as a "limited run," the new Broadway hedge, reminiscent of the provincial troupe of Vincent Crummles in Dickens's *Nicholas Nickleby* wherein a play could be repeatedly extended due to "popular demand," finally opened on Broadway in March 2014. It ran 137 performances and earned Tony and Drama Desk nominations for Tyne Daly.

Mothers and Sons was significant for Terrence in another way. He remembered that one day while the show was running, he got out of a cab in front of the Golden Theatre on Broadway and looked up at the marquee. There was a sign that said, "The 20th Broadway Production by Four-Time Tony Award Winner Terrence McNally." He said that after all those years—and all those productions—this was the first time he felt that he had truly arrived on Broadway. And he was being heard at his most heartfelt.

VI.

It wasn't a new play, but in 2014 *It's Only a Play* got a new life on Broadway as a star-studded hit that finally found its audience. The play was largely rewritten, though the concept and the structure remained intact. Given its timely satire, all the jokes were updated, and it got a lavish production.

A year or so before the show bowed on Broadway, producer Susie Dietz was working with a small theater in Los Angeles, called the Skylight Theater. They had done several successful productions, including a mounting of *Some Men* that had featured Ed Asner and Stacy Keach playing two elder gays being interviewed by clueless young people. It had been a hit.

Dietz suggested that, as a fundraiser, Terrence and Tom should come out to Los Angeles, and they would do a weekend of Terrence's work. During that weekend, *It's Only a Play* came up, and Dietz said that perhaps they should "refurbish" the play and maybe try to make it happen on Broadway:

> I think we did a living room reading of it, just to hear it. I know Thomas Sadoski was in it, and Griffin Dunne, and some really good people. Jack Cummings came in and directed it, and I think we had, like, three hours of rehearsal. We did two performances, and people were rolling out of their chairs. We didn't think it was going to do well in Los Angeles because it's such a New York play, such a Broadway play. And, my God, these people were just enthralled.
>
> And I think that's the experience that made Terrence say, "yeah, let's do this. I'll change some things and make it more relevant to today."

Tom, with Ken Davenport and Roy Furman, were the lead producers, with Dietz on the team. Jack O'Brien was the director. Logan Reed who was billed as "Author's Assistant" recalled that Terrence had to be convinced to make it an all-star cast, but the producers felt that that was essential if the show was going to sell. The Who's Who of Broadway that was cast included F. Murray Abraham (the poison-penned theater critic), Matthew Broderick (the playwright), Stockard Channing (the drug-taking, fading star), Nathan Lane (the TV star who turned down a role), and Megan Mullally (the producer). Rupert Grint (the British director) known as Ron Weasley from the *Harry Potter* movies, was making his Broadway debut, and the billing said "introducing Micah Stock (the Broadway hopeful, coat-checker)," fresh from his first outing with Terrence in *And Away We Go*.

What Reed remembered was how hard Terrence worked on making the comedy work. He said that Terrence would sit at a table working on the jokes again and again, down to the smallest word. He also remembered that with all that talent—and all those egos—on the stage, Jack O'Brien was the perfect director to manage all of that and create harmony among the cast. He said that everyone was aware that the stakes were high and especially for Grint who was making his Broadway debut. Reed says that on breaks he and others on the production team would go out into the alley where Grint was smoking and give him pep talks.

Stock, who got a Tony nomination for his role, loved the process of working on the show and remembered how the whole company came together, welcoming him in to the Broadway community.

> The whole thing was a master class because everyone in the company was an entirely different actor with an entirely different process.
>
> I remember that Nathan and I ran the first scene in the play every day, and we developed a superstition where we had to run through the scene speed demon style before everything. Whenever we didn't do it—when Nathan didn't want to do it that day—something would happen, and he said, "We gotta run it." I got to play a team sport with Nathan every day, and that was important to him as well. Nathan was just so generous, and he wanted me to be as funny as he was.

Stock said that Lane was really the reason he got the part. Terrence and O'Brien wanted him, but it was when Lane said, "Give it to the kid," it was Lane's confidence in him that got Stock the part—and propelled his career. Stock loved working on the show and had complete appreciation for his castmates. He was in awe of how Stockard Channing, for example, could work an audience to get a laugh.

Audiences, including most of the critics, loved it, too. It came at the right time culturally, as it happened. Widespread obsession with celebrities and entertainment had permeated the culture with outlets like TMZ and innumerable blogs, and shows were devoted to the doings—good and scandalous—of celebrities. It was the perfect time for a Broadway audience to laugh at it all. Originally announced as an eighteen-week engagement running from August 2014 to January 2015, it was extended to June. In December, *Variety* reported that the show had recouped its $3.9 million investment and was grossing more than $1 million each week.

The play has also become a staple of regional and community theaters as a reliable moneymaker. As usual, it just took time for the world to come around to what Terrence was up to.

VII.

Terrence and Director John Doyle had become friends during *The Visit*. At some point, Terrence told Doyle that he had a play that "wasn't quite in his bottom drawer" that he had been looking at recently and doing some work on, and would Doyle take a look at it?

Doyle at the time was the artistic director of Classic Stage Company (CSC), and he read the play, which was *Fire and Air*. He thought that it was about how art evolves, about how classic dance became dance as it's known today, and complex artists, and he thought it would be perfect for CSC.

In the play, Terrence returned to one of his favorite topics: how theater happens—and what it costs, personally and spiritually. The plot centers on impresario Sergei Diaghilev, his *Ballets Russes*, and his artistic and sexual relationship with dancer Vaslav Nijinsky. The deeper issues developed through the play are the relationships of artists to one another, to their art, and to the culture, and reflect in the relationship between Diaghilev and Nijinsky.

The central question of the script is whether art and artists are inseparable. Terrence would appear to argue that they are. It's obvious that Diaghilev loved Nijinsky, but that love was not requited, and Nijinsky was more an opportunist than a lover. After all, Diaghilev was much older, overweight, and covered with boils, but the play suggests that their creative partnership was the high point of their respective careers.

When Nijinsky marries a dancer from the corps on a South American tour, Diaghilev cuts all ties—only to have the role of lover and muse filled by a young dancer, Léonide Massine. The play also chronicles the collateral damage suffered by others in Diaghilev's inner circle, including his cousin and manager Dima, his childhood nurse Dunya who still attends him, and his friend and benefactress Misia. They are the scorched moths around Diaghilev's candle, loyal to the end, though each suffers for that loyalty.

A central theme of the play is how art challenges conventional culture, something that Terrence would have known very well. When Diaghilev presents *Le Sacre du Printemps* (*The Rite of Spring*), the audience boos. It's shocking to them and upends their sense of what dance should be. Talking to the audience, Diaghilev says, "I shall be brief," he tells the crowd. "You are idiots. You have been shown a masterpiece . . . I detest you." How many times would Terrence—or many other visionary artists—have longed to confront an audience in that way?

Doyle and Terrence assembled a group of friends to have a reading, including Nathan Lane, Sarah Jessica Parker, Tyne Daly, John Glover, and others. As Doyle said, none of them came with the intention of doing the play; it was just to help a friend. It certainly wasn't a first; Terrence would often gather actors he loved in his living room on 9th Street so he could hear the play out loud.

After the reading, Doyle and Terrence worked through the play scene by scene, editing as they went along. The play had started with a larger cast, but it was pared down to six characters, and the show went into rehearsal.

Because of the way CSC worked, Doyle said, there wasn't the time to do a workshop, but Terrence was thrilled to be working in that small theater, and said it was one of his favorite spaces, virtually in his neighborhood. Doyle accurately summed up Terrence's lifetime of work, saying, "There always was that bit of Terrence that was kind of downtown, and his approach wasn't about the next Broadway gig, or the next Tony. It's about making work. Certainly that piece [*Fire and Air*] felt like a part of his canon of work about great artists."

Doyle remembered the process as wonderful and fully collaborative. The cast included John Glover, Douglas Hodge, Marsha Mason, and Marin Mazzie, in her last role, and Doyle said they all wanted to do it because they would be working with Terrence on a new play.

Terrence was very present and, as Doyle describes him, very generous with the work. Marsha Mason, who played Dunya the nurse, who looks after Diaghilev throughout his life, said the process was "paring away and paring away" until they got down to the truth and clarity of the piece.

Terrence loved listening to the actors and the process of working with them, though, as always, he would be very clear about what he wanted, and made a lot of what Doyle called "wonderful changes."

> But what I loved was at a certain point—I remember we were rehearsing over the holiday period—he said, "Okay, I'm going to go away now."
>
> And he vanished for about eight days.
>
> I thought, "God, you know exactly what you're doing because there comes a point in any rehearsal period when the writer should not be in the room, where the actor has the freedom to say, 'Do I really have to speak these words?' It's that period when the creatives feel you're walking through mud before you get to some clarity. And he knew not to be there tremendously during the preview period."

The play opened at CSC on February 1, 2018. It got mixed-to-negative reviews, but the run was extended by a week to accommodate enthusiastic CSC audiences.

There was one sad note out of this production. As noted earlier, *Fire and Air* was Marin Mazzie's last role. She had appeared in more than a dozen Broadway shows, including a Tony-nominated performance in *Kiss Me, Kate*, opposite Brian Stokes Mitchell. During the rehearsals and performances of *Fire and Air*, she was dealing with ovarian cancer. She had been diagnosed in 2015, and she and Terrence called themselves "cancer buddies" as he was dealing with his own lung cancer. Logan Reed remembers that she missed a few performances of *Fire and Air*, but she was determined to see the production through, even as her disease was taking its toll. She died on September 13, just over six months after the show closed.

In June of 2019, the Zach Theater in Austin, Texas, hosted a world premiere of a revised *Fire and Air*. The nonprofit theater has been a center for creative theater in Austin since 1937 and is near the Harry Ransom Center at the University of Texas in Austin where Terrence's archives are kept.

The revised play was tightened and focused more on the politics surrounding the *Ballets Russes*. The relationship between Diaghilev and Nijinsky was expanded, and though the basic structure of the play stayed the same, Terrence would sharpen the elements of the approach to art and its role in life.

It would be his final play.

It was called *Immortal Longings*.

10

The Love Story

I.

IT IS A TRUTH universally acknowledged that any tale of a life in the theater has to include a love story. For Terrence, that didn't happen until he was sixty-one. As fate would have it, he would meet Tom Kirdahy at a panel discussion in the Hamptons on "Theater from a Gay Perspective" sponsored by the East End Gay Organization. Terrence was on the panel with Edward Albee and Lanford Wilson. Terrence, who was still frustrated that he was being identified primarily as a "gay playwright" went anyway to support the organization he'd been a member of from its earliest days. Kirdahy, who was just thirty-eight at the time, said that when they were in the green room that they "just clicked." Terrence, as we've seen, had certainly had relationships and referred to himself as a "serial monogamist."

Terrence hadn't had serious relationships when he was in high school or his early college days. The sex he had had in high school, as discussed earlier, was with friends, and it had no deeper meaning outside of the sex. He had "tricked" (had casual sex) with men while he was in college, but it was when he met Edward Albee that he became serious about having an adult relationship. At the time there were no cultural models for a same-sex relationship, and the kind of relationship Cal and Will would have in *Mothers and Sons* was inconceivable. Still, Terrence did fall in love and tried to make it work.

> I was a student at Columbia, which was a demanding program, and I didn't want to fail out of Columbia, and I took my writing

in my courses very seriously. So, our time together the first couple of years was somewhat limited. I was at my own apartment several blocks away on Barrow Street. Edward lived on Abingdon Square, just below 14th Street.

I would say, "I can't see you this weekend. I have to write my paper on *King Lear.*"

Terrence and Edward weren't living together while Terrence was in college, but later they did, and it became apparent to Terrence during that time that they were both drinking too much. As noted earlier, he had said, "What kind of relationship do you really have if you're both drunk most of the time?"

Though Albee was known to be gay in the theater circles, he wasn't out publicly, and Terrence was forced to hide, something he didn't want to do. He was around, however, during *Virginia Woolf*, and says that during the preparation for *The Ballad of Sad Cafe* "we were a 'quote,' functioning couple." Things got really bad, he said, when Albee was in the process of putting together *Tiny Alice*, "which eventually led to me meeting someone else—someone else being Bobby Drivas—and breaking up. It was very unfriendly." However, in 2019, Terrence was still protective of the details of his private life with Albee. He didn't participate in the Mel Gussow biography of Albee. "When the book came out I was one paragraph, and I was a pretty significant part of Edward's life. I know things about Edward I would never tell another soul." He added that those facts never appeared in another book, and he questioned whether revealing them would have any relevance to understanding or appreciating Albee as "an important man of letters in the American theater." They are stories that will remain untold.

Though Terrence was doing his own writing at the time, he and Albee rarely talked about either of their work. "Playwrights don't go around mentoring one another. I think people often think they do, but the last thing we want to talk about is theater."

The relationship with Robert Drivas was also complicated. He was three years older than Terrence and an established actor by the time they met. Terrence cast him in *Bump* and wrote *Sweet Eros* for him. Drivas also directed *Bad Habits*. However, virtually nothing is known about Terrence and Drivas's private life, other than Drivas also was not open about his sexuality and that Terrence said he would be "invisible" with Drivas in any kind of public setting. The relationship fell apart, but they remained close until Drivas's death at age fifty in 1986. What Terrence remembered was that Drivas was very private and embarrassed about his battle with AIDS, something not uncommon at that time, particularly among men who had built careers in show business and were heavily invested in being straight. Ultimately, his disease outed him, at least in the theater world.

The relationship with Dominic Cuskern followed, and as described earlier, it ended when Cuskern met the man to whom he's still married to in 2022. The two remained friends, and, as noted, Terrence helped Cuskern establish his career as an actor, and they stayed close until Terrence's death.

What followed was one of the most confusing relationships of Terrence's life, certainly to any observer in his orbit. Wendy Wasserstein had been a student at Yale School of Drama when Terrence was there during *The Tubs* in 1974. Wasserstein's thesis play *Uncommon Women and Others*, about a group of students at Mount Holyoke, was produced Off-Broadway in 1977, and she would win the Tony Award for *The Heidi Chronicles* in 1989. Wasserstein and Terrence became close in 1987, and they would stay so for the next several years. They were romantically involved, at least according to Terrence, and his friend Don Roos said,

> She was always smiling and laughing and warm whenever I met her, and it was just a surprise when he told me that they were romantically involved. At the time I was extremely judgmental thinking it's a bad time to be gay, so lucky for you, you can switch. I was thinking this isn't his best self. Wendy was an extraordinary person, and the mysteries of desire are real. I don't think they were kidding themselves. I think they genuinely loved one another, but of course nobody knows what goes on in a relationship.

Terrence told Edgar Bronfman that he and Wendy were a couple and that he was a gay man in a relationship with a woman. "He didn't say that he wasn't bisexual, but he was trying to make that point that he was still Terrence," Bronfman said.

Terrence and Wendy were inseparable and wrote several things together, including *Sam Found Out* for TV and a play *The Girl from Fargo*, which was published in the *New York Times* in an article that reinforced the closeness of their relationship, only fueling the gossip theater people love only too well.

Julie Salaman in her book *Wendy and the Lost Boys* speculates that perhaps, as Roos thought, that Terrence was interested in a romantic relationship because of the times and AIDS and that he was "seeking an alternative that was less dangerous." That speculation was fueled by their closeness developing around the time that *Frankie and Johnny* was having its premiere at MTC, with Frank Rich's review in *The New York Times* taken by some as corroboration of Terrence and Wendy's relationship:

> The playwright examines his characters' connections with a new forthrightness and maturity, and it's just possible that, in the process, he's written the most serious play yet about intimacy in the age of AIDS.

Perhaps, while not maintaining the work was not autobiographical, Terrence did like to address issues that he was grappling with personally in his plays. How could he not?

Salaman does say that Wasserstein claimed that she and Terrence discussed having a baby. That's potentially misleading. If they discussed it, there's no evidence that they would have agreed. Kirdahy, Bronfman, and Roos say that Terrence had no interest in having a child, and Bronfman adds,

> Wendy was pressuring him. Wendy wanted a child. Wendy wanted a child with Terrence. I think she wanted to be married to Terrence,

and I think that's when Terrence pulled away because he said I can't be somebody I'm not. I care for her, and maybe in my own way I love her, but I'm a gay man. Maybe in the absence of anything else, this might go on for a bit, but at the end of the day I am who I am, and I can't pretend that I'm not.

Wasserstein was devastated by the breakup of the relationship. She went on to become a single mother in 1999 and never revealed the identity of her daughter Lucy Jane's father, but whoever it was, it was not Terrence. Terrence had been consistently outspoken to both Roos and Bronfman that he had no interest in having children, and Tom asserted that Terrence was not the child's father. (This is not especially uncommon for people who have grown up in alcoholic homes and have endured difficult relationships with parents and romantically. Besides, Terrence was much more interested in his work than parenting.) Wasserstein died from lymphoma in 2006, and Terrence spoke at her memorial service at Lincoln Center.

Even less is known about Terrence's relationship with Gary Bonasorte. Bonasorte was one of the founders of Rattlestick Theater Company. By all accounts from people who knew them they were happy together, and Bonasorte was referred to as "a sweetheart." In the few notes and scraps that exist, he called Terrence "puppy." Terrence had known that Bonasorte was HIV positive from the time they met, and he was unabashedly out. However, Terrence was identified only as Bonasorte's "companion" in the obituary in the *New York Times* in November 2000 and quoted as saying Bonasorte had died from "complications from lymphoma."

It would be approximately seven months later, that Terrence would feel that "click" backstage on a summer afternoon in the Hamptons.

II.

As the story goes, when they met, Kirdahy and Terrence did, indeed, click. "I mean clicked, instantly," Kirdahy said.

Terrence and Tom celebrate at Sardi's after Mayor Bill DeBlasio proclaims November 4 Terrence McNally Day.
COURTESY TERRENCE MCNALLY ESTATE

Before the event started, we were deep in conversation, and we just made each other laugh. Then the event happened, and it went extremely well. Afterwards he said on his way out, I'd love to give you a ring. I'm leaving for Machu Pichu, but when I get back, can I call you? And I just said sure, I'd be delighted.

I was like, Oh Terrence McNally just asked me if we wanted to hang out. I did not think it was a date. I didn't. I didn't think anything more than that this incredibly nice, charismatic guy said, let's get together when I'm back.

Both Terrence and Tom were single at the time. Bonasorte had died from AIDS the previous November, and Tom wasn't in a relationship and moreover had just gotten clean and sober. They had both gone through seismic changes in their lives. Tom continued:

I was sort of vulnerable and open, and he was vulnerable and open, and we were both game for taking a risk on love. Then he came back from his trip, and we had our first date on July 29, 2001. We had pasta at his home in Bridgehampton, and we were together ever since.

I learned that night that he was sober, and he learned that I had done AIDS work for almost two decades. We talked a lot about being in recovery. We talked about the impact of HIV on our personal lives, our community, and our country, the world. It was such a fun night. But it was intense because we talked a lot about alcoholism and AIDS. We laughed all night long and we had a few tears, and just instantly we were a couple.

Terrence said he had never believed in love at first sight . . . until he met Tom.

Excited as Tom was, he was concerned about losing his identity, and he told Terrence that he had his own dreams and goals. Suddenly, though, Tom was thrust into Terrence's world, and it could be intimidating—and a little scary. He met Nathan Lane on his second date with Terrence. He was meeting people like Angela Lansbury, Chita, Kander and Ebb, but as glamorous and exciting as that was, it made him more determined to stay in his work. "I just had to not sacrifice who I was, what my values were, and there was never any pressure from him."

But things were changing, as Tom said,

> He was so proud of me and the work I did. I was working on Long Island, doing an HIV project on the east end, which I had moved out there to do. Terrence's work kept us in New York, and I was doing a reverse commute. I was in court every day, and I was getting tired. I was going to the theater every night, and I was really falling in love with the work he was doing.

As he was getting more and more interested in Terrence's world, every once in a while, Tom would ask to sit in on rehearsals. They were together more and more, and it was clear to both of them that they were just falling more in love with each passing day.

For Thanksgiving that year, Tom traveled to Terrence's home in Key West. It was a wonderful time, but he was headed back to New York for work:

> Terrence said, "I have to tell you something." And I got that feeling in my stomach I didn't know if I was being dumped or I didn't know what was happening. I didn't think that because we had just had this incredible week together and he said, "I've been diagnosed with lung cancer and I'm going to be having surgery.
>
> "And I struggled with how and when, to how, when, and if I should tell you, this is all so new, and this is a lot on you, but you need to know this." In that moment I just said, I, I want to be by your side. If you'll have me. I don't want to impose myself, but I really want to be with you through this. And he said, I'd really love that.
>
> That changed everything. Two weeks later he had his first surgery that was December 10, 2001. I started spending a lot more time with his friends because I was by his side just about all day, every day. And I really knew how to be a hospital advocate because of my AIDS work.

Tom began soaking up all the information about what was going on with Terrence's work and his health and trying to help Terrence stay on top of all his projects. At the time it still never occurred to him that he would be a producer; he was using his legal skills to gather information and organize things.

Tom and Terrence went to London together for the opening of *The Full Monty* in 2002 and they were having a wonderful time, but Terrence's lung collapsed. Tom, who was in the middle of a huge trial, had to call his colleagues and say he wasn't going to be back because of a medical emergency. (Fortunately, he was able to get an adjournment.)

Tom started thinking about what he wanted his life to be:

> I really remember being in his hospital room and thinking this man is the most important thing in my world, and I don't ever want to be absent for anything. I have to find a way to incorporate my professional life with my personal life, and I knew I didn't want to be a lawyer any more.

After twenty years in the legal trenches, Tom was tired of the grind. Theater had always been one of his great loves, and he had studied dramatic literature as an undergrad. Tom broached the idea of learning to be a producer to Terrence, and Terrence was supportive, but was clear that Tom would have to do the work himself. In 2019, Terrence said that he had supported the idea but at the time had no idea if Tom would like it . . . or be good at it. He wasn't even completely sure of all that producers do. Still he made some calls, notably to Susie Dietz and asked if Tom could hang around and shadow her.

Tom was happy to start there, as he was clear that he never wanted to be the "meddling spouse"; he believed that one has to earn their place in a room. He was willing to lick envelopes, sit in the back of the room. Susie Dietz said to him, "You will bring me coffee, but you're also smart. You'll give me notes, and you'll give me reports." *Some Men* became the first show that Tom worked on.

It was working out, this being a producer thing. Tom said Terrence was incredibly supportive, even when Tom wasn't sure he could do it. When John Doyle was working with Tom and Terrence on *Fire and Air*, he was apprehensive at first and wondered if there would be "pillow talk" at home but said no such thing ever happened, at least not to his knowledge or that impeded Doyle's work. Almost immediately, Doyle realized that Tom was a creative, smart producer who had great instincts and was delightful to work with.

Perhaps Tom shouldn't have worried. In part, he credits his sobriety—and the hard work that entailed—for his being able to take on the challenges of a career change. He says if he hadn't been sober, he never would have been able to put that panel together that changed his life. With sobriety, he got his life back together, got his friends back, ultimately a new career and a renewed political fervor. As he says of sobriety, "it changed everything." Most importantly, "I found the love of my life."

He would also find he really did have a gift for producing—and become beloved within the theater community in his own right. Did Tom and Terrence have to learn to negotiate the personal and professional aspects of their relationship? Of course they did. In an interview with *Broadway Direct* in 2015 as *The Visit* was preparing for Broadway, Tom joked that Terrence sometimes referred to him as "management." Still, despite the inevitable issues that come up on any project, they found a resolution, and Tom fully believed that in their professional collaboration they brought out the best in one another. (They established that in their personal relationship almost from day one.)

Tom would quickly, for the theater, rack up an impressive list of shows as a producer, including *The Visit*, *It's Only a Play*, and the revival of *Frankie and Johnny*, as well as the Tony-winning *Hadestown*, and the Off-Broadway hit revival of *Little Shop of Horrors*. Tom Kirdahy Productions is among the most important producing organizations in the theater, something in which Terrence took great joy.

III.

If Terrence had been forced to hide in previous relationships, with Tom, it was exactly the opposite. For the first time, he was able to love openly with his full heart. As described previously, gone was the naïve, and tragic, hopefulness of Clarence in *Bump,* the barely suppressed anger and resentment of Buzz in *L!V!C!,* the lies of the couples in *Lips Together* and even the unrequited—and abused—passions of Maria in *Master Class.* Having brilliantly charted the landscape of relationship dysfunction for nearly four decades, Terrence suddenly found himself in a world with a man that fully accepted him and loved him for who he was.

This love awakened a political fervor in Terrence, and he became a powerful advocate for marriage equality. In a column for the *Huffington Post,* he expressed with some vehemence that he and Gary had only been "boyfriends" with no automatically granted legal rights. As he wrote, "Spouses have rights; boyfriends have none." This was essentially Cal's speech from *Mothers and Sons* cited earlier.

Terrence was no stranger to being vocal and active. In 1990 when controversy broke out over the National Endowment for the Arts (NEA) supporting an exhibit on AIDS that included photographs of gay men, and there were calls to have the NEA take its name off the exhibit, Terrence was speaking and writing columns. When the St. Patrick's Day parade in New York continued to ban participation by gay groups, Terrence again wrote. He was vocal as the sex scandals of the Catholic Church were revealed, and he took the church to task for its position on gay people. He spoke at AIDS walks, Gay Pride rallies, and anywhere he could to promote equal rights for gay people, their legitimacy and outrage at being second class citizens.

With marriage, though, the activism became directly personal. As he watched what was happening in the world, and as his relationship with Tom deepened, he was keenly aware that his feelings and their partnership were as valid as those of any heterosexual marriage and required full recognition on that level. Terrence readily acknowledged in 2019 that the relationship with Tom had caused him to rethink and reevaluate what gay relationships could be—and that they were legitimate in the eyes of God. He wanted them to be legitimate in the eyes of the state as well.

On December 20, 2003, Tom and Terrence were married in Vermont. Tom described it:

That was a civil union. That was the most married you could be in the United States at that time. In some ways, we wanted to just have a nice weekend in Vermont. So, I said, there's this beautiful inn . . . At that point in time, Terrence had been through, I think, three surgeries and all sorts of treatment. He had been very, very sick, but he turned a corner, and it felt like, we have time, like he's going to live. He was doing really well.

He became almost obsessed with protecting me. I worked providing free legal services for people with HIV, so I had nothing. Marriage was not legal. We were fully in love, and there was the promise of his wellbeing in the future. So, he wanted to take every possible step to protect me, and that's part of why we went to Vermont.

They each wrote short notes to read to one another, and it was really playful. Tom never knew how it happened, but on the way up to Vermont, he said the *New York Times* found out that they were doing this and said they wanted to put it in their wedding announcements. At first, they were surprised, but then they realized that perhaps this would help the movement and be part of the "cry for change" that was happening in the culture. They set it up to be done in the lobby of the inn, and Tom said:

It suddenly became so much more than we anticipated. I was nervous that the patrons [of the inn] might see us and judge, but the opposite happened. A lot of people stayed. People were crying. People clapped. It was beautiful.

When we said the words out loud, "in sickness and in health till death do us part," it became so much more than we ever thought it would be.

At that point, Tom and Terrence knew they had to get involved in the fight for same-sex marriage on a larger scale. Tom said that with a twenty-five-year age difference between them, for Terrence the idea that a gay man born in 1938 was able to marry the man he loved was something that he never imagined would happen in his lifetime.

There was still some uneasiness, though, as Tom described because when they would drive from New York to Key West, they were nervous driving through states where they knew their marriage wouldn't be recognized. He said they even considered taking their rings off when they stopped in a restaurant in South Carolina. It was a little scary, and they thought it could be dangerous. They opted not to, but with marriage not recognized in every state, every same-sex couple was potentially experiencing this kind of concern.

Terrence kept up the pressure wherever he could, leveraging his celebrity and, for once, seeing that being a "gay playwright" actually worked in his favor in terms of being heard. In an op-ed published in the *New York Times* in November 2004, he wrote:

> I am not asking a Catholic priest to marry us. I am asking that when I die my property passes to Tom without penalty. I am asking that we can file joint income tax returns. Nothing less, nothing more. I realize that doesn't sound very romantic, but it's finally what it comes down to. Homophobia is not going to vanish when we are given our full civil rights. I would prefer that you accept me as a gay man but I insist that you give me full status as a citizen in a committed relationship.

They upped the ante on their work and writing and advocating for change, especially when the government was considering a constitutional marriage amendment in 2006, which would have defined marriage as between one man and one woman. Terrence and Tom responded and felt the need to keep up the pressure, and their talents meshed perfectly. As Tom said at Terrence's memorial service:

> We each had a front row seat at injustice for both of us. Love and rage were the engines that drove our lives. Rage at second-class citizenship, injustice, and governmental indifference as everywhere

people were dying. And love for both of us—the unshakeable belief
in the power of love to heal the wounds of loss.

They became involved with Edie Windsor, whose marriage to Thea
Spyer was recognized by New York State, but when Spyer died, the federal government did not recognize the marriage and denied Windsor
the tax exemption claim for surviving spouses because of DOMA. The
case was eventually heard by the Supreme Court, and Tom and Terrence attended the hearings; Windsor was a dear friend of both of theirs.
DOMA was struck down as unconstitutional with the decision coming
on June 26, 2014, just in time for Gay Pride celebrations in New York.
That decision opened the door to challenging same-sex marriage in the
states, and one year later on June 26, 2015, the decision *Obergefell v.
Hodges* ruled that same-sex marriage was constitutional and such marriages must be recognized nationwide.

Before the Windsor decision, Terrence and Tom were married for a
second time on April 6, 2010, in Washington, D.C., at the Kennedy
Center while they were producing *Nights at the Opera*, Terrence's three
plays about the opera: *The Lisbon Traviata*, *Master Class*, and *Golden Age*.
Tom says that their civil union was later turned into a marriage—and
they gave a huge party that their friends and families had been disappointed to miss. Tom said it was one of the happiest days of their lives.

And then when *Obergefell* was announced:

> We were sitting in the living room when that got announced, and
> Peter McNally and his wife Vicky were here visiting. And I con-
> tacted Mayor Bill DeBlasio, who was my college roommate, and
> I said, I know you're doing this press conference. I know you're
> marrying some people. Can we join? Can we get remarried, and he
> said, "come on down."
>
> We reaffirmed our vows the day that federal equality was granted
> on the steps of City Hall.

Fifty years previously, Terrence had been vilified as a man daring to
say that he was gay without guilt or shame. In 2015, he stood on the

steps of City Hall, in front of God, the mayor, and most importantly the man he loved and faced down the forces that would have kept him hidden . . . the forces out there.

IV.

The next years were happy ones for Terrence and Tom. As Tom said, so much of their early courtship had begun when Terrence was in the hospital battling cancer. They talked for hours and hours, and Tom said that in hindsight it was a wonderful way to begin a relationship, and they learned so much about each other—in very challenging circumstances.

Terrence told Tom that as soon as he was well enough he wanted to take Tom to Italy, "so together we could experience the kind of beauty that would make me weak." Travel became a staple of their relationship, whether going to Maine for a weekend or traveling overseas. Terrence and Tom also traveled to India, which had been the beginning of Terrence's spiritual journey.

They went to the theater everywhere and would see anything. Jack Cummings remembers going with Tom and Terrence to see a community theater production of *The Sound of Music* while they were work-shopping *And Away We Go* in Ojai. They had stopped into a coffee shop and seen a poster, and decided they had to go.

They held hands wherever they went, happy always to be physically connected as well as emotionally and spiritually.

By late 2019, Terrence's health was declining. From his surgeries, he had about a quarter of one lung left, and often depended on portable oxygen. He still went to the theater, but he regretted that he was unable to climb the stairs to go to some intriguing Off-Off Broadway show that he had heard about in a loft.

And then a pandemic hit. Not knowing what the best course was, Tom and Terrence decided to go to Florida and wait it out. It was a long drive and a difficult one, stopping for food, restrooms where Terrence had trouble moving, and all the while the unknown threat of infection lingering everywhere. Tom described doing his best to sanitize public restrooms because so little was known about COVID-19 and how it was spread. Once again, there was something out there that threatened them in ways that they didn't, couldn't, know, and it was bumping louder and closer with each passing day.

They made it to Florida and had a few days of peace together in a place they loved. When they could no longer go and sit by the water—something Terrence loved—Tom said, they would sit on the bed and imagine themselves there. Terrence's ability to set a scene was not diminished, and Tom described how vibrantly real the images Terrence was creating appeared to both of them. It gave them joy as the situation looked more and more dire.

Terrence continued to decline and had to be moved to the hospital. He spent a few days in isolation and was only able to talk to Tom on FaceTime. It was tough for both of them. On March 24, with no possible chance of recovery, the final journey to whatever was "out there" had begun. Terrence had tested positive for COVID-19, and he was being taken off oxygen. Tom was in the hospital room, softly playing Maria Callas, holding Terrence's hand, talking to him, letting him know how much he is loved. The monitor was going.

Bump.

Bump.

Bump.

Silence.

In July of 2014, Jack Cummings had had a long conversation with Terrence. The conversation turned to death. Tom was in London, and it was clear to Cummings that Terrence was seriously not well. Cummings could tell that Terrence was sensing something, that perhaps for the first time his end was in sight, though at the time, it was still a ways away.

Terrence had for a long time been afraid of death. Well, if not of death completely, of losing the voice he had had through a career spanning nearly sixty years. He had been increasingly aware of growing older and the world moving on, though he greeted the new generation of plays and playwrights enthusiastically. Tyne Daly, who remained close to Terrence and talked to him often said, "We mostly now talk about being old. We talk about what it feels like to be marginalized in the world we've lived in a lot and how to still be of use." Even so, Terrence always had a new project on his mind, a new way to be heard, some new way to express what was in his mind and heart.

However, as Cummings sat with Terrence out on Long Island and talked to him over Independence Day weekend, Terrence seemed more philosophical about his inevitable end. "I remember he said something so beautiful to me, and I thought 'one should be so lucky.' He said, 'when I go, I just want to hear Tom's voice.'"

And he did.

EPILOGUE

I.

TERRENCE'S BELOVED Shakespeare was fond of writing epilogues. So in his honor, we'll give it a go. Unlike Shakespeare, the goal is not to ask the reader to overlook the flaws in the foregoing work and beg your indulgence—and get you to clap, anyway. However, as noted at the outset, no work of this sort can ever be definitive or even comprehensive. There are plays not mentioned, librettos skipped over, events only referred to in passing. After all, in his career, Terrence wrote some thirty-six plays and fourteen librettos that were published or produced. That can't even begin to cover the myriad other projects that were never completed, abandoned partway through, or existed only as a few lines written on a piece of notepaper.

In the Harry Ransom Center at the University of Texas in Austin, there are some sixty-four acid-free boxes of old Terrence's papers. It was Mrs. Mac who convinced Terrence that he should move his papers to those archives after she began her distinguished career there.

The Ransom Center archives hold the papers and effects of many American writers and artists. "Impressive" doesn't even begin to express it; "overwhelming" is more like it. In our world which moves so quickly and in which people and works are so easily forgotten, it is a remarkable monument to the creative spirit and the creative process. (If you want to picture the entire archive, think of the end of *Raiders of the Lost Ark* when the Ark in a box is slid into stacks of boxes that seem to go on

Terrence was known for writing gracious notes (and sometimes not so gracious). A note sent to the author after a review of Dedication.
PHOTO BY CHRISTOPHER BYRNE

forever.) It is about as close to a physical demonstration of creativity and art that one will ever find.

Terrence's boxes hold clippings, letters, speeches, award citations, scripts at various stages of development. Sheets of paper, some nearly seventy years old, no matter how gently they're handled under the caring

10 Plays To See
1. King Lear
2. The Seagull
3. Long Days Journey Into Night
4. Death of a Salesman
5. Our Town
6. The Glass Menagerie
7. Hamlet
8. Angels In America
9. The Zoo Story
10. Guys and Dolls

Terrence McNally

Terrence's handwritten list of plays that everyone who loves the theater should see.
COURTESY JEFF KAUFMAN

eyes of the Ransom Center staff, sometimes brittle, sometimes already falling apart as entropy does its thing.

No book could begin to contain the thousands of pages, the outpourings of love on cards and letters. To read the words of dozens of actresses who have played Maria in *Master Class* in productions all over the world and what it meant to them as artists and women is profoundly moving. There are tributes Terrence wrote for everyone from Chita to Albee to Marin Mazzie, Nathan Lane, and countless others that Terrence presented at dinners and galas and gatherings. With his generous heart and loving good humor, he had turned his talents to celebrating people he truly loved and who had inspired him.

There are citations from his induction into the Theater Hall of Fame in 1995, and one of the awards of which he was most proud, his induction into the American Academy of Arts and Letters in 2018, the highest honor an American writer can receive.

There are programs from productions of his plays around the United States and around the world, and mementos like buttons from *A Dancer's Life* that say, "I Just Saw Chita!" and autographs from Joan Sutherland, and, yes, Maria Callas, the letters mentioned earlier from Ethel Merman and Katharine Hepburn. To see all of this is to see how expansive a life Terrence had, how many people he touched, and what he meant to them. There is a parody of *Master Class* written by playwright Stephen Karam and sent to Terrence when Karam was in school. It's pretty funny, and Karam would go on to win the 2016 Tony Award for Best Play for *The Humans*.

There are notes and scraps, and lists of play titles, one-line descriptions of situations that might be funny, in all a chronicle of a mind and imagination that was always looking for what was next—and a heart that, for the most part, was always open, even when it was vulnerable and could be hurt.

There is one thing of Terrence's down at UT that's not in his archives. It's in the archive of the author Carson McCullers. It's a gold Zippo lighter engraved to Terrence. Eric Colleary, the curator of the vast collections at the Ransom Center says he asked Terrence about why that should have been among McCullers's effects. Apparently, McCullers had visited Albee and Terrence on Fire Island in the early sixties. She wasn't able to walk that well at the time, and Terrence had to get her back and forth to the ferry in a classic red wagon on the boardwalk. His lighter disappeared after what was a difficult visit. "Bitch stole my lighter," Terrence had told Colleary. These are the stories too good to lose.

Like Shakespeare's Agincourt, a life, and in particular Terrence's life, cannot be crammed between two covers any more than a massive battle can be expressed on an "unworthy platform." And yet, we try. The effort is all.

When this book is published, the audio files of the people who were so generous with their time will become part of the archive. The stories of these major figures in modern American theater would fill twenty volumes, at least. The common thread through all of them, though, is their love for Terrence, for his work, and for how they grew as artists working with him.

II.

A collection of papers and Playbills may be an admittedly incomplete record of this thinking, process, and product, but Terrence's legacy isn't in boxes stored in an immaculate, climate-controlled building. It's very much out in the world. It's in the lives he touched, the actors he inspired, and the ways in which the modern theater was shaped in a very large part by his work.

It was in his love for the theater, which was always foremost in his mind. As his close friend Don Roos said, "He was an acolyte of the theater. He was just so honored to be a part of it." He cared deeply about the theater and wrote columns about where it was going, the challenges of the theater for a contemporary audience and its essential role in inspiring minds and, when necessary, changing hearts.

He opened the door to topics and playwrights who came after him possible—something not lost on others. Matthew López, who won the Tony Award for *The Inheritance*, a play about three generations of gay men, readily acknowledges Terrence's influence on the theater and the subject matter of plays as an inspiration for him. Could it have happened another way? Perhaps, but it didn't.

López also says that when he was starting out, he was connected to Terrence—one of the only playwrights who answered a "mail merge query" that he sent out and who told him, "You don't have to go to graduate school to be a writer. You have to write to be a writer." López was an unpaid assistant on *A Man of No Importance*, an invaluable training ground, and with Amber Ruffin wrote the book for the musical adaptation of *Some Like It Hot*, which premiered on Broadway in 2022 and incorporated a touching and outspoken element of gender fluidity that would have been unthinkable in the 1959 movie and would not have been possible without Terrence's work that continually shattered conventions and taboos.

Terrence was fiercely loyal to the people he loved and pushed them. Logan Reed, who had been Terrence's assistant and later a director, remembered that Terrence was contacted by a theater group in Hawaii that wanted to put on *It's Only a Play*, but they couldn't afford royalties, and it was for a fundraiser, and it was featuring a local newscaster. Terrence agreed . . . if Reed was hired as the director.

We've seen how Joe Mantello was pushed (or perhaps prodded) into new forms, and that Terrence would not allow *L!V!C!* to be made into a movie unless Mantello was hired to direct and they used the original cast (Nathan Lane was unavailable and was replaced by Jason Alexander), how Jake Heggie established himself as a leading contemporary opera composer and was influenced by his work with Terrence. Terrence would not allow *Frankie and Johnny* to be revived on Broadway without Arin Arbus as director, and Audra McDonald and Michael Shannon, playing the parts. He used his weight whenever he could to ensure that his artistic vision was realized—and that those he respected and admired would be given a seat at the table.

Terrence wanted everyone he worked with to love the theater to the extent he did, to know its history and traditions that had gone before. That reverence is seen in *And Away We Go*, where the actors come out, introduce themselves and kiss the stage. It's a tradition for a singer making their debut in one of the great opera houses to literally kiss the stage at the curtain call, to honor the tradition and express gratitude for the work. There are references to all that history in so many of Terrence's characters from Buzz in *L!V!C!* and even Chloe in *Lips Together*, who even if she is only a community theater actress, knows the roots of the form and feels connected to it. As a man of the theater, Terrence loved and respected it throughout his life; it was an indelible part of him, and he wanted that for everyone he encountered.

Logan Reed said when he was working as Terrence's assistant that if Terrence would mention a playwright like Molière or Marivaux, and Reed didn't know them, Terrence would say, "read him." Terrence continued to be inspired by Chekhov throughout his entire life, and Shakespeare as well. In his last years, he was trying to learn favorite

Shakespeare speeches by heart, though he admitted he wasn't very good at it, though he said he just loved saying the words, the progression of them, and the sounds they made inspired him.

Mostly, though, Reed summed up what many said about Terrence,

> The thing I will always remember about Terrence the most was his childlike curiosity and wonder, like an artist. It was like he was seeing everything for the first time. That's why Terrence was able to write what he did. Everything always fascinated him.

Reed said that as a director, he watched how Terrence would go so deeply into his characters, and it forced Reed to be deeply curious about every aspect of a play and how to approach the work.

Terrence loved actors . . . *loved* actors. He would develop "actor crushes" and be completely enamored of what that person did and upset if they "left" him to do movies, as we saw earlier. Nathan Lane, Christine Baranski, John Benjamin Hickey, John Glover . . . the list goes on and on. Virtually every actor who ever worked with Terrence felt how he invested in them and how he trusted them. In turn, working with Terrence, they found the art in themselves. Stanislavski warned actors "to love the art in yourself, not yourself in the art," an admonition that Terrence lived and modeled.

Much has been written and discussed about the "McNally actors," the ones who seemed to know intuitively how to interpret Terrence's writing and bring it to life. Though it's often talked about as something mystical, it's really very simple: pay attention to the words and the punctuation. It was always right there. For Terrence, the role of the actor was to find the playwrights' poetry and music. It's why he hated method acting so much because, "it taught people to be disrespectful of what the playwright set down."

Those actors who trusted Terrence and trusted his words found their characters in them. So many of them said that as actors, their goal was to serve the playwright, and through that they found their own unique artistry.

In describing that he said,

What's so funny is I've never had a serious conversation about a play of mine with Nathan, Zoe Caldwell, Kathy Bates, Christine Baranski, you know, all the wonderful actors I've worked with. They just get it.

So, what are you talking about? Where to have lunch today.

Zoe Caldwell said, "I know what you're talking about. All I do is follow your punctuation, right? When there's a comma, I act a comma. A semi-colon is a semi-colon. There's a dash I know what these things mean and like music from the composer—*moderato, allegro, pizzicato.*

Exactly.

For Terrence the play as always first on the page. López, however, describes a script as a "theoretical document" and only becomes a play when it's realized on stage. Terrence agreed, and often said that a script is not a play.

Audra McDonald says that Terrence was very important to her as an artist, and they developed a close, personal friendship over the years as well:

> Terrence was so much a part of my formative years as a professional actor. I was 24 when I met him. I feel like [working with him] was the textbook. It shaped me; it's molded me as far as feeling comfortable enough to trust my own ideas and trust my instincts.
>
> This incredible playwright whose words we were all so privileged to say and whose characters, we were also privileged to play that in my time working with him, I learned and developed such a sense of trusting what I have to give, and that's because that's because Terrence loved that collaboration so much with actors and loved empowering actors and young directors. You don't have to be the biggest one out there. You are the one I want because what you have is special.

Michael Urie, who might arguably be called a "second generation" McNally actor, said that discovering Terrence's work as a high school student in Plano, Texas, was essential to him as he was beginning to understand himself as a queer actor.

> When I discovered *Love! Valour! Compassion!,* it was about the same time I discovered *As Is, Angels in America,* and *Torch Song Trilogy.* These gay plays were mainstream, and I started to explore what modern theater was in the late nineties when I was in high school. I discovered these playwrights and discovered these plays and started to really figure out myself, but also, especially with McNally. I never really got the plays of John Patrick Shanley or Sam Shepherd, which were the other options.
>
> But here was Terrence McNally, and when you're figuring out your sexuality in Texas, you can't just do gay plays. Terrence wrote so many plays, and you could always find something new to work on and something new to play with or read—plays about women, plays about men, plays about straight people, and he was like at such a, a great gateway into all kinds of things.

Urie credits Terrence's work with allowing him to explore and express his authentic self as an actor, saying that in a previous generation, he would have had to hide his queer identity, or "butch it up," or be relegated to stereotypical comic, and (by twenty-first-century sensibilities) demeaning roles. Urie draws a straight line from the doors opened by Terrence's work to Urie's ability to star in a gay romcom, the Netflix Christmas movie *Single All the Way.* "Without Terrence's work, I wouldn't have been able to get those parts."

Terrence for his part greatly admired Urie's work, calling him "fearless" and praising his comic ability. After meeting him, Terrence wanted to write something for Urie—as happened often with actors he admired. He got to. It wasn't much, but for a benefit reading of *Some Men* in 2019 for Rattlestick Playwrights Theater—the troupe founded in part by Gary Bonasorte and to which Terrence remained devoted throughout his life.

Urie says,

The scene wasn't in the original play, but Terrence said, "I want to do this, but only if you'll play the role. And it's Mayor Pete [Buttigieg] and Chasten in bed talking about Pete running for President." And it is the sweetest, most wonderful piece of writing. It's probably one of the last things he wrote, and we got to do it on stage just for him. It was one of the most meaningful moments for me as an actor, getting to premiere something of Terrence's for him.

Urie's emotion in telling this story matches that of so many people whose stories of Terrence are among their most treasured—and in the theater, that's saying a lot.

As a writer, over the course of his career, Terrence said that he found that he was able to get simpler and simpler, and that became the goal: "I remember once saying the five greatest lines in dramatic literature are in *King Lear* when Cordelia says, 'Never, never, never, never, never.' With the simplicity you get the realization of the word 'never.'"

Small wonder he would spend the time to analyze a word, a phrase, and a joke until it was just right for the script—and would help the audience hear him. If there was anything that drove Terrence, it was the quest for powerful, effective communication.

For all these reasons and more, Terrence was awarded a special Tony for Lifetime Achievement in 2019. The video of his acceptance speech is available on YouTube, and the printout he read from ("typescript" is a charming but antiquated word) is in his archives. As he said,

> Lifetime achievement. Not a moment too soon.
>
> . . . I love my playwright peers—past, present, and especially future. You're chomping at the bit for your turn. Your diversity is long overdue and welcome. It's a club with open admissions. The only dues are your heart, your soul, your mind, your guts, all of you.
>
> Your commitment to this ancient art form assures me that what we do matters. The world needs artists more than ever to remind us what kindness, truth and beatify are. O brave new world that has such people in it. Shakespeare's talking to all of us.

In those simple lines, Terrence sums up his entire career and philosophy. Though his breathing made it a challenge to even deliver the speech, and he was on a portable oxygen tank, his passion and belief were undiminished. No wonder the audience at Radio City Music Hall gave him a prolonged ovation, and he was heard by an international audience.

He meant every word, too. At the end of his life, Terrence was very excited to see how the theater was growing with diversity, new writers, women directors, and playwrights of all genders, races, and ethnicities. He hadn't sensed that kind of excitement since his early days in the 1960s when Off-Broadway was such a big deal in New York. He said this excitement didn't necessarily translate to Broadway—at least not initially, but what he saw was a burst of creativity happening in response to the very things he and his cohort saw happening on Broadway sixty years before—overly commercialized and pandering to audiences rather than challenging them. It made him happy and hopeful, though he characteristically was extremely humble about how much his work and his fearless artistry had been a model for this new generation.

Terrence changed playwriting. He took the abstractions that had been popularized in the Off-Off-Broadway movement including the acknowledgment that theater is not real but can reveal real truths and took them mainstream. He used theater to comment on itself, and while that wasn't new, he elevated the trope. He was "meta" before meta was a thing—and in 2022, so many pieces thrive on their theatricality, and, once again, the audiences have caught up to Terrence.

Terrence's impact on LGBTQ+ rights will be felt for a long time. It was always his honesty and ability to understand the humanity at stake, not just the civil rights, that motivated him. He took the risk to be out and open when it would have been easier to hide. He demanded that people look at the corroding forces of bigotry and hatred that denied people the freedom to experience and express themselves fully. He spoke up on stage and off, and the only times he ever used his celebrity was when it would serve others as well as himself. Yet he didn't yell and demand; he just kept showing up and insisting that he be heard. He used the power of his words—and the power of the theater—to engage people in what he thought should always be obvious to everyone: we all deserve to love and be loved, no matter who is the object of those affections. He told the truth, not because he chose to as a revolutionary act but because as a man, he always felt he had no choice. He was heard, people listened, and the world changed.

Perhaps, though, Terrence's greatest legacy for artists is how he kept getting up and going on. No matter what critical storms he faced, no matter what controversy, no matter what disappointment, or loss; if he was knocked down, he kept going. He was always looking for what was new. He lived in the present—and he was fully engaged in it—and always looked for what was next. He wrote what he needed to write— what he *had* to write. His passionate belief in the art and the art form gave him a life in the theater . . . and the theater gave him life.

It is, perhaps, a bit of *reductio ad absurdum* to try to reduce a life to one word, but with Terrence, it's possible. That word is love. It was the difficult love he had in his family, the love of theater from an early age, that moment when opera spoke to his heart, the love of learning and language, and then the love of being able to create, to move people, and be heard. Even in a brutal business that doesn't always love one back, he kept going. He loved with his whole heart, even when it turned out to not be what he had intended. It was finally the ability to love Tom, freely and openly that gave his story a happy ending—Odysseus home from the war. There wasn't a single conversation for this book where someone didn't mention the word love. People loved Terrence, as much as they admired him, and they trusted his love for them onstage or off. That love empowered a generation of artists and enabled so much innovation and creativity—all of which delighted Terrence, even when it was difficult or he didn't agree.

These are just parts of Terrence's legacy, the parts we can see. Terrence would probably be most excited about the parts that can't be seen—the unknown and unknowable numbers of young people who will, through accident or intention, discover one of his scripts. They will read it, perhaps on a summer day alone, curious, in the shade of a tree, not at first knowing what they're getting into. But they will slowly and inexorably be drawn into Terrence's genius and his world.

. . . And their lives will be changed forever.

ACKNOWLEDGMENTS

THERE ARE SO many people to thank who helped this project find its way. First and foremost, however, I have to thank Terrence himself. We were acquainted over many years, and I interviewed him several times for articles. He was always generous, warm-hearted, and interested. He shared his memories, insights, and connections, which made this job a lot easier. It was only after he had died that I heard from other people I spoke to how important this book was to him, which was flattering. Like everyone, I only wish I had had more time with him.

Terrence's husband Tom Kirdahy was similarly generous and honest, and we should all be so fortunate at some point in our lives to know someone with as good and generous a heart as Tom. Even as he grieved his loss, he made time to talk and support the project.

My editor Chris Chappell at Rowman & Littlefield rescued this project when it looked like the pandemic would put the kibosh on it and has been a great supporter. Editorial assistant Barbara Claire and production editor Meaghan Menzel were invaluable, as was Talley Brown for reading the draft.

My agent Maryann Karinch, who many years ago saw the potential for a book in a tossed-off remark in one of my theater reviews, was intrepid in finding a home for this project, and did it with grace and good humor.

I can't begin to thank the theater folks who made time to talk to me. Their generosity with their time and their recollections made this book what it is. Terrence was so eager that I talk to each of them and would want to know if and when I'd connected with them. If they're quoted in here, I owe them a huge debt of thanks. It was an honor to be able to talk to so many people I've admired for so many years. Each of them deserves their own book. And for those who managed to dodge emails, emissaries, and entreaties over the better part of two years, rest assured Terrence loved you anyway.

Behind the scenes, Santino D'Angelo from Tom Kirdahy Productions, and who works on Terrence's foundation, helped at every step of the way. Rosie DiVincenzo at Manhattan Theatre Club was tireless in helping me have contact and to make sure I accurately reflected Terrence's long relationship with that organization. Eric Colleary, PhD, Cline Curator of Theatre and Performing Arts at the Harry Ransom Center at UT Austin and his whole staff made me feel welcome and could not have been more helpful as I delved into Terrence's archives.

To the family and friends who indulged me in my excitement and listened to the stories, thanks for your interest and patience. Among them Jennifer Deare who sent me a picture of her well-worn acting edition of *Apple Pie* the day this project got the go-ahead, and who has been one of my greatest champions throughout my career. Michele Litzky, Linda Kraus D'Isa, Barbara and Scott Siegel, Lori Schulweis, David Kennerly, Stephen Slovenski, and Ashley Rogers are the best cheerleaders a writer could ever hope to have—especially when we were all locked down for so long, and it seemed like this story would never get told. And, of course, my partner Michael G. Jackson, whose intelligence, wit, and passion for theater delights and inspires me every day.

The last time I saw Terrence was in November 2019. We had had a long conversation, and he had grown tired. I helped him with his oxygen that he had increasingly relied on—he had about a quarter of one lung left at the time, as he said, but it didn't diminish his spirit. We wished each other happy holidays and said we'd pick up the conversation in the New Year when he returned from Florida. "I should still be here," he said. Sadly, he wasn't.

For all those whose lives were touched by Terrence directly or through his work—and for those yet to come—we owe him a debt of gratitude that we were so lucky to be so deeply touched by this man of much importance.

WORKS BY TERRENCE MCNALLY

THE FOLLOWING LIST was partially compiled from available materials in the Harry Ransom Center at the University of Texas in Austin, Texas. Dates are either first productions or on scripts or noted on other archival material.

1960—*The Roller Coaster*, one-act play
1962—*This Side of the Door*, one-act play
1963—*The Lady of the Camellias*, two-act play, adaptation
1964—*The Play of Malcolm*, one-act play
1965—*And Things That Go Bump in the Night*, three-act play
1967—*Next*, one-act play
1967—*Tour*, one-act play (debuted in *Collision Course*, 11 short plays)
1968—*Botticelli*, one-act play
1968—*Witness, one-act play*
1968—*Sweet Eros,* one-act play
1968—*¡Cuba, Si!*, one-act play
1968—*Noon*, one-act play. Produced in *Morning, Noon, and Night* with one-acts by Leonard Melfi and Israel Horovitz
1970—*Bringing It All Back Home*, one-act play
1971—*Where Has Tommy Flowers Gone?*, two-act play
1972—*Let It Bleed*, unpublished one-act play
1973—*Whiskey*, one-act play
1974—*Bad Habits,* two-act play

1975—*The Ritz,* two-act play (Previously, *The Tubs*)

1978—*Broadway, Broadway,* two-act play (Previously *Bye Bye Broadway*)

1985—*It's Only A Play,* two-act play (Revised version of *Broadway, Broadway*)

1987—*Frankie and Johnny in the Clair de Lune,* two-act play

1987—*Prelude and Liebestod,* one act play

1988—*Andre's Mother,* one-act play (debuted in *Urban Blight*)

1988—*Street Talk,* one-act play

1988—*Hope,* one-act play. Produced in *Faith, Hope, and Charity* with one-acts by Leonard Melfi and Israel Horovitz

1989—*The Lisbon Traviata,* two-act play

1989—*Up in Saratoga,* three-act play

1991—*Lips Together, Teeth Apart,* three-act play

1993—*The Wibbly, Wobbly, Wiggly Dance That Cleopatterer Did,* one-act play

1993—*A Perfect Ganesh,* two-act play

1994—*Love! Valour! Compassion!,* three-act play

1995—*Master Class,* two-act play

1996—*Dusk,* one act play, one part of *By the Sea, By the Sea, By the Beautiful Sea*

1998—*House,* one-act of two-act play, the other act by John Robin Baitz

1998—*Corpus Christi,* one-act play

1999—*Some Christmas Letters,* one-act play

2002—*Ghost Light,* one-act play produced in *Short Talks on the Universe*

2004—*The Stendahl Syndrome,* two one-act plays, *Full Frontal Nudity & Prelude and Liebestod*

2005—*Dedication or The Stuff of Dreams,* two-act play

2005—*Crucifixion,* one-act play

2006—*The New York Times,* one-act play

2007—*Some Men,* two-act play

2007—*Deuce,* one-act play

2008—*Unusual Acts of Devotion*, two-act play

2012—*Golden Age*, two-act play

2013—*And Away We Go*, two-act play

2014—*Mothers and Sons,* one-act play

2018—*Fire and Air,* two-act play

2019—*Immortal Longings*, two-act play

MUSICALS

1960—*A Little Bit Different*, score by Ed Kleban

1968—*Here's Where I Belong*, score by Robert Waldman, lyrics by Alfred Uhry

1984—*The Rink*, score by Kander & Ebb

1987—*Bingo!*, Music by Skip Kenner, lyrics by Michael Korie

1991—*All Together Now*, partial musical developed with Stephen Sondheim

1993—*Kiss of the Spider Woman*, score by Kander & Ebb

1995—*Pal Joey*, unproduced adaptation, book further adapted for concert adaption for *Encores!*

1998—*Ragtime*, score by Ahrens & Flaherty

2000—*The Full Monty*, score by David Yazbek

2002—*A Man of No Importance*, score by Ahrens & Flaherty

2005—*Chita Rivera: The Dancer's Life*, new/additional music by Ahrens & Flaherty

2011—*Catch Me If You Can*, score by Mark Shaiman & Scott Wittman

2015—*The Visit*, score by Kander & Ebb

2016—*Anastasia*, score by Ahrens & Flaherty

OPERAS

1985—*Plaisir d'Amour*, music & lyrics by Skip Kenner

2000—*Dead Man Walking*, Jake Heggie

2005—*At the Statue of Venus: A Musical Scene for Soprano and Piano*,
    Jake Heggie
2015—*Great Scott*, music by Jake Heggie

TELEVISION

1968—*Apple Pie* (*Tour*, *Next*, and *Botticelli*), teleplay adaptation
1969—*Last Gasps*, teleplay
1976—*Next*, pilot unproduced
1978—*Positively Tenth Street*, pilot, unproduced
1979—*Bad Habits*, treatment for teleplay, unproduced
1979—*The 4:58*, teleplay, adaptation of a Cheever story
1983—*The Education of Young Harry Bellair, Esq*, pilot with Norman
    Lear, pilot unproduced
1983—*XXIII Skidoo*, pilot with Norman Lear, unproduced
1984—*Mama Malone*, 13-episode TV series
1984—*Teacher's Break*, pilot, unproduced
1984—*Man to Man*, pilot, unproduced
1980s—*Better and Worse*, pilot, unproduced
1988—*Native Tomatoes/Local Peaches*, pilot, unproduced
1988—*Sam Found Out: A Triple Play* (one act teleplay written with
    Wendy Wasserstein)
1988–1989—*L/S/M/F/T*, unproduced pilot
1990—*Andre's Mother*, teleplay
1991—*Sand Between the Sheets*, teleplay, unproduced
1992—*The Last Mile*, teleplay
2000—*Mr. Roberts*, part of *Common Ground on HBO*, one-act, pre-
    sented with pieces written with Harvey Fierstein and Paula Vogel

SCREENPLAYS

1976—*The Ritz*, screenplay
1980—*Iris and Luigi Meet the Wolfman*, screenplay unproduced
1986—*Goin' to the Chapel*, screenplay, unproduced

1986–1987—*Puccini*, screenplay, unproduced

1980s—*Boo!*, treatment, unproduced

1990–1991—*Banana Peels*, screenplay, unproduced

1991—*Frankie and Johnny*, screenplay

1993—*Paying Up*, with Jon Robin Baitz, Nora Ephron, Beth Henley, Michael Hoffman, Wendy Wasserstein, screenplay, unproduced

1996—*A Perfect Ganesh*, screenplay, unproduced

1997—*Love! Valour! Compassion!*, screenplay

UNDATED

Untitled play about George and Ira Gershwin c. 1952, 1953

The Playwright, play, unproduced c. 1960

The Summer People, play, partial, unproduced c. 1961

The Play of Lorna: Three Scenes with Prologue and Epilogue, play, unproduced c. 1962

Sweet Eros, screenplay, unproduced c. 1968

¡Cuba Si!, screenplay, unproduced c. 1968

Goin' to the Chapel, screenplay, unproduced c. 1968

Three Driven Women, teleplay, unproduced c. 1990

Honkytonk, musical, unproduced, score Jim Wann c. 1998

UNCATALOGUED

Speeches

By-lined articles, columns

Tributes.

INDEX

Page references for photos are italicized.

Melfi, Leonard, 87
Melton, James, 7
Memed, My Hawk (novel), 77
Memoir in Plays (McNally, T.), 55, 291
Meneghini, Giovani, 48
Mercer, Mabel, 48
Merman, Ethel, 3–4, 90
Merrily We Roll Along (Sondheim), xii, 36, 219
method acting, 54
Miami Vice (TV show), 17
Midler, Bette, 91
Millennium Approaches (Kushner). *See Angels in America*
Miller, Arthur, 6
Miller, Mitch, 208, 211–12
Minnelli, Liza, 18, 133–34, *207*, 215–22
The Mirror Has Two Faces (film), 15
Misery (film), 134–35
Miss Saigon (musical), 228
Mitchell, Brian, 239, 320
Mitchell, Jerry, 249
Moby Dick (McNally, T.), 275, 287
Mona Lisa and the Matador (McNally, T.), 53
Monday Night Football, 16
monogamous relationships, 323–27
The Moon Is Down (Steinbeck), 55
Moran, Martin, 1–2
Mordente, Tony, 210
Moreno, Rita, 93, 97
Morning, Noon, and Night (triple play), 87–88
Morris, Jay Hunter, 293
Moss, Adam, 245
The Most Happy Fella (musical), 213
Mothers and Sons (McNally, T.), 2, 21, 314–15
MTC. *See* Manhattan Theatre Club
Mullaly, Megan, 161, 316
Murder, She Wrote (Lansbury, Angela), 304
Murdoch, Rupert, 196–97
Murphy, Donna, 239
muses, 21, 79–83, 115

music: finding, 266; influences from, 7–8, 29; in opera, 22, 29–30; poetry and, 347; in show business, 300–301; on television, 11–12; Tony Awards for, 215; writing, 223, 272–73; YMCO, 281. *See also specific music*
musicals: audiences of, 213; on Broadway, 214–15, 251–52; collaboration for, *207*, 207–14; to Dietz, 300; Golden Age of, 3; to McNally, T., 205–7; National Alliance of Musical Theatre Festival, 225; New Musicals program, 229–30; opera and, xiii; passion for, 206; production of, 222–25; show business and, 225–34; theater and, 6; Tony Awards for, 76, 108, 205; writing, 122, 214–22. *See also specific musicals*
Myers, Sam, 19
My Fair Lady (play), xii, 45
My Favorite Year (play), 237
My Six Loves (film), 68

National Alliance of Musical Theatre Festival, 225
National Endowment for the Arts (NEA), 333
National Public Radio (NPR), 139
NEA. *See* National Endowment for the Arts
Nelligan, Kate, 105
Neuwirth, Bebe, 203
New Musicals program, 229–30
New York City: audiences in, 137; Biltmore Theater in, 197–202; Columbia University in, 42–52, *43*, 77–78; culture of, 46–48; gay culture in, 51–52, 181–82; HIV/AIDS in, 151–52, 161, 163; legacy in, *328*, 351; Off-Broadway plays in, 110–11, 306–7; playwrights in, 58–59, *59*; politics in, 112–13; protests in, 79–80; relationships